"I found the book to be an extremely well-researche
I saw it as a very powerful work to connect the dots
ent facets of a dynamic, live and inspiring Continuou
built upon people interactions."

Eric Piquant, Continuous Improvement Coach

"I found *Why Care?* to be a very stimulating read. It should provoke an informed debate that leads to measurable change."

Ken Nelson MBE, LEDCOM CEO

"*Why Care?* brings to the fore the key fact that Continuous Improvement cannot succeed without thriving individuals! It is not so much about the tools and techniques and more about genuinely caring for people and creating a culture where people feel safe to be/become the best versions of themselves. The book is full of wonderful nuggets of gold. It gives organizations a road map on how to take care of their employees. This is especially important to tap into people's discretionary effort."

Ciara Carlin, Operations and Process Improvement Manager

"Well done to the authors of *Why Care?* for appropriately placing the individual front and center in the enabling and sustaining of CI cultures. For far too long the focus has been overly and overtly on tools and techniques, projects and results – whilst important elements in their own right, they have unfortunately been put to the fore of people. Faced with the immense challenges associated with integrating Lean with Digital Transformation and Industry 4.0, as well as with the demands of contemporary workforces, managers and leaders must now more than ever be truly 'mind-full' of their people and individuals. This book should greatly assist those managers and leaders to understand why they need to care, and to reflect and recalibrate on how to lead and manage more effectively and respectfully."

Darrin Taylor, Lecturer in Management & Lean Program
Director South East Technology University

"The 'people side' of continuous improvement has, for too long, lacked adequate attention, yet it is crucial. This book makes a compelling argument for a deep focus on the 'people side,' and combines a wealth of information, ideas and practical resources that can be used by anyone, at any level in an organization, to increase that focus. Recommended reading for anyone interested in helping their organization thrive."

Nuala O'Hagan, CI Coach

"What a need I had of this book at the beginning of my career! Almost 30 years later, leading teams and projects in different countries or activities, I still have a lot of 'aha' moments. The importance of psychological well-being is still a neglected area and understanding how to bring it into your personal and professional life is fundamental. A brilliant book pointing out why, how and what to do to continuously progress in minimizing the most important waste of our time, the lack of thriving individuals."

Catalin Manoli, Factory Director, Danone

"While in companies, we sometimes witness debates and opposition between the deployment of CI and a human approach, this book reconciles the two. It shows how by placing the individual at the heart of the system and helping them to develop, we manage to create an environment of trust, kindness, high standards and professionalism that propels the individual into a powerful, committed collective and allows the company to accelerate its pace of progress. In the future, teams that develop in this way will be the cornerstone of successful organizations in an increasingly Volatile, Uncertain, Complex and Ambiguous (VUCA) environment."

Olivier Marsal, Industrial Director, Hermès

"I'm captivated by this book, not only for its intriguing nature but also for its capacity to explore a vital question regarding continuous improvement. While the significance of people is frequently acknowledged, individuals often get absorbed in the technical aspects of work, neglecting the social components. However, our present work systems are more akin to a double helix rather than distinct social and technical columns. The technical & social are interwoven and inseparable. This book admirably addresses this issue by starting with the fundamental question: 'Why Care?'"

Skip Steward, Vice President, Baptist Memorial Hospitals

"To unlock the true potential in every individual in your organization, you need to create an environment of trust and psychological safety. *Why Care?* gets to the heart of what it takes to truly understand every individual's mental fitness so you can then create a team of high trust, respect, psychological safety, and continuous improvement. A must read for every leader or aspiring leader."

Stephen Dargan, Cultural Transformation Executive

"*Why Care?* is an excellent book on such an important topic in today's world. Psychological safety is essential in achieving excellence within an organization. The book explores the latest thinking and practical approaches to help. I recommend *Why Care?* to anyone, regardless of position or role in an organization."

Brad Jeavons, Author, Speaker, and Organization Improvement Consultant

"This book does a terrific job in peeling away layers within an organizational ecosystem, through the strata of the 'Why Care Model' to look at how a psychologically (un)safe environment can support or undermine a culture of Continuous Improvement – for individuals, teams, leaders, and for the enterprise. I look forward to sharing these practical approaches, frameworks and tools with my clients – and using them to fill critical gaps that many transformation programs would otherwise miss."

Indi Ray, Principal Consultant, Vedas Advisory

"In the research I have carried out with the authors of this book, we found that you won't create a sustainable culture of improvement by focusing on the well-being of your people alone, but equally you won't create a culture of improvement if you don't focus on the well-being of your people. Within the People Value Stream approach, we found that the key was not to start with how we manage people, but to start with your people, how they think, what they need, the value they bring as unique individuals, the safe environment they require and what they need to thrive. This inside-out thinking requires teams, leaders, and the whole organization to focus on these individual requirements for psychological well-being to create an environment where everyone can thrive. This requires a sort of mass customization of our leadership. The authors have skillfully explored why this is so, what is required, as well as how to do this. It escapes me how anyone can consider trying to create a sustainable culture of continuous improvement without reading this book first."

Professor Peter Hines, Enterprise Excellence Network

Why Care?

We live in an ever-changing world in which organizations find it increasingly difficult to stay ahead of the changes needed to be successful without thriving people. The authors believe that when people are valued and respected it improves their overall mental well-being and workplace experience, which in turn, makes them more motivated to help meet the purpose and objectives of the organization and adapt to external drivers.

This book explores how mental well-being and a culture of continuous improvement are intertwined and mutually reinforcing. The authors contend that to create a sustainable culture of continuous improvement there must be an organization-wide focus on mental well-being at the individual level. A culture of continuous improvement nurtured in the right way, however, will indeed support mental well-being and help create a thriving organization.

The key benefit of the book is demonstrating how important mental well-being is for sustainable organizational success. It explores this through many different lenses such as the individual, teams, leaders, and the organization as a whole, and explains the key elements needed for success. Leaders at all levels are able to understand why mental well-being is critical and how to nurture it in the workplace.

In addition, the book explains the importance of diversity, equality, inclusion, and belonging, and how this is integral to mental well-being and a thriving organization. This book provides unique insight into how mental well-being and a culture of continuous improvement are intertwined, explaining how thriving people and a thriving culture of continuous improvement create a thriving organization.

Why Care?

How Thriving Individuals Create Thriving Cultures of Continuous Improvement Within Organizations

Chris Warner
Caroline Greenlee
Chris Butterworth

A PRODUCTIVITY PRESS BOOK

First published 2024
by Routledge
605 Third Avenue, New York, NY 10158

and by Routledge
4 Park Square, Milton Park, Abingdon, Oxon, OX14 4RN

Routledge is an imprint of the Taylor & Francis Group, an informa business

ISBN: 978-1-032-53765-8 (hbk)
ISBN: 978-1-032-53764-1 (pbk)
ISBN: 978-1-003-41347-9 (ebk)

DOI: 10.4324/9781003413479

Typeset in Garamond
by Deanta Global Publishing Services, Chennai, India

Contents

About the Authors xiii
Acknowledgments xv
Charity Donations xvi
Glossary of Key Terms xvii
Foreword xix

Introduction **1**
Background 1
Our Purpose in Writing This Book 2
Target Audience 2
A Changing World—VUCA 3
Economic Impact of Poor Mental Health 3
The Case for Investment 5
The People Value Stream 8
Physical Health 9
Continuous Improvement Culture 10
The Why Care Model 13
Thriving Plan Process Explained 17
Why Care Book Website 21

1 Why Care about the Brain? **22**
Introduction 23
Structure of the Brain 23
Brain and Decreased Individual Psychological Well-Being 25
Psychological Capacity and the Window of Tolerance 30
Brain and Increased Psychological Well-Being 31
Brain and Increased Psychological Well-Being in Teams 35

Brain and Increased Organizational Psychological Capacity 39
The Brain and Diversity...42
Brain and CI...46
Conclusion...52
Key Points from Chapter 1 52

2 Why Care about Thriving DEIB? 54
Introduction..55
What Is DEIB? 55
Culture and Systems...55
Intention and Action 56
What Is Diversity?...57
What Is Equity?...60
What Is Inclusion? 62
What Is Belonging? 64
Why Does DEIB Matter for Business? 66
How We Can Make a Tangible Difference...68
Behaviors..72
How Can CI Help..72
PDCA 75
Conclusion..81
Key Points from Chapter 2 82

3 Why Care about Psychological Well-Being? 83
Introduction..84
Psychological Well-Being Consists of Various Elements.......................86
The Impact of Personal Factors on PWB..88
The Impact of Workplace Factors on PWB...90
The Cost to the Organization of Not Managing Workplace Factors.......92
PWB Is Impacted by Severe and/or Prolonged Stress...........................94
PWB Has an Impact on Psychological Capacity...................................96
Psychological Capacity Has an Impact on Continuous Improvement 97
Psychological Capacity Is Not Limitless 98
The Thriving Matrix...101
The 12 Design Principles of the Thriving Matrix 103
The Three Constraints of the Thriving Matrix.....................................120
Psychological Health and Safety (PH&S)..136
Risk Register..142
Psychosocial Injuries Need to Be Treated a Lot More Seriously..........143
Key Points from Chapter 3 145

4 Why Care about Thriving Individuals? 146
Introduction 147
Individuals Should Assess the Impact of Their Unique Personal Factors 149
Individuals Should Assess the Impact of Their Unique Workplace Factors 150
Individuals Should Become More Informed about the Various Elements of PWB 152
The Ten Elements of PWB 154
Factors Combine and Interact to Impact PWB 158
Examples of Two-Factor Combinations 158
The Links between Individuals and the Ten Elements of PWB 160
A Thriving Plan for Every Individual 181
Key Points from Chapter 4 188

5 Why Care about Thriving Teams? 189
Introduction 190
What Is a Team? 190
Continuous Improvement and People 192
Teams and Well-Being 192
Team Psychological Health and Safety 192
Workplace Hazards 193
Team Culture 198
Visual Management Boards and Huddles 203
Qualitative Measures of Success 204
Huddles 205
A Thriving Team Plan 208
Conclusion 211
Key Points from Chapter 5 215

6 Why Care about Thriving Leaders? 216
Introduction 217
Stages of Maturity 219
Key Features of Leaders in Stage 3 222
Coaching 231
Leadership Behaviors 236
DEIB and Leaders 238
Summary Role of Leaders in PWB And CI 240
Leader Thriving Plan 240
A Final Thought 240
Key Points from Chapter 6 243

7 Why Care about a Thriving Improvement Culture? 244
Introduction 245
The Improvement System 247
The Role of Ideal Behaviors 248
Social and Technical Elements of the CI System 249
The Improvement System Can Be Used to Implement the PH&S System 288
The Improvement System Elements Can Be Mapped to Specific Psychosocial Hazards 288
Key Points from Chapter 7 291

8 Why Care about the Thriving Organization? 292
Introduction 293
What Organizations Need to Do 298
Key Points from Chapter 8 303

9 Summary and the External Environment 304

References 309

Index 323

About the Authors

Chris Warner is an author, speaker, and coach. He has been applying and teaching the Lean methodology within the automotive and mining industries for the past 30 years. His career has allowed him to work globally within numerous large multinational organizations. He received senior executive training and accreditation at the Toyota Motor Company on the Toyota Production System.

Chris has been one of the foremost thinkers on the application of the Lean methodology within the mining industry. He authored the first book on Lean within the mining industry *Flick the Switch: Five Principles to "Flick the Switch" from Good to Great within Mining*. Chris is a mental health advocate and has shared his own story dealing with mental health challenges to many people. As a co-author of *Why Care?* he seeks to help bring more awareness of the critical role mental well-being has in ensuring organizations create a thriving culture of continuous improvement. www.chriswarner.com.au

Caroline Greenlee is passionate about developing people and partnering with organizations to learn together how best to achieve exceptional performance. She has extensive first-hand experience working as a Lean/Continuous Improvement Coach across a wide range of sectors, coaching individuals and teams to achieve great outcomes, both personally and professionally. Her background in Lean is complemented by her work in Learning and Development and Organizational Development. Her HR Masters specialized in Management and Leadership, and is underpinned by real-life experience working as a leader for over 20 years. She is a qualified Executive Coach, a certified Systemic Team Coach, a member of International Coach Federation, a member of the British Psychological Society, an EFQM examiner, and a Six Sigma Green Belt. www.sustainablepeopleperformance.com

Chris Butterworth is a multi-award-winning author, international speaker, and coach. He is a certified Shingo Institute master-level facilitator and a Shingo Institute Faculty Fellow and examiner. He coaches executive teams and transfers continuous improvement knowledge across all levels of organizations. He has extensive leadership and consulting experience in a wide range of sectors. Chris is the winner of Best New Speaker of the Year Award for The Executive Connection (TEC) for his talk on Lean Thinking. He is the co-author of the three widely acclaimed Shingo publication award-winning books *4+1: Embedding a Culture of Continuous Improvement*, *The Essence of Excellence: Creating a Culture of Continuous Improvement*, and *Why Bother? Why and How to Assess Your Continuous Improvement Culture*. He is also the editor of the Shingo Institute book *Enterprise Alignment and Results*. www.cbenterpriseexcellence.com

Acknowledgments

We would like to express our thanks to the many people who have helped shape our thinking for this book and further assisted us in many different ways. In particular, we would like to call out Peter Hines, Sandie Butterworth, Elle Butterworth, Nicole Gallant, Indi Ray, Gary Peterson, Skip Steward, Stephen Dargan, Brad Jeavons, David Hamill, Niamh Shiells, Graham Whitehurst, Tracey Whitehurst, and Jason van Schie.

Charity Donations

A proportion of all author proceeds from this book will be donated to a range of mental health charities around the world, including Black Dog Institute (www.blackdoginstitute.org.au) and T.A.M.H.I. (www.tamhi.org).

Glossary of Key Terms

Eighth Waste = Lack of Thriving Individuals The waste of an individual not thriving. The outcome of people not utilizing their full emotional and cognitive capacity for improvement due to a lack of psychological safety and poor management of psychosocial hazards.

Hansie A Japanese word that means introspection or observation of one's reflection. The word "Han" means to change or turn over, while "Sei" means to look back upon and examine oneself. It is about acknowledging one's own faults and always trying to correct them.

Psychological Capacity The amount of emotional and cognitive energy available for use by an individual at any point in time.

Psychological Flow The melding together of action and consciousness; the state of finding a balance between the level of a skill and the challenge of a task. It is rewarding and fulfilling.

Psychological Health and Safety The application of a risk management framework to psychosocial hazards. One that actively works to prevent harm to the psychological health of workers in negligent, reckless, or intentional ways, and promotes psychological well-being.

Psychological Well-Being (PWB) An individual's ability to think, feel, and behave in a manner that enables them to perform effectively in their work environment, their personal lives, and in society at large.

Psychosocial Hazards Those aspects of the design and management of work, and its social and organizational context, that have the potential to cause psychological and physical harm if not managed correctly.

Psychosocial Risks These occur due to exposure to psychosocial hazards. A psychosocial risk is the potential of a psychosocial hazard of causing psychological harm.

Psychosocial Safety A shared belief held by members of a team that the team is safe for interpersonal risk taking. The shared belief that you won't be punished or humiliated for speaking up with ideas, questions, concerns, or mistakes.

Thriving Plan An action plan tailored to each level and context to enable thriving, subject to continuous PDCA. The action plan is based on a thorough understanding of the current status—what's working well and areas for development using tailored assessments.

Foreword

About seven years into our Lean conversion at O.C. Tanner, I was struck by the confidence radiating from our team members as I watched them coming and going during a shift change. It had not occurred to me that one of the most important outcomes of a culture of continuous improvement (CI) would be that not only would people learn to solve problems in their teams and find new and better ways to provide more value to their clients, but also their personal lives would thrive more than ever! Of course, that would happen! I stood there in wonder, watching them, seeing them in a whole new light, and could easily imagine them going home and owning and solving problems in their families, in their communities, in their churches, and in their schools.

Our people and our culture definitely grew up together. As I watched them continue to grow together over the next two decades, I often paused to contemplate the underlying forces that have made it all possible. Every chapter of this book reinforced and added to my thinking on this subject.

Many companies come to visit our factories in an attempt to better understand how to do the important things described in this book. I often hear the statement, "We launched a CI program and it was very well received. But a couple of months later it was dead. I don't know what happened!" I tell them, "I know exactly why it died. Your culture killed it!" According to the Shingo Model, a CI Culture requires Respect for Every Individual and Humble Leadership. The behaviors that naturally flow from these two principles create the psychological safety and the autonomy that power CI.

Every year, the O.C. Tanner Institute publishes new data on workplace culture in our Global Culture Report. (You can find them on our website.) A couple of years ago, there was impressive data on psychological safety and autonomy that reinforces and amplifies these authors' statement that "thriving individuals have high levels of psychological well-being, thereby unleashing psychological capacity to work on CI."

I will add that mental well-being is essential for CI, and that CI creates mental well-being. It is a very virtuous cycle. The O.C. Tanner Global Culture Report (2024) says that strong psychological safety comes with a 347% increase in the probability of highly engaged employees, a 277% increase in the probability of a highly rated employee experience, and a 33% decrease in the incidence of moderate-to-severe burnout. Those are big, significant numbers. We cannot overstate their importance.

Similarly, giving employees high autonomy in their work comes with 94% engagement, compared with only 32% engagement with low autonomy. And those who report even a medium sense of autonomy show a 200% increase in psychological safety. Further, those who report a high sense of autonomy show a stunning 586% increase in psychological safety (O.C. Tanner Global Culture Report 2024).

It is definitely time for modern leadership. The authors describe a global explosion in volatility, uncertainty, complexity, and ambiguity (VUCA). Couple that with technology that now allows all workers to see and respond to critical business data, and it no longer makes sense to employ a line leader who believes she can make better and faster decisions than the people who are closest to the work.

The modern leader now has a higher calling of ensuring that the culture is safe, enduring, and empowering. Their best contribution is to provide teams with problem-solving tools and coach team members to be more creative problem solvers. When leaders let teams hold themselves accountable for their results, they can then spend their time helping team members to reach the highest level of accountability on powerful cultural expectations. One of the most meaningful activities on my executive Leader Standard Work sends me to the Gemba to strengthen our culture and look after the emotional well-being of every team member.

Another powerful point in this book is that we all need to do a better job of seeking to understand and support each individual around us in their unique set of life experiences. "The workforce is made up of people with different backgrounds, circumstances, identities, and experiences." I fully agree that managing Psychological Well-Being is never a "one size fits all."

At O.C. Tanner, it is easy to see our diversity, and you quickly become aware of our global geographical diversity when you hear our numerous accents. But you would have to work side-by-side with our team members before you realized how safe it is for the myriad diversities we enjoy.

As the authors state in Chapter 3, "Continuous improvement cannot exist in an atmosphere of fear and self-preservation. It requires the freedom to speak and be heard, to be insatiably curious, and to relentlessly challenge bureaucracy."

Recognition and appreciation are powerful tools for a company and must be leader-supported, but they are strongest when they are people-led. I know of no better way to help employees feel a sense of connection to each other and to feel like they belong to a larger whole. When recognition happens regularly in teams, the odds of having a strong community increase by 508%! And when employees have a strong workplace community, the odds increase by 785% that the employees will feel like they belong (O.C. Tanner Global Culture Report 2024, pp. 75–79).

As you read this book, I believe you will find yourself convinced by the data that this is what the world needs from our companies and institutions. Companies will achieve their greatest success when they build, as the authors state in Chapter 6, an "existentialist culture built on the shared understanding that the organization exists to help people achieve their higher purpose."

It is no surprise to me that:

- 60% of employees worldwide say their job is the biggest factor influencing their mental health.
- managers have just as much of an impact on people's mental health as their spouse (both 69%)—and even more of an impact than their doctor (51%) or therapist (41%).
- 81% of employees worldwide would prioritize good mental health over a high-paying job, and 64% admit they would take a pay cut for a job that better supports their mental wellness.

We occasionally have employees who leave O.C. Tanner for more money. I hate to see them go. I love to see them come back! And I love to hear them tell anyone who will listen how different other employers are from O.C. Tanner. As you read this book, see if you do not come to believe that you have the capability (and the responsibility) to create a thriving culture of CI, where your people can grow and thrive.

Gary Peterson
Executive Vice President, Supply Chain & Production
O.C. Tanner

Introduction

Background

The idea for this book was sparked by two of the authors (Chris and Chris) undertaking a week-long onsite continuous improvement (CI) assessment together. Reflecting on the learning and what was a wonderful experience, we came to the realization that no matter how brilliant the CI system and the leadership commitment in any organization is, there is something else integral to building and sustaining a culture of CI.

That "something else" is ensuring the psychological well-being (PWB) of every individual in the organization. We realized that CI and PWB are two sides of the same coin and therefore CI can't succeed unless individuals are thriving. Further, individuals won't thrive unless they have a safe working environment, where psychosocial hazards are recognized and proactively managed. CI done correctly can help to create this environment, providing support for stronger PWB and thriving individuals.

Consequently, we decided to write a book exploring how PWB and CI are intertwined. Then COVID-19 arrived. At around the same time, Professor Peter Hines led a lot of research work into the People Value Stream and published several academic papers, supported by Chris Butterworth, Caroline Greenlee, and Cheryl Jekiel. One of the "flows" in the People Value Stream is "the Mental and Physical Well-Being Flow," which we explore further in this book. We would like to acknowledge and thank Peter for his work, insights, and support for this book.

Three years on from our on-site assessment and the world is a very different place. PWB has become a mainstream hot topic and is recognized as being critical for organizational success. We needed help with the book, and Caroline Greenlee, who worked closely with Peter on his research, kindly agreed to join us as a co-author.

DOI: 10.4324/9781003413479-1

Our Purpose in Writing This Book

Our purpose in writing this book is to explain why PWB is critical for a sustainable CI culture. We believe that while the importance of PWB in the workplace has gained prominence, there is limited work explicitly linking PWB with CI. We will explain the key elements needed to support PWB, how to implement these in any organization, and how these key elements are explicitly linked to a culture of CI.

We put forward three key insights:

1. A thriving culture of CI is essential for organizations to successfully respond to opportunities and threats in the volatile, uncertain, complex, and ambiguous external environment. A thriving culture of CI starts with eliminating the eighth waste of individuals not thriving.
2. Thriving individuals can maintain a positive state of PWB, thereby unleashing psychological capacity to work on CI. As everyone is unique, maintaining this positive state will require a partnership approach between the individual and the organization, starting from the inside-out with the individual.
3. To maximize the number of thriving individuals, assessments need to be undertaken at all levels (individual—team—leader—organization), which will feed into Thriving Plans at each level, linked to the CI system and subject to a never-ending cycle of Plan, Do, Check, Act. Crucially, this starts with the individual and is embedded through ideal behaviors and leveraging the social and technical elements of the CI system to work in synergy.

We hope readers of this book will find many valuable insights that will enable their organizations to have thriving individuals who can flourish, thereby empowering their organizations to also thrive.

Target Audience

The target audience for this book is a wide range of people, from senior leaders to subject matter experts. We aim to provide insights, templates, and frameworks that will enable organizations to either start on the journey of embedding PWB at the heart of their culture or enhance what is already in place.

Some specific examples of people who we believe will find this book valuable include:

- Organizational culture leaders.
- Subject matter experts in CI.
- Business leaders at all levels.
- Improvement leaders and teams.
- Executive teams who want to increase people engagement and productivity.
- People dealing with mental health issues at work.
- Organizations seeking to transform their culture.
- Organizations seeking to embed a thriving culture of CI.

A Changing World—VUCA

There has been a global explosion in volatility, uncertainty, complexity, and ambiguity (VUCA). The pace and complexity of work has continued to increase in the wake of the COVID-19 pandemic.

With the advent of the Fourth Industrial Revolution (sometimes referred to as Industry 4.0), we are experiencing an ever-accelerating pace of change. This was summarized by Canadian Prime Minister Justin Trudeau in his speech to the World Economic Forum in Davos in 2018, where he pointed out that "the pace of change has never been this fast, yet it will never be this slow again." Recent advances in artificial intelligence prove his point and changes to the work environment continue to accelerate in ways we are only just beginning to understand.

As such, organizations need to be able to adapt and respond quickly to this ever-changing environment. To navigate this unprecedented new economic landscape, they need to improve how they maximize the limited psychological capacity (the amount of emotional and cognitive energy, available for use, at any point in time) of every person in the workplace.

Economic Impact of Poor Mental Health

There is growing evidence from around the world that mental well-being has an impact on both the economy in general and on an organization's ability to provide both their required services and shareholder returns. Some of the more recent publications provide startling statistics.

The Organization for Economic Cooperation and Development (OECD) published a report in 2022: *A New Benchmark for Mental Health Systems: Tackling the Social and Economic Cost of Mental Ill-Health.* It states that:

> The economic and social costs of mental ill-health are significant. On average, half of people experience a mental health condition at some point in their lifetime. Living with a mental health condition makes it harder to stay in school or employment, harder to study or work effectively, and harder to stay in good physical health. These individual and social costs also have a clear economic dimension—up to 4.2% of GDP—with more than a third of these costs driven by lower rates of employment, and lower productivity at work.

In a global study published in 2023 by the Workforce Institute titled *Mental Health at Work: Managers and Money*, the authors found that 20% of workers say their job negatively impacts their mental health. They found that 81% of employees worldwide would prioritize good mental health over a high-paying job, and 64% say they would take a pay cut for a job that better supports their mental wellness. It is an issue across all generations, with around 70% of Millennials, 69% Gen Z, 56% Gen X, and 46% Boomers likely to "trade in a well-paying job" for better mental health.

The UK government commissioned research that calculated that 300,000 people lose their jobs annually in the UK due to mental health issues, with around 15% of people at work having symptoms of an existing mental health condition (Stevenson and Farmer 2017). They show that this has an annual cost to employers of between £33 and £42 billion and an additional cost to the government of between £24 and £27 billion.

More recent work shows that the impact is increasing. In 2020, Deloitte UK published a report *Mental Health and Employers: Refreshing the Case for Investment.* It found that a sixth of UK workers were experiencing a mental health problem at any one time and that "stress, anxiety and depression thought to be responsible for almost half of working days lost in Britain due to health issues." They estimated that employees' poor mental health costs UK employers £42–£45 billion each year.

Similar statistics are available in Canada (Deloitte Insights) in 2019: "The business costs of poor mental health in the workplace are staggering, with

30 of every 1,000 Canadian employees missing work for mental health reasons each week." Deloitte estimates that it costs the Canadian Economy at least CAD$50 billion annually, with around 500,000 workers unable to work each due to poor mental health.

The Australian Productivity Commission's mental health report, published in November 2020, estimated the direct economic cost of mental ill-health and suicide at between A$43 billion and A$70 billion, with an additional A$151 billion due to the cost of disability and premature death.

In 2019, the World Health Organization formally classified "burn-out" as an "occupational phenomenon," describing it as:

> Burn-out is a syndrome conceptualized as resulting from chronic workplace stress that has not been successfully managed. It is characterized by three dimensions:
>
> feelings of energy depletion or exhaustion;
>
> increased mental distance from one's job, or feelings of negativism or cynicism related to one's job; and reduced professional efficacy.
>
> Burn-out refers specifically to phenomena in the occupational context and should not be applied to describe experiences in other areas of life.

Research in the US undertaken by Indeed (*Employee Burnout Report*) shows burnout is increasing. In a pre-pandemic survey of over 1,500 people, 47% of respondents said they were experiencing burnout. In 2021, this number rose to 58%.

Something must change.

The Case for Investment

In 2022, the US Surgeon General published a *Framework for Mental Health and Well-Being* that stated:

> Work is one of the most vital parts of life, powerfully shaping our health, wealth, and well-being. At its best, work provides us the ability to support ourselves and our loved ones, and can also provide us with a sense of meaning, opportunities for growth, and

> a community. When people thrive at work, they are more likely to feel physically and mentally healthy overall, and to contribute positively to their workplace.

There is growing evidence of the positive return on investment from mental well-being programs at work. A study by Deloitte (*Deloitte Insights* 2019) demonstrated that over a six-year period, the stock value of companies in Canada with high health and wellness scores grew by some 235% compared to the overall S&P 500 index growth of 159%. In the same report, Bell calculated that every $1 of investment in mental well-being programs in the year 2018 yielded a return of $4.10.

Similar figures are reported by Deloitte for the UK (Deloitte 2020), with an average investment return ratio of five to one. The report also noted that the return is much higher—almost 11 to 1—when the focus is on "preventative large-scale initiatives, and on using technology or diagnostics to tailor support for those most in need."

The Australian Productivity Commission's 2020 *Mental Health* report estimates that their recommended reforms would deliver up to A$18 billion in benefits per year, mainly from improvements to people's quality of life, plus a further A$1.3 billion a year from increased economic participation and productivity. These benefits would require up to A$4.2 billion of expenditure per year.

There is also increasing awareness of the ROI and wider benefits of investing in mental well-being. Pressure from investors to tackle the issue of mental well-being is growing. For example, in 2022, CCLA—the UK's largest charity fund manager—published its *Corporate Mental Health Benchmark Global Report*, ranking the 100 largest global companies based on their approach to mental well-being at work against 30 distinct criteria. Of the Top 100 companies, employing a total of almost 19 million people globally, 90% acknowledged workplace mental health as an important business issue. The report states that:

> The average number of people employed by the 100 companies in this benchmark is 188,000. That equates to an average annual loss per company of £310 million (US$356 million) from mental ill health in the workplace.

While the costs of mental health are shocking, the reported figures, in reality, massively underestimate the true impact. What is not quantified in any of the statistics is the loss of improvement ideas that people do not contribute to the organization. We lose not only their labor contribution, but also their ideas on how to improve. This lost potential is likely to be worth far more than the wage bill.

Another factor to consider is the wider implications for long-term, sustainable success. For example, the 2023 Edelman Trust survey of over 36,000 people in 28 countries found that:

- 58% buy or advocate for brands based on their beliefs and values.
- 60% choose a place to work based on their beliefs and values.
- 64% make investment choices based on their beliefs and values.
- 88% of institutional investors subject environmental social and governance factors to the same scrutiny as operational and financial considerations.

In other words, organizations need to *care* if they want to attract long-term, repeat customers, great employees, and investors.

One of the many inputs used to create the CCLA criteria was the ISO 45003 Standard Occupational Health and Safety Management—Psychological Health and Safety at Work—Guidelines for managing psychosocial risks. First published in 2021, ISO 45003 gives guidance on managing psychological health and safety risks within an occupational health and safety management system. It covers the many areas that can impact a worker's psychological health, such as ineffective communication, excessive pressure, poor leadership, and organizational culture. It is the authors' view that, just as ISO 9000 has become a minimum standard for many leading organizations, the increasing awareness of the critical importance and impact of mental well-being will eventually lead to demands from employees, customers, stakeholders, and investors that organizations implement, as a minimum, the standards called for in ISO 45003.

Another relevant perspective in terms of ROI is the business concept of the triple bottom line. This concept puts forward the idea that businesses should measure not only their financial performance but also their social and environmental impact. This can be summarized into "three Ps": profit, people, and the planet.

According to Kelsey Miller (2022 HBS Online):

> The triple bottom line does not inherently value societal and environmental impact at the expense of financial profitability. Instead, many firms have reaped financial benefits by committing to sustainable business practices.

Using the CCA Benchmark tool and ISO 45003 standard are examples of how organizations can measure and seek to improve one of the most important people elements—well-being.

The People Value Stream

In the paper, *Human Centred Lean*, Hines (2022) explores the concept of the People Value Stream. For the People Value Stream approach to be successful, the most important area is to help employees understand what they want, convey this "voice of the employee" to the organization, and develop a path to achieving it. This involves them flowing (in a similar way to goods or services in a Product Value Stream) throughout their career. One of these flows is that of mental and physical well-being. These flows are designed to be employed in the Lean sense of "flow" (to remove impediments to seamless movement) as well as in the Mihaly Csikszentmihalyi's (1990) psychological sense of "personal flow" (a state of mind in which a person becomes fully immersed in an activity and is using their skills to the maximum to achieve an optimum experience).

Hines et al. put forward that:

> The Mental & Physical Well-being flow will have the largest impact on employee wellness as it creates a self-developed "plan for every person" and a customized self-delivered "single person flow."

In this book, the authors seek to build on the concept of the "plan for every person" and propose how organizations can create a "thriving plan for every individual" and the organization as a whole.

In the follow-on paper "The Mental and Physical Well-Being within the People Value Stream," Hines et al. argue that it is important to create a positive psychological environment in order for an individual to thrive. This environment should take into account the needs of the organization, but fundamentally start with the needs of the individuals within it. In other words, the starting point should be the meaning and subsequent "voice of the employee" and how employees might be encouraged to be self-reliant, purposeful, and highly engaged (Smiles 1866/2017). Borrowing Ryan's and Deci's self-determination theory, when this is successfully achieved, people are "inspired, striving to learn; extend themselves; master new skills; and apply talents responsibly" (Ryan and Deci 2000).

Self-determination theory therefore involves "the investigation of people's inherent growth tendencies and innate psychological needs that are the basis for their self-motivation and personality integration, as well as the processes that foster those positive processes" (Ryan and Deci 2000).

The essence of the People Value Stream approach is the self-development and growth of the individual with the support of leadership, an individual's team, and the organization's culture.

Physical Health

Hines et al. recognize and demonstrate that physical health is intertwined with mental health. For example, Perkbox (2018) found that 79% of 1,815 surveyed British adults in employment commonly experience work-related stress, and that this is the most common type of stress in the UK. These effects have been compounded during the COVID-19 pandemic (Malini et al. 2021) and recent cost of living crisis (Tetlow and Bartrum 2022).

According to multiple studies such as Atkinson (2000) and Cartwright et al. (1997), workplace stress is recognized as a key contributor in 75%–90% of all primary-care doctor visits. The longer these stress responses persist, the more damage to one's health. In the short term, stress leads to stomach disorders, back pain, musculoskeletal problems, headaches, skin problems, loss of sleep and energy, and emotional distress.

According to Carney and Getz (2009), if stress persists over the long term, it can lead to heart disease. People with low level of control over their work, whether actual or perceived, will trigger the fight-or-flight response, with the ensuing impact that men who feel little or no control over their work are 50% more likely to develop heart disease and 100% for women (Bosma et al. 1998). Hence, mental and physical health issues are highly intertwined.

The impact of poor physical health is daunting. UK government estimates show that in 2018–19, approximately 581,000 workers were injured in workplace accidents and the UK lost 28.2 million working days due to work-related ill health in the same period (hse.gov.uk 2019). A recent survey conducted by Personal Group (2021) indicated some worrying trends with regard to the prioritization of work over well-being, with the average British worker having worked more than four days whilst genuinely ill in the previous year, and over half of UK employees (52%) admitting to delaying seeking medical advice because they didn't want to take time off work.

The authors fully acknowledge the critical importance of physical health but due to the extensive literature already published on this subject, we have focused on mental well-being, with recognition that physical well-being is an essential requirement.

Continuous Improvement Culture

A sustainable CI culture is not about tools and techniques. It is about embedding principle-based ideal behaviors and ensuring that business systems are constantly refined to support these behaviors.

When there is no focus on culture and the required behaviors, an improvement culture fails to sustain itself. As pointed out by Hines P. et al. (2022 August), a CI culture will not just happen by chance. A CI culture needs to be proactively managed and constantly reinforced. To quote ex IMB Chairman Lou Gerstner from his book *Who Says Elephants Can't Dance?*:

> Culture is not just one aspect of the Game, it is the Game.

If culture is not defined and proactively managed, an organization will have multiple cultures often working against each other. With no proactive management of the desired culture, there will be no single culture. Instead, culture will be determined at a local team level, either by the leader of that team or even the strongest individual in the group. To quote Schein:

> The only thing of real importance that leaders do is manage culture. If you don't manage culture, it manages you and you may not even be aware of the extent to which this is happening.
>
> **(Edgar Schein, Sloan Management)**

Culture can be difficult to pin down. There are literally hundreds of definitions, and many leadership teams seem to struggle to clearly define what it means for their organization.

Mann has a very useful description of culture:

> Consider culture in a working organization to be the sum of people's habits related to how they get their work done… it is the

> result of the management system… to change it, you must change your management system.
>
> **(David Mann 2005, pp. 3–4)**

Martyn and Crowell in their book *Own the Gap* point out that:

> While organizations openly express the desire to make daily improvements part of their culture, no more than 5 to 10% of the organizations we visit exhibit the types of behaviors we expect to see from a true culture of continuous improvement. These behaviors begin with team members clearly understanding the specific challenges of their area of responsibility, and culminate in a palpable sense of excitement and passion to engage in actions to improve the current state.
>
> **(Mike Martyn & Bryan Crowell, *Own the Gap*, 2012, p. 3)**

Whilst leadership behavior is undoubtedly critical, it is not enough on its own. A cultural transformation will succeed only if it engages the whole workforce and a wide range of stakeholders, such as trade unions, regulators, and external communities.

Most of us know intuitively when we are working in a positive, supportive environment compared to when we are not. What helps us to understand this is the behaviors that we see exhibited by colleagues and leaders on a day-to-day basis. As such, defining and managing behaviors is the key to managing culture.

Many organizations base these behaviors on a set of Principles. For example, the two Cultural Enabler Principles from the Shingo Institute are: respect every individual and lead with humility.

The principle of respect for every individual is fundamentally about seeing people as people. This may seem simplistic but pause and ask yourself how often you really see and think of the person you are talking to at work unless they are a close work colleague. Instead, we often label people by the job they do—"the data entry clerk" or "the guy on the shop floor." One charity in Australia encourages us to think about "a person without a home" rather than label someone as homeless. First and foremost, they are a person and they don't have anywhere to live. If you pause and think in this way, you will respond emotionally in a very different way to the next person you see without a home. Respecting every individual is not about creating a soft cozy environment where everyone is nice to each other and nothing ever gets challenged. In fact, it is quite the opposite. If someone is behaving in a way that is not showing respect, then it is incumbent on the organization to create a culture where this is called out and dealt with—in a timely and respectful manner.

Leading with humility requires the strongest of individuals to be prepared to admit that, even though they are a leader, they do not know all the answers and can learn from everyone else around them. It is often misunderstood as servile or soft leadership, but it is not this at all. True, leading with humility requires the individual to show vulnerability, and the ability to do this requires courage and strength of character. A key aspect of leading with humility is what is often referred to as servant leadership. One way to think about this concept is to recognize that the role of the leader is to serve the people in the organization so that they can better serve the customer.

The behaviors that are informed by these principles are essential to a culture of CI and these behaviors must be constantly nurtured and managed. One of the key insights from the Shingo Institute is that ideal results require ideal behaviors. Ideal results are defined as being sustainable over the long term and deliver excellence from multiple perspectives including social, environmental, the individual and the organization.

Traditionally, we determine how we are tracking against results with Key Performance Indicators (KPIs), which usually tell us what has already happened and what we need to fix after it has gone wrong. Increasingly, organizations try to identify leading indicators that help predict when a KPI may be going off track. An enormously powerful form of a leading indicator is a Key Behavioral Indicator (KBI), which aims to tell us whether the ideal behaviors that we need to achieve the results are in place. Measuring KBIs gives us a way to manage ideal behaviors and to highlight potential issues where our systems are not fully supporting the ideal behaviors and need to be reviewed. KBIs need to change over time. For example, they might start with a simple yes or no about a particular behavior. Once the behavior has been established, the KBI might change to a frequency measure (e.g., number of x). Once the behavior has been established as a habit, then the KBI can change to a measure of quality or value. KBIs need to be constantly reviewed and updated to ensure they are supporting desired ideal behavior. Throughout the book we will give examples of ideal behaviors and potential KBIs.

Creating and sustaining a culture of CI is no easy thing. It takes a lot of hard work, tenacity, and humility to succeed. On the plus side, the rewards can be very fulfilling both from a business and personal perspective. The business is likely to grow, with customers readily expanding their requirements and returning for more great service and employees getting high levels of satisfaction and motivation from a culture that values them.

Organizations that achieve this have a major focus on deploying and embedding the ideal behaviors needed to achieve their desired CI culture (Hines and Butterworth, *The Essence of Excellence*, 2019). Success is not about tools and techniques but about creating an environment where people can thrive.

It is the authors' contention that it is impossible for organizations to achieve a sustainable CI culture without a deep understanding of what is required to create a psychologically safe environment where psychosocial hazards are understood, and psychosocial risks are proactively managed.

A culture of CI needs to be co-created from top down and bottom up—it is the listening and partnership approach that is important. We will explore some key ways to do this in the following chapters.

The Why Care Model

The Why Care Model (Figure 0.1) is central to the book and is represented by an orb. The orb shows a three-dimensional view of all the key elements that will be discussed in the subsequent chapters. At the center of the model—the nucleus—are thriving individuals. It is from within the core of the model that it finds its strength. The ability of an organization to successfully respond to internal performance pressures as well as external demands will depend on the strength of its core—the PWB and the capabilities of every single individual within their workplace. Like the nucleus of an atom, thriving individuals provide the organization with the stability and energy to prosper. It is from within the deepest confines of the organization, from within every workplace where people are doing the work, that the organization finds its strength.

Like the human body, a weak core leads to instability and suboptimal strength. The entire body is left susceptible to internal and external pressure. Build a strong, stable core and you build a strong, stable structure

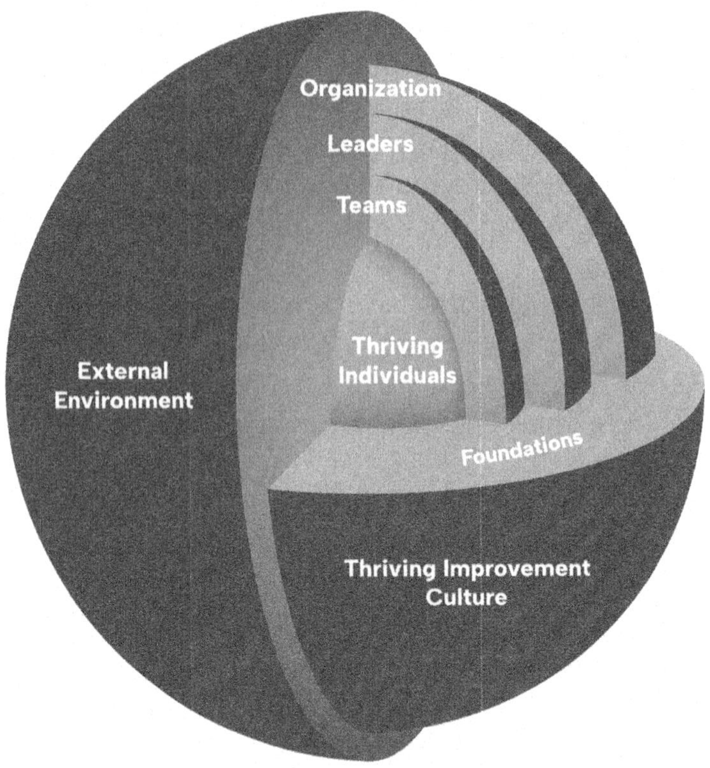

Figure 0.1 The Why Care Model.

that can meet its potential, whether it is an atom, a human body, or an organization. There are millions of organizations across the world with people working for them. The most successful organizations have proven repeatedly to have a strong core; a strong foundation of thriving individuals that help the organization to withstand almost insurmountable pressures. These organizations can leverage the emotional, cognitive, behavioral, and social strengths and maturity of every individual and team to meet challenges head-on.

This strength isn't assumed but rather deliberately developed over decades as a strategic pillar to ensure that the purpose of the organization is never compromised. The organization comes to rely on this internal fortitude to remain stable, even when faced with a turbulent external environment, whether this is adapting to the challenges of a global pandemic, tsunamis that cripple supply chains, geopolitical tensions, or disruptive technologies. Irrespective of the source of pressure, the organization knows that pressure is inevitable, and it needs to make sure it has a core strength, a resilience, an organizational muscle to be able to stand firm and absorb and manage an emerging crisis and/or constant VUCA.

It does this by prioritizing the PWB of every individual, from CEO to cleaner. It is PWB that ensures the core is stable. It is from within a thriving emotional and cognitive state that every individual within the organization can apply creative genius to pre-empt and manage business risk as well as implement ideas for improving performance. Mobilized en masse across the organization, PWB creates a thriving culture of improvement. This culture of improvement interfaces with the external environment and can rapidly interpret, absorb, and respond to pressure in the appropriate manner. This ability or capability is dependent on the energy created by thriving individuals who are constantly utilizing their knowledge and skills to improve their work and helping others solve complex problems. They come to work to do their job well and improve it at the same time. Weak energy, emanating from the core, leads to weak improvement culture. Weak improvement culture leaves the organization susceptible to harm, whether financial or reputational.

Unfortunately, many organizations don't focus on developing a core strength, with tragic moral and economic consequences. They believe people are a means to an end, a machine that can be used to force short-term results. They assume that they can maneuver through any crisis or constant VUCA without a deep focus on developing and maintaining the PWB and capabilities of the people who work for them.

When pressure is placed on their doorstep, they don't have the innate resilience to manage it. They respond reactively, placing additional pressure on the people they have neglected to try and get them out of a hole. This pressure destabilizes the organization because people are pushed so hard to mitigate weak systems and processes that they break. When people start breaking, the entire organization starts buckling. This puts further pressure on those who are doing the work to perform.

The time has come when the PWB of people cannot continue to be ignored in the pursuit of mitigating a crisis or pursuing a performance aspiration. PWB needs to be proactively managed so that the organization has at its disposal a bank of emotional and cognitive energy for use to manage change. A positive state of PWB enables optimum psychological capacity (emotional and cognitive energy) that can be utilized to ensure the organization thrives. Psychological capacity, however, isn't a limitless resource that can be constantly tapped into by the organization to get it out of a difficult predicament. It therefore needs to be deliberately managed.

The core of the organization—thriving individuals—is, therefore, not something that merely evolves out of nothing. It needs to be seen as a continuum of maturity. This maturity is different for every organization and team. Some have a collective group of people who are thriving, where their PWBs are being intentionally managed, one person at a time.

For other organizations, the opposite is true. Their core consists of people who are fearful, traumatized, self-preserving, and constantly guarding themselves against a never-ending flood of toxic behaviors and poorly designed and managed work environments. People aren't helping the organization improve because all they are doing is trying to survive. The last thing on their minds is improvement. Every morsel of emotional and cognitive energy is quarantined for making sure they can get through the day. Surviving is the opposite of thriving.

An organization will never thrive if its corridors are filled with people just trying to survive. An organization thrives when it helps those within its corridors thrive. The center of the Why Care Model, thriving individuals, is the core theme of the book. It is an "inside-out" mindset and approach to business. It's the belief that no organization can achieve greatness without looking after its core—every individual in its workplace.

Creating a thriving core is both an individual and organizational responsibility. The individual has a role to play in maintaining and/or improving their own PWB and the organization is responsible for supporting and protecting this PWB. The individual does this by implementing a "thriving plan," combined with regular "PWB Assessments" (refer to Chapter 5 on the Individual). The organization does this by ensuring people have a voice, have confidence their voice will be heard, and know that their workplace is psychologically safe. The organization is also responsible—legally, morally, and economically—for protecting every individual from psychological harm. This is done by embedding a psychological health and safety system, which we discuss in Chapter 4. The combination of individual and organizational effort in managing and improving PWB is the key enabler for building a strong core. Thriving individuals are those who have thriving PWB.

Surrounding the Why Care Model core are the teams, leaders, and organizational layers. These layers have a dual purpose: firstly, as a supportive and protective covering; and, secondly, as a means for the individual to find meaning in their work.

In the first case, the organization, the individual's leader, and team members are all responsible for helping the person to thrive. The organization, the individuals' leader, and their peers can have a positive and/or negative impact on their PWB. For this very reason, they all need to take responsibility for helping to maintain and improve it.

In the second case, the individual needs to be able to work with the team, leader, and organizational layers to understand their role and unique contributions toward collective success. Understanding this golden thread—of how they fit into the bigger organizational purpose—enables them to apply their unique knowledge and skills toward being an active partner in improving performance and managing business risk. Importantly, it is the safety provided by the protective layers that enables the individual to unlock their potential. Both protection and meaning are intertwined like rope. The inside-out improvement energy is enabled by a safe psychological climate that has been deliberately created by teams, leaders, and the organization.

The foundational elements of the Why Care Model include an understanding of how the brain works, including diversity, equity, inclusion, and belonging (DEIB). These foundational elements, which include deeper understanding of PWB, will be discussed in their own chapters. The authors believe that a base understanding of brain function, DEIB, and PWB is essential for explaining how thriving individuals can create thriving cultures of CI.

Each layer within the Why Care Model Figure will be explained step by step through the book. This will include how PWB and the organization's improvement system work together to increase the productivity of knowledge. The knowledge economy depends on an increase in quantity and quality of ideas for improvement and innovation. An organization's future will depend on it. The authors will illustrate the interdependent relationship between PWB, an organization's improvement system, and knowledge productivity through a model referred to as the Thriving Matrix. This will be further discussed in Chapter 3.

Another key element of the book is the creation of Thriving Plans at the individual, team, and organizational levels. Each of these plans is explained in detail in the relevant chapter but they all follow the same process.

Thriving Plan Process Explained

Why?

The aim of a Thriving Plan is to understand what is working well, and how it could be even better. Following a reflection on current status, an action plan should be defined, detailing the vital few (1–3) priority actions, which would have the greatest impact. These should then be implemented and reviewed for effectiveness.

What?

A Thriving Plan consists of three elements (inputs, process, and outputs), supported by a never-ending cycle of Plan Do Check Act (PDCA). An overview of how to develop Thriving Plans is shown in Figure 0.2.

It is vital that all three elements work together.

- Inputs on their own = good understanding of current status and trends.
- Inputs + Process = good understanding of current status and trends + a sense of which habits and behaviors are leading to those outcomes, as well as what could be done differently to achieve different outcomes.
- Inputs + Process + Outputs = good understanding of current status and trends + a sense of which habits and behaviors are leading to those outcomes, as well as what could be done differently to achieve different outcomes + definition of 1–3 priority actions which will shift the dial, with accountability mechanism of PDCA.

PDCA considers:

- Have the previously defined 1–3 priority actions been completed?
- If they weren't completed, explore why and what can be learned.

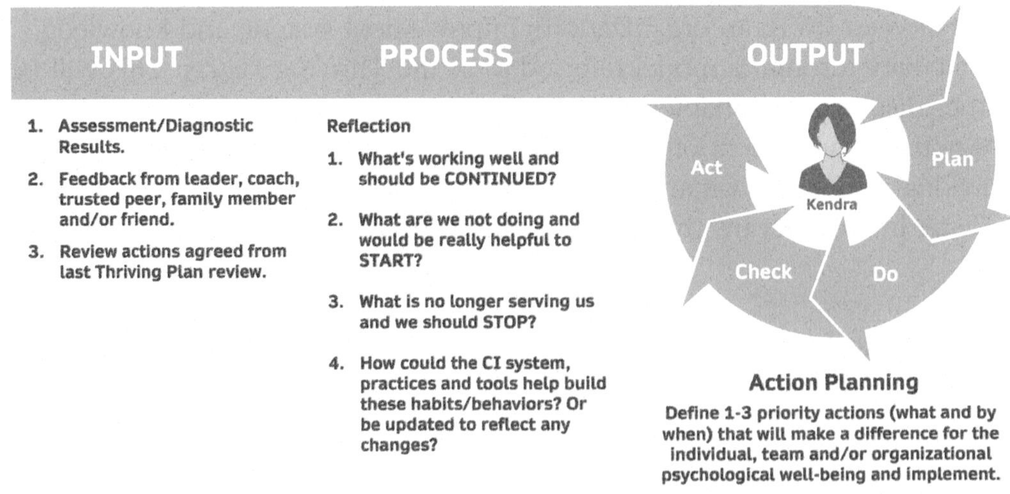

Figure 0.2 Overview of how to develop Thriving Plans.

- If they were completed, did they give the outcome you expected?
- If not, explore why that might be and what can be learned.
- What is your learning overall, and how can this be applied for the next cycle?

Who?

This is designed so that you can walk through the process yourself, a self-reflection exercise linked to the concept of Hansei outlined in more detail in Chapter 5. Or it can be completed with a trusted peer or leader. When completing it with someone else, it is important that it is a high-trust relationship with psychological safety.

How?

This should be approached with a caring lens. There will already be lots of things working really well, and these could be amplified to even greater effect. Often, strengths are taken for granted and the concept of a Thriving Plan allows us to take a step back and recognize what those strengths are and how well they are serving us. Equally, we are all a work in progress and have areas for development. Staying curious—asking either ourselves, or someone else, open questions, actively listening, and staying out of judgment—is crucial.

Questions to help guide your thinking are listed below.

- Looking out over the next [insert time period, e.g., 4–6 weeks], what 1–3 areas of PWB need to be working at optimum?
- Considering those 1–3 priority areas of PWB:
  - What's working well and should **CONTINUE**?
  - What are we not doing and would be helpful to **START**?
  - What is no longer serving us and we should **STOP**?
  - What might the first step be?
  - What might stop progress, and how might you get around that?
  - What does support look like?
- And considering all of that, how could the CI system, practices, and tools help to build these habits/behaviors? Or be updated to reflect any changes?

We would recommend that there are only 1–3 priority actions defined to be completed in the next time period. The emphasis is on choosing to focus time, attention, and precious psychological capacity on the vital few things that will shift the dial, rather than creating a long list of things to do. Creating a long list can risk individuals feeling disheartened or demotivated when only a small portion has been completed. Also, there can be an emphasis on the "low hanging fruit," with the ensuing difference in PWB and no consequent increase in psychological capacity, no movement toward a thriving culture of CI, or thriving organization.

To help clarify everyone's role in Thriving Plans, we've listed some key points:

Roles and Responsibilities

- Individual/Leader/Team to define, commit, and follow through on actions—importance of ownership and accountability.
- Leader/peer to coach and not fix or "rescue."
- It is not counseling or therapy. If these services are needed, a leader/peer can signpost to additional help.

Session 2 Onward

The second, and any subsequent, Thriving Plan reviews should start with looking back at the 1–3 priority actions agreed at the last session and considering the following questions:

- Where have you made most progress?
- Where have you made less progress than you would have hoped?
- What can you learn from that?

When?

We would recommend that the inputs are completed as required, and that the process and action plans are reviewed and updated every 4–6 weeks at individual, team, and leader levels, and quarterly at the organizational level. Any actions defined should be able to be completed within this timeframe with the resources available, with larger projects broken down into key milestones that can be completed within the review cycle.

Why Care Book Website

Many of the templates in the book are designed to be interactive and, in some cases, have too much content to display in their entirety on the printed page. As such, we have created a website where these tools can be accessed and the instructions in the book followed to complete them. The website is www.whycarebook.com.

Chapter 1

Why Care about the Brain?

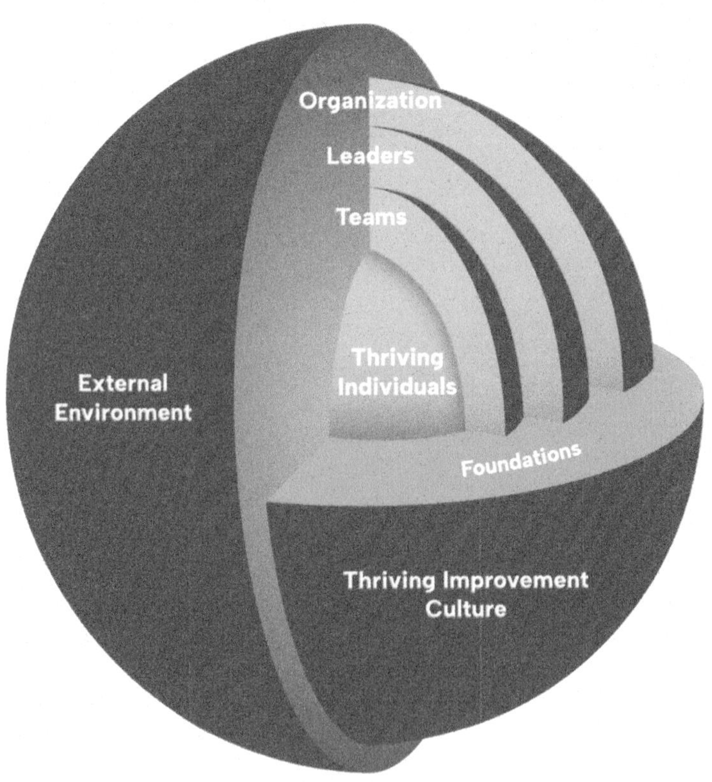

Figure 1.0 The Why Care Model—Foundations.

DOI: 10.4324/9781003413479-2

Introduction

As Daniel Pink (2009) says in his famous TED Talk about *The Puzzle of Motivation*, there is a mismatch between what science knows and what business does. Neuroscience, and the study of the brain, is not a module commonly taught on leadership or in CI programs. Yet, it is fundamental for our understanding of how we and others feel, make decisions, and act. Every individual's brain is unique and has developed based on our personal experiences. Understanding how the brain operates is critical for engaging people, and for creating the conditions for each individual to thrive. CI methodologies and research to date have tended to presuppose the engagement of the prefrontal cortex, or what's commonly called the rational, or executive functioning part of the brain, without being explicit about the conditions needed for this to be possible. In this chapter, we will explore why understanding neuroscience and biology is important for creating a thriving culture of CI. We will start with how the brain works and processes information. We will then explore the link between the brain and psychological well-being (PWB) and psychological capacity at individual, team, and organizational levels. We will then look at what this fundamental understanding means for creating sustainable CI cultures where individuals and organizations can thrive.

Structure of the Brain

Just as you wouldn't want a mechanic tinkering with your car who had no idea of what was under the hood, so too do we need an understanding of what's "under the hood" of the individuals in our organizations if we are to create environments where individuals can thrive. The modern workplace is predicated on the misconception that we are rational beings who sometimes feel. But we are actually feeling beings who sometimes think and this is rooted in our biology. To get to the top "smart" part of our brain, we have to go through the lower part, which is mainly concerned with feelings. Feelings are not something which we can turn on or off—our biology means that our brains are designed to act and feel before we can think. That means that we need to pay attention to feelings if we want individuals to contribute, continuously improve work, to innovate, and to thrive.

This tension between the thinking and feeling parts of the brain is described in detail by Professor Steve Peters in his excellent book *The Chimp*

Paradox. He explains that in the womb, two different brains, the frontal (Human) and limbic (Chimp: an emotional machine), developed independently and have two different ways of thinking. The Chimp starts with feelings and impressions and then uses emotional thinking, whereas the Human searches for facts and establishing the truth and uses logical thinking.

It is important to note that when the two disagree, the Chimp is the more powerful and gets control. Many comedy sketches illustrate the ludicrous nature of two people trying to communicate while speaking different languages and yet we do this in the workplace on a daily basis. How often have you seen someone try to persuade another person of the validity of their argument with facts and figures, only for the other person to get more irate? Maybe you have been on either end of that scenario for yourself? When your Chimp is in the driving seat, the Human won't get a look in. How then do we bridge the divide to create a safe environment for constructive dissent?

In the first instance, it is about creating a gap, a space, a pause to respond rather than react. This is called self-management in Emotional Intelligence. It's about becoming consciously aware of what's happening and not running on autopilot. The brain is essentially a prediction machine—it uses past experiences to predict and construct your view of the world. Without you being consciously aware, your brain is scanning to see how what it is faced with now links to what it has experienced before. That is why really getting to know people at work as individuals matters—what are their values, beliefs, experiences? This will help to understand their behavior and their triggers—are they drawing on experiences which are helpful and constructive, or unhelpful and destructive?

Brain Chemicals

Understanding brain chemicals matters for PWB, as well as understanding how you can help and support colleagues and the individuals you lead. Some of the main brain chemicals and their function are detailed below.

Oxytocin

Often known as the "cuddle hormone," oxytocin helps with bonding and attachment and is associated with honesty. When we face a stressful situation, oxytocin lowers our blood pressure and reduces the levels of hormones that make us feel more stressed.

Dopamine

Dopamine, the feel-good chemical, is linked not only to our levels of motivation and desire, but also our willingness to keep going, even when it is tough, as it shifts our energy levels and our mindset. We each have a different base level of dopamine and introverts get more dopamine from less social interaction.

Adrenaline and Cortisol

Adrenaline prepares your body to deal with stressful or dangerous situations. An adrenalin rush leads to an increased heart rate, higher blood pressure, and extra oxygen is sent to the brain, increasing alertness.

Cortisol, a stress hormone, helps us have energy early in—and stay focused throughout—the day and it is important for our immune system. It is released during stressful situations to give your body an energy burst and is harmful if released for long periods of time.

Brain and Decreased Individual Psychological Well-Being

Our brain has an impact on our levels of PWB and psychological capacity, either positively or negatively. We'll first explore how the brain can decrease our PWB and psychological capacity, looking at scanning for threats, stress, and trauma.

Our brains are primed to be alert as a key survival mechanism, and we are predisposed to focus on the negative because, unconsciously, we're always scanning for threats. The knowledge that the brain has a predisposition to think negatively, and to react more strongly to negative stimuli, has important implications for leaders and for CI. For CI to thrive, we need to take away any sense of threat, both physical and psychological, as the higher parts of our brain shut down when we're stressed. This can be done through creating routines and rhythms and a sense of psychological safety where it is safe to take a risk, admit a mistake, or propose new ideas.

Stress

We tend to use the term "stress" almost synonymously with threat and always with a negative connotation but it is how we experience stress that matters for our PWB. Kelly McGonigal (2013) found that "when you change your mind about stress, you can change your body's response to stress." How we interpret the physiological changes—increased heart rate, increased breathing, constricted blood vessels as a result of the adrenalin and cortisol flooding our system—matters. These are not signs that we can't cope but are signs that the body is getting energized. They are helpful for performance, change your physical response, and give you a performance edge. And research by Alia Crum (2022) found that viewing stress as a challenge and recognizing its benefits for focus and ability to process information led to better health outcomes, better well-being, and higher performance. As part of thriving CI, we need to frame things as challenges if we are to leverage the benefits of a positive stress mindset. It is also important to understand that the level of challenge differs from one person to the next.

According to Kelly McGonigal (2013), one of the most under-appreciated aspects of the stress response is that stress makes you social. Oxytocin is released in the stress response, motivating you to seek support, crave physical contact with your friends and family, enhance your empathy, and be more willing to help and support the people you care about. Creating high-quality relationships, and strong bonds within teams at work, is crucial for PWB, and for building individual and collective resilience. Remember not all stress is created equal. To create the positive outcomes of tolerance and resilience, it is important that the stress is "dosed," i.e., it is predictable, moderate, and controllable. Its undesirable sibling is stress which is unpredictable, extreme, and prolonged, which leads to sensitization and vulnerability.

We have already seen that our brain is constantly scanning for threats and, when we perceive danger, our threat response, also known as the "fight-or-flight" response, is activated. In its most extreme form, this is commonly called the "amygdala hijack." According to David Rock (2009), the threat response is "both mentally taxing and deadly to the productivity of a person—or of an organization." This is because the fight-or-flight response uses up oxygen and glucose from the blood, diverting them from other parts of the brain, thus impairing analytic thinking, creative insight, and problem-solving just when you need those capabilities the most.

Crucially, it is the perception of threat which triggers the fight-or-flight response and this does not require a huge scary monster to be present but can be triggered in social situations. Our perception of the way we are treated by others evokes the same neural responses that drive us away from predators and numerous studies now show that the brain equates social needs with survival. This has profound implications for organizations, and how people act and interact. When threat responses are triggered, individuals' brains become far less efficient. But when people feel safe, that they belong, when there is a degree of certainty and autonomy, when there is equity and fairness, a reward response is induced. To create PWB for individuals, and thriving cultures of CI, psychological safety must be primordial if we are to maximize creativity, innovation, and discretionary effort. CI philosophies, systems, and practices need to be designed, and reviewed, with psychological safety, belonging, certainty, autonomy, equity, and fairness in mind. Equity and belonging will be explored in greater detail in Chapter 2 and PWB in Chapter 3.

How to Control Stress

Friederike Fabritius (2022), author of *The Brain Friendly Workplace*, explains that most of us are under the misapprehension that the brain alone controls stress, which is somewhat inaccurate. She recommends that to control stress you first control your body and exercise is a great way to do this because rhythm is regulating.

We can build this rhythm into the workplace through the use of music, walking meetings, stand-up meetings, and stand-up desks. CI regularly uses stand-up meetings, which is great, and some Gemba activity could be considered to be walking meetings as well. Consciously building this rhythm into how we do things will help to enhance PWB and thriving cultures of CI.

Burnout

Chronic stress leads to burnout and, according to Sangeeta Agrawal and Ben Wigert (2018), burnout affects two-thirds of full-time workers at any given time. As we saw in the Introduction, burnout is an occupational phenomenon resulting from chronic workplace stress that has not been successfully managed.

According to Christina Maslach and Michael Leiter (2016), burnout has three critical dimensions:

1. Exhaustion Dimension: wearing out, loss of energy, depletion, debilitation, and fatigue.
2. Cynicism Dimension: negative attitudes toward clients, irritability, loss of idealism, and withdrawal from professional obligations.
3. Inefficiency Dimension: reduced productivity, low morale, and inability to cope.

Christina Maslach (2016) and Paula Davis (2023) have identified the biggest drivers of burnout at work:

1. Lack of autonomy and flexibility.
2. Unmanageable workload and self-sacrifice promoted as the model of work.
3. Lack of community—loss of shared common meaning and purpose at work, loss of feeling of belonging, destructive competition among co-workers, and fear as the primary experience of work.
4. Unfairness.
5. Values disconnect.
6. Lack of recognition and employees feeling they are not meaningful change agents.
7. Burnout is simply business as usual.

Rest is an essential buffer from burnout, not just physical rest but any activity which quietens the mind and lets you get into "flow"—sport, yoga, cooking, reading, and time outside in nature are particularly helpful. But burnout cannot be mitigated by rest alone—rest is a countermeasure, to use Lean language, and the root cause is systemic.

So, what then can be done to prevent, and manage, burnout? It starts with caring for the individual, with making it ok to not to be ok. Prevention starts with managers and leaders looking at what in the system, and ways of working, is leading to burnout. Paula Davis's (2021) research found that it is the seemingly small things which make a difference. Asking people how they are, and really listening to what is being said, and what is not being said. Leading with humble curiosity, and being intentional about how you start and end your day. All these small things can positively impact morale.

Google's Project Aristotle (2012) found that psychological safety is the number one factor of effective teams, followed by structure, and clarity about roles and responsibilities. CI is built on the cornerstone of regular debriefing through huddles. How can we do these with a lens not just on the "what" but also the "how"? How can we ensure team members feel supported, that they feel that they can speak up? How can we create transparency and clear, agreed expectations? Asking questions, seeking input and explaining why as well as what, and then allowing as much autonomy and flexibility as possible around the "how" are all key. A focus on what's working well and how that could be amplified at both team and individual level is also crucial. Borrowing from design thinking principles and starting with empathy is incredibly powerful not just for building trust and connection but for ensuring effective, sustainable solutions. This means starting problem-solving by stepping into the other person's shoes and seeing things from their perspective.

It also requires an inside-out approach focused on the individual. It is about getting to know and connect with individuals on a deeper level, understanding their values and interests. It is about helping them to build those personal values and interests into their work through job crafting. Job crafting involves using your individual skills and interests to adapt and shape your job. This makes work more meaningful for the individual and significantly reduces the rate of burnout.

Impact of Trauma on the Brain

Trauma, the lasting effects of emotional shock and continued hypervigilance, has an instantaneous impact on our cognitive ability and functional IQ. If we want to leverage the full potential of creativity and innovation, we must pay attention to psychological capacity. When we are alarmed, we lose a potential 40 points on our IQ, rising to a 50 points loss for fear. Paying attention to how people feel and creating environments where people feel calm and regulated are foundational for PWB and for thriving cultures of CI. Trauma also changes our brain, and how that impacts each of us will be different as we each have a unique brain. What we all have in common, however, is the importance of connectedness to others, both as a buffer to current stressors and to heal from past trauma. Belonging matters. This is why having friends at work, having high-trust relationships with your colleagues and your leader, is so crucial, and the CI system can be leveraged to support this.

Dr Richard Tedeschi (2020), a world-renowned expert on the subject of post-traumatic growth, shows how the very negative experience of trauma can lead to positive benefits. These benefits include personal growth, new possibilities, improved relationships, appreciation for life, and spiritual growth. Whilst not everyone will have experience of trauma, the principles hold true about creating the conditions for learning, whether that's during problem-solving, at huddles, or when learning new skills. Creating the opportunity for people to get "into the right headspace" at the outset is so important for PWB. It is also critical to use the CI system to shine a light on what is possible and what is already working really well. Another area to consider is helping people to find their individual purpose, how that links to their role in the team and the organizational purpose as a whole.

Psychological Capacity and the Window of Tolerance

We all have fluctuating levels of psychological capacity and our levels can vary depending on the situation. A useful way to understand our levels of psychological capacity is using the concept of the "window of tolerance" which was developed by Dan Siegel (1999). He proposed that everyone has a range of intensities of emotional experience which they can comfortably deal with at any given moment—their "window of tolerance." People with a wide window of tolerance can think, feel, and behave flexibly whatever the situation. When we move outside of our "window of tolerance," how we think, feel, and act can be disrupted as illustrated in Figure 1.1.

The upper boundary is a state of hyperarousal where you feel anxious, angry, and out of control, and you may want to fight, or flee. The lower boundary is hypoarousal, where you start to feel overwhelmed and begin to shut down or freeze. The further you move out of your window of tolerance, the harder it is to regulate. Your window of tolerance is a measure of your psychological capacity and, once we start to move outside of our window of tolerance, our capacity to problem-solve, to innovate, and support others is reduced.

Building your awareness of strategies for how to return to your window, and proactively expand it, are key for maintaining emotional equilibrium. Some strategies are summarized in Table 1.1.

HYPERAROUSAL ZONE	FIGHT OR FLIGHT IS ACTIVATED Angry, Fearful, Anxiety, Panic, Emotionally Overwhelmed, Racing Thoughts, Difficulty Concentrating, Tension, Shaking, Unable to Rest, Sleep Issues
WINDOW OF TOLERANCE	OPTIMAL AROUSAL ZONE Feel Present, Feel Safe, Feel Open and Curious (versus defensive and judgemental), Awareness of Boundaries, both Yours and Others, Feel and Think Simultaneously and Choose Response to suit the situation
HYPOAROUSAL ZONE	Feeling Numb "I just can't Think", Lethargic, Low Energy and Exhaustion, Body Starts to Shut Down - Blood Pressure Drops, Slow Digestion, Feeling of Emptiness and Disconnected, Depression FREEZE RESPONSE IS ACTIVATED

Figure 1.1 Window of tolerance.

Table 1.1 Strategies to Return to Window of Tolerance

Self-Regulate Hyperarousal	*Self-Regulate Hypoarousal*
Breathing exercises to slow your breathing down	Anything that stimulates the senses—smell is the fastest way to the brain
Physical activity—walking, throwing a ball, dancing, jumping	Movement
Warm water	Cold water
Music—soothing, calming	Stress ball
Visualization	Rocking, dance
"54321" method—name 5 things you can see; 4 you can feel; 3 you can hear; 2 you can smell (or imagine); and 1 you can taste (or imagine)	

This has important implications for organizations, notably for leaders. Firstly, leaders need to recognize where they are in their window of tolerance before they try to support others. Just like on the plane, where they tell you to put on your own oxygen mask before you help others, you cannot support and help someone else to regulate if you are dysregulated. Knowing your triggers, and what pulls you outside of the window, is key, as is proactively managing those triggers. As Dan Siegel says, "you've got to name it to tame it." Secondly, an inside-out approach focused on the individual is needed. This involves really knowing those whom you lead, asking how they are today and seeing if they seem within their window of tolerance. It means knowing their triggers, and proactively helping them to expand their respective windows too. A regulated workforce is a high-performing workforce. The CI system allows for these regular check-ins through Gemba on a one-on-one basis and huddles as a collective.

Brain and Increased Psychological Well-Being

We have seen how our brain is predisposed to focus on the negative and the impact of threats, stress, burnout, and trauma. How then might those be mitigated and how can we use the power of our brain to increase our PWB and psychological capacity? It all starts with our mindset—how we look at situations, how we frame challenge, and how we talk to ourselves. Our mindset is important, as is being mindful and choosing where to focus.

Mindset

Our mindset matters and the interplay between how we think, feel, and act is at the cornerstone of Cognitive Behavioral Therapy. How we think (our thoughts) affects how we feel and act. How we feel (our emotions) affects what we think and do, and what we do (our behavior) affects how we think and feel.

For individuals to thrive with high levels of PWB, and to create thriving cultures of CI, we must pay attention to this interplay. We must actively surface what people are truly thinking and feeling. Creating environments where individuals can be vulnerable requires high levels of trust and psychological safety. It also requires an inside-out focus on the individual as we are all unique. The CI system, and tools, can be used to build that connection one-on-one, and to get a sense of how each person is feeling every day, as that will impact their thinking, behavior, and actions.

Growth Mindset

Carol Dweck's (2016) ground-breaking work on the power of a growth mindset has important connotations for PWB. She discovered that when companies embrace a growth mindset, employees report feeling more empowered and more committed with increased levels of collaboration and innovation.

So, what is a growth mindset, and how does it differ from its counterpart, fixed mindset? A fixed mindset is the belief that your abilities and talents are fixed—you either "have it or you don't." With a fixed mindset, effort doesn't matter as it won't change your inherent intelligence and abilities. There is a desire to play it safe in case you look foolish—approval from others matters and the end result is more important than the learning process.

Growth mindset, on the other hand, is the power of "yet." It is the belief that our abilities and understanding can be developed: I can get smarter, more intelligent, and more talented by putting in time and effort. Challenges are a natural part of the learning process and should be welcomed and sought out. Learning is more important than approval. Failing has been reframed as learning. A useful acronym for this is: F—first; A—attempt; I—is; L—learning.

In Carol Dweck's (2014) TED Talk on *The Power of Believing That You Can Improve*, she showed the impact of mindset on the brain; notably, the electrical activity from the brain as students confronted an error. With the fixed-mindset students, there was hardly any activity; they ran away from the error, rather than engage with it. But the students with the growth mindset engaged deeply. Their brain was on fire with "yet," processing the error, learning from it, and correcting it.

How then can we create growth mindset cultures in our organizations? Microsoft, under Satya Nadella's leadership, is deliberately emphasizing learning and creativity. Across companies with a growth mindset culture, there is a focus on effort as well as output. They recruit for potential, rather than pedigree, and a significant portion of time is spent on coaching and developing everyone to reach their potential, rather than a select few. The CI system provides a fantastic opportunity to model a growth mindset and to amplify the power of "yet." The CI system can be used to invite learning, growth and development for all, through huddles and problem-solving, through Gemba, and through individual coaching and mentoring.

It is important to remember that growth mindset is not binary—it is not something that you do or don't have. Rather, it is a continuum where you could have a growth mindset about one element and a fixed mindset about another. Changing habits takes time and energy and growth mindset must always keep people's cognitive capacity in mind. Thriving cultures of CI start with an individual's psychological capacity, with an inside-out approach tailored to their specific needs rather than a cookie-cutter approach of "one size fits all."

Power of Self-Talk

We all have a voice in our head. For some of us, sometimes, it is a positive affirming voice; our best coach. At other times, it is our inner critic, focused on the negative, telling us we're going to fail. This happens particularly when things are tough—when the stakes are high, and difficult emotions are involved. Contrary to popular belief, the inner critic does not drive us to achieve. Rather the negative self-talk—what psychologist and neuroscientist Ethan Kross (2021) calls "chatter"—is a marvelous saboteur when it comes to focused tasks, negatively impacting our health, our mood, causing us to fold under pressure and straining our social connections.

So, how then can we manage it? Ethan Kross has recommended a plethora of tools which we can use to manage our self-talk and incorporating these into our CI practices, such as Gemba and huddles, is crucial for increasing PWB and psychological capacity. Ensuring that people's emotional needs are met is vital. This requires high trust relationships. Just as stress is contagious, so too is calm. Staying out of drama, providing perspective, and remaining optimistic and hopeful are all helpful.

There are tools and techniques which we can employ at an organizational level: creating order in our environment—5S in action (a workplace organization method which translates as sort, set in order, shine, standardize, sustain); increasing our exposure to green spaces—walking meetings in nature, or even photos of green places in the workplace. Finally, create spaces which elicit a sense of awe—even photos of breathtaking scenery, or videos of people achieving incredible feats within the organization. Considering these tools and techniques as we build team and CI meeting areas can help shift the dial on PWB.

Mindfulness

Research by psychologists Matthew Killingsworth and Daniel Gilbert (2010) of Harvard University found that "people spend 46.9% of their waking hours thinking about something other than what they're doing, and this mind-wandering typically makes them unhappy." They found that the ancient philosophical and religious traditions are right. They teach that happiness, or PWB, is to be found by living in the moment, where practitioners are trained to resist mind-wandering and to be present—"be here now."

Several organizations have introduced mindfulness training and mindfulness apps abound. But what exactly is it, and what are the benefits? Mindfulness is about paying attention to your inside, about the seemingly opposite elements of focus and distance. It is about being present in the moment and being able to stand back and watch your thoughts without the usual commentary. Mindfulness actually makes the area of the brain associated with happiness and well-being stronger and it allows people to operate more effectively in unpredictable environments, essential in today's VUCA world. Daniel Goleman and Richard Davidson's research (2018) illustrates the benefits of mindfulness:

- It allows you to stay calm and open minded: Mindfulness practices, such as breathing meditation, are associated with decreased volumes of gray matter in the amygdala, thus reducing the tendency to interpret an uncertain environment as a threat and react defensively. It improves mental agility, shifting attitudes from "we've always done it that way" to one of curious experimentation of "let's see what happens if we try a new approach."

- Cognitive ability: Mindfulness improves short-term memory and the ability to perform complex cognitive tasks. It also frees people to think outside the box, leading to more effective decision making and collaboration.
- Focus and clarity of thinking: As Nobel laureate Herbert Simon (1971) observed, "a wealth of information creates a poverty of attention" and never have we had so much information so readily available. The regular practice of mindfulness can reduce mental wandering and distractibility by strengthening our awareness of the present moment and our mental processes and behaviors (known as meta-awareness).

Offering mindfulness training, and starting meetings with a mindfulness practice, can all help to increase the time we spend in the present, which is crucial for PWB and for creating thriving cultures of CI.

Brain and Increased Psychological Well-Being in Teams

Understanding how our brain operates matters not only for our own levels of PWB and psychological capacity, but also for the people around us. We'll explore the role of the brain in building trust and psychological safety—the glue of effective teams—as well as the importance of kindness for building connection and belonging.

Brain, Trust, and Psychological Safety

According to Jamil Zaki and Oriel FeldmanHall (2022), deciding to trust someone is like gambling—trying to suss out intentions, possible actions, reactions, and the risk of betrayal. And, given the brain's bias toward the negative, the fear of betrayal leads us to be risk-averse, missing opportunities for connection, for collaboration, and for building relationships. Trust is the waterline for building deep, meaningful connections. Without trust, what we see is a façade and precious psychological capacity is wasted on maintaining our own façades and in trying to connect with other people's façades. Trusting relationships positively impact our physical and psychological well-being, and are foundational for building resilience.

Psychological safety is covered in depth in Chapter 3. In brief, it is feeling safe to speak up, to challenge, and to take risks. Crucially, it isn't just about the actions of one person, but research shows that it is about a shared set of agreed behaviors and goals. This thinking aligns with CI and the Shingo Institute's emphasis on "ideal behaviors." The CI system and practices should be designed with psychological safety in mind, with "ideal behaviors" taking into account what's needed to maximize individual psychological capacity and psychological safety.

Remember that our brains evolved to be good at sensing danger, and are even better at helping us avoid it. This applies in any environment where we don't feel safe. The human brain is a social organ which is shaped by social interaction. Naomi Eisenberg's (2003) research showed that the feeling of being excluded provoked the same reaction in the brain that physical pain might cause. Feeling unsafe engages the limbic circuit and amygdala, knocking our prefrontal cortex offline. Instead of being able to perform at our best, we avoid the perceived danger and focus on self-protection, with vital psychological capacity diverted inward, limiting engagement and commitment. Teams and organizations need everyone's optimum psychological capacity to perform, innovate, and grow. Attending to psychological safety is not soft and fluffy; it is essential for increasing team psychological capacity and PWB and it is rooted in our biology.

Today's more enlightened organizations understand that human beings aren't machines, that we can't always be "on" and perform at optimum. If we are to encourage thriving and PWB, for individuals, teams, and whole organizations, we need to normalize talking about anything which is impacting psychological capacity. If something is impacting your ability to do your job, then that conversation is relevant to work.

Our brains have an overarching, organizing principle to "minimize danger and maximize reward." The SCARF model developed by David Rock (2008) details the five qualities that minimize the threat response and enable the reward response. These are Status, Certainty, Autonomy, Relatedness, and Fairness. We will now explore each of the elements of the SCARF model, why it matters for the brain, and which behaviors can help move us toward the reward response and away from the threat response. Actively designing CI systems and practices with this in mind will increase individual and team PWB, and engender thriving cultures of CI.

- Status: As humans, we are constantly assessing how social interactions either enhance or diminish our status. We are biologically programmed to care about status because it favors our survival. The perception of status increases when people are given praise and when they master a new skill. Values have a strong impact on status—respecting all employees irrespective of earnings or level will have a positive impact.

- Certainty: When we encounter the familiar, our brains conserve energy by shifting into autopilot. Mild uncertainty attracts interest and attention, sparking curiosity and energizing us to solve problems. Increased uncertainty is uncomfortable for our prediction machine—our brain expends extra neural energy, which diminishes memory, and undermines performance. All of life is uncertain—it is making the perception of uncertainty manageable which is key. This is done through transparent practices and by breaking complex projects into small steps.
- Autonomy: Because human brains evolved in response to stressors over thousands of years, they are constantly attuned, usually at a subconscious level, to the ways in which social encounters threaten or support the capacity for choice. Presenting people with options, or allowing them to organize their own work and set their own hours, provokes a much less stressed response than forcing them to follow rigid instructions and schedules.
- Relatedness: Fruitful collaboration depends on healthy relationships, which require trust and empathy. In the brain, the ability to feel trust and empathy about others is shaped by whether they are perceived to be part of the same social group. Loneliness and isolation are profoundly stressful. Research by John Cacioppo and William Patrick (2009) showed that loneliness is itself a threat response to lack of social contact, activating the same neurochemicals that flood the system when one is subjected to physical pain. Teams of diverse people must be deliberately put together in a way that minimizes the potential for threat responses. Trust cannot be assumed or mandated, nor can empathy or even goodwill be compelled. These qualities develop only when people's brains start to recognize former strangers as friends. This requires time and repeated social interaction. Leaders who strive for inclusion, and minimize situations in which people feel rejected, create an environment that supports maximum performance.
- Fairness: The perception that an event has been unfair generates a strong response in the limbic system, stirring hostility and undermining trust. As with status, people perceive fairness in relative terms. In organizations, the perception of unfairness creates an environment in which trust and collaboration cannot flourish. Fairness is served by transparency. Leaders who share information in a timely manner can keep people engaged and motivated. It is also important that leaders do not play favorites, or reserve privileges for people who are like them.

Brain and Kindness

Dr David Hamilton (2020) is a leading expert on kindness and his research shows that kindness is the physiological opposite of stress. We're genetically wired to be kind, as it helps to build connection and a sense of belonging. But it also generates changes in key parts of brain chemistry, increasing our levels of oxytocin, serotonin, and dopamine leading to what's commonly called "Helper's High," or what psychologist Jonathan Haidt (2005) coined "elevation." "Elevation" is the warm, uplifting feeling that people experience when they see unexpected acts of human goodness, kindness, courage, or compassion. It draws us in to help others and to become a better person ourself. Interestingly, we feel "elevation" when we see others being kind and carrying out unexpected acts of goodness, what's called the "Mother Teresa Effect." Shining a light on everyday acts of kindness helps to form a buffer against stress, as well as making you feel happier and more empathetic. It even elevates our immune system and is contagious.

Being kind does not require some grand gesture. In fact, the everyday small acts of kindness are more powerful due to their increased frequency. David Hamilton (2020) also points to the importance of intention—you need to intentionally be kind, taking your ego out of it by completing anonymous acts of kindness as well. Intentionally building kindness into CI systems and practices enhances PWB and buffers against stress, thus increasing prefrontal cortex thinking and our ability to be creative and problem-solve.

Self-Compassion

It isn't just being kind to others which matters; we also need to be kind to ourselves. Kristen Neff (2011) has carried out extensive research on self-kindness, or self-compassion, which she defines as having the same compassion for yourself as you would for others. Self-compassion enhances PWB, psychological capacity and resilience, increasing our ability to deal with challenges and uncertainty.

She talks about "the illusion of perfection" and how perfectionists experience enormous stress and anxiety about getting things exactly right, and how devastated they feel when things don't go to plan. Crucially, perfection is an illusion. It is unattainable and research (Neff 2011) indicates that perfectionists are at much greater risk for eating disorders, anxiety, depression, and a whole host of other psychological problems.

The counter to perfectionism is what Brené Brown (2018) calls "healthy striving for excellence", coupled with self-compassion. Kristen Neff has identified the three elements of self-compassion, outlined below.

- **Self-kindness versus self-judgment**: Self-compassion entails being warm and understanding toward ourselves when we suffer, fail, or feel inadequate, rather than ignoring our pain, or flagellating ourselves with self-criticism. Remember, Suffering = Pain × Resistance and when reality is accepted with sympathy and kindness, greater emotional equanimity is experienced.
- **Common humanity versus isolation**: The very definition of being "human" means that one is mortal, vulnerable, and imperfect. Therefore, self-compassion involves recognizing that suffering and personal inadequacy is part of the shared human experience—something that we all go through rather than being something that happens to "me" alone.
- **Mindfulness versus over-identification**: Self-compassion requires taking a balanced approach to our negative emotions so that feelings are neither suppressed nor exaggerated, and putting our own situation into a larger perspective. It also stems from the willingness to observe our negative thoughts and emotions with openness and clarity, so that they are held in mindful awareness.

Building your own self-compassion and encouraging others to do the same will lead to more healthy striving, increased PWB, and increased psychological capacity. Thriving cultures of CI should be designed with striving for excellence and challenge as guiding principles, rather than seeking the illusion of perfection.

Brain and Increased Organizational Psychological Capacity

In today's VUCA world, the pace of change has increased exponentially. In order to adapt and respond effectively to this ever-changing environment, organizations need to increase their organizational psychological capacity, i.e. the sum of the available psychological capacity of every person in the organization. The role which the brain can play in increasing this organizational psychological capacity centers on two areas. First is brain plasticity and learning, as the pace of learning determines the capacity to adapt and respond to change. Second, it's about understanding the neuroscience of habits as habits form a huge chunk of what we do every day.

Brain Plasticity and Learning

The *Encyclopedia Britannica* (2023) defines neuroplasticity as the "capacity of neurons and neural networks in the brain to change their connections and behavior in response to new information, sensory stimulation, development, damage, or dysfunction."

Andrew Huberman (2021) points to the fact that we can decide that we want to change our brain. In fact, he goes on to say that learning is neuroplasticity. An oft-cited example of neuroplasticity is the increased size of the hippocampus in London taxi drivers, illustrating the potential to learn and improve, and the importance of regular, reinforced learning. Designing CI practices to reinforce learning, with lots of practice and feedback, is key.

Each brain grows most where it is already strongest. As Joseph LeDoux (2019), a professor of neuroscience at New York University, memorably described it in an HBR article (2019), "added connections are therefore more like new buds on a branch rather than new branches." Through this lens, learning is akin to building, brick by brick, on what you're already good at. This lends scientific credence to the theories of strength-based leadership, and working with individuals to amplify and reinforce what they're already really good at. We should work on our strengths whilst also ensuring there are no "fatal flaws," or weaknesses which would completely undermine those strengths.

To maximize organizational psychological capacity we need to start with an inside-out approach focused on each individual and their personal strengths and creating a thriving plan for every individual to grow and develop. "Trained neurons fire more quickly, process faster and recover quicker, ready to fire again. Faster neurons = faster thoughts, a crucial component of intelligence, and vital for the pace we are challenged to operate at today" (Morgan Jones et al. 2018).

The Neuroscience of Habits

Morgan Jones et al. (2018) consider employee habits as the "muscle memory" of an organization and they have a huge influence on behaviors, ways of working, and organizational psychological capacity. "Good habits and behaviors generally lead to good outcomes, just as bad habits and routines can lead to bad outcomes" (Jones et al. 2018). We talk about habits, but, from a neuroscience perspective, what are they? Andrew Huberman (2022) explains that habits are things that our nervous system learned, not always consciously, and they are a big part of who we are. It is estimated that up to 70% of our waking time is made up of habitual behavior.

The goal of all habits is to make them as automatic as possible, and one tool, used frequently by athletes, is visualization. Wendy Wood and Dennis Rünger (2015) found that thinking about the specific sequence of steps required to execute that habit decreased limbic friction and increased the likelihood of the habit happening. This is not, as popular mythology would have us believe, because our brains cannot tell the difference between what we think and what happens but because you set in motion the same neurons required for the execution of that habit. Building visualization into CI practices increases automaticity and the likelihood of developing good habits.

"The brain automates everything it can to conserve energy. Change requires vastly more energy to pay conscious attention" (Morgan Jones et al. 2018). The transition required to move from beginner to competent requires, firstly, disrupting and bringing awareness to the new habit we would like to learn, as illustrated by the Conscious Competence Learning Model (Figure 1.2). Remember learning to drive and how conscious you were, listening when to change gear and the amount of concentration and energy expended to complete even the most basic maneuvers. Think now to the last time you were behind the wheel of a car and your mind was probably mostly elsewhere and the journey was a blur. Introducing, and changing, habits starts with awareness. Knowing this is crucial for how we train people, and introduce and embed CI systems and practices.

What if, on the flip side, you want to break habits which are no longer serving you, so called "bad habits"? As anyone who has tried to break a habit knows, they are hard to give up as they have generally become intuitive and are done without conscious thought. Just as visualization works for creating habits, it works for breaking habits too. Becoming aware that you are engaging in the behavior which you want to change is the first step. Then you try to capture the steps which led you there and insert a "circuit breaker." For example, pick up my phone, recognize the steps that led me there, and replace that with picking up a book instead. This changes the nature of the neural circuits so you can rewrite the script for the habit you want to change. Understanding this is crucial for embedding standard work, and managing change.

John Medina and David Rock quoted in Morgan Jones et al. (2018) examined the development of habits that drive desired behaviors and collectively create a thriving culture of CI.

1. The brain is a connection machine—It is phenomenal at making connections especially around trends in data and targets as well as abstract connections of cause and effect.
2. No two human brains are alike—Each of our brains has developed uniquely due to various experiences, external influences, and family/societal influences.
3. Constrained conscious processing capability—The brain filters the amount of information it requires for processing by using previously formed frames of reference to categorize and remove less important or irrelevant information. Most of the brain's power is in the subconscious part of the brain, where habits are located, whereas conscious thoughts occur in the newer part of the brain, the prefrontal cortex, which by comparison is volume constrained on the brain's processing power.
4. The brain does not unlearn—The brain does not unlearn things, except due to medical trauma. The brain creates new neural pathways that drive new thinking and this informs new behaviors. Initially when we are learning new things, we must be conscious about the new thing we want to do. This information stays and is processed in the prefrontal cortex or conscious part of the mind. Then, over time, this neural pathway becomes stronger as it is performed repeatedly and eventually moves into the subconscious. A true habit is something we do without having to consciously think about it.
5. Stressed brains don't learn or listen—Under stress or perceived danger, blood (containing much of the brain's fuel) flows away from the prefrontal cortex to the major muscle groups in preparation for fight or flight, reducing the ability of the individual to think rationally, make connections, and, most importantly, to listen. In the threat state, the brain's ability to solve problems and collaborate effectively is severely reduced.

The Brain and Diversity

Diversity is explored in more detail in Chapter 2, but here the focus is on how understanding our brain matters for managing diversity. We'll also explore some different types of diversity and how to use that understanding to maximize PWB and psychological capacity.

Bias

If you have a brain, you have bias. That's because bias is an evolutionary adaptation designed for survival—is this person a friend, or a foe? Biases are unconscious and can be helpful in making quick judgments using minimal cognitive effort. But they can also blind us to new information, or mean that we don't take account of valuable options when making important decisions.

Because of the very fact that they are unconscious, educating individuals about bias does little to change things, as you can't watch out for what you can't see. So, what can be done? The Neuro Leadership Institute's research indicates that the answer lies in the collective, as organizations and teams can become aware of bias in ways that individuals cannot. They have condensed over 150 different biases into the SEEDS Model ® (NLI):

1. Similarity: The tendency to view people who look or think like us more favorably than people who are different.
2. Expedience: The tendency to rush to conclusions in an effort to minimize cognitive effort.
3. Experience: The tendency to believe that how we see the world is inherently truer than someone else's perspective.
4. Distance: The tendency to assign greater value to those things that we perceive to be closer to us, rather than further away.
5. Safety: The tendency to over-account for negative outcomes instead of positive ones.

When identifying and mitigating biases in organizations, David Rock and Heidi Halverson (2015) recommend that we keep four general principles in mind to help broaden our perspective beyond our own specific viewpoint:

1. Bias is universal. If you believe you are less biased than other people, that's probably a sign that you are more biased than you realize.
2. It is difficult to manage for bias in the moment you're making a decision. You need to design practices and processes in advance.
3. In designing bias-countering processes and practices, encourage those that place a premium on cognitive effort over intuition or gut instinct.
4. Individual cognitive effort is not enough. You have to cultivate an organization-wide culture in which people continually remind one another that the brain's default setting is egocentric and that better decisions will come from stepping back to seek out a wider variety of perspectives and views.

The CI system can be used as a framework to help prevent bias and invite a wide variety of perspectives, creating space for deliberate thought and reflection.

Diversity

We have learned that no two brains are the same but there are common traits which different groups share.

Introverts and Extroverts

Susan Cain's (2012) TED Talk on *The Power of Introverts* and her book *Quiet* (2012) highlighted the bias which introverts suffer. She says that our workplaces are designed primarily for extroverts, who require higher levels of stimulation and who think best in company. Introversion and extroversion are a spectrum, with those who fall in the middle called "ambiverts"; in other words, they're equally at home in both worlds. But what do those different worlds look like? Figure 1.3 depicts the introversion-extroversion spectrum.

According to Susan Cain (2012), between a third to a half of the population are introverts. If we are to maximize organizational psychological capacity, how do we effectively harness the creativity and input of

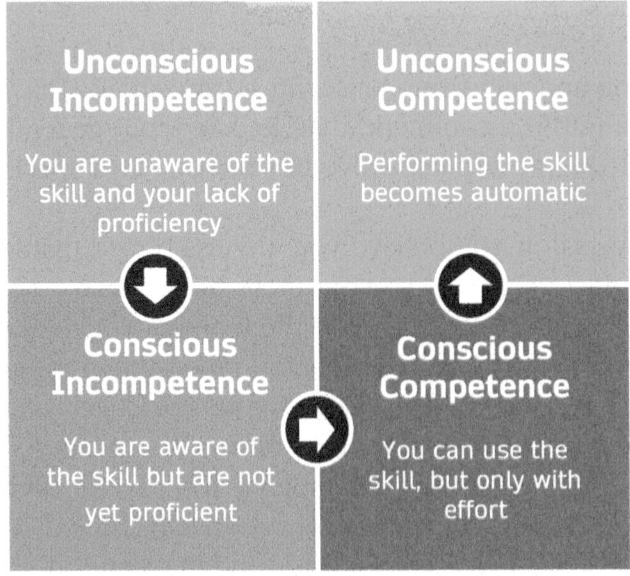

Figure 1.2 Conscious competence learning model.

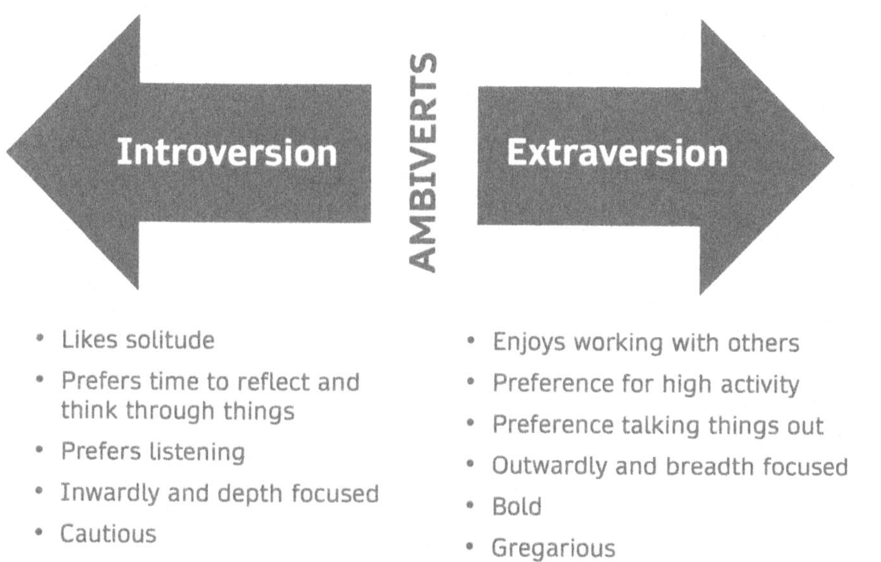

Figure 1.3 Introversion-extroversion spectrum.

the 30–50% of the workforce whose ideas may be drowned out at the minute? The environment matters. We need to design workplaces which simultaneously allow for collaboration and company, as well as solitude and thinking time in quiet spaces. We must create working models which don't assume that creativity and problem-solving happen in the moment, brainstorming in a room together. Instead, we should share information in advance to allow for thinking and reflection time for those who prefer that. We have to allow individuals to work autonomously and then share, using text tools as well as speech to collaborate. We should problem-solve using asynchronous communication with leaders speaking last. The different tools in CI can be leveraged to take advantage of this difference and ensure everyone can perform at their optimum, thus increasing organizational psychological capacity.

Neurodiversity

The term "neurodiversity" is being used with increasing frequency. What do we mean by it? The Chartered Institute of Personnel and Development (CIPD 2018) defines neurodiversity as "a biological fact of the infinite variety of human neurocognition." Pioneering organizations, such as JP Morgan, Microsoft, Deloitte, EY, and Google, have neurodiversity-at-work initiatives to harness the value that thinking differently brings. This is crucial if they are to harness the talents of the 15–20% of the global population who are neurodivergent.

Each approach differs by organization but some common strands include the importance of the work environment. How can we avoid sensory overwhelm, create quiet spaces, and permit the wearing of noise-canceling headphones and working from home where possible? Written communication is preferable, as is clear, concise language. In terms of development, providing a personalized, strengths-based approach, which allows for self-directed learning, is key. It is also important to allow individuals to fully utilize their strengths through techniques such as job crafting. Managerial support needs to balance flexibility and autonomy with high levels of awareness and understanding. For high levels of PWB and a thriving culture of CI, neurodiversity needs to be considered in designing the system and in all interactions. The cornerstone of effective CI starts with understanding what individuals need to maximize their psychological capacity—an inside-out approach.

Brain and CI

We have discovered how the brain works and processes information, and why an understanding of neuroscience and biology matter for creating a thriving CI culture. A thriving culture of CI starts with thriving individuals with high levels of PWB and psychological capacity. Let's explore how we can use the CI system, methodologies, and tools to create thriving, brain-friendly workplaces.

CI, by its very nature, can help create certainty as there is often a clear framework of what will happen when. Making the what, the why, and the how as transparent as possible will help to further reduce any perceived threat and create a sense of safety and certainty. For example, the why of Gemba is to connect with people at their place of work, check in on how they are feeling, look at what is happening, listen to their concerns and ideas, and learn together. Making this explicit reduces the fear that it is to check up on someone, to "police" their work, and to catch them out.

For day-shift workers, the optimum time for Gemba, huddles, and problem-solving is morning to early afternoon when the brain is more alert. 5S already considers elements of workplace design, creating order which helps for brain functioning. This could be expanded with team CI areas having photos of green spaces, stunning scenery, and people within the organization achieving amazing feats.

Leaders are the linchpins of a CI system, almost like conductors in an orchestra, ensuring that all of the different tunes are played at the right time. They too are human and subject to all of neuroscience and biology. It could be helpful for the leader to check-in with how they are feeling before they start each workday, to consider where they are in their window of tolerance—what are their levels of PWB and psychological capacity? It may also be helpful to start the day with a mindfulness exercise, or by taking a few deep breaths and becoming intentional about what they'd like to achieve, and how they need to be for that to happen.

We will now consider how to reorient CI methodologies to help create a brain-friendly environment, conducive to thriving.

Behaviors

We saw how automatic and unconscious most of our brain processing and habits are, so it is important to embed behaviors which create thriving brains. Thriving brains increase PWB and psychological capacity and lead to thriving cultures of CI and adaptable, resilient organizations. Some examples of brain-friendly behaviors are listed below. This is not designed as an exhaustive list, but rather one to get you started. We would recommend personalizing your own list to suit the needs of the individuals in your team in your organizational context at this time.

- In every interaction, I pay attention to my own and others' feelings and take them into account before I act.
- When I start to feel emotionally hooked, I consciously pause and think before I respond.
- I consistently make a conscious effort to be present and focus on the here and now.
- When coaching and mentoring others, I focus on what's possible, and what's already working well.
- Every day I practice a growth mindset and the power of "yet." For example, "I don't know *yet*..."
- Every day I coach others to fully develop to their potential.
- I consistently respect every individual, irrespective of position or status.

Brain and Gemba

Gemba is an opportunity for the leader to listen with all of their senses to what is being said and not said to ascertain where the other person sits in their window of tolerance, or psychological capacity, at that point in time. Gemba is explored in more detail in Chapter 6 and should be seen first and foremost as a means of connection. It is an opportunity to get to know the other person better as an individual, to check in and ask how they are feeling, looking for signs of stress and burnout. It is a chance to demonstrate compassion and kindness, to validate their feelings, to help broaden their perspective if they seem "stuck," to coach and explore options, and to help them stay optimistic and hopeful. Connection builds a sense of belonging and is fundamental to creating psychological safety, and connection and relationships are fundamental for resilience. Connecting with someone on a personal level builds trust, and lets them share what's really going on beneath the waterline as depicted in Figure 1.4.

High-trust relationships and psychological safety allow individuals to share problems and challenges, voice ideas, be creative, and problem-solve. Trust is built in small moments over time and Gemba is the perfect

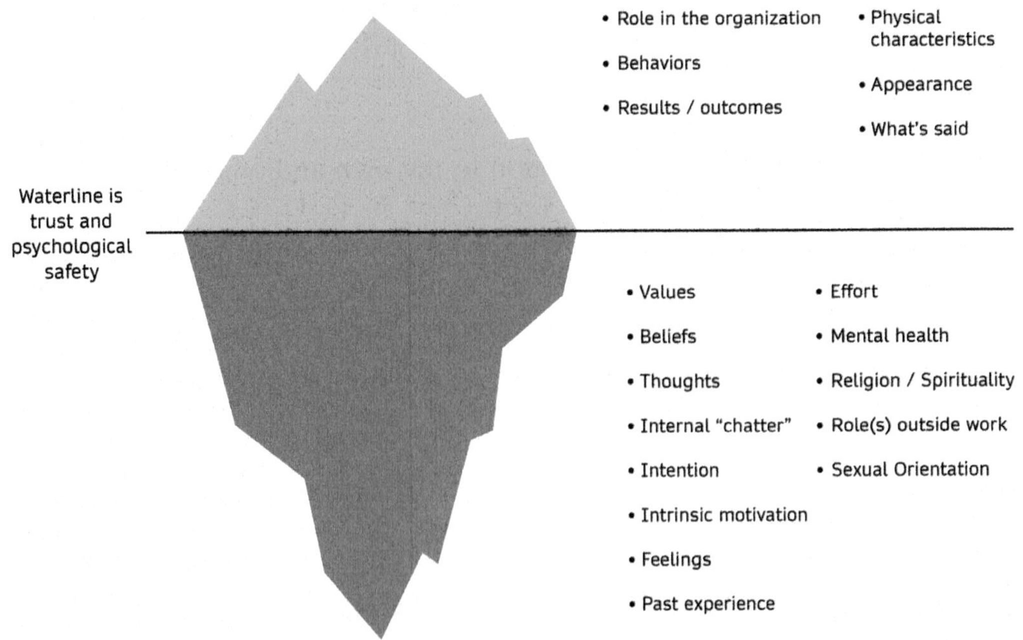

Figure 1.4 Visible and hidden identity.

opportunity to build trust and for both parties to make deposits into the "marble jar," to borrow Brené Brown's (2018) metaphor.

Brain, Visual Management Boards, and Huddles

> More than 50 % of the cortex, the surface of the brain, is devoted to processing visual information.
>
> **(David Williams 2012)**

> Data visualization—whether quantitative or qualitative—speeds up the processing of information within the brain by a factor of 3–4 times. It also increases the possibility of insight.
>
> **(Duclerci and Mauel cited in Morgan Jones et al. 2018)**

The power of using Visual Management to aid cognitive processing is clear, but could we take that even further? Visual Management Boards (VMBs) define what the team needs to achieve to be successful—the Measures of Success and, in some instances the how, with ideal behaviors. Imagine the power of having a portion of the board dedicated to the team's well-being, even something as simple as a traffic-light system. One financial services organization uses this. The principle is that if anyone feels below optimum, the light goes "amber" at a minimum, or "red" based on the individual's feedback and whether it is within the team's locus of control to support that person in that given situation.

We've seen the power of kindness and gratitude and the ripple effect it has. Dedicating a portion of the VMB to everyday acts of kindness would help to shine a light on what's already happening, and hopefully encourage even more kindness. One healthcare organization has made a "kindness tree" where a small tag is hung on the tree with a message of gratitude for a colleague and their act of kindness which has positively influenced individual and collective PWB. Pivoting the CI system to be more holistic and consider what individuals need to thrive rooted in neuroscience and biology will lead not only to thriving individuals, thriving cultures of CI, but also sustainably excellent organizations. It starts with co-creating a thriving plan for every individual, considering their current PWB and psychological capacity.

Huddles

The regular, repeatable rhythm of huddles creates the opportunity for regular debriefing. Regular debriefing helps create a sense of certainty, which can be further heightened by the huddle being regarded as a safe space. Having psychological safety directs blood flow to the prefrontal cortex and allows the executive functioning part of the brain to come online. Safety and certainty can be further enhanced by using huddles as an opportunity to be transparent and share information with the team in a timely manner, as well as providing role clarity.

The leader's approach is crucial—modeling vulnerability and situational humility by acknowledging they do not have all of the answers, and being willing to say, "I don't know." Starting conversations with explaining the why behind decisions and initiatives, and allowing the team as much autonomy and flexibility on the how, is vital for building a sense of engagement and ownership.

The leader should be mindful of the inbuilt power difference within the organization and do what they can to reduce it and encourage equal status. For example, can they rotate who leads different portions of the VMB and huddle? Can the leader stand at the back, as a true coach? Think of sports teams—the players are on the pitch executing the game plan and the coach is on the sideline providing feedback and encouragement.

Leading with humble curiosity is crucial for people to feel safe and to stay in the executive functioning part of their brain. Gentle questions such as "tell me more about," "help me understand," and "I'm wondering about" can be particularly effective. Using an appreciative inquiry and strengths-based approach shines a light on what's working well and how that could be amplified to have an even greater impact, rather than always focusing on the gap.

As we saw from the research on growth mindset, recognizing effort and not just results, is crucial to build confidence and increase resilience. Having a tolerance for failure and modeling healthy striving versus a drive toward perfection also helps increase confidence and resilience and encourages appropriate risk-taking. Openly inviting dissenting opinions helps draw more people in. Allowing different methods of contributing, rather than just speaking in front of the group, will create the conditions for introverts and neurodiverse employees to feel more comfortable in participating. This will further increase their PWB and psychological capacity.

Sincerely thanking folks for their efforts, having team members genuinely show their gratitude for one another, and giving unexpected rewards and recognition (versus contingent rewards—"if… then…") all help to create brain-friendly environments with high levels of PWB and psychological capacity. It is important to create an environment where people feel they belong. The huddle can help with this, for example, by dedicating a portion of the huddle on a frequency, such as fortnightly or monthly, to consider belonging. This time can be used to step back and reflect on how well the team is functioning, what is helping create belonging and cohesion, and what could be done differently. This is explored further in Chapter 5.

Some organizations start their huddles with a short mindfulness practice. Mindfulness invites individuals to slow down and check in with how they are feeling and showing up today at work. Taking a few deep breaths slows down the parasympathetic system. Other organizations start with warm-up exercises, building in the regulating notion of rhythm, which can be further heightened by adding in music. Or you could even start with mindfulness and end with music and exercise if you want to maximize the benefits. Alternatively, you could select whichever method you feel appropriate based on what you have picked up from people during your Gemba.

Brain and Problem-Solving

By its very nature, problem-solving can be fraught with fear and uncertainty—will I be judged? Will I be considered inadequate? Will I be found out? Will I be sanctioned? Setting the scene will help to quell fear and increase psychological safety. For example, starting the problem-solving session by saying something along the lines of:

> We are here today because X has happened and we want to try and discover what led to that. We want to discuss how we might prevent it from happening again, or at least reduce the likelihood of it happening again. The aim of the session is not to apportion blame or to judge, but to be curious as we know we are all doing our best.

The onus is on the problem-solving facilitator to create psychological safety and to make it safe to speak up. They need to model vulnerability and situational humility and don't need to know all of the answers. In fact, it is often best if the facilitator has little to no knowledge of the issue. Then, they can be inherently curious, without any bias or prior knowledge.

Asking lots of open questions and using design thinking principles, such as empathy maps, to consider how the problem looks from different perspectives can be particularly valuable. It is also helpful to be kind and generous in our assumptions. It can be beneficial to take a break, to go for a walk and come back, or to do a short mindfulness practice if it is becoming too intense or you sense people are starting to feel overwhelmed or stressed. Remember we cannot do our best thinking when stressed and problem-solving requires everyone's best thinking if it is to be truly effective.

When analyzing and formulating action plans, it is advisable to actively invite dissenting opinions to reduce bias and groupthink. One organization discovered that, culturally, this proved a challenge for people. Creating a prop (a gavel in this instance), which was handed across to a particular individual as a prompt to present the argument from a different perspective, was particularly effective at inviting dissent. Also, presenting action plans as experiments to learn more and modelling growth mindset principles—using the word "yet"—can be particularly effective. For example, "We don't know *yet* what caused A, B, C. How might we find out more?"

Traditional problem-solving has happened where the problem has occurred. But with geographically dispersed teams, and a move toward a knowledge economy, there is the opportunity to make problem-solving asynchronous. Asynchronism allows introverts to reflect in advance and the balance of text and talk is beneficial for neurodiverse people as well.

Conclusion

Hopefully this chapter has helped to close the gap between what science knows and what business does. The knowledge economy, and the pace of change, require all of us to function at our best. We have aimed to offer an opportunity to see how the CI system, practices, and tools could be utilized differently incorporating neuroscience research to increase PWB, psychological capacity, and to create thriving teams, organizations, and cultures of CI.

Key Points from Chapter 1

- The structure of the brain is organized to act and feel before thinking—we are feeling beings who can only think when we feel safe. Thriving cultures of CI need to attend to individual feelings, and enhancing PWB and psychological safety, as a priority.

- Each individual's brain is unique and we each have a different window of tolerance depending on our history, biology, and the situation we're in. Starting from the inside-out, understanding and proactively managing individual triggers is key. A regulated workforce is crucial for PWB, psychological capacity, and thriving cultures of CI.
- Having trusting relationships is beneficial for us as individuals. Trusting relationships improve both our physical health and PWB. Kindness helps to form a buffer against stress, as well as making you feel happier and more empathetic. It even elevates our immune system and is contagious.

Chapter 2

Why Care about Thriving DEIB?

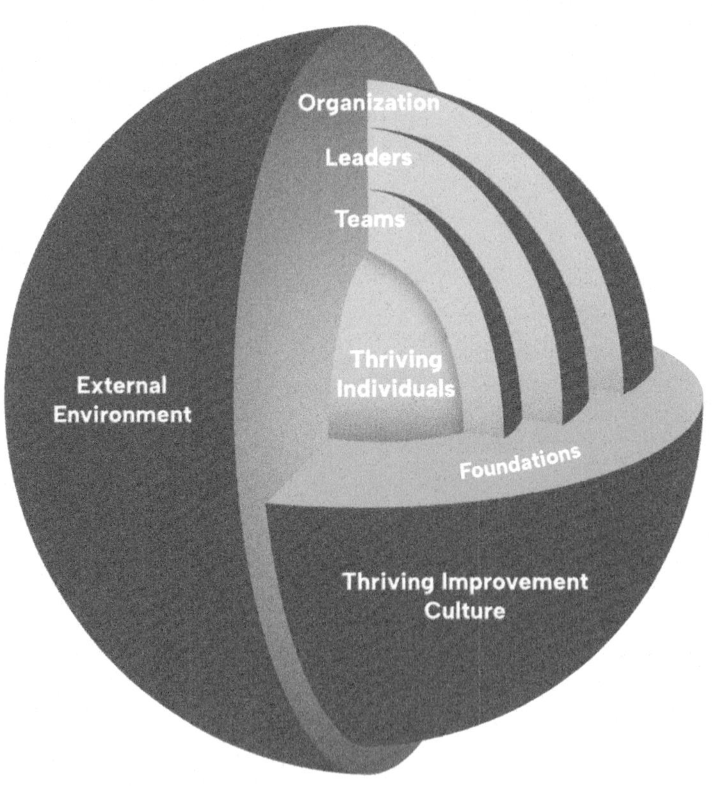

Figure 2.0 The Why Care Model—Foundations.

 DOI: 10.4324/9781003413479-3

Introduction

Diversity, Equity, Inclusion, and Belonging (DEIB) are crucial organizational issues. They have clear links to psychological well-being (PWB), psychological capacity, and to thriving cultures of continuous improvement (CI), and organizational performance. In this chapter, we will explore what diversity, equity, inclusion, and belonging mean and why they matter for us as individuals and for business. CI and DEIB are rarely discussed in the same sentence. Yet there is huge potential for the CI system, and tools, to help create thriving cultures of DEIB, and for CI practitioners to recognize that DEIB is not the preserve of HR, but is integral to CI work. We will consider how CI and DEIB can work together to create PWB, increase psychological capacity, and create true cultures of belonging which are the foundation for a thriving culture of CI and innovation. All this needs to start with an inside-out approach focused on the individual, versus the "cookie-cutter" approach which predominates.

What Is DEIB?

DEIB is often misregarded as initiatives, or programs, but it is really about behaviors and practices. DEIB needs to be part and parcel of how we do things. It is about making the workplace human-centered, and crushing the false dichotomy between people and performance. DEIB is not a zero-sum game where one group loses and the other wins. It is about making the workplace better for everyone.

Culture and Systems

We talk about culture as an almost mythical, ethereal concept, but it is the sum of the mindset and behaviors of everyone every day in the workplace. Like lobsters put into a pot of cold water and slowly boiled, we've come to accept the workplace as a standard and have forgotten that it is a social construct, with many of its customs belonging to a bygone era. We wouldn't even contemplate using machinery from the Industrial Era, yet many of its structures and management practices linger in our modern workplace. Therefore, for DEIB work to have maximum impact, it needs to operate on two levels—a systems level and a cultural or behavioral level.

As James Clear (2018) says: "You do not rise to the level of your goals. You fall to the level of your systems." And, until now, as Deepa Purushothaman (2022) highlights, "we've had a system where, in order to succeed, you have to give up who you are" with a consequent reduction in psychological capacity, and PWB. The focus to date has been tinkering around the edges of existing systems but we need to carefully consider which ones we need to deconstruct. We can use CI to reconstruct organizational systems differently to create a modern workplace where everyone can thrive.

Intention and Action

We know that to have a brain is to have bias, but what checks and balances can we build into our systems, our behaviors, and our practices to create that space, that pause which is so crucial? We know from Chapter 1 that everything passes through the limbic, feeling part of the brain before reaching the prefrontal cortex, the executive functioning part. According to Robert Sapolsky (2018), when we see difference, our automatic and internal stress system is activated within fifty milliseconds. It is seconds later before the reasoning parts of the brain catch up to affirm, or refute, this reflex anxiety. We know that our brain is trying to keep us safe, but it is also holding us back from being objective and inclusive, and we behave in ways counter to our intentions, values, and beliefs. Lisa Kepinski and Tinna Nielsen (2023) call this the "knowing-doing gap."

We have a "knowing-doing gap" at both an individual and organizational level. Human resources (HR) leaders know their laudable intentions; employees only see their actions. This huge disparity is highlighted in the difference between employee and HR leaders' perceptions of progress on DEIB (Gallup 2022 cited in HBR 2023): 97% of HR leaders strongly agree that "diversity needs create real change," compared to 37% of employees; 60% of HR leaders strongly agree that "inclusion needs respect me," versus 44% of employees; and 65% of HR leaders strongly agree that "belonging needs care about my well-being," compared to 24% of employees. Clearly, the focus must be on how employees feel. We must start with an inside-out approach with the individual at the center. In the language of CI, individuals are the customers of DEIB.

This inside-out approach, with the individual at the center, means a human-centered workplace where respect, compassion, and kindness are prized in the same way as analytical and technical skills. As Nazir Afzal (2022) says, this requires being "woke" in its truest sense—"the opposite of being asleep, seeing the injustice in inequality." DEIB is the work of every one of us. It requires everyone to lead from every seat with courage. The root of the word "courage" is the Latin word for heart, which reminds us that to do this work we need to lead with our hearts. We have to care.

The cultural shift requires unlearning of beliefs, practices, and habits and relearning new ones to create PWB. This allows individuals to feel they really belong and increases their psychological capacity, which is essential for thriving cultures of CI and innovation.

What Is Diversity?

We have talked about DEIB, but what exactly do we mean by diversity? Diversity is about people; it is about human difference. The UK Equality Act (2010) defines a diverse organization as one where "the workforce is made up of people with different backgrounds, circumstances, identities and experiences. Its people are representative of the organization's community."

Visible and Invisible Diversity

Visible diversity is simply the intrinsic forms of diversity which we can easily see, such as race and gender. However, as Figure 2.1 shows, there is more diversity below the surface.

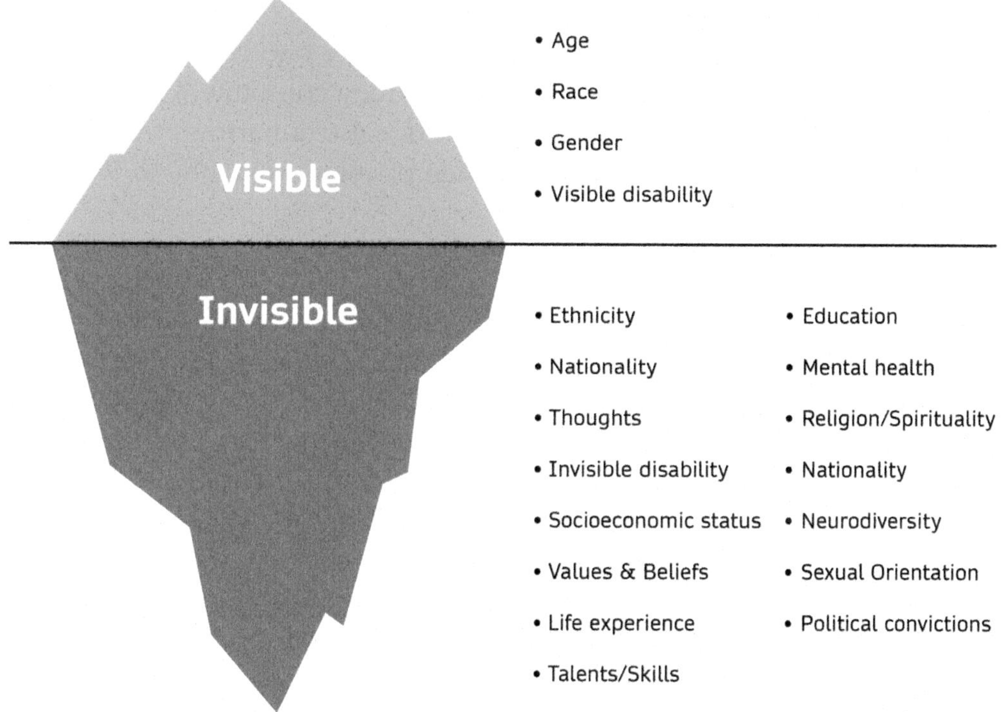

Figure 2.1 Visible and invisible forms of diversity.

To date, there has tended to be a focus on visible diversity and, even here, progress is woefully inadequate. According to the World Economic Forum (WEF 2023), at the current rate of change, it will take another 151 years to close the global economic gender gap.

And when we look at ethnic diversity, the situation is even more stark:

> As of 2022, ethnic minority representation in Chief Executive, Chief Financial and Chair roles stood at 3.7 per cent. This amounts to an increase of one additional ethnic minority leader since 2014.
>
> **(Nazir Afzal 2022)**

Intersectionality

Visible and invisible diversity considers each of the components of diversity in isolation. But, as the CIPD (2022) highlights, people have multiple identities that are interlinked in a complex way, which is why looking at intersectionality is so important. Research by McKinsey (2019) shows that in the US, for every 100 men who are promoted from entry level to manager, only 79 women receive the same promotion. It reduces even further to 60 for women of color, and there is insufficient data available on LGBTQ+ and disability inclusion. The higher up the corporate ladder one goes, the dominant voice, by a significant majority, is white men—they constitute 33% of entry-level roles, yet 61% at C-suite level. For men of color, it narrows from 19% at entry level to 13% at C-suite and, for women of color, from 19% to 5%.

Narrowing of Diversity

What is causing this narrowing of diversity and voice? Neuropsychologists use the term "affinity bias" to show how we unconsciously gravitate toward people like ourselves. According to Nazir Afzal (2022), many argue that affinity bias turns meritocracy into "mirrorocracy." How can a significant portion of the workforce thrive when they have no seat at the table nor any voice? How can you thrive when your talents are not recognized, and you have no space to develop and grow?

We also need to broaden what we consider "professional" and "managerial" if we are to fix the "broken rung," the first step up to manager. The narrow definition of professional is adversely impacting anyone who does not fit the straitjacket description of a manager. According to research by Deloitte (2013), this is even impacting white men as well, with 45% of straight white men currently "covering" at work (i.e., hiding their true identity). This is impacting individual PWB and draining precious psychological capacity.

Confidence and Competence

According to Ruchika Tulshyan and Jodi-Ann Burey (2021), we often falsely equate confidence—most often, the type demonstrated by white male leaders—with competence and leadership. Employees who can't (or won't) conform to male-biased social styles are told they have imposter syndrome. According to organizational psychologist Tomas Chamorro Premuzic (2021), men tend to think they are smarter than women, globally. Yet arrogance and overconfidence are inversely related to leadership performance. In today's VUCA world, leaders need to build high-performing teams. They need to create "we" cultures not "me" cultures, with a focus on high-trust, high-quality relationships with high levels of psychological safety.

Imposter Syndrome

So, what exactly is imposter syndrome? According to Ruchika Tulshyan and Jodi-Ann Burey (2021), it is a relatively common feeling of discomfort, second-guessing, and mild anxiety in the workplace, which is pathologized, especially in women. As white men's careers progress, not only are their work and intelligence validated, but they also have role models to emulate, and others rarely question their competence, or leadership style, whereas anyone who does not fit the narrow definition of professional and managerial is told to be assertive, but not too assertive, and not in that way. Walking this tightrope to find the almost elusive "Goldilocks" zone of professionalism is exhausting, draining psychological capacity, and negatively impacting PWB.

Systemic

Diversity is a systemic issue which cannot be fixed by individuals alone. It must be regarded as a strategic organizational imperative if we are to create environments where individuals can thrive. Thriving individuals can unleash their full psychological capacity to solve the organization's problems, to create and innovate. How CI can be used to help create this environment will be considered later in this chapter.

What Is Equity?

Equity or equality? And what's the difference? Equality is about sameness. Equity is about fairness. Equity is about allocating the resources and opportunities required to reach an equal outcome. The focus is on outputs and outcomes, versus inputs. It is also about eliminating what Marshall Chin and Alyna Chien (2006) call "systemic disparities" to create a meritocracy in terms of power and status. Inequity is predicated on a scarcity mindset—that there are limited resources and, if others have some, there is less for you. A meritocracy, however, is predicated on an abundance mindset—there is enough for everyone.

Power and Status

Power and status matter. It is the people who have power and status who allocate resources, design the system of work, create policies and procedures, define which behaviors are ok and not ok, and make available opportunities and support. It is also important because the "areas of the brain that are used to act fairly are less engaged the more power someone has" (Neuro Leadership Institute 2023). This means that we have to consciously design our workplaces to ensure there is equal voice, and transparency as the NLI's research (2023) indicates that transparency increases the likelihood of acting equitably.

Once again, we need to go back to the drawing board and redesign our workplaces to create equitable environments where individuals can thrive with high levels of PWB and psychological capacity.

Psychological Safety

We know from Google's Project Aristotle (2012) that psychological safety is the number one factor in determining team effectiveness and it, too, is impacted by equity. Research by Tirzah Enumah and Mike Arauz for August (2023) shows that the amount of psychological safety experienced by different team members is not distributed equally by default. Societal, situational, and cultural factors can deplete individuals' psychological safety in ways that are often invisible to members with more. This can result in vastly different, and inequitable, individual experiences within the same team. Organizations that want to create equal access to psychological safety must have an inside-out approach to meet different people's different needs.

Current Status

According to Jeremie Brecheisen (2023), sadly, only 30% of employees strongly agree they are treated fairly at their company. We have all heard of the glass ceiling for women and Ruchika Tulshyan (2022) vividly describes the image of a concrete ceiling for women of color. And diversity expert Trevor Phillips (2023) says that people of color seem to be superglued to the floor. Opportunities for these underrepresented groups tend to only come during difficult times. This is known as the "glass cliff" phenomenon. Nazir Afzal (2022) emphasizes the willingness to sacrifice those employees regarded as less valued and more dispensable—women and racial minorities.

And when women and people of color are given equal opportunity, they do not receive equal compensation. Brené Brown and Ruchika Tulshyan (2022) highlight that, for every dollar that a white man makes, Asian women make 85 cents, white women make 77 cents, Black women make 61 cents, Native American women make 57 cents, and Latinx women make 54 cents. Donald and Charles Sull's research (2023) indicates that the exodus of female leaders, dubbed the Great Breakup, is attributable in part to the persistent pay gap.

Toxic Culture

Donald and Charles Sull's research (2023) shows that women are 41% more likely to experience toxic workplace culture than men. They have defined toxic culture as consisting of five elements: lack of inclusion, disrespect, cutthroat behavior, abusive management, and unethical behavior. They draw a direct link between lack of power and experience of toxic culture.

Inequity—Statistics

Women are not the only ones to suffer unfair treatment. According to research by McKinsey (2020), ethnic diversity appears to have been less of a focus than gender for many organizations. Sue Unerman et al. (2022) highlight how prevalent inequity is with one in three people having experienced bias, harassment, or inappropriate behavior at work. This rises to 50% of 18–24-year-olds, 40% BAME, 61% disabled, 70% neurodiverse, 53% of people diagnosed with mental illness, and 48% of LGBTQ+. And that's if they have managed to get a job—the unemployment rate for people with disabilities is nearly double that of those without.

What Is Inclusion?

Diversity is a group of different people. Inclusion is about creating space for each member, listening to, and valuing their perspective. Without feeling valued and psychologically safe, individuals' PWB is negatively impacted, psychological capacity is reduced, and CI is stifled.

Inclusion or Exclusion

You either have inclusion, or you have exclusion. People either feel that they have space and voice, or they feel that they have no space and no voice. When people are not included, they are seen as "other." In ancient times, they would have been regarded as outside the tribe, when being excluded was tantamount to being sentenced to death.

We now use the term "othering" to describe the process of emphasizing differences and using those differences as justification for hierarchies. "Othering" creates power and systemic disparities where those who are different are often regarded as less than.

And who decides who is included, and who is excluded? It is those in power who have designed the system of work as it exists today. This is reflected in the McKinsey research (2020) which shows that, while over 50% of employees believe that sentiment on diversity is positive, this falls to 29% for inclusion. Clearly there is still a lot of work to do. So, what should we be considering when we look at inclusion?

An Inclusive Organization

The UK Equality Act (2010) defines an inclusive organization as a place where

> difference is valued, and people feel they belong without having to change who they are at work. Anyone, regardless of their identity, background or circumstance, has equality of access, treatment and outcomes at work, including equal opportunity to develop, progress and be rewarded. People are treated fairly, with dignity and respect.

Bringing your "whole self" to work, and being accepted for who you are, unleashes psychological capacity to solve problems and innovate, bringing benefits to individuals and organizations. Yet Sue Unerman at al.'s research (2022) shows that one in three people feel that they can't bring their whole self to work, with more women than men feeling this is the case.

The energy wasted in trying to fit in is known in academic circles as the "Glass Slipper Syndrome," where individuals "code-switch," i.e., change their behavior to fit the cultural norm. Vital psychological capacity is consumed with maintaining a façade, eroding PWB and causing organizations to miss out on the value of diverse perspectives and viewpoints.

Inclusive Mindset and Behaviors

Inclusion starts with mindset and intention, which show up in our behaviors. Inclusion is about how you think, feel, and act and—as we saw in Chapter 1—these are interconnected, and it starts with feeling. Donald Sull et al.'s research (2022) shows that *feeling* disrespected at work has the largest negative impact on an employee's overall rating of their corporate culture. Culture matters for employee engagement, for retention, discretionary effort, psychological capacity, and for PWB, and it all starts with inclusion. You must consciously design the workplace for inclusion, and for psychological safety. You must consciously create space to question the rule of thumb and truly value different perspectives.

An Inclusive System

For inclusion to work, it requires all layers of the system—individual, team, leader, and organization to work together. Crucially, it starts inside-out with the individual, and how they feel. This means that the other levels—the team, the leader, and the organization—must be flexible enough to meet the myriad needs of different individuals. The system of work must flex rather than the individual conforming to the status quo. The status quo is built on traditionally masculine traits and the cultural norms are based on authority, status, and compliance. This patriarchal alpha environment is not conducive for PWB for a large proportion of employees, including many men.

For inclusion to truly work, everyone must be included—we cannot "other" white men and make them a homogenous group. They will not see the value of diversity and inclusion through being shamed and excluded. We must show how we all benefit from an inclusive culture, where we are each regarded as an individual with individual needs, wants, and desires, where others truly care, and where we feel that we matter.

This does not mean that there is no accountability. In fact, it is the complete opposite. It opens the space to have brave conversations, to be challenged, and to be held accountable for what we say and do, and CI can be an important accountability lever.

What Is Belonging?

We're biologically hardwired for belonging and, according to Brené Brown (2021), research shows that the pain and feelings of disconnection are often as real as physical pain. The feelings of belonging matter, with the need to belong in the workplace coming second only to the need to belong at home. And a huge proportion of employees don't feel this is the case—the EY *Belonging Barometer* (2019) suggests that 40% of adults experience feelings of isolation at work. This impacts on your PWB and psychological capacity. When we feel isolated, the fight-or-flight response kicks in, releasing adrenalin and cortisol. Tunnel vision takes over and our thinking ability reduces. When we feel we belong, however, our body releases oxytocin, serotonin, and endorphins, which are conducive to social bonding and which enhance our PWB.

Our Whole Self

We saw that, to feel included, we need to be able to bring our "whole self" to work. Our "whole self" is who we are when we feel safe. As Jodi-Ann Burey (2021) highlighted in her TED Talk, it is easier to be who you are when that is the same as everyone else around you.

Three Levels of Belonging

To truly belong at work, belonging needs to happen on three levels as depicted in Figure 2.2.

The characteristics of belonging at each of the three levels are outlined in Table 2.1.

Micro Belonging Cues

Belonging shows up in micro belonging cues. As Daniel Coyle (2019) highlights, we're biologically primed to pay attention to largely unconscious physical signals, such as proximity, eye contact, body language, turn taking, and tone. These small cues are important as they send a clear signal that

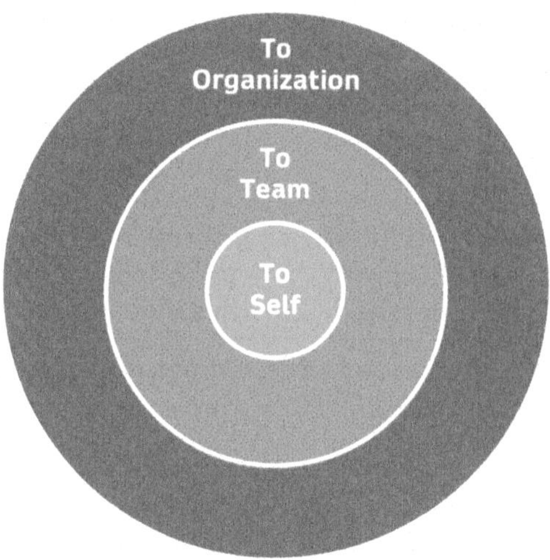

Figure 2.2 Three-layer model of belonging.

Table 2.1 Characteristics of Three-Layer Model of Belonging

Level of Belonging	*Characteristics*
To Self	Able to be real self Able to be vulnerable High levels of self-compassion
To Team	High levels of trust and psychological safety Feel connected to, and supported by, co-workers, including leaders Brave conversations Active listening Social accountability
To Organization	Shared sense of purpose Everyone has a voice Power with and power to Space for everyone to be their whole selves

you matter, you belong, you are cared for. David Epstein (2022) calls these micro belonging cues "connective tissue for the group brain."

Benefits of Belonging and the Impact of Not Belonging

The impact of belonging for an organization is huge, as is the lost potential when there is "othering," or "fitting in." Table 2.2 summarizes the benefits of belonging and the impact of not belonging.

Table 2.2 Benefits of Belonging and the Impact of Not Belonging

Benefits of Belonging	*Impact of Not Belonging*
Recruit and retain talent	Full benefits of diversity are not harnessed
Individuals can thrive and play to their strengths—full psychological capacity and discretionary effort is unleashed	Individuals are in a state of anxiety with reduced psychological capacity and negative impact on PWB
Can speak truth to power—decisions are based on true state versus curated image	Unquestioning acceptance of status quo—diminished risk management and reduced problem-solving
Can anticipate change	Performative culture—emphasis on spin versus truth. Culture of "emperor's new clothes"
Individual and organizational resilience	Individuals suffer burnout and physical health issues leading to absence and increased employee turnover

David Epstein (2022) sums it up when he says, "what efficiency was to the Industrial Revolution, relationships are to the present era." This echoes Josh Bersin (2022) who stated that we are now in the era of heart, rather than brains or muscles, which is why a belonging culture must be *the* culture at work.

Why Does DEIB Matter for Business?

In today's VUCA world, we need the psychological capacity, insights, ideas, capabilities, and discretionary effort of every individual. Without DEIB, we don't fully understand our customers, or our communities; we don't attract, or retain, the best talent; we don't innovate to the same degree; we don't have the adaptive organizational resilience we need to survive. And that impacts the bottom line.

Research from McKinsey Global Institute (2015) found that advancing women's equality can add $12 trillion to global growth. This potential is reflected in organizational results. A 2018 study by Boston Consulting Group found that increasing diversity in leadership teams increases profits. In short, when diversity increases, so too does a company's performance.

DEIB is about being good humans and it is also good for business, as Figure 2.3 shows.

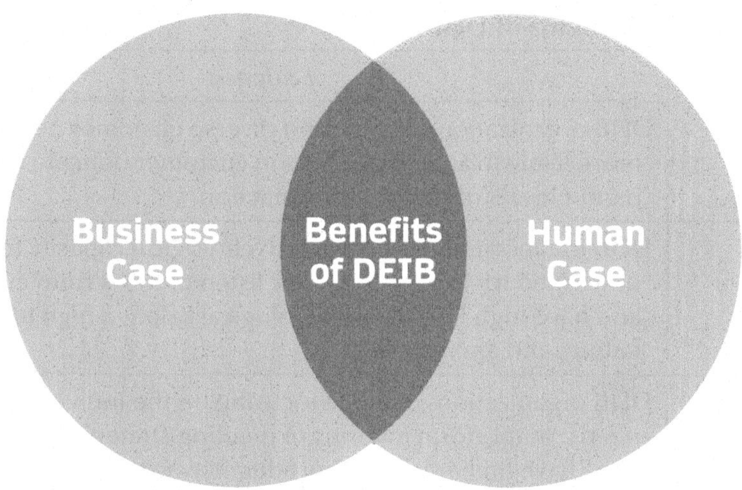

Figure 2.3 The benefits of DEIB.

Business Benefits for DEIB

The business case for DEIB is stark. The benefits are clear and progress has been far too slow despite calls from both employees and consumers. Later in the chapter, we will explore how we can accelerate the much-needed progress, and how CI can be leveraged to maximize advancement. The business benefits of DEIB can be seen in Table 2.3.

Why Does DEIB Matter for Us All?

The business case for DEIB is clear, but why does it matter for all of us as individuals? Feeling that you belong, that you can bring your whole self to work, increases PWB. Feeling you belong allows for precious psychological capacity to be utilized for work, for CI, and makes for a happier, more resilient workforce.

Research by McKinsey (2021) shows there is a huge gap between what people value versus what employers think they value. Employers' blind spots center on DEIB matters: feeling valued by the organization and your manager; a sense of belonging; having caring and trusting teammates; potential for advancement; and autonomy around how and when you work. It is imperative that we close this gap, both for business performance and because of the human impact. As Brené Brown (2021) says, in the absence of love and belonging, there is always suffering.

Table 2.3 Business Benefits of DEIB

Benefit	*Evidence*
Understand Customers Better	DEIB organizations understand diverse customer needs, and are more likely to anticipate shifts in customer demand and have higher levels of customer satisfaction.
Innovation	DEIB organizations allow vital psychological capacity to be unleashed for innovation. They listen to ideas from every level and have high levels of psychological safety, a high tolerance for failure, and are resilient.
Productivity and Performance	DEIB organizations, despite focusing on the individual and their needs, outperform in terms of meeting strategic business goals. They have higher levels of productivity with lower levels of attrition and absence.
Attraction of Talent	DEIB organizations are magnets for top talent.
Employee Retention	Feeling a sense of belonging at work is crucial for employee retention according to evidence from "The Great Resignation."
Employee Engagement	In DEIB organizations, individuals feel respected, valued, and that they matter. In this environment, individuals can thrive and grow and they willingly go the extra mile. Integrating DEIB into organizational Employee Engagement strategies, and joining the dots between engagement and DEIB, is vital.

The next section will explore how we might pivot the untapped potential of the CI system and tools to create diverse, equitable organizations where people are included and belong without having to fit in, or hide.

How We Can Make a Tangible Difference

It is evident that to really shift the needle on DEIB, we need systemic change. The change needs to happen at four levels (as depicted in Figure 2.4), starting with an inside-out approach with the individual at the heart.

We will now consider what to do at each of the four levels to foster PWB and increase psychological capacity from a DEIB perspective, to allow for a thriving culture of CI. Sounds good, does it not? It is not a utopia—it is possible. It needs intention and action, with all four levels working together synergistically, starting with the individual.

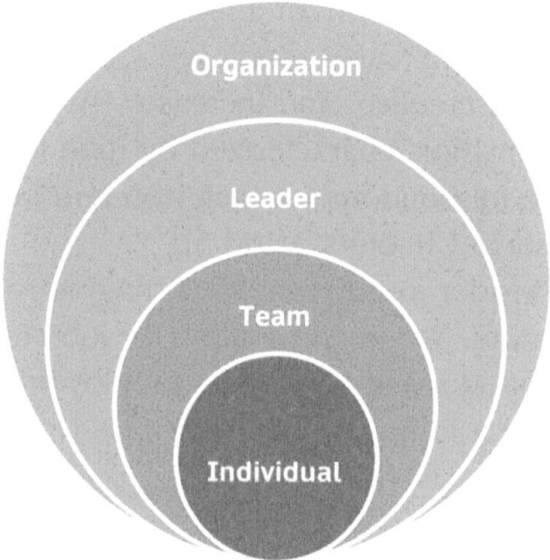

Figure 2.4 Four levels of change for DEIB.

Organization

The focus at an organizational level needs to be on systems, culture, and power. To date, the onus has been on individuals to engender change, but, as William Deming (1993) said, a bad system will beat a good person every time. Too much work thus far has been tinkering around the edges but, when dealing with systemic issues, there must be a willingness to dismantle and rebuild systems of work to create diverse, equitable, and inclusive cultures of belonging. There must be a willingness to share power—power to and power with, rather than power over.

Leadership

Leaders are the linchpins for implementing policies and practices equitably, ensuring psychological safety, creating environments of inclusion and belonging, and holding individuals accountable for their behavior. Organizations must recognize, and celebrate, a variety of different leadership styles and models. This will help to ensure that diversity does not narrow as you reach the top.

Team

Potential Project's *Mind at Work* study reveals that those who are socially connected at work are 14% more satisfied with their job, with employee satisfaction rising almost 50% when an employee has a best friend at work. Social well-being not only increases employee satisfaction and engagement, it also reduces absenteeism, and increases PWB. Psychological safety and high-quality relationships, characterized by high levels of trust and mutual respect, are the foundations for inclusion and belonging and will be explored in more detail in Chapters 3 and 5.

We also need to consider job design, to reimagine roles and responsibilities with DEIB in mind. We need to allow for job crafting, and to see leading initiatives and workstreams, such as Employee Resource Groups, as integral to work and not additional responsibilities.

Individual

The inside-out approach, starting with the individual, requires everyone to lead from every seat, what the Navy SEALs call "extreme ownership." Every individual has a part to play in what we think, say, and do. The individual is at the center as we are all unique. We have unique experiences, backgrounds, needs, and desires which influence how we see things, and how others see us. A one-size-fits-all approach will not work. Yuval Noah Harari (2018) writes in *21 Lessons for the 21st Century*:

> Even if you personally belong to a disadvantaged group, and therefore have a deep first-hand understanding of its viewpoint, that does not mean you understand the viewpoint of all other such groups. For each group and subgroup faces a different maze of glass ceilings, double standards, coded insults and institutional discrimination. A thirty-year-old African American man has thirty years' experience of what it means to be an African American man. But he has no experience of what it means to be an African American woman, a Bulgarian Roma, a blind Russian or a Chinese lesbian.
>
> **(Sue Unerman et al. 2022)**

The first step is increasing self-awareness and getting to know your own biases. Amy Gallo (2022) recommends taking a quiz to get a better sense of your susceptibility to hidden biases. One such quiz has been created by Project Implicit, a non-profit started by researchers at Harvard, the University of Washington, and the University of Virginia, which you can find at: https://implicit.harvard.edu/implicit/takeatest.html.

DEIB work is not easy, and it requires courage. With this increased self-awareness can come shame and grief, because there's a loss. There's a loss of innocence and how you once viewed the world, and there may be a loss of community. Developing shame resilience and self-compassion are crucial to navigating this difficult emotional terrain, as is increasing your empathy—stepping into someone else's shoes and walking a mile in them to see the world from their point of view.

Psychological Well-Being—Mental and Physical Health

The opposite of belonging is fitting in, changing and hiding your true self. This leads to cognitive dissonance, the mental conflict that occurs when your beliefs don't line up with your actions. Cognitive dissonance has an impact on PWB, reduces psychological capacity, and impacts physical health.

As we saw in Chapter 1, the fight-or-flight stress response, which can be induced by cognitive dissonance, can drive maladaptive coping strategies that manifest physically. According to Deepa Purushothaman and Valerie Rein's (2023) research, persistent symptoms include skin rashes, digestive challenges, heart issues, migraines, fertility issues, adrenal fatigue, and chronic fatigue.

Terrifyingly, Donald Sull et al.'s (2022) findings show that, when employees experience injustice in the workplace, their chances of suffering a major disease (including coronary disease, asthma, diabetes, and arthritis) increase by 35%–55%.

Individual Psychological Safety

PWB and psychological capacity require psychological safety. This concept is explored in detail in Chapter 3 and the focus here is on how different equity factors impact an individual's psychological safety. An article published in August 2023, *Looking at Psychological Safety Through an Equity Lens* by Tirzah Enumah and Mike Arauz, put forward a model that can be used to map your own equity lens. It shows how different elements, such as race, gender, sexuality, native language, and positional authority, combine. This model can be a helpful guide when considering how to build psychological safety with others as each individual has a different starting point and unique needs to enable psychological safety.

Psychological safety is crucial for creating DEIB cultures. Research by Henley Business School (2021) shows that fear is one of the main barriers. It is fear of being judged which holds people of color back from reporting discrimination, and fear of causing offence which prevents white employees from truly engaging with DEIB work. It is crucial that we create psychologically safe environments to open up dialogue, and demonstrate empathy and understanding to enable progress.

Behaviors

We know what the behaviors look like when there isn't DEIB; there is harassment and discrimination, and people are neither respected nor valued. But which behaviors create DEIB cultures? Building on Ruchika Tulshyan's (2022) BRIDGE framework, a suggested list of behaviors is below:

- Be okay with being uncomfortable.
- Reflect on what you don't know.
- Invite feedback.
- Defensiveness does not help.
- Grow from mistakes.
- Expect that change takes time.
- Choose courage over comfort.
- Use inclusive language.
- Demonstrate respect by being curious rather than judgmental—listen more than you speak, ask questions rather than make statements.
- Practice microaffirmations—small acts and gestures of inclusion and belonging.
- Act to interrupt bias and highlight positive behaviors.
- Be an ally—build equal, supportive relationships with underrepresented, marginalized, or discriminated individuals or groups with the aim of advancing inclusion and lifting their voice(s).
- If in doubt, flip it to test it. Flipping it interrupts the heuristics and shortcuts we normally take and gets us to appraise things afresh. For example, change "he" for "she" and vice-versa.
- Be proportional when responding—strike a balance between the severity of the nature of an act and the corrective measure applied in response to it.

How Can CI Help

CI and DEIB are often on parallel paths. If they were to work synergistically, there could be huge benefits for helping individuals to thrive. Thriving individuals have high levels of PWB and lots of psychological capacity to devote to creating thriving cultures of CI and transformative cultures of DEIB. How CI systems and tools could be pivoted and reorientated to include DEIB will now be explored.

Voice of the Customer

CI has the voice of the customer at its heart. It can be considered as a "true-north concept," guiding decision making and prioritization. Who, how, where, and when this information is gathered is crucial. If we were to do this with a DEIB lens, we would consider to what extent the people involved with this process are representative of our current and potential future customers. We would also consider the data being collected and analyze it for diversity and intersectionality. Care would be taken when conducting surveys, focus groups, and observations to ensure diverse representation of the people involved, both participants and facilitators, and to ensure equitable and inclusive practices and language.

An example of this is Dove's Real Beauty campaign from 2004 when Dove realized that there was a gap between what people wanted from beauty products and what was available on the market. It is considered to be one of the most successful marketing campaigns, demonstrating diversity in terms of age, ethnicity, and body shape. It was a resounding success, as it won several advertising prizes and sales doubled in three years.

Strategy Development and Deployment

Strategy Development and Deployment is about defining what the organization wants to achieve in relation to its vision and purpose. The main steps of the Strategy Development and Deployment process are summarized in Figure 2.5.

Including DEIB at all levels will ensure DEIB is integrated and embedded into the organization's strategy deployment process. The information flow, up and down, solicits feedback from each level and ensures a listening approach. This actively demonstrates respect for each individual and values their unique perspective. Co-creating the strategy and measures of success is vital to overcome othering and to build true DEIB cultures with a shared sense of purpose. Integrating DEIB measures of success into the wider organizational goals shows it is a key lever for organizational performance and helps to embed a DEIB culture.

CI helps to ensure that we start with the end in mind, with a shared understanding of what success looks like and how that translates into specific goals, both marginal gains and a step-change in performance. CI can also be used to make explicit what good looks like—to achieve X by when. Figure 2.6 illustrates operationalizing a DEIB Strategy using a CI system, blending goals, behaviors, tools, and culture.

The CI system is designed to operationalize goals and aspirations into tangible targets, to track progress, and—crucially—to define the behaviors required. Good behaviors achieve good outcomes. To create a DEIB culture, the strategy must be operationalized in a relational way, involving all levels, across all value streams, and at all stages of an individual's life cycle at work. Leaders must listen to the diverse perspectives on which qualitative and quantitative measures would be valuable to track and why.

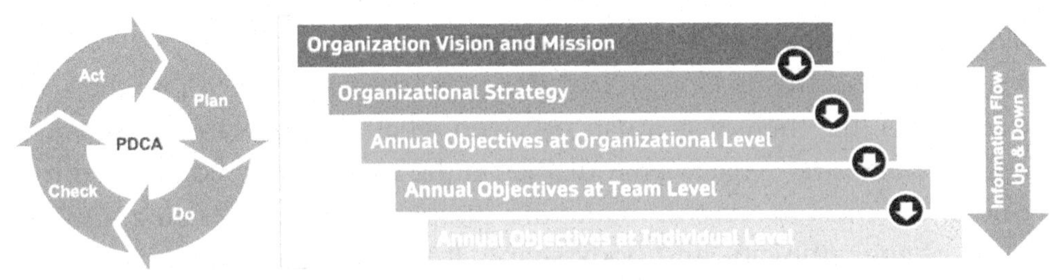

Figure 2.5 The strategy development and deployment process.

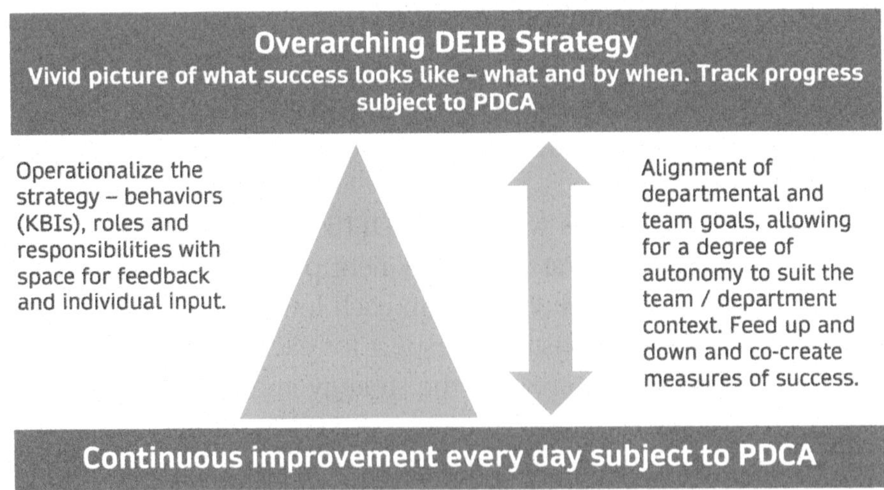

Figure 2.6 Operationalizing a DEIB strategy using CI.

There also needs to be the autonomy for teams to have specific measures of success depending on their current situation or the context within which they are operating.

Examples of some metrics are listed below:

- Quantitative—demographic representation, counting the number of ethnic groups, gender, abilities, sexual orientation, etc.
- Qualitative—employee feedback. For example, employee engagement surveys; retention, promotion, and bonus levels for underrepresented groups.

CI systems and tools can be used to great effect to analyze both quantitative and qualitative data. They have the flexibility to show both the big picture and delve into cross sections of the data, by team, by gender, by ethnicity, as well as allow for intersectional analysis. The analysis should balance shining a light on what's working well so that it can be recognized and amplified, along with looking for opportunities for improvement.

PDCA

Using the Plan, Do, Check, Act (PDCA) approach (Figure 2.7) ensures that progress against goals is reviewed regularly, and that action plans

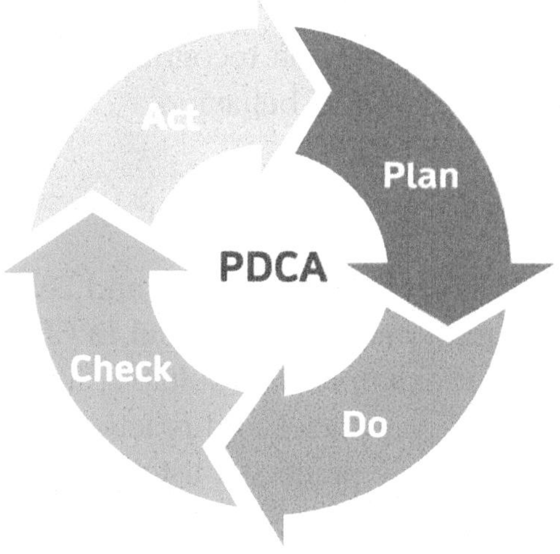

Figure 2.7 PDCA approach.

are instigated in the case of any gaps. Action plans should be based on a nuanced understanding of root causes of the problem, and should involve all individuals to ensure a complete understanding of the issue. It is important to involve a diverse group of people to co-create solutions, and develop ideas for progress.

This approach would significantly help close the gap between spend on DEIB and impact. The WEF estimates that, in 2020, companies worldwide spent $7.5 billion on DEIB-related efforts, and it is projected to more than double to $15.4 billion by 2026. However, there is minimal impact, especially at the higher levels of organizations.

Visual Management and Huddles

Communication is key, and time should be allocated to discuss DEIB strategy, measures of success, and action plans as leaders signal what is important to them by how they allocate their time. Whilst hearing from leaders is important, employees really need to see it and experience the DEIB strategy being lived for themselves. The changes must be visible and meaningful.

Using the principles of Visual Management, including DEIB goals, and measures of success on Visual Management Boards at all levels across the organization will increase transparency. It will also ensure that there is regular discussion on DEIB at huddles. Using CI's suite of analytical tools will ensure data is used to drive focused action plans. These should really start to shift the dial, particularly if there is psychological safety and everyone has a voice in what needs to happen.

Communication could also focus on recognizing what's working well and intentionally modeling desired DEIB behaviors.

Gemba

Gemba is a chance for leaders to Look, Listen, and Learn, and build connection and belonging. It is explored in more detail in Chapter 6. Leaders can Look, Listen, and Learn for examples of equitable, inclusive practices, and where there are gaps between policies and practices on paper versus lived experience. Leaders can actively practice a listening approach, and regularly ask questions focused on belonging.

Gemba is a fantastic opportunity to build high levels of trust, practice empathy, and be open to seeing things from another person's perspective. Doing Gemba with DEIB as an intention should only heighten that, as will slowing down and resisting the urge to rescue and fix. Instead, it is important that each individual feels heard and accepted. As the inimitable Dr Edith Eger (2021) says "love is a four-letter word—spelled T-I-M-E".

Behaviors

Behavioral deployment with a DEIB lens would ensure that the behaviors are enabling a DEIB culture and that there are no inhibitors, such as biased or non-inclusive language used.

Problem-Solving

When problem-solving, how do we ensure that we have diverse representation on our problem-solving teams? How do we approach problem-solving with a DEIB lens, with the intention to co-create and seek out diverse voices and opinions? How do we use inclusivity to work at the pace of the people concerned and avoid action bias from people in privileged positions?

We can use our problem-solving skills to be comfortable with vulnerability and to sit with the problem. Einstein is purported to have said, "If I had an hour to solve a problem, I'd spend 55 minutes thinking about the problem and five minutes thinking about solutions." And we can demonstrate equity, inclusivity, and belonging when defining which actions we will take. This means consciously considering who will complete each action and by when, co-creating action plans as equal partners.

Equity Value Stream Mapping

To understand how well the organization is creating a DEIB culture, Jeremie Brecheisen (2023) recommends carrying out a fairness audit. This involves benchmarking key equity issues, such as promotion rates, pay gaps, and development gaps to name but a few, and comparing them with external best practices. It is also extremely important to look inside the organization and measure employee perceptions about equity issues to understand what's working well and what isn't.

McKinsey (2020) recommends that, to reverse the narrowing of diversity at senior levels, organizations seek to understand where the pinch points in the talent pipeline are greatest. Value Stream Mapping (VSM) could be extremely powerful when used to this end.

Classic VSM was popularized by Mike Rother and John Shook (1998). It captures all of the actions required—both value added and non-value added—from the start to the end of a process in a visual manner, showing each process step and information flow. Typically, the focus is on value-added and non-value-added work. Our proposal is that you use VSM to reduce the eighth waste of lack of thriving, with a specific focus on equitable practices. The aim would be to complete equity VSM for all stages of the individual's lifecycle at work as outlined in Figure 2.8. However, here, we will focus on Recruitment and Selection (R&S) by way of an example.

The first stage would be to identify the number of VSMs that need to be completed as part of the R&S process. At a high level, the VSMs needed for

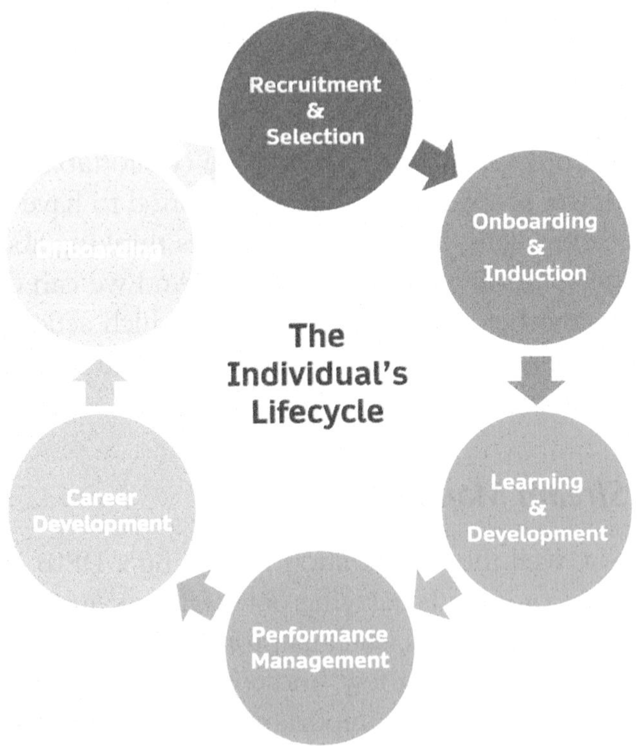

Figure 2.8 Individual's lifecycle at work.

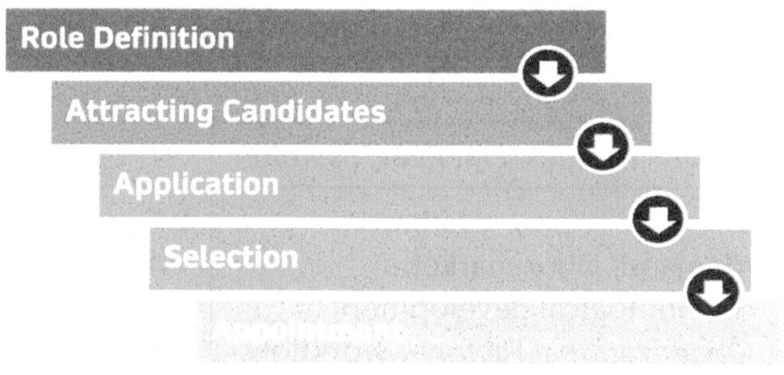

Figure 2.9 VSMs needed for recruitment and selection.

R&S are depicted in Figure 2.9. Having a diverse team complete the VSM is essential.

The next stage is to consider the steps which are needed within each Value Stream—what needs to happen. To illustrate how to do this, we'll hone in on role definition.

Firstly, we would consider the macro steps in role definition, before considering which systems, policies, and practices are involved with each step. All of this is concerned with "what." But, as we have seen, we all have a unique view and inherent bias, so "who" needs to be considered as well.

Table 2.4 provides a framework of what that could look like at a high level. Each of these components could then be broken down further. The first phase of that breakdown has been done for job analysis. The next step would be to look at each of the policies, practices, and systems within each of the four factors—External, Organizational, Human, Motivation and Growth—in more detail, looking for examples of equity and inequity.

Reorienting a tool, which is common in many organizations, would allow biased and inequitable policies, practices, and systems to be highlighted, and actioned, without the need for external consultants to complete "fairness audits." It would also integrate DEIB work into the lens of value-added and non-value-added work. Inequitable practices are most definitely non-value-added.

Once the current state has been mapped, the next step is to map the ideal state. After that, map the targeted future state and the action plans required to make that happen, as illustrated in Figure 2.10.

Some questions that could be asked as part of a fairness audit to identify current state and ideal future state are:

Table 2.4 Equity VSM Framework—What and Who

Equity VSM: R&S, Role Definition		
Category	*What—Policies, Practices, Systems*	*Who*
1. Job Analysis	*External Factors*—customer demand, labor market, technological development *Organizational Factors*—workflow, range of tasks and associated skills, capabilities, and resources *Human Factors*—Ergonomics, workload, work-life balance, including flexible working *Motivation & Growth*—meaningful work, autonomy, personal, and career growth	External Factors—HR Manager, Operations Manager Organizational Factors—HR Manager, L&D Manager, Manager of area concerned Human Factors—HR Manager, Manager of area concerned, H&S Manager Motivation & Growth—HR Manager, Manager of area concerned, L&D Manager
2. Job Description		
3. Person Specification		
4. Advert		

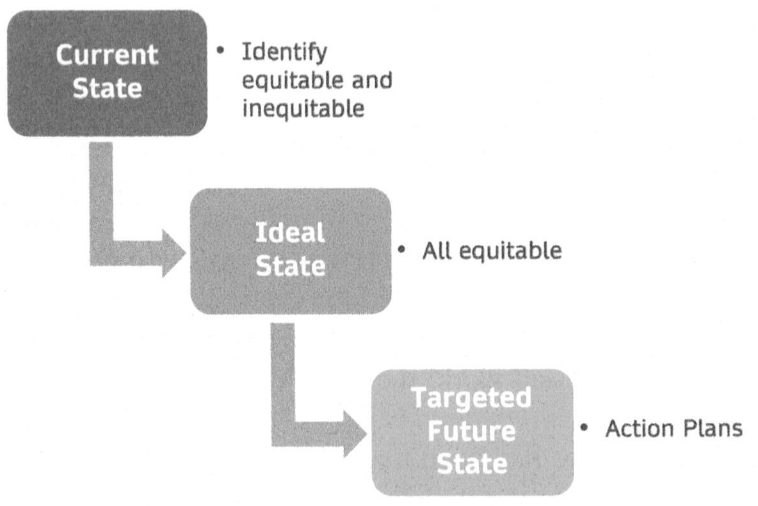

Figure 2.10 Current state to future state in VSM.

- What is the employee sentiment regarding the following statements: I feel I am treated fairly; I feel I am treated with respect; I feel valued; I feel that my work matters?
- Who progresses in the organization? Assess promotion rates at all levels and compare the percentage of diverse groups at each level from entry level through to C-suite. Does it narrow? If so, explore why using a listening approach.
- What are the pay gaps? How can these be eliminated?
- Who has power and status? Who has no power and status? Which systems, policies, and practices are creating this outcome and how can they be recreated with a DEIB perspective at the center?
- To achieve equity in terms of opportunities, which groups need additional resources to achieve that? What do the resources look like? Consider resources such as time, money, and support.
- Which behaviors are rewarded, and which are sanctioned? How do these enable a DEIB culture? If not, what needs to change?

The output of these can then be used to create a prioritized action plan, focusing on the actions which are easy to do, and which will have a high impact on creating a DEIB culture.

Conclusion

DEIB is crucial if we are to eliminate the eighth waste of lack of thriving, to create PWB and increase psychological capacity. Unleashing psychological capacity allows for thriving cultures of improvement and excellent organizational performance, agility, and resilience. We cannot create thriving cultures of CI without DEIB. And we need to start from the inside-out with the individual. We also need to look with new eyes. As Nazir Afzal (2022) highlights, structural injustice is tragically so ordinary and commonplace that people often struggle to see how deeply embedded injustice is in the fabric of organizations.

The CI system and tools can be reorientated and used to help make the much-needed breakthrough in DEIB and help integrate it into the way we do business and measure organizational success. There is huge potential, and we hope this will help you to realize this potential in your organization.

Key Points from Chapter 2

- DEIB is foundational to PWB and unleashing psychological capacity.
- DEIB starts with an inside-out approach, focused on the individual and what they need to optimize psychological capacity and for them to feel psychologically safe.
- To create thriving cultures of improvement you need psychological safety, which starts with DEIB. The CI system, tools, and practices can be used to create and embed psychological safety and transformative DEIB cultures.

Chapter 3

Why Care about Psychological Well-Being?

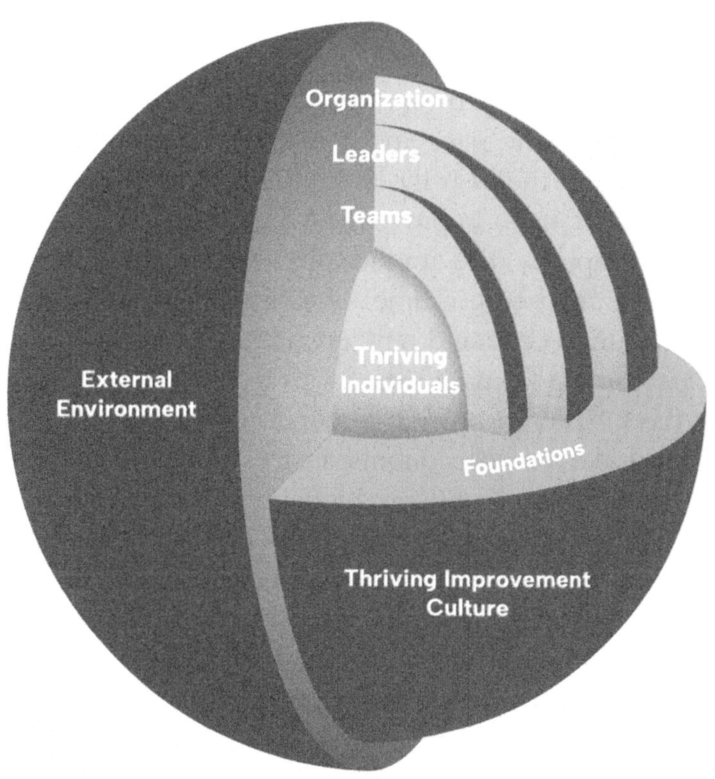

Figure 3.0 **The Why Care Model—Foundations.**

DOI: 10.4324/9781003413479-4

Introduction

Chapter 3 will focus on psychological well-being (PWB) as a foundational element within the Why Care Model. PWB is defined as an individual's ability to think, feel, and behave in a manner that enables them to perform effectively in their work environment, their personal lives, and in society at large. The chapter will also include how PWB interacts with an organization's continuous improvement (CI) system in creating a thriving improvement culture. A thriving improvement culture is one that is growing, developing strongly, or vigorously flourishing, helping the organization to proactively manage change, both internally and externally.

The authors believe that understanding the relationship between PWB and improvement is well overdue: it is a moral and economic imperative. The constant demand for organizations to improve performance while simultaneously managing the external environment is changing the very nature of work.

There has been a global explosion in volatility, uncertainty, complexity, and ambiguity (VUCA). The pace and complexity of work has continued to increase in the wake of the COVID-19 pandemic. The pressure continues to increase for organizations to improve how they engage and leverage the limited psychological capacity (the amount of emotional and cognitive energy, available for use, at any point in time) of every person in the workplace to help navigate this unprecedented new economic landscape.

Pressures are coming from all sides, with many factors having the potential to impact the PWB of people and, therefore, an organization's performance. These include: macro-economic factors, such as inflation, fiscal policy, employment levels, and international trade; geopolitical factors, such as the Russia-Ukraine war, protectionist trade policies, and energy transitions; technological factors, such as the rise of artificial intelligence and cybercrime; social factors, such as rising cost of living, healthcare availability, climate change, and threats to biodiversity; personal factors, such as family conflict, trauma, coping skills, neurochemistry, temperament, grief, socio-economic status, education, gender, health, and cultural traditions; and workplace factors, such as organizational culture, role clarity, job demand, leadership support, inclusion, and belonging.

People commence work each day with their own personal factors already consuming a large portion of their psychological capacity. These factors have their own associated PWB impact. The boundaries between personal and work life have blurred over recent years, with many people working more from home. The likelihood of personal factors merging into work life is therefore so much higher.

Organizations, on the other hand, are also constantly being faced with their own unique internal and external factors. These factors can flow on and impact the individual (e.g., layoffs, restructures, changing roles, higher job demands).

People are, therefore, faced with two sources of potential strain that can impact their PWB: firstly, the factors they bring into the workplace; and, secondly, the factors they are exposed to from within the workplace (Figure 3.1).

Leaving these factors unmanaged can leave the individual susceptible to harm, which can impact their ability to cope; in worst cases, leading to psychological breakdown and suicide. The ripple effect flows through to family and communities, leading to family breakups, financial loss, and withdrawal from support networks.

Caring about the PWB of individuals, although primarily a moral duty of care, is also a critical input for caring about the health of the organization's bottom line. The two are becoming far more intertwined and intrinsically linked. The more pressure that is placed on organizations to perform, the more pressure that is placed on individuals to deliver these results.

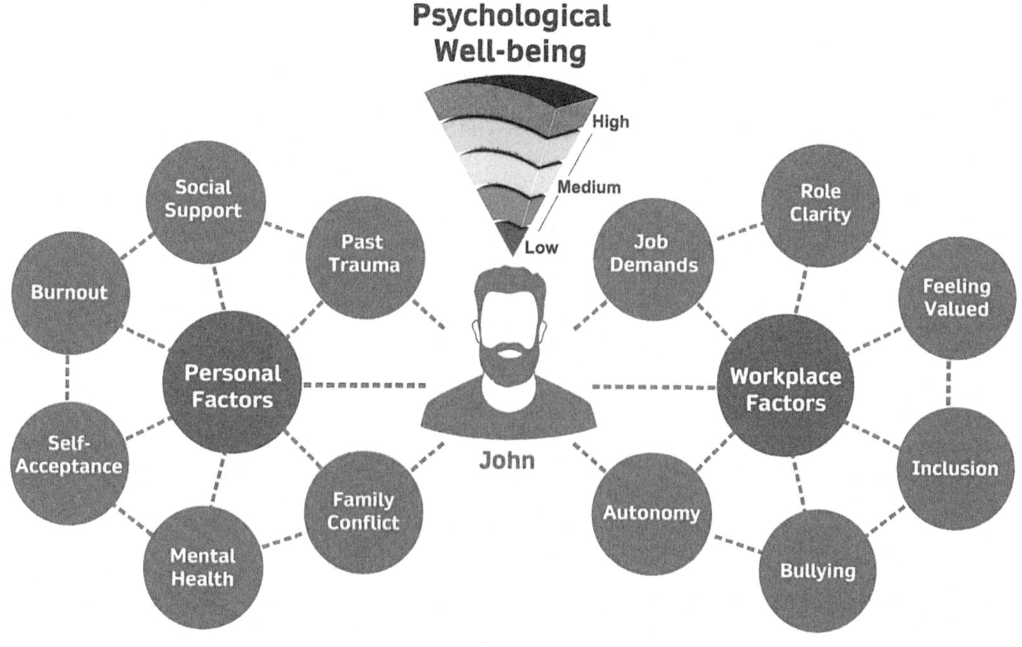

Figure 3.1 PWB is impacted by personal and workplace factors.

PWB cannot be collateral damage in the pursuit of achieving excellent results. It is not "either/or" but "and." The goal is to ensure that excellent results are an outcome of leveraging the input of positive PWB. Pushing the well-being of people to breaking point to produce a positive result is no longer acceptable. Both need to prosper to meet ethical, social, and organizational expectations.

> Employee well-being contributes to a thriving workplace culture. But true employee well-being is more than just healthy employees and physical wellness. It means helping employees feel their best, do their best, and bring their most authentic selves to work. Companies must be places where employees feel a sense of connection and belonging; a place that creates peak moments where employees feel the company cares about and appreciates them. Centra Health did just that.
>
> **(Amy Martin and Aubrey Varraux, *Wellbeing and Recognition: The Heartbeat of Thriving Workplace Cultures*, 2023)**

For any organization to thrive in the current environment, they must embed a culture of CI. This is simply not possible without proactively supporting the PWB of every individual within their employment.

Psychological Well-Being Consists of Various Elements

PWB consists of numerous elements that focus on the emotional, cognitive, behavioral, and social aspects of a person's life. Together, these elements provide a holistic understanding of the state of a person's well-being. Each element exists on a continuum and can either be lacking or thriving (e.g., no sense of direction in life versus deeply driven and guided by purpose).

The health of each element and/or combination of elements can increase or reduce PWB. Improving the state of merely one element will, however, not make a substantial inroad into increasing overall psychological capacity. A comprehensive approach is needed that monitors the condition of all elements. The goal is to regularly assess the health of each element as a proactive measure to ensure positive well-being is maintained. A positive state of well-being ensures optimum levels of psychological capacity to thrive in life (Figure 3.2).

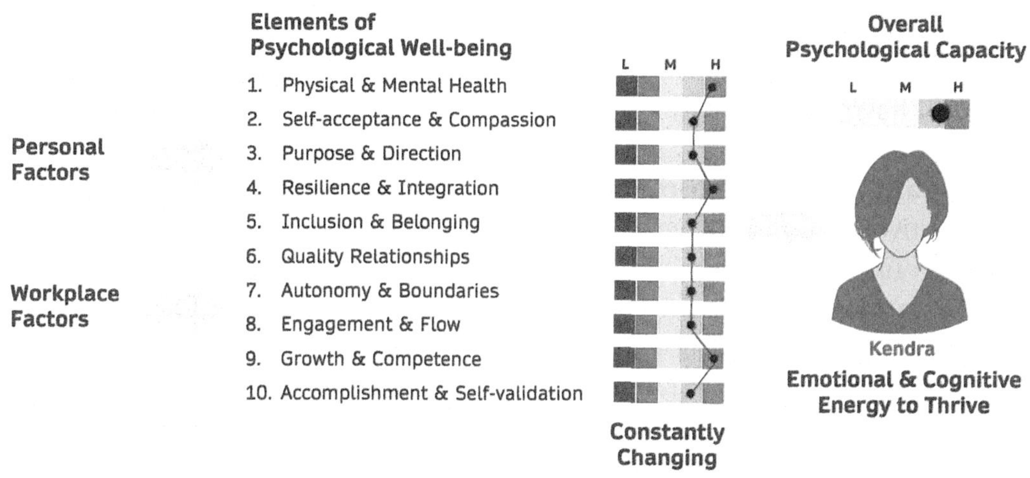

Figure 3.2 PWB impacts an individual's psychological capacity.

The ten elements selected draw insight from various well-established models, such as the PERMA model, which was introduced by Dr. Martin Seligman in 2012 to increase and measure well-being. This model defines well-being in terms of positive emotion, engagement, relationships, meaning, and accomplishment (PERMA). In addition, the model for PWB proposed by Carol Ryff was also referenced. The model consists of six components: self-acceptance, autonomy, purpose in life, personal growth, positive relations, and environmental mastery.

The 10 Why Care Elements of Psychological Well-Being

1. **Physical and Mental Health**—Feeling confident in your physical and mental health and taking the steps to maintain and/or improve it. The ability to thrive in life because of the positive state of your physical and mental health.
2. **Self-Acceptance and Compassion**—Embracing all of who you are, whether physical or mental. You are kind and understanding rather than harshly self-critical when you fail, make mistakes, or feel inadequate.
3. **Purpose and Direction**—Having a clear sense of direction in life with strong goal orientation and conviction that life holds meaning.
4. **Resilience and Integration**—Having the ability to adapt to difficult or challenging life experiences. Having the ability to seamlessly weave together all aspects of your life.

5. **Inclusion and Belonging**—Feeling valued and respected for who you are and being able to contribute your perspectives and talents. Knowing you have access to the same opportunities as others, have a voice at the table, and are heard.
6. **Quality Relationships**—Developing caring, trusting, and supportive relationships with others where there is mutual support and encouragement.
7. **Autonomy and Boundaries**—Your ability and capacity for self-governance and self-direction, including your ability to set limits for what is ok and not ok, even if this means disappointing others.
8. **Engagement and Flow**—The level of involvement and commitment you have to a task. The amount of time and fulfillment you get from being in flow ("in the zone"), total absorption in what you are doing.
9. **Growth and Competence**—Learning and pushing yourself to experience new things to fulfill your potential. Developing and applying your knowledge, skills, and abilities to solve problems and achieve worthwhile tasks.
10. **Accomplishment and Self-Validation**—Celebrating achievements in your life and regularly reflecting on the accomplishment of goals. Encouraging yourself, acknowledging your strengths, successes, progress, and effort.

The Impact of Personal Factors on PWB

Our personal life factors emerge the day we are born. Some of these factors remain constant (e.g., race, personality, and temperament), some can change over time (e.g., age, coping skills, self-esteem, attitude, beliefs, interpersonal relationships), and some get added (e.g., new trauma/grief, health factors, education).

These unique factors are split into biological, psychological, and social categories (Figure 3.3). The categories represent the whole person, including their physical body, emotions, thinking, behaviors, and social context of their life.

The impact of these factors on PWB is unique to the individual. We all have, for example, different genetic codes, upbringings, family situations, childhood experiences, levels of education, personalities, beliefs, coping mechanisms, lifestyles, social support, and socio-economic status. The impact of these factors on PWB is dynamic and constantly changing.

The Biopsychosocial Model (Table 3.1) provides insight into what some of these factors are.

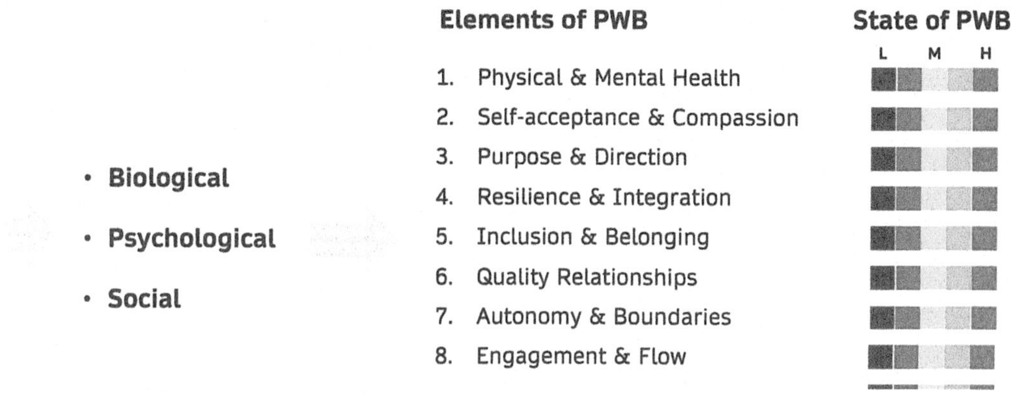

- **Biological**
- **Psychological**
- **Social**

Elements of PWB | **State of PWB** (L M H)

1. Physical & Mental Health
2. Self-acceptance & Compassion
3. Purpose & Direction
4. Resilience & Integration
5. Inclusion & Belonging
6. Quality Relationships
7. Autonomy & Boundaries
8. Engagement & Flow

Figure 3.3 **Personal factors (biological, psychological, and social) impact and individual's state of PWB.**

Table 3.1 **The Biopsychosocial Model**

Biological	*Psychological*	*Social*
Age	Self-acceptance	Cultural traditions
Gender	Grief	Family history
Lifestyle	Emotions	Living environment
Neurochemistry	Behaviors	Access to care
Genetics	Perceptions	Socio-economic status
Physical health	Past trauma	Support network
Immune function	Beliefs	Education
Flight-fright response	Coping skills	Marital health
Body mass index	Self-worth	Work relationships
Temperament	Mental health	Working conditions
Physiology	Learning and memory	Domestic violence
Stress reactivity	Meaning in life	Financial resources
Disability	Motivation	Marginalized group
Nutrition	Attitude	Community support
Fatigue/burnout	Resilience	Social causes

> The biopsychosocial model was first presented in 1977 by George Engel. His landmark idea described a dynamic interaction between pathophysiological, psychological, and social variables, and highlighted the hypothesis that, the workings of the mind, could affect the body, as much as the workings of the body, could affect the mind.
>
> **(Timothy Cocks, "Everything Old Is New Again, on a History of the 'Biopsychosocial Model,'" 2018)**

"Biopsychosocial" is comprised of "bio" (physiological pathology), "psycho" (thoughts, emotions, and behaviors such as psychological distress, fear/avoidance beliefs, current coping methods, and attribution), and "social" (socio-economical, socio-environmental, cultural factors, family circumstances, and benefits/economics). This model suggests that biological, psychological, and social factors are all interlinked and important in promoting health or causing disease.

Although each factor has its own influence on PWB, it is usually the combination of factors and how they interact with each other that can have the biggest impact. The quantity of possible combinations of factors is almost impossible to predict. No two people are the same. It depends on their unique biological, psychological, and social makeup and is constantly changing, based on new personal and workplace events and experiences.

For example, the intersecting of genetic vulnerabilities, past trauma, and interpersonal relationships can have a much bigger impact on a person's well-being than any one of these on their own. These personal factors can have positive or negative influences on an individual's well-being. It is important for the individual to be self-aware and understand how these factors can influence their health. This will help the person develop a plan to lock-in positive factors and eliminate and/or manage negative factors.

The plan can be discussed with a family member, friend, leader, trusted peer, and/or coach for feedback and guidance. The more a leader can understand the "whole person," the better. By understanding the individual more deeply, the leader can be more intentional in providing fit-for-purpose support. Biopsychosocial factors need to be valued. They are the individual's unique blueprint and represent the complex, but critical, diversity that is required for an organization to thrive.

The Impact of Workplace Factors on PWB

Two concepts will be focused on regarding ensuring positive PWB within the workplace: firstly, the level of psychological safety within a team; and secondly, how well a Psychological Health and Safety (PH&S) system has been embedded for preventing psychosocial hazards from harming people (Figure 3.4).

Psychosocial hazards pertain to anything in the design, management, or social context of work that has the potential to cause psychological harm/injury. A psychological injury includes a range of cognitive, emotional, and

Workplace Factors

- **Psychological Safety**
  Conducive Atmosphere
- **Psychological Health & Safety (PH&S)**
  Conducive Workplace

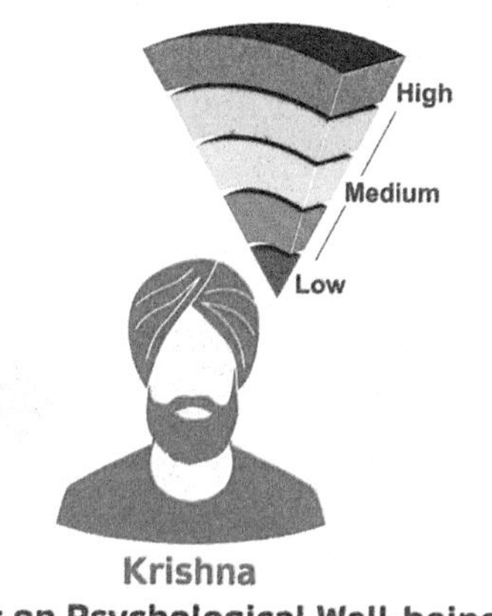

Impact on Psychological Well-being
Conducive Mindset

Figure 3.4 Workplace factors focus on psychological safety and PH&S and their impact on PWB.

behavioral symptoms that interfere with a person's life and can significantly affect how they feel, think, behave, and interact with others.

Psychological safety is defined as the

> shared belief held by members of a team that it is ok to take risks, to express their ideas and concerns, to speak up with questions, and to admit mistakes—all without fear of negative consequences, it is felt permission for candour.
>
> **(Amy Edmondson, *The Fearless Organization*, 2019)**

Psychological safety is an atmosphere where people feel safe to speak up, solicit feedback, own up to mistakes, and challenge the status quo without fear. It is critical for embedding a workplace atmosphere that is conducive to creating a thriving culture of CI and innovation. CI cannot exist in an atmosphere of fear and self-preservation. It requires the freedom to speak and be heard, to be insatiably curious, and to relentlessly challenge bureaucracy.

PH&S is the application of a risk management framework for identifying, risk assessing, eliminating, and/or controlling sources of work-related stress. The authors believe that PH&S needs to be elevated to the same level of importance that has been placed on physical health and safety and prioritized as a compulsory strategic imperative. The importance thereof is evident in the recent release of a global standard for PH&S (ISO 45003). It is the first global standard that helps organizations identify and control work-related hazards and manage psychosocial risks within an occupational health and safety system.

ISO 45003 was published on June 9, 2021, and is a product of 74 countries coming together, with the goal of making the workplace more psychologically safe and healthy. Much of ISO 45003 sets out how psychosocial hazards arise, addressing how the workplace is organized, the social factors at work and the work environment itself.

People are constantly being faced with psychosocial hazards, also known as workplace stressors. These stressors stem from multiple sources. Some originate from the design and management of people's work, and others are rooted in the social fabric of the work environment and include, for example, relationship conflict, weak leadership, and inappropriate behaviors.

These hazards have remained hidden and unmanaged for a long time, causing untold psychological harm to millions of people. The impact of prolonged exposure to these workplace-stressors can cause physical and psychological breakdown, which can take a lifetime to recover from. The implementation of the ISO 45003 standard helps organizations protect individuals from being harmed by these hazards.

The Cost to the Organization of Not Managing Workplace Factors

Organizations are being forced to prioritize and increase their focus on the design, management, and social context of their workplaces. Not doing so increases the risk of people being exposed to psychosocial hazards. Prolonged and/or severe exposure to these hazards can lead to severe stress, which can then lead to psychological injury and reduced PWB.

The focus of this book is less on the physical aspects of well-being; however, the link between physical and PWB is unequivocable. Poor PWB can lead to both physical and psychological injuries (e.g., injury at work, high blood pressure, fatigue, or depression). Our body and mind are not separate, so any impact to the mind can have an impact to the body and vice versa.

A physical injury, chronic illness, or not feeling good about your health can cause psychological harm, including low mood, post-traumatic stress disorder (PTSD), and/or anxiety. Anxiety in turn can cause physical problems, such as headaches, feeling dizzy, and constant heart palpitations. Physical and PWB are intertwined and operate interdependently (Figure 3.5).

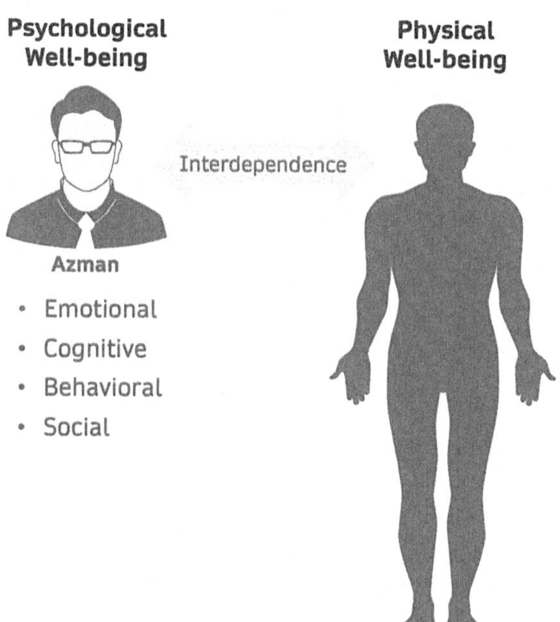

Figure 3.5 Physical and psychological well-being are interdependent.

"Work related stress, depression, and anxiety account for 44% of work-related ill-health and 54% of working days lost in the United Kingdom. Over 11 million workdays are lost each year because of stress at work" (Health and Safety Executive, n.d.).

Job stress is estimated to cost American companies more than $300 billion a year in health costs, absenteeism, and poor performance, with 40% of job turnover being due to stress. According to the US Center for Disease Control and Prevention (CDC), absenteeism alone costs US employers $225.8 billion annually, or about $1,685 per person. The Canadian Policy Research Networks estimates that stress-related absences cost Canadian employers about $3.5 billion each year.

A workplace saturated with psychosocial hazards can result in many different outcomes, such as increased accidents, fatalities, higher absenteeism, exhaustion, presenteeism, short-and long-term disability, increased turnover, insurance claims, increased number of grievances or lawsuits, and decreasing satisfaction and commitment. These factors in turn have significant impacts to health and safety of individuals and performance of the organization (Figure 3.6).

Presenteeism, for example (when people are at work in body, but not in mind), can lead to serious physical injuries or fatalities. The act of not being

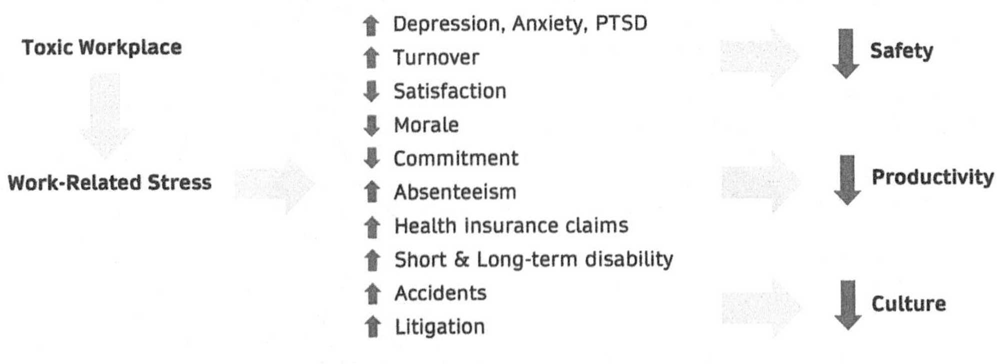

Figure 3.6 Workplace factors can negatively impact the individual and organization.

present at work, or distracted, can lead to catastrophic outcomes for the individual. The workplace needs to be a safe place for every individual.

The organization has a duty of care to make sure it meets its obligation to care for the health and safety of every individual. Meeting this commitment ensures families, communities, customers, and shareholders are subsequently taken care of. Workplace factors need to be managed with chronic unease (a state of unrelenting watchfulness, a persistent suspicion that all is not well, that something could go horribly wrong at any moment).

PWB Is Impacted by Severe and/or Prolonged Stress

Severe and/or prolonged stress can have a detrimental impact on people's PWB (Figure 3.7).

Stress is defined as a "state of emotional or mental strain/tension resulting from adverse or demanding circumstances" (*Oxford English Dictionary*). Stress can be caused by factors both inside and outside of the workplace. Irrespective of source, stress impacts all elements of PWB, which influences how a person thinks, feels, behaves, and interacts with others at any point in time.

Inappropriate levels of stress can impact a person's sense of purpose, inclusion, and belonging. It can break down relationships and stunt personal growth. It can reduce confidence and make people doubt their capabilities. It takes people out of psychological flow (a state of mind in which a person becomes fully immersed in an activity) and reduces their effectiveness. The ability to effectively manage stress is a key enabler for ensuring PWB, which

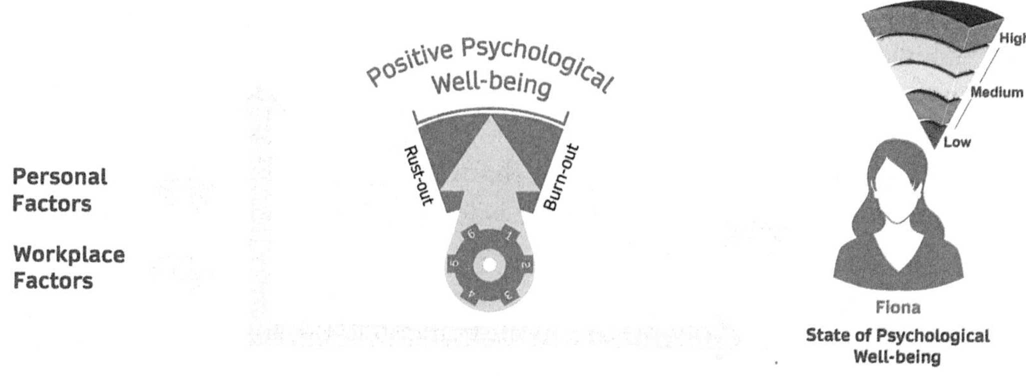

Figure 3.7 Personal and workplace factors can cause severe and/or prolonged stress that can negatively impact PWB.

in turn is a key enabler for ensuring optimum psychological capacity for personal and organizational improvement.

> Work-related stress is the physical, mental, and emotional reactions that occur when people perceive the demand of their work exceeds their ability or resources to cope. Work-related stress if severe and/or prolonged can cause both physical and psychological harm. The longer the work-related stress continues unresolved, the higher the risk that a psychological injury can occur.
>
> **(SafeWork SA 2020 Mental Health)**

Organizations, therefore, have an accountability to ensure they prevent and/or control psychosocial hazards from impacting the health and safety of the people who work for them. Managing workplace stress can literally be a matter of life and death.

A broad-brush approach to helping people manage stress at work is not effective, simply because it is such an individualized experience. The unique nature of people's genetics, past experiences, and personal and workplace circumstances requires a deeply personal approach. The myriad of personal and workplace factors at play, including how they interact with each other, requires a multi-pronged approach. This includes the creation of a psychologically safe workplace climate, embedding systems to prevent psychosocial hazards from causing psychological harm, and embedding regular touchpoints with individuals to assess and manage their PWB.

Many people enter the workplace already dealing with the effects of psychological harm. People may have developed these injuries through past personal and/or workplace events. Organizations need to acknowledge and accept this as a norm going forward. They need to plan for it and ensure the necessary capabilities and support mechanisms are in place to support this groundswell of need. The duty of care is to ensure the individual and organization thrive.

> The fact that some people are more vulnerable because of events connected with their personal lives does not relieve an organization and leaders of their responsibility and obligations to prevent occupational risks.
>
> **(*FPS Employment, Labour, and Social Dialogue*, 2016)**

PWB Has an Impact on Psychological Capacity

PWB is constantly changing. This natural instability has a knock-on impact to psychological capacity (Figure 3.8).

The emotional and cognitive energy required to thrive in life is therefore not limitless. It is susceptible to many interacting personal and workplace factors. As each well-being element is impacted (positively or negatively), it changes the overall psychological capacity available for use by the individual.

Worry, fear, uncertainty, poor relationships, not feeling included, lack of growth, and limited control over decisions that impact people's work are all examples of how PWB can be negatively impacted. If they are left

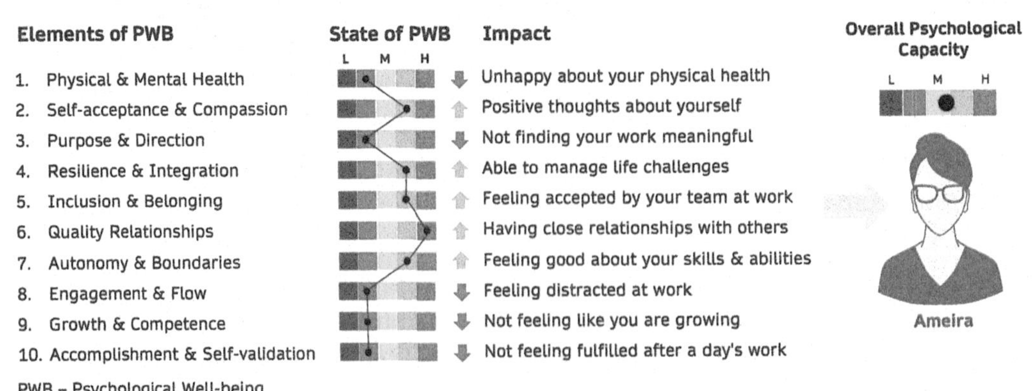

Figure 3.8 PWB has an impact on psychological capacity.

unresolved for a prolonged period, this can substantially reduce the person's capacity to thrive.

Feeling a deep sense of purpose in life, feeling included, personal and career growth, autonomy to make decisions about one's life, and strong relationships with others are examples of how PWB can be positively impacted, providing energy to thrive.

The elements of PWB have a cumulative impact on psychological capacity. Some elements may increase capacity and others may erode these gains. The objective is to ensure that well-being is being increased across all elements, rather than just a few. These then need to be carefully maintained to avoid any drop in scarce psychological capacity.

Psychological Capacity Has an Impact on Continuous Improvement

The ability of any organization to stay abreast of change requires the full use of every person's knowledge, skills, and abilities. Every person within the organization needs to see themselves as having two jobs: their day job and improving their day job. Improvement needs to be treated as equal to what people do (work equals improving work) versus nice to have or an addition to work.

This ideal, however, is dependent on an individual having optimal psychological capacity.

> Don't expect people to produce if you don't first cultivate an environment that enables well-being and regeneration of human energy. A recipe for workplace despair is having high performance expectations in a system that erodes well-being and extracts the energy needed to perform.
>
> **(Zach Mercurio, *The Invisible Leader*, 2017)**

Improvement requires emotional, cognitive, behavioral, and social energy. The act of identifying and implementing improvements, while at the same time being good at your day job, requires effort and effort requires energy. Sustainable improvement requires deep thinking, challenging the status quo, interpersonal risk taking, cross-functional engagement, and relationship building. Solving complex problems requires

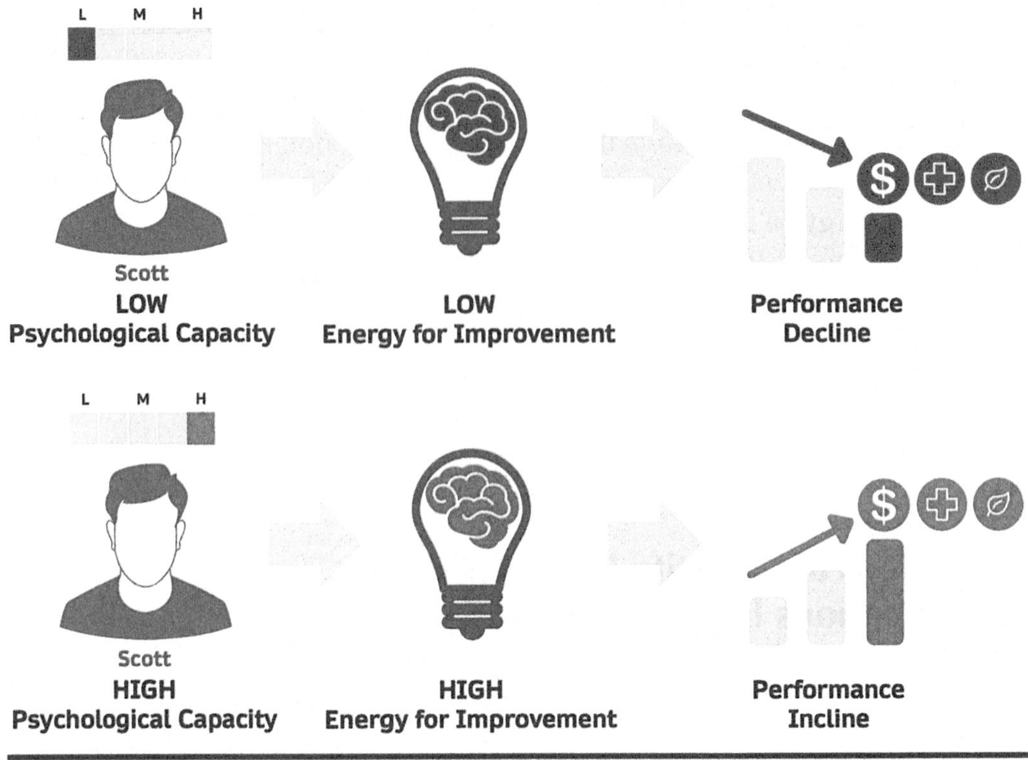

Figure 3.9 Psychological capacity enables CI.

perseverance and a "never-give-up" mindset. Energy drives creativity and creativity drives CI.

Positive PWB is the energy source that enables people to think creatively, behave ideally, and connect deeply. It ignites and increases psychological capacity, which in turn can be used to continuously improve and innovate (Figure 3.9).

A thriving improvement culture requires bucketloads of psychological capacity. Filling the bucket is the outcome of managing psychological well-being, one person at a time.

Psychological Capacity Is Not Limitless

As previously stated, the personal and work lives of people have melded much closer together since the COVID-19 pandemic. The line between personal time and work time has almost disappeared, which has put further strain on how psychological capacity is allocated.

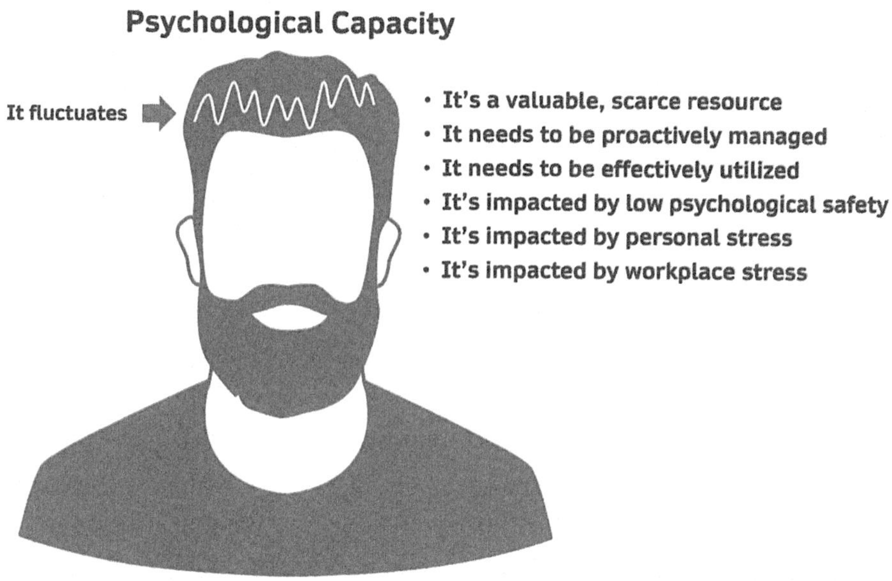

Figure 3.10 Psychological capacity isn't limitless and is constantly changing.

People do not start work each day with an unlimited reservoir of capacity to use (Figure 3.10).

Their state of PWB can change from day to day, based on personal and workplace factors. The normal stresses of life, whether personal or in the workplace, drain energy. A drop in energy reduces our ability to cope, be productive, contribute fully, and reach our potential.

This circumstantial volatility can sometimes be predicted but in most cases it is unforeseen. The unpredictable nature of life can destabilize—in worst cases dissolve—psychological capacity. The risk, in either event, is that people struggle to cope. Take the following scenario:

> John comes to work and is shouted at in front of his peers by his manager, leaving him feeling disrespected and devalued. His emotions take a knock. Feelings of anger, resentment, and embarrassment flood his emotions. His psychological well-being starts dropping.
>
> The next day, John goes to work avoiding his boss and sheepishly walks through the workplace. He does not feel psychologically safe anymore. He starts focusing his emotional and mental energy toward surviving versus thriving. Psychological capacity that should have been used to excel at work is now being used to manage

> work-related stress. His confidence drops, which reduces his ability to be the best version of himself. Both individual and organization lose.
>
> John feels unfulfilled at work, which flows through to his family life. The organization loses because John stops contributing his ideas for improvement because he feels devalued.
>
> Combine this workplace situation with a death in John's family and his emotional and cognitive capacity will drop dramatically, impacting his ability to manage his life.
>
> The organization cannot afford to not support John through this difficult time. They do so because they care about him as a human being that needs help. In addition, they know that John takes great pride in his work and not being able to work or work at previous levels of performance could impact his PWB even further. Finally, they help John because they know that having him stable and healthy helps the organization succeed.

Organizations need to treat psychological capacity as a scarce resource, an asset for driving the organization forward. Understanding and effectively managing psychological capacity should be one of the most important activities prioritized by leaders. Every person working for a leader will have their own unique, constantly moving, profile of PWB (Figure 3.11) based on personal and workplace factors. Leaders need to understand each person's profile and help manage it. Psychological capacity isn't limitless and requires proactive management.

There are only so many hours in a day and there is only so much energy a person can make available to execute and improve work. If a person works eight hours a day, 261 days a year (excluding weekends), then the organization has 2,088 hours of psychological capacity available for use. Multiply this by 100 people and we have 208,800 hours of collective psychological capacity. The challenge organizations face is how to make use of this contractual capacity in the best way possible to simultaneously benefit the individual and organization.

No longer can organizations merely provide fruit bowls in the communal area, offer gym memberships, childcare vouches, paid annual leave, discounts at retailers, bean bags, free coffee, after-work drinks, team days, corporate wellness calendars and campaigns, outsourced professional support services,

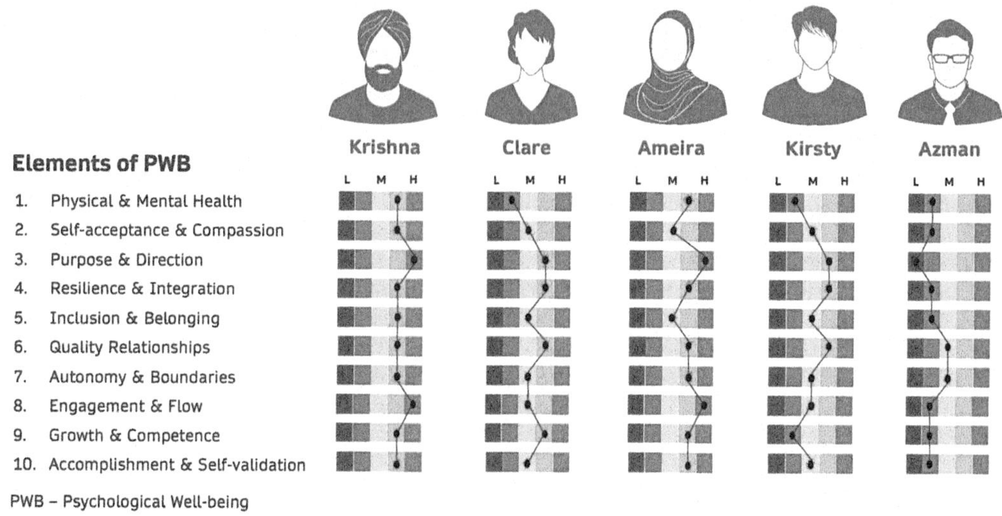

Figure 3.11 Psychological capacity needs to be managed one person at a time.

or online tools to proactively manage PWB and subsequent capacity. They need to dig deeper and be a lot more proactive in ensuring the design and management of work, including social environment, is conducive for positive PWB. This includes developing an employee well-being strategy that can be proactively implemented in an intelligent and genuinely impactful manner.

Individuals can never be expected to continue increasing their resilience when the workplace is the cause of their psychological challenges. "We need to stop just pulling people out of the river. We need to go upstream and find out why they're falling in" (Desmond Tutu, *Going Upstream with Positive Psychology in Our Schools*, 2022).

Psychological capacity needs to be treated as a valuable resource. It needs to be proactively managed, one person at a time, as a critical input to ensuring the aspirations of both the individual and organization are met.

The Thriving Matrix

The Thriving Matrix (Figure 3.12) was developed to show the relationship between three factors: (1) Continuous Improvement System; (2) Psychological Well-Being; (3) Knowledge Productivity. For each of the three, there is a continuum of maturity from one to five (low to high).

The Matrix illustrates that achieving a thriving culture of CI (Point A) is an outcome of a thriving CI system (Point B), effectively utilizing the available psychological capacity of thriving individuals (Point C).

Psychological capacity is increased when the organization and leaders proactively focus on improving the PWB of every person within the workplace. The goal is to achieve high *system flow* (seamless flow between the technical and social aspects of the organization's CI system), high *psychological flow* (individuals being completely absorbed, focused, and involved in their work, being "in the zone"), and high *knowledge flow* (flow rate of improvement ideas).

Knowledge flow is severely constrained if system flow and psychological flow are low. The opposite is also true; knowledge flow is unconstrained and increases when system flow and psychological flow are high.

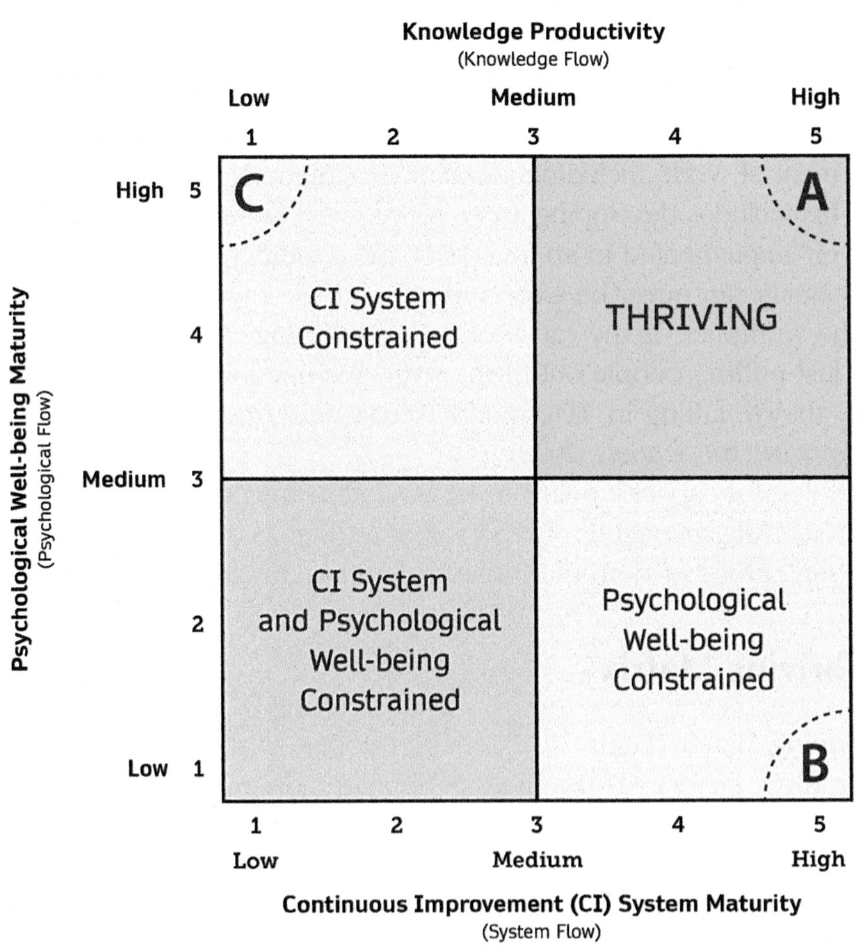

Figure 3.12 The Thriving Matrix.

Table 3.2 Twelve Principles of the Thriving Matrix

Knowledge Productivity	*Psychological Well-Being*	*Continuous Improvement System*
1. Knowledge productivity needs to be measured.	6. Managing PWB is critical for people to feel valued and respected.	10. Embedding an improvement system ensures optimum use of psychological capacity.
2. The flow rate of knowledge needs to be increased.	7. Positive PWB should be used to increase psychological flow.	11. The system should be glued together by role-modeling ideal behaviors using KBIs.
3. The cycle time for idea implementation needs to be reduced.	8. Embedding a system for preventing psychological harm improves PWB.	12. The system needs to be regularly assessed to determine its effectiveness.
4. Ownership for improvement needs to be created to reduce cycle time.	9. Creating a psychological safe workplace enables improvement and innovation.	
5. People need to feel valued for improvement to be fully owned.		

KBIs: Key Behavior Indicators; PWB: Psychological Well-Being.

The 12 Design Principles of the Thriving Matrix

The Thriving Matrix was created based on twelve design principles (Table 3.2). These have been categorized based on the three axes of the matrix: Knowledge Productivity, Psychological Well-Being, and Continuous Improvement System.

Knowledge Productivity

1. Knowledge Productivity Needs to Be Measured

The productivity of capital, equipment, and people are measured and tracked rigorously as key indicators of performance. Knowledge is, however, not explicitly treated as an organizational asset and therefore seldom gets measured.

Knowledge, and the effective use thereof, has become the currency of the 21st century. The knowledge economy (or the knowledge-based economy) is an economic system in which the production of goods and services is based principally on knowledge-intensive activities. The key element of value is the greater dependence on people and their intellectual property for the source of innovative ideas and problem-solving.

Organizations need to capitalize on this "knowledge" to improve performance. Knowledge utilization needs to, at minimum, match internal gap closure requirements and at least keep up with (but ideally be faster than) the pace of change from the external environment. Knowledge productivity is, therefore, the actual rate (hours it takes) for ideas to be implemented to close gaps in internal performance and manage the external environment.

A simple idea implementation plan can be used by the team to set targets and track actual results (Table 3.3).

Table 3.3 Idea Implementation Plan

	Idea Implementation Plan		*Jan*	*Feb*	*Mar*	*Apr*	*May*	*Jun*
1	Total quantity of people in the team	Mostly fixed but adjust as the team size changes	15	15	15	15	15	15
2	Target ideas implemented per person per month	Agreed with the team. Raise the target as each person's waste elimination skills improve*	5	6	7	8	9	10
3	Target ideas implemented for the team per month	Set by team based on historical performance	75	90	105	120	135	150
4	Total working hours in a month for an individual	Adapt based on unique situation (8 hrs × 22 days in a month = 176 hrs)	176	176	176	176	176	176
5	Cycle time (hours) to implement an idea for an individual	Goal is to reduce cycle time—Knowledge Productivity (176 hrs/ agreed target of ideas per month)	35	29	25	22	20	18

* Eliminating waste that the individual can implement themselves (micro improvements). Ideally in less than 48 hours.

Row 1 on the plan is the quantity of people on the team. Row 2 is the agreed target quantity of ideas every individual needs to implement for the month. Row 3 is the total target for the whole team. Row 4 is the total hours an individual works in a month and can be adjusted based on a team's specific situation. Row 5 is the hours it takes for an individual to implement an improvement idea (hours worked/implementation target per month). The team may want to reduce this cycle time (row 5) by increasing the implementation target per month (row 2), thus improving their knowledge productivity. Increasing targets should not be rushed. It needs to be done in parallel with a good understanding of the team's capacity and demand. The goal is to ensure the improvement ideas are kept small and focused on the elimination of waste that frustrate people every day when doing their work.

The idea implementation plan can be used by leaders at all levels within the organization when talking to their teams about CI. Teams can look at actual results from previous months to agree on target cycle times for the following month.

The purpose of the plan is to help mold an improvement mindset. Hoping that improvement will be integrated into work will not drive a change in the way people think about their jobs. Making improvement part of daily work needs to be a habit that is practiced over and over. It needs to become so natural that it emerges without any conscious thought but, rather, muscle memory. This culture of improvement is deliberately created.

2. The Flow Rate of Knowledge Needs to Be Increased

The goal is to ensure a steady flow of knowledge; more specifically, the flow of improvement ideas—a steady, continuous stream of improvement ideas that can be used for driving excellence. These ideas need to come from every person in the organization, not merely from a few improvement professionals. Thousands of ideas should be constantly generated. Like a fast-flowing river, the flow of ideas needs to cascade within and across all teams in the organization.

Tracking the quantity of ideas against set targets helps the organization understand the health of their knowledge flow. The goal is to track this over time and see if the trend is increasing. If the rate is dropping, then leaders should ask why and encourage their teams to keep making improvements part of what they do every day.

The flow rate of knowledge is a key indicator of how engaged people are in the workplace and how well the organization is leveraging the collective intellect of all its people.

This is why we need a targeted number of ideas to be submitted per person per month. If we keep a constant, steady supply of ideas flowing through the company, improvement will be inevitable.

(Norman Bodek and Bunji Tozawa, *The Idea Generator*, 2001)

3. The Cycle Time for Idea Implementation Needs to Be Reduced

A steady flow of improvement ideas, however, is not enough. These improvement ideas need a high conversion rate. Ideas need to be converted into solutions much quicker, reduced from months and weeks to days.

This is done by reducing the time (cycle time) between an idea being identified and the idea/solution being implemented (Figure 3.13). Having ideas sit in an idea management system for months, if not years, is of no use to the individual to make their job easier or to the organization to improve performance. Ideas need to be kept alive. They need to be made visible, spoken about often, and tracked to determine the time it takes to implement.

4. Ownership for Improvement Needs to Be Created to Reduce Cycle Time

Reducing the cycle time occurs when idea implementation is unconstrained. Idea implementation becomes unconstrained when all people own improvement as part of their daily work. People do not seek permission to improve their work; they just do it because it makes their job easier. They don't need

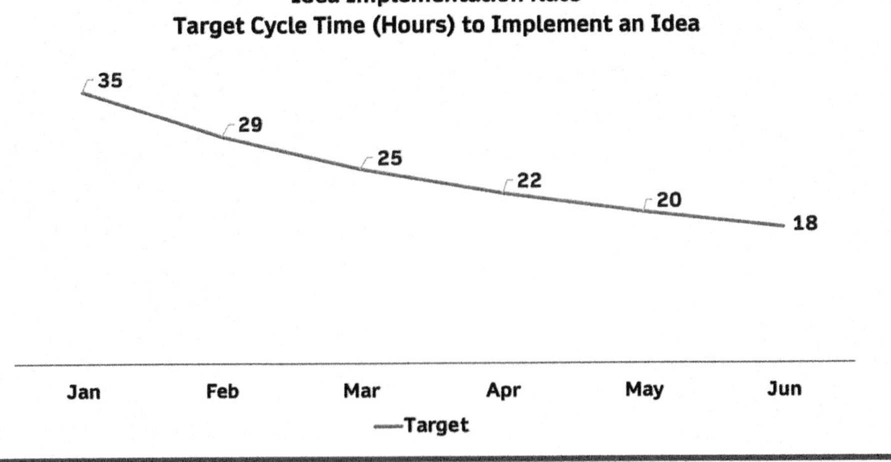

Figure 3.13 Reduce the cycle time to implement an idea.

lots of money or project teams to implement ideas. They do it themselves by using their knowledge and experience of the processes they work with. They apply their unique knowledge and creativity to solve problems rapidly for themselves and with other team members without waiting.

A thriving CI culture is defined as one in which *all* people are improving *all* processes, *all* the time, at *all* levels of the organization. Improvement is not seen as the job of a few "improvement professionals" (Six Sigma Black Belts, Lean practitioners, Reliability Engineers, Financial Analysts, etc.), but the responsibility of every person working within the organization. Waiting for a few improvement professionals to solve problems will take far too long to keep up with the current pace of change. As previously stated, every person should be informed that they have two jobs—firstly, doing their day job; and secondly, improving their day job (Figure 3.14).

Work is seen as equal to improvement versus it being an add-on. The goal is to learn in the flow of work—this is when learning happens in the moment and as part of a regular workday. Learning is the job. It is not something that is scheduled for an hour each week or a day each month.

Leaders need to engage with every individual within their workplace, to Look, Listen, and Learn. They need to encourage improvement ownership and remove bureaucracy so that people can see their improvements come to life. This drives up ownership because people can see the benefits of their idea implementation.

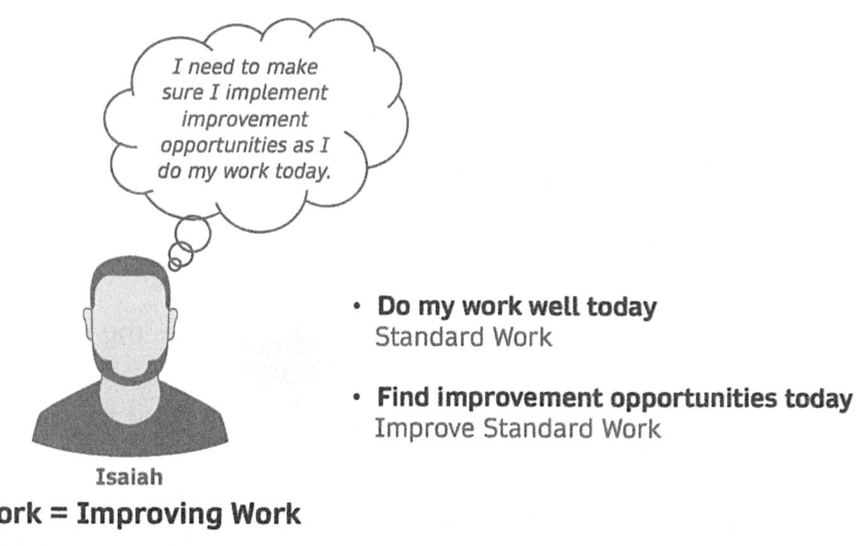

Figure 3.14 People have two jobs—doing their work and improving their work.

5. People Need to Feel Valued and Respected for Improvement to Be Fully Owned

People, however, will not own improvement if they do not feel valued. Expecting people to apply their discretionary effort in using their creative genius toward improvement, when they are not feeling valued, is unrealistic and naive. When people feel valued, they are more likely to be engaged in their work and feel more driven and satisfied with performing their work.

People need to know that who they are—their whole self—is accepted, included, and appreciated. They also need to know that what they do at work is recognized and seen as an important contribution to making the organization succeed. They need to know that their voice matters. They need to know that they are heard.

If people are not treated with dignity and respect, and recognized as the true experts of their work, they will hide and diminish their contributions to improvement. Thriving individuals are those who work within an atmosphere of autonomy, where their unique nature, style, and ideas are treated with utmost care. They feel psychologically safe to take risks without worrying about making a mistake. They feel supported by their team members and leaders, and know that being vulnerable by sharing their improvement ideas is ok and not something to be feared. "No passion so effectively robs the mind of all powers of acting and reasoning as fear" (Edmund Burke, *A Philosophical Enquiry into the Origin of Our Ideas of the Sublime and Beautiful*, 1756).

People shouldn't fear challenging the status quo; it should be encouraged. The obligation for respectful dissent should be promoted as a critical enabler for CI. People should come to work each day excited about finding new ways to improve their work and help others do the same. Ensuring full ownership for improvement is, therefore, an outcome of every individual feeling deeply valued for who they are and their unique knowledge, skills, and ideas for improvement (Figure 3.15).

Feeling valued drives up PWB, which in turn increases the psychological capacity to improve. An organization can never expect people to willingly contribute their wealth of knowledge, experience, and skill when all they are doing is trying to survive at work because they do not feel they are worth much. People will self-preserve and hide when the workplace isn't psychologically safe and/or if people are constantly being exposed to psychosocial hazards.

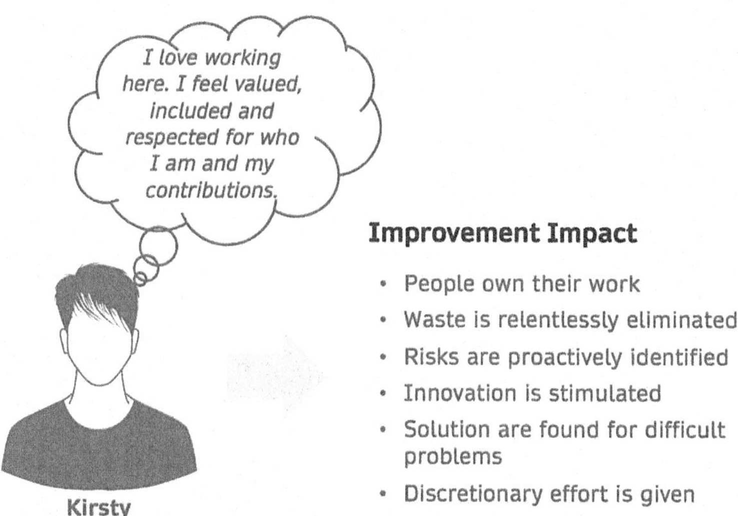

Figure 3.15 Individuals help create thriving cultures of improvement when feeling valued.

Psychological Well-Being

6. Managing Psychological Well-Being Is Critical for People to Feel Valued

The state of every person's PWB needs to be regularly assessed. This can include feedback, guidance, and support from family members, friends, trusted peers, and/or coaches. The biggest impact on an individual's PWB at work is, however, their one-up leader—the person they report to.

> Managers have just as much of an impact on people's mental health as their spouse (both 69%)—and even more of an impact than their doctor (51%) or therapist (41%).
>
> **(The Workforce Institute at UKG, *The Impact of Work on Mental Health*, 2023)**

Leaders have two responsibilities: first, to help their team members manage their PWB; and second, to reflect and improve areas in their own leadership style that could be contributing to any negative impact. Leaders need to be courageous and acknowledge that they could be the reason for harm. This could be from not proactively preventing psychosocial hazards harming individuals, to not helping create a psychologically safe workplace or role-modeling behaviors that promote care.

PWB is best understood and supported through one-on-one relationships. Regular meetings should be held between the leader and the individual to understand their current state of PWB and any proactive steps that can be taken to ensure positive outcomes (Figure 3.16).

It is important that during these meetings the leader acknowledges any shortcomings they may have in not preventing negative impact on a person's PWB. Showing vulnerability and sincere care helps to build the relationship and increases trust. People will share more of what they are feeling and going through when they see that the discussion is not merely to tick a box but rather a sincere engagement to see where support can be provided.

The leader will not be able to extract valuable well-being information from the individual if there is no trust in the relationship. Trust is earned in small moments. If this has been eroded over time, then the leader will struggle to know the real psychological state of an individual.

Building and maintaining trust is, however, a competency and leaders can work at improving the trust between them and the people they lead. Understanding and consistently demonstrating trustworthy language and behavior will help leaders earn and keep the trust of the people they lead.

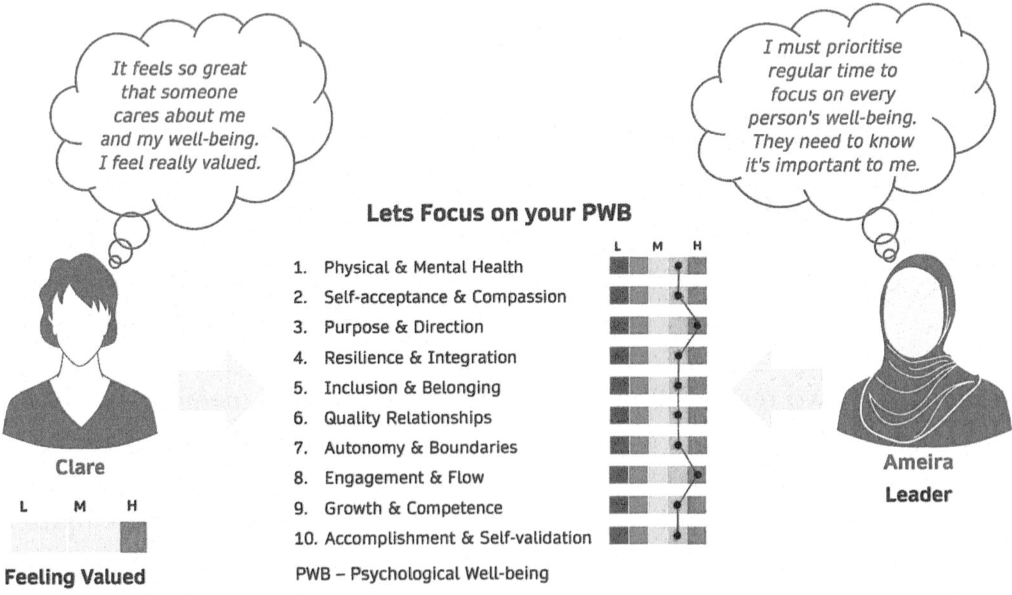

Figure 3.16 Individuals feel valued when their well-being is treated as a priority by their leader.

> Trust is defined as choosing to risk making something you value vulnerable to another person's actions.
>
> **(Charles Feltman, *The Thin Book of Trust*, 2008)**

People will openly share their well-being state if they feel it is safe to do so. If they feel that the information will be used in a negative way and spoken about behind their back as a weakness, then they will never share the truth about how they are feeling. Proactively managing well-being is non-negotiable for ensuring individual and organizational success.

7. Positive Psychological Well-Being Should Be Used to Increase Psychological Flow

Positive PWB increases psychological capacity. The goal is the optimum utilization of this available capacity. Assuming an organization has 2,088 hours of unconstrained capacity available per year per person, how much of this total time is being used to help the organization prosper?

It will depend on the amount of time during this period that the individual is operating in psychological flow or "in the zone." Psychological flow captures the positive mental state of a person being completely absorbed, focused, and involved in their activities at a certain point in time, as well as deriving enjoyment from being engaged in that activity. Psychological flow is characterized by the complete absorption in what a person does, and a resulting transformation in one's sense of time.

Flow is the melting together of action and consciousness; the state of finding a balance between a skill and how challenging a task is. It requires a high level of concentration; however, it should be effortless.

> Flow is being completely involved in an activity for its own sake. The ego falls away. Time flies. Every action, movement, and thought follows inevitably from the previous one, like playing jazz. Your whole being is involved, and you're using your skills to the utmost.
>
> **(Mihaly Csikszentmihalyi, *Flow: The Psychology of Optimal Experience*, 1990)**

People can have a substantial impact on the organization's performance when they are in regular flow, when the relationship between their work demand (challenges) and their capacity (skills) to fulfil this demand is in balance (Figure 3.17).

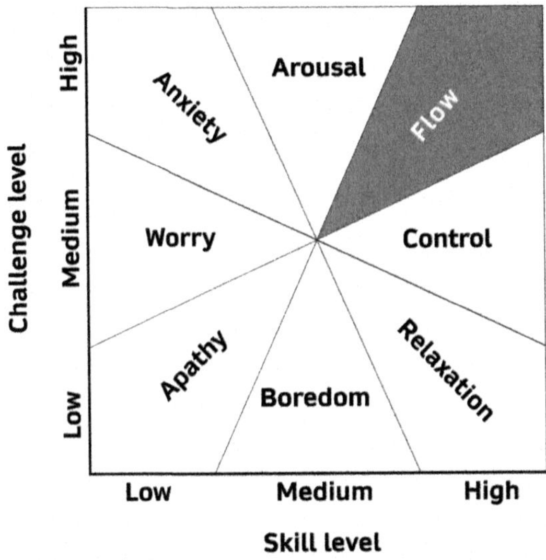

Figure 3.17 Psychological flow is the ideal balance between skill and work challenges.

High work demand without the skills to fulfil this demand can lead to anxiety, which reduces PWB. Low work demand with high skills leads to a lack of job satisfaction and not fulfilling potential.

A flow state is achieved when the demand and skill levels are high. People draw confidence from their skill levels and can take on challenging work. The outcome of consistent flow is a positive impact on various elements of psychological well-being. People feel they are growing from having to achieve challenging goals. They also get a sense of pride from knowing their skills are recognized.

The more people are in flow, the more they feel engaged with their work and feel a sense of fulfillment at the end of a day's work. This all drives up PWB. This positive state of well-being helps people display ideal behavior and work well with others in solving complex problems. The goal for every leader is to help the individual use as much of their available capacity in the most effective manner. They need to help people focus on what matters most—enjoying their work and leaving work each day feeling like they made a difference.

A lack of psychological safety and the presence of psychosocial hazards in the workplace draws people away from being in flow. Instead of focusing on their work, they are consumed by emotions, thoughts, and actions to guard themselves against harm. Self-preservation is the enemy of improvement. The goal is to make sure as much of the 2,088 hours of employed psychological capacity is used in the most rewarding, productive way possible.

Personal and workplace stressors take people out of psychological flow. It reduces the effective use of their knowledge, skills, and abilities because they are focused on things other than their job. Increasing psychological flow is a key enabler for creating a thriving culture of CI and innovation.

There are a few simple actions a leader can take to help individuals stay in flow:

(a) Scheduling regular one-on-one time with their direct reports to discuss any stress they are experiencing in their personal life, linked to any of their biopsychosocial factors. This could just be offering a listening ear, showing empathy, and/or helping people think through their circumstances. In addition, they can discuss whether there are any persistent workplace stressors that are impacting the individual and how they can help eliminate and/or control these factors impacting their PWB.
(b) Conducting regular, informal visits to the place where individuals are working to connect and do informal check-in; periodic pulse checks on people's PWB.
(c) Spending time working through the individual's capacity and demand profile. Talking through how they manage their time, including whether they believe they have the appropriate resources, including skills, to meet the demands of their work.

8. Embedding a System for Preventing Psychological Harm Improves Well-Being

Focusing on the design, management, and social context of people's work is an important foundation for ensuring positive PWB. This is done through the implementation of a system for ensuring the psychological health and safety of every person in the organization.

The global standard ISO 45003 Psychological Health and Safety in the workplace was published on June 9, 2021, by the International Standards Organization. The standard is intended to help organizations identify and control work-related hazards and manage psychosocial risks within an occupational health and safety system (Figure 3.18).

Psychosocial risks occur due to exposure to psychosocial hazards. Psychosocial risk is defined as the potential of a psychosocial hazard to cause harm.

Figure 3.18 Eliminating and/or controlling psychosocial hazards improves PWB.

> Psychosocial risks may arise from poor work design, organization and management, as well as poor social context of work, and they may result in negative psychological, physical, and social outcomes such as work-related stress, burnout or depression.
>
> **(European Agency for Safety and Health, *Psychosocial Risks and Mental Health at Work*, 2021)**

Organizations will now be held accountable for implementing the standard. The goal is to prevent psychological harm. Preventing harm ensures PWB is maintained and/or improved.

Too often, people are put in a job and told to get on with it, without having any process for ensuring they have the appropriate resources to execute and improve their work—a "sink-or-swim" mindset. The design of their work includes factors such as job clarity, job control, and the balance between job demand and capabilities. These all influence the individual's sense of fulfillment at work.

If, for example, they have role ambiguity, lack of job control, and not enough resources to perform their work, this can increase stress, which, if left unresolved for an extended period, can erode a sense of worth that can further lead to emotional and cognitive exhaustion. This in turn can lead to psychological harm, which could take decades to recover from.

The individual loses because they feel inadequate, incapable, and an imposter. The organization loses because valuable psychological capacity is dissolved.

9. Creating a Psychologically Safe Workplace Enables Improvement

In addition to embedding a system for managing the psychological health and safety of every individual, a work environment needs to be constantly assessed for its levels of psychological safety.

The psychological climate within a workplace needs to be one that values every person's unique biopsychosocial factors, knowledge, experience, and skills. People need to know they matter and feel significant. They need to feel a sense of inclusion and belonging. They need to feel valued and respected for who they are and what they can contribute.

This in turn fills the individual with self-worth and confidence, believing that they are not an imposter but rather play an important role in helping the team be successful. This confidence and sense of psychological freedom opens the door for people to be curious and freely challenge the status quo without fear. Less fear means more time to express themselves and actively contribute (Figure 3.19).

It also provides the landscape for people to be in psychological flow. The less fearful people are, the more they can focus on getting stuff done. A psychologically safe workplace increases the likelihood of successful improvement and innovation because people are not worrying about what others may think of their ideas. They know that ideas, no matter how small, are valued and never judged or trivialized. They are expected to raise and implement improvement ideas every day to help themselves and their team meet ever-increasing customer demands.

Psychological safety increases the opportunity for people to learn from mistakes because taking calculated risks isn't frowned upon but rather expected as a workplace norm. This constant learning, over time, yields higher quality outputs, which increases the person's sense of growth and accomplishment. People are more likely to express their ideas, concerns, and mistakes if they feel that doing so is ok.

Leaders need to role-model behaviors that promote psychological safety.

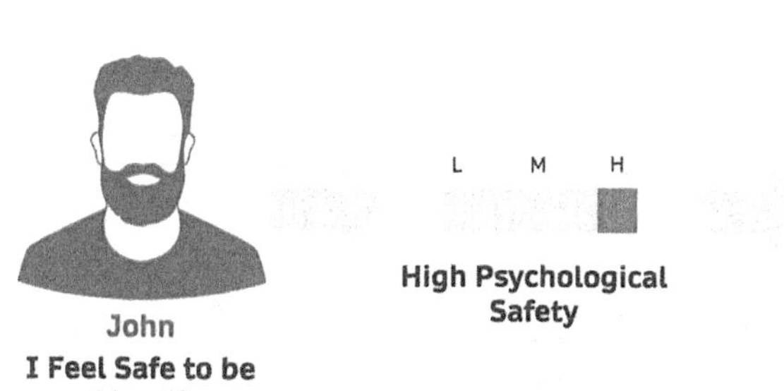

Improvement Impact

- Freedom to challenge the status quo
- Freedom to raise concerns
- Freedom to acknowledge mistakes
- Ownership of improvement
- Increasing volume of improvement ideas
- Active cross functional problem solving
- Proactive risk management
- Increased customer satisfaction

Figure 3.19 Psychological safety provides the atmosphere for improvement to thrive.

> For knowledge to flourish, the workplace must be one where people feel able to share their knowledge. This means sharing concerns, questions, mistakes, and half-formed ideas.
>
> **(Amy C. Edmundson, *The Fearless Organization*, 2019)**

Continuous Improvement System

10. Embedding a CI System Ensures Optimum Use of Psychological Capacity

A system consists of a collection of elements (social and technical) working together to achieve a specific purpose. The purpose of the CI system is to make sure everybody owns improvement. Without a CI system, it is very difficult for individuals and teams to channel their ideas and convert them into solutions, and to focus on what matters most.

There are nine "wastes" that we look for when thinking about any improvement. The eighth waste is the *waste of individuals not thriving.* Thriving individuals love coming to work. Their purpose connects to the organization's purpose, and they get deep fulfillment from being able to bring their full self to the workplace to help make the organization better.

Unfortunately, many people are not thriving when they enter the workplace but rather surviving. A lack of thriving remains one of the biggest wastes that plagues an organization's performance. The amount of insight that remains hidden within the heads of people because they don't feel safe to contribute their ideas, and/or they don't have the systems to raise and implement them, is immeasurable.

The value available by identifying and utilizing these ideas is enormous and can play a key role in helping organizations to improve performance. If an organization has 1,000 people and they each have 10 years' experience in their field of work, then the total available knowledge is 10,000 years (Figure 3.20).

The key word is "availability." Availability of knowledge remains worthless unless it is used for value creation. Imagine the performance impact on the organization if all these years were valued and systemically leveraged.

> In the same way that an electricity grid supplies power to a city, so too does the conjoined thinking-grid of switched-on people supply energy to an organization. A city is left paralysed when it experiences electricity shortages. In the same way, an organization

Average Years of Experience

20	20	200	2,000	20,000	200,000	2,000,000
19	19	190	1,900	19,000	190,000	1,900,000
18	18	180	1,800	18,000	180,000	1,800,000
17	17	170	1,700	17,000	170,000	1,700,000
16	16	160	1,600	16,000	160,000	1,600,000
15	15	150	1,500	15,000	150,000	1,500,000
14	14	140	1,400	14,000	140,000	1,400,000
13	13	130	1,300	13,000	130,000	1,300,000
12	12	120	1,200	12,000	120,000	1,200,000
11	11	110	1,100	11,000	110,000	1,100,000
10	10	100	1,000	10,000	100,000	1,000,000
9	9	90	900	9,000	90,000	900,000
8	8	80	800	8,000	80,000	800,000
7	7	70	700	7,000	70,000	700,000
6	6	60	600	6,000	60,000	600,000
5	5	50	500	5,000	50,000	500,000
4	4	40	400	4,000	40,000	400,000
3	3	30	300	3,000	30,000	300,000
2	2	20	200	2,000	20,000	200,000
1	1	10	100	1,000	10,000	100,000
	1	10	100	1,000	10,000	100,000

People in the Organisation

Figure 3.20 The grid of available knowledge.

> is left limp and lethargic to increase internal performance as well as manage the external environment without regular provision of creative thinking from every person working within the organization. Imagine the collective organizational insight discharged from the thinking of hundreds, if not thousands of people. Consider the transformational capabilities dormant within your organization.
>
> **(Chris Warner, *Flick the Switch*, 2014)**

The objective of the CI system is to define and embed behaviors, principles, practices, and tools for ensuring that the knowledge and skills of every person is valued, harnessed, and shared for individual and organizational success.

A mature CI system helps people thrive by ensuring ideal behaviors saturate the workplace. These ideal behaviors drive positive PWB which in turn increases the psychological capacity that can be used for improvement.

The CI system then helps people convert their ideas into tangible outcomes, focused on what matters most. The system, therefore, has dual objectives: first, ensuring people are valued and treated as true experts of their work; and second, channeling this positive PWB and increased capacity to concrete outcomes.

11. The System Should Be Glued Together by Role-Modeling Ideal Behaviors Using Key Behavioral Indicators

Ideal behaviors deliver ideal results. The lubricant that keeps all the technical and social gears working well together, as one engine, is ideal behavior. A behavior is something that can be observed and recorded—a good sense check is: could we video record it happening?

We can manage ideal behaviors using Key Behavioral Indicators (KBIs). For example, an ideal behavior might be "everybody implements two improvement ideas per month." The KBI could be the percentage of people that have implemented two improvement ideas per month. This would change over time as the behavior matures. Ideal behaviors deliver ideal results (Figure 3.21). By focusing on defining ideal behaviors, and measuring them through KBIs, we achieve the ideal result of creating a culture of improvement.

12. The System Needs to Be Regularly Assessed to Determine Effectiveness

The ability of the CI system to have a positive impact on PWB and drive tangible outcomes is dependent on its maturity. By "maturity," we mean the system's ability to operate consistently as a self-reinforcing network of social and technical elements.

A mature system has all its elements (social and technical) elegantly synchronized, with each knowing its role in meeting the system's purpose of making improvement part of everybody's job. Immature CI systems are

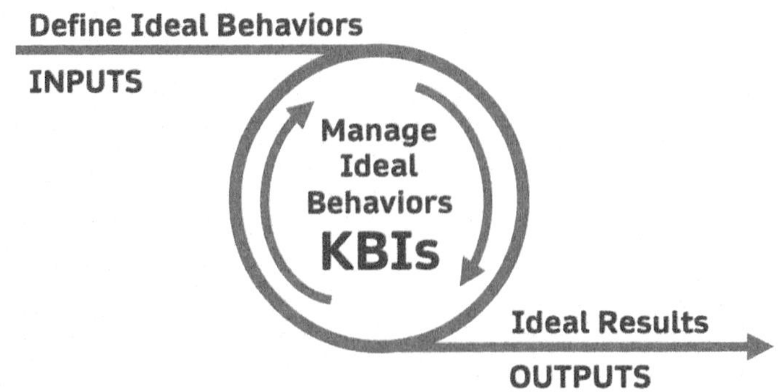

Figure 3.21 Ideal behaviors deliver ideal results.

not designed and/or deployed well. Both are important—the design and the implementation.

A well-thought-out design, anchored by philosophy, principles, practices, and required behaviors, is the first step. This needs to be followed by a well-thought-out implementation approach. The design is worthless unless it has an appropriate, fit-for-purpose deployment model and process attached to it.

The final ingredient is making sure the appropriate coaching resources are put in place for the implementation. This includes processes for regular feedback on how successful the design, implementation approach, and coaching are in lifting maturity (Figure 3.22).

The maturity of every stage, from design to implementation, needs to be regularly assessed. An assessment methodology should be developed, with criteria for each social and technical element. This should include information describing what low and high maturity is. The number of maturity levels will depend on the assessment process being used. Maturity assessments usually have four to five maturity levels and a good source of reference for their design is Butterworth et al. *Why Bother* (2022).

It is important to understand the difference between maturity and performance. They are linked but have subtly different meanings. Maturity is how well the social and technical elements of the system are working together as a self-reinforcing engine. Performance is the outcome of a "state of maturity," where sustained results are being produced through the system. There is an inflection point in the maturity continuum where tangible results will start to become evident. It is important for the organization to be very clear on where this inflection point is to ensure the system remains a vehicle for CI.

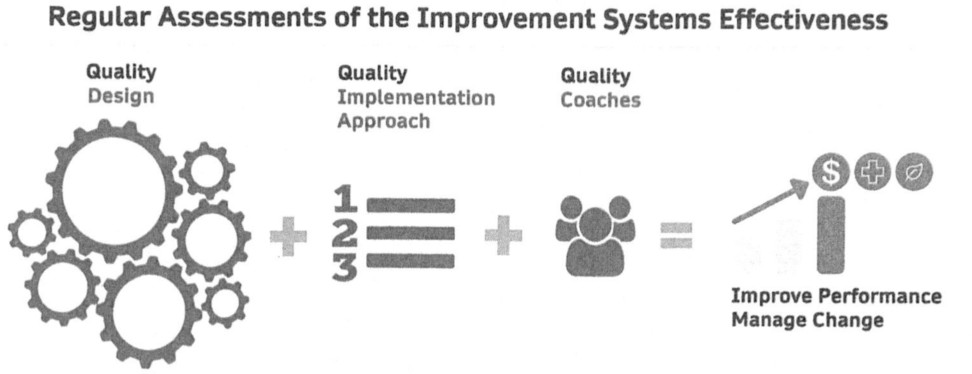

Figure 3.22 The CI system needs to be regularly assessed for effectiveness.

The Three Constraints of the Thriving Matrix

Thriving CI, the key enabler for thriving within a knowledge economy, can be constrained in three ways (Figure 3.23):

1. Low CI system and psychological well-being maturity.
2. High psychological well-being and low CI system maturity.
3. High CI system and low psychological well-being maturity.

These constraints can represent themselves at an organizational and/or team level. An organization could have a well-structured and maturing CI system but still be in the early stages of understanding how to manage and lift overall PWB across all its workplaces.

A team, on the other hand, could be great at managing their PWB but not mature at embedding and utilizing an CI system to leverage the available psychological capacity.

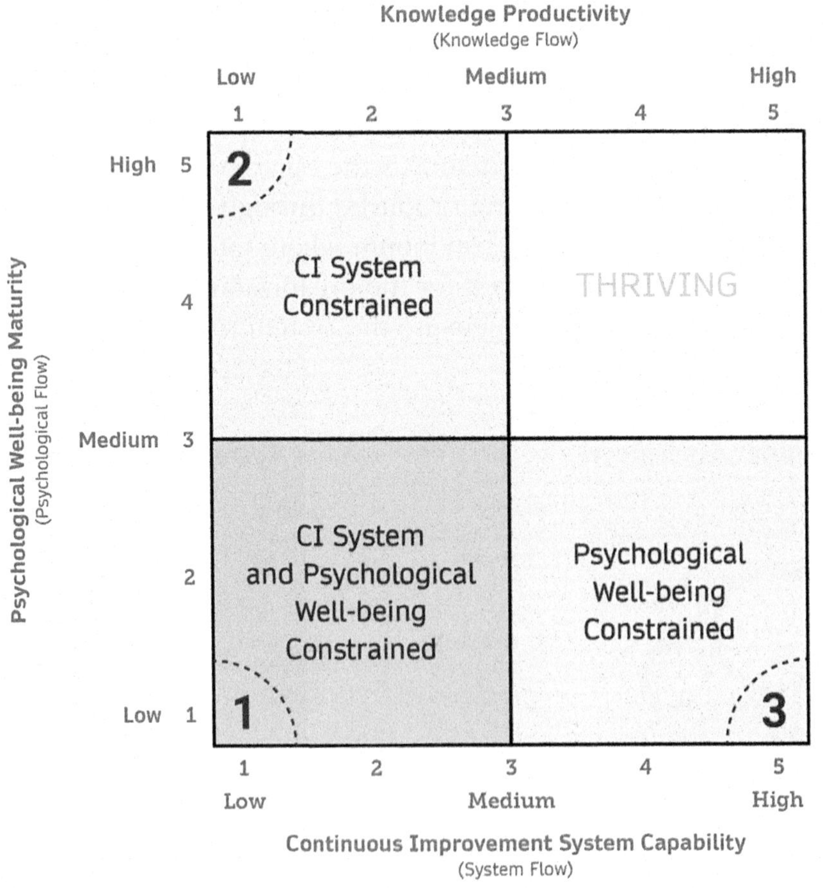

Figure 3.23 The three constraints within the Thriving Matrix.

In either case, there is a high likelihood that good practice is already available that can be used for others to Look, Listen, and Learn for themselves. Identifying these pockets of excellence and communicating it across the business, for possible replication, will rapidly increase maturity levels. People need to approach these places of good practice with curiosity, focusing on the associated behaviors that are driving the positive outcomes.

The Goal of the Organization Is to Move toward the Thriving Quadrant

The goal is for an organization and its leaders to move progressively toward the top right-hand location of the matrix—referred to as the "Thriving Quadrant" (Figure 3.24).

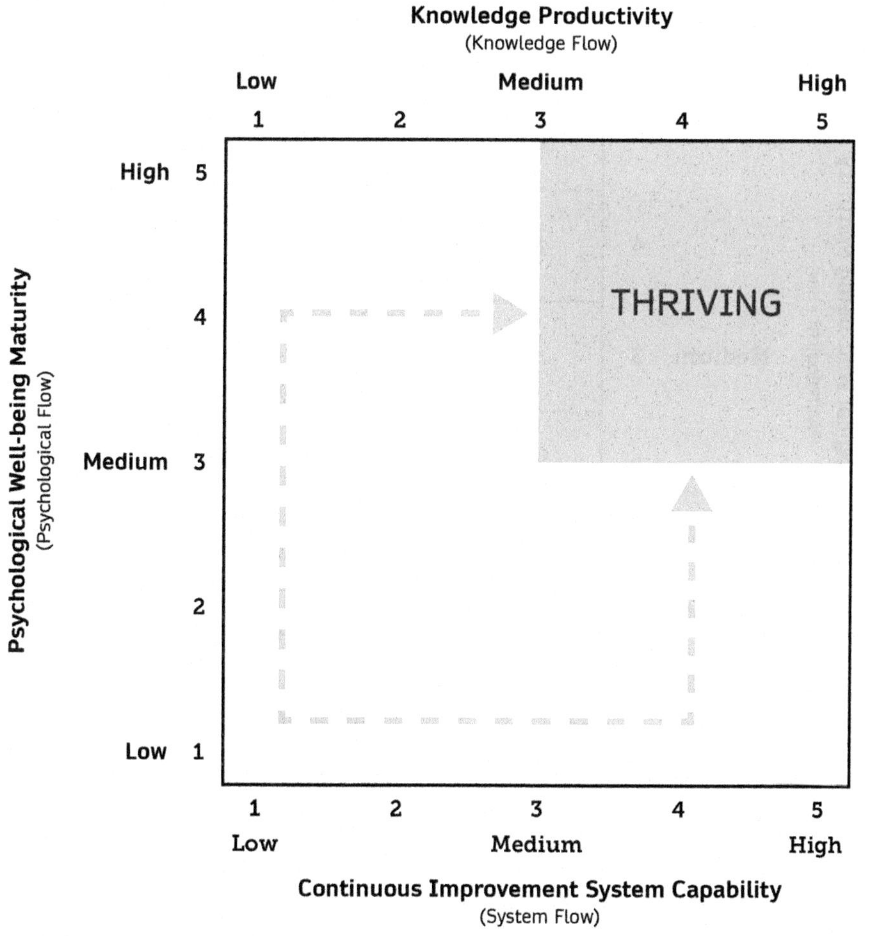

Figure 3.24 The Thriving Quadrant.

The Thriving Quadrant represents the ideal state. It is where the organization has created a thriving culture of CI, enabled by thriving individuals. It is the location on the matrix where the organization can keep up with, and ideally stay ahead of, an increasing pace of change.

Moving toward the quadrant cannot be done overnight and is the outcome of many years of deliberate focus on maturing the organization's CI system and the psychological well-being of every individual. This maturity must occur in parallel, to increase the organization's ability to proactively manage change. Increasing the CI system maturity while having low psychological well-being will not move the organization closer to the Thriving Quadrant.

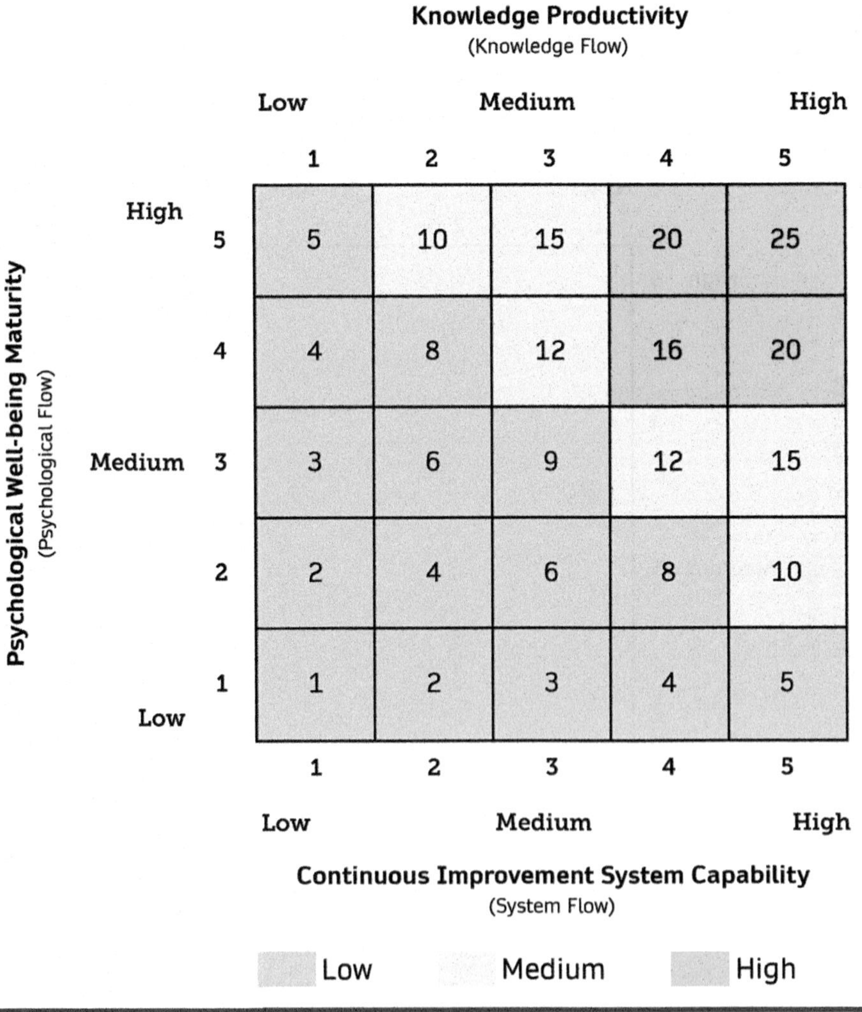

Figure 3.25 The Maturity Grid.

A maturing CI system needs to leverage the increasing psychological capacity of all individuals, enabled through the deliberate focus on maturing their PWB. It is within the Thriving Quadrant that a high volume of ideas is being rapidly converted into solutions that benefit the individual and organization.

A simple Maturity Grid (Figure 3.25) shows the importance of improving maturity for both PWB and the CI system. The numbers increase at the intersection points along the vertical and horizontal axes. Maturing along one axis and not the other does not move the dial. There needs to be parallel maturity. It is only when there is a high CI system and a high PWB maturity that an organization can move into the Thriving Quadrant.

A thriving CI system, utilizing a thriving mindset, will create a thriving culture of improvement. It is a thriving CI culture that can buffer the organization from the increasing levels of VUCA being seen across the world.

The objective is to become more proactive in managing change versus always struggling to close performance gaps in key performance indicators and constantly lagging in responding effectively to the pressures of the external environment.

The ability of the organization to pre-emptively manage change is the result of multiplying PWB maturity by the organization's CI system maturity (Figure 3.26). Example A shows a maturity level of 4 for the CI system and 5 for PWB maturity. Multiplied together, this equals a knowledge productivity

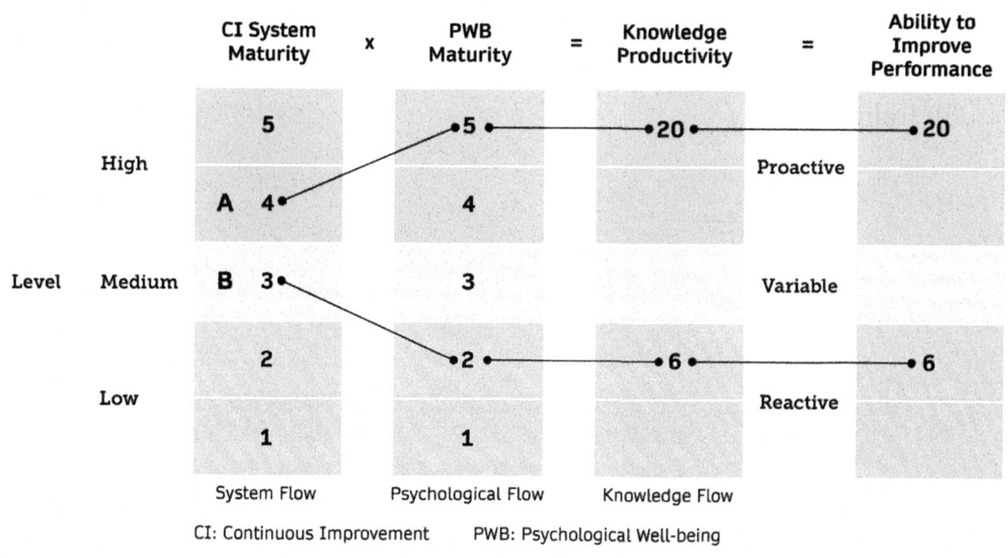

Figure 3.26 The ability to improve performance requires high knowledge productivity.

maturity of 20. Example B shows a maturity level of 3 for the CI system and 2 for PWB maturity. Multiplied together, this equals a knowledge productivity maturity of 6. The goal is to mature both at the same time so the organization can increase knowledge flow and become much more proactive at improving performance.

The Thriving Quadrant Has Five Characteristics

There is a very specific atmosphere within the Thriving Quadrant; an atmosphere that consists of five characteristics (Figure 3.27).

These include:

1. Leaders are role-modeling the behaviors required to remain in the Thriving Quadrant, including:
   - Deeply caring for individuals' physical and psychological well-being.
   - Actively promoting and improving psychological safety.
   - Actively promoting and improving psychological health and safety.
   - Role modeling diversity, inclusion, equity, and belonging.
   - Constantly reflecting on whether they are leading with humility and curiosity.
   - Constantly developing their improvement and coaching skills.
   - Constantly developing their communication skills.
   - Constantly developing their emotional intelligence.
2. Knowledge productivity is being measured as a critical leading indicator on how well the organization is leveraging the collective knowledge of all individuals.

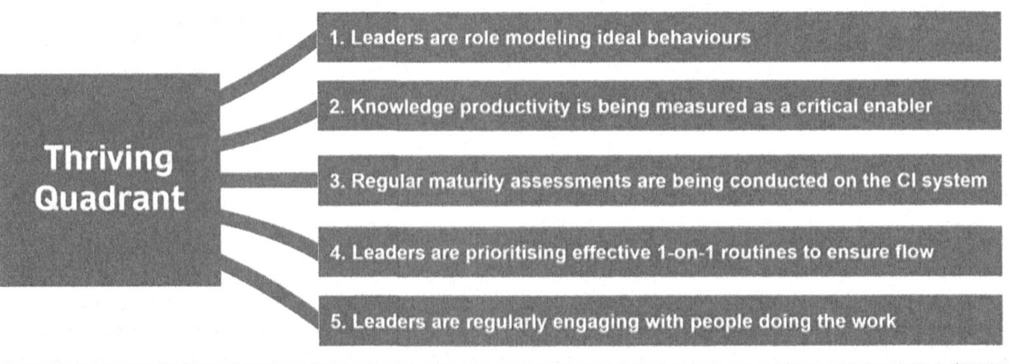

Figure 3.27 The Thriving Quadrant consists of five characteristics.

3. The organization is prioritizing regular assessments of the maturity of the CI system. This is being done through formal internal and external evaluations.
4. Leaders are using their one-on-one routines with individuals to understand needs and proactively ensure people are kept in a "flow state."
5. Leaders are regularly engaging, as part of their standard work, with the people who are doing the work to understand the "real situation" of how waste is impacting on their psychological state.

Psychological Well-Being Maturity

Psychological well-being (PWB) is defined as an individual's ability to think, feel, and behave in a manner that enables them to perform effectively in their work environments, their personal lives, and in society at large.

As previously stated, there are both personal and workplace factors that can influence an individual's PWB. The focus for the remainder of this chapter is to focus on two workplace enablers that, if prioritized and matured, will have a big impact on the state of an individual's PWB. The goal is to ensure that the workplace does not cause psychological harm. Every single individual working within an organization needs their PWB protected and supported (Figure 3.28). It is a moral, legal, and economic imperative.

Two enablers:

1. Create a psychologically safe workplace environment.
2. Embed a psychological health and safety system across the organization.

1. Create a Psychologically Safe Workplace Environment

The thriving organization of the future is one where *all* people working there feel that their unique skills are valued and utilized. People work seamlessly with each other, both within and across locations, to get work done that matters. People are driven by purpose and meaning, operating dynamically in applying their knowledge and skills in driving the organization forward.

There are high levels of engagement, with each person being empowered to make improvements to their work. They feel fulfilled at the end of a working day because they have made a difference.

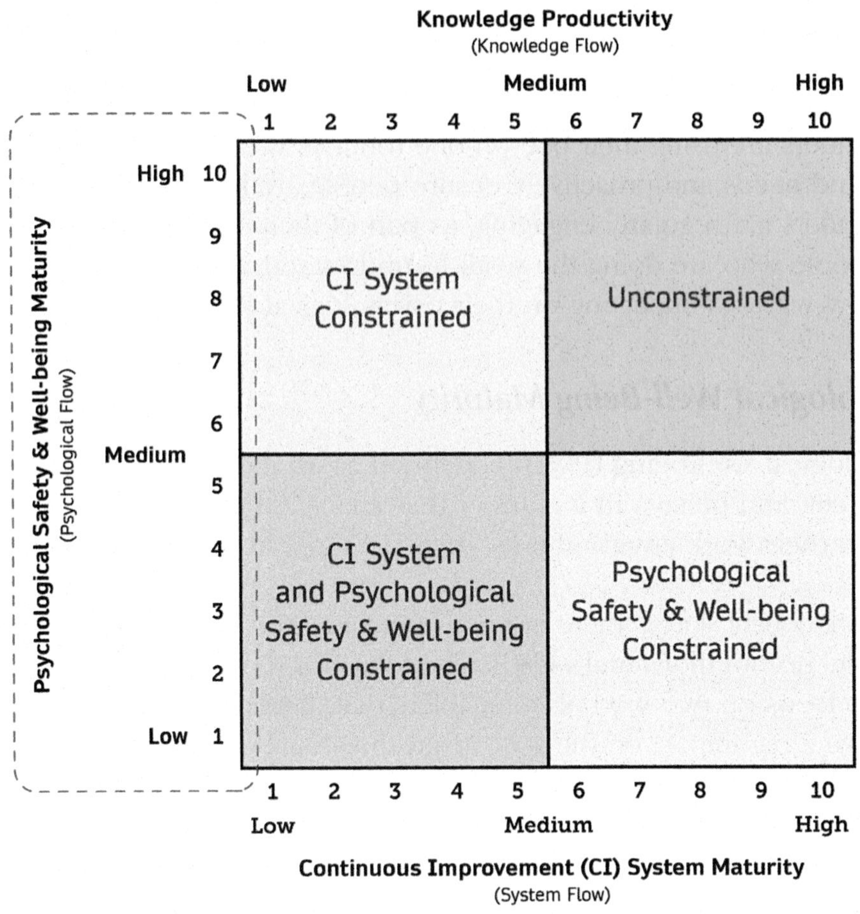

Figure 3.28 PWB maturity is a key enabler for knowledge productivity.

It is this inner sense of fulfillment that keeps people energized and curious. Without energy and curiosity, there is no improvement; with no improvement, there is organizational stagnation. It is a motivated, curious mind that will push longer and harder to find creative solutions to problems.

People treat the organization as if they own it, constantly giving of their intellect and time to help it adapt to constantly changing internal and external demands. They approach each day deeply connected to the organization's purpose, finding ways to solve problems collaboratively much faster than their competitors.

There are organizations today that have created this thriving environment. One of the key ingredients, common in all of them, is that they have high levels of psychological safety. Psychological safety refers to an individual's perception of the consequences of taking an interpersonal risk, or a belief that a team is safe for risk-taking in the face of being ignorant, incompetent, negative, or disruptive.

In a team with high psychological safety, team members feel safe to take risks around their teammates. They feel confident that no one on the team will embarrass or punish anyone for admitting a mistake, asking a question, or offering a new idea.

In 2012, Google conducted a study on what makes teams successful (Project Aristotle). They spent two years studying 180 real and diverse teams at Google. These were not experimental teams but real teams doing "real" work in a corporate setting. They conducted over 200 interviews. They analyzed over 250 different attributes of teams. They defined what comprised a team. They also defined how to measure team effectiveness. They measured it in terms of the leader, team manager, and team members' performance and opinions. They collected both quantitative and qualitative data and used their brainpower to analyze the data. They sought to find the "algorithm" that would predict what makes teams successful.

What they discovered from the study was that how the teams worked together made the biggest difference. They identified five factors common to effective teams at Google. These included psychological safety, dependability, structure and clarity, meaning, and impact.

Psychological safety is presented as the most influential factor of the five in creating successful teams. Google has built its culture on the idea of psychological safety. If people at Google were to be hired for knowledge, innovation, and the ability to stretch to the edge of seemingly impossible aspirations, then the culture to speak up would have to be comfortable so that people would vocalize and contribute their thoughts and ideas. Google wanted people to feel safe to take risks and be vulnerable in front of each other.

These messages are constantly reinforced by leaders to every person—dream big, reach, experiment, and try. People are encouraged to try new things, working together across boundaries. Succeeding or failing isn't the measurement, but rather what was learned and what was experienced in the process of the learning. Google relentlessly promotes the importance of trying new things in the service of ambitious goals. It is this workplace atmosphere that keeps organizations such as Google ahead of the rest.

A lack of psychological safety can be found at the root of many noteworthy organizational errors and failures.

(Amy Edmondson and Jeff Polzer, "HR News Roundup: Weeding Out Psychopaths; Dysfunction at Work; Health Benefits Survey Results, and More News," 2016)

Three Examples of Where a Lack of Psychological Safety Had Catastrophic Consequences

1. Boeing 737 Is Grounded

In March 2019, the Boeing 737 MAX passenger airliner was grounded worldwide after 346 people died in two crashes. First, it was the Lion Air Flight 610 on October 29, 2018. The second flight was the Ethiopian Airlines Flight 302 on March 10, 2019.

There were 387 Boeing 737-model aircraft at that time, which served 8,600 flights per week for 59 different airlines. All of them were grounded, causing severe damage to Boeing's reputation worldwide. The groundings became the longest ever of a US airliner. Boeing also had to suspend the production of the 737 MAX airliner indefinitely.

In November 2018, Boeing launched a new automated flight control system for the 737 MAX airliner. Later, in the post-mortem done by FAA and NTSB, they found that employees had serious concerns about the automated flight control system. They didn't feel comfortable enough to voice their concerns against the backdrop of a multibillion project's delivery timeline pressures.

Later in the interviews, the employees said they were afraid to speak up as they thought they might lose their job. Whether that would really happen or not, it clearly shows that these people didn't feel psychologically safe at work.

2. Chernobyl Disaster

In 1986, the Chernobyl power plant suffered a major disaster that directly killed 31 people and is estimated to have indirectly killed over 4,000.

Whilst the plant itself possessed an inherently unsafe design, the culture in Russia at the time didn't encourage the raising of concerns or speaking up about mistakes. A fear of authority and the need to please political masters resulted in a fear-driven culture.

During a simulated power shutdown, operators who were not fully equipped to deal with the situation made a series of protocol mistakes, including shutting off or ignoring safety systems. This resulted in a steam explosion, followed by a nuclear explosion.

The cause of the disaster was in large part due to a lack of psychological safety, resulting in operators not speaking up about their concerns. Of course, there is no root cause, but we know that the official findings state that the RBMK reactor could only have been operated in an environment where there was no safety culture.

3. Space Shuttle Columbia Explodes

On January 16, 2003, the Space Shuttle *Columbia* blasted off into space on its 28th mission. A piece of foam broke off from the outside of the rocket and hit the wing area during lift-off.

On Tuesday, January 21, five days after the launch, a team of engineers at NASA had their first formal meeting to assess the potential damage from the piece of foam that had struck the wing. They agreed that NASA should immediately observe the wing area impacted, even if the impact was minor.

The team of engineers selected Rodney Rocha, an experienced but mild-mannered engineer, to convey their recommendation. Rodney Rocha attempted to inform his superiors and request them to observe the wing's possible damage, but he was simply brushed aside. One manager told Rodney Rocha to stop being a "Chicken Little"—referring to the cartoon character who was always running around afraid and warning others that the sky was falling. Despite his severe concerns about the mission's safety, he had no choice but to keep quiet.

On February 1, 2003, the Space Shuttle *Columbia* disintegrated into pieces while returning to Earth. Seven astronauts, including mission specialist Kalpana Chawla, died in the tragic accident.

NASA suspended any further space flights for the next two years while investigating and eliminating what could have caused the disaster. The investigation confirmed that the cause was the friction caused due to the damaged tiles on the wing; the same damage that Rodney Rocha and his team of engineers were trying to bring to the mission control's attention.

The Unseen Implication of a Lack of Psychological Safety

The repercussions of a lack of psychological safety cascade from an organizational to an individual level.

Consider the mental and emotional anguish that Rodney Rocha at NASA would have gone through trying, without success, to inform his superiors of the safety risks of launch. As an engineer he would have been trained to be precise, to look for potential failures, and to proactively find solutions to prevent catastrophe. He would have sat through hundreds of hours of tertiary training and spent years refining his skills at work.

Rodney would have taken much pride in his knowledge and experience and would have simply wanted to do a good job each day at work. He would have wanted to simply be heard, to feel like somebody was listening to what he had to say. Rodney would have welcomed dialogue, would have cherished the opportunity to explain his thoughts.

Consider the internal disappointment and frustration Rodney would have felt by having no choice but to keep quiet. Consider the absolute inner devastation when Space Shuttle *Columbia* exploded, knowing that it could have been prevented if only the leaders at NASA had listened to him.

We do not know the psychological impact to Rodney by this experience. Did he develop prolonged depression, anxiety, or post-traumatic stress disorder? Did it trigger suicidal thoughts due to deep guilt? Did it impact negatively on his home life and lead to a divorce? Did it lead to him losing his confidence in his skills, second-guessing his decisions? Did it forever break his trust in leadership? Did it lead to him losing his job and financial stability? We don't know.

What we do know is that there is a high probability it would have had an impact on his psychological well-being. What we also know is that it all could have been prevented if an atmosphere of psychological safety had been created for him to freely speak up and be heard.

Rodney is an example of what millions of people are facing within the workplace every day. Whether these be workplaces within healthcare, manufacturing, banking, military, not-for-profit, education, government, mining, or any other industry. People struggle to be authentic, to freely speak without fear. Most people are in self-preservation mode, stepping into the workplace a reduced version of themselves. Most of their time is spent managing interpersonal risk and perception, rather than proactively applying their intellect to manage organizational risk. Low psychological safety reduces people's ability to thrive and help the organization prosper (Figure 3.29).

People end up worrying more about what not to say than what needs to be said to make things better. People spend inordinate amounts of time worrying about what others think of them, especially those higher up in the organization. People will readily speak up if they are confident that it will be well received. Why? Because people like making a good impression.

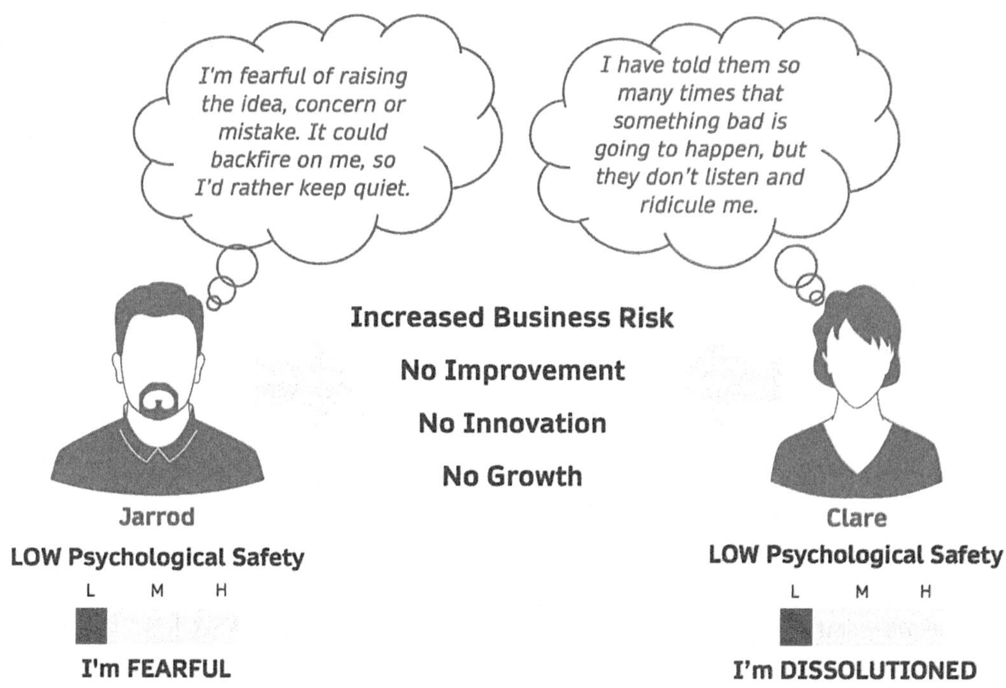

Figure 3.29 Low psychological safety reduces people's ability to thrive and help the organization prosper.

The problem, however, is that making a good impression does not always agitate the norm, a prerequisite for creating a culture of improvement—the expectation that everybody will constantly challenge the status quo.

It is within the uncertainty of response that a lot of value resides. This value will never become available without an atmosphere of freedom where people deeply know that they will not be labeled or criticized for ideas, questions, concerns, or mistakes. This atmosphere is predominantly created by leaders and takes time to mold and mature.

It can take years to develop psychologically safe workplaces and seconds to shatter. Psychological safety is extremely fragile. It is cultivated through daily, repeated experiences of being heard, not being retaliated against, and not being punished. Subtle responses like eye rolls, tone of voice, and negative body language can chip away at psychological safety, creating an environment where people are afraid to speak up. Someone who is too afraid to speak up feels powerless and becomes prone to learned helplessness, an insidious force in organizations. People don't speak up because of risk to reputation, risk of being perceived as ignorant, risk of being disruptive, and/or risk of failing. When people can and do speak up, those risks are lessened and result in behaviors like collaboration, experimentation, and open feedback—the key ingredients for creating a thriving culture of CI.

In Rodney's case, he was using his full psychological capacity (emotional and cognitive energy), skills, and abilities when warning the leadership team at NASA about the potential safety risks associated with the Columbia launch. His confidence would have been high, and he would have had no fear of communicating his concerns.

This, however, would have changed over time. The unwillingness of his superiors to acknowledge his concerns and being mocked by being referred to as "Chicken Little" would have slowly worn him down. His frustration in not feeling heard (a basic human need) would have slowly dissolved his psychological capacity. The possibility is high that he would have started worrying about being labeled a catastrophizer, which would have potentially reduced his confidence and willingness to continue speaking up.

Consider the loss. Rodney would have lost confidence, reducing his workplace contributions. This in turn would have made NASA lose because a highly skilled individual within the organization had stopped helping them manage business risk. The implications for the organization, as we know, were catastrophic, as it can be for any organization in their own context. "Psychological safety is the ability for someone to employ or express themselves physically, cognitively, and emotionally" (William Kahn, *Psychological Conditions of Personal Engagement and Disengagement at Work*, 1990).

Negative impacts of psychological safety on psychological well-being:

- Not being able to express oneself can lead to a person shutting down and denying their best self.
- Feeling shamed by a leader or colleague when a person expresses an original thought can sink their self-esteem and lead them to feel bad about themselves and their abilities.
- Noting or making mistakes can make a person feel bad. Not being able to report them can make the person feel much worse.
- Lack of emotional support in the workplace can leave a person feeling abandoned and alone: not an environment to offer their best work.
- Feeling alone in a place where a person is meant to feel connected can bring on symptoms of despair and depression.
- Fearing going to work—whether a person is underworked or overworked—can develop anxiety and fear symptoms.
- Quality of life can be affected if a person spends eight hours of every day not feeling appreciated or valued by peers and leaders.

- Sleep can also be affected—and lack of sleep has been shown to heighten emotional responses and lessen rational thinking.
- Not being able to think clearly, because a person is under stress most of the time, may affect their emotional ability to do their job.
- Stress levels may mount because it becomes too exhausting to deal with the toxic work environment.

When there is no psychological safety at work, a person can feel:

- Reluctant to stand out.
- Scared of being wrong.
- Fearful of offending their manager.
- They'd prefer to hold back rather than share.
- Terrified of saying or asking something that makes them look bad.
- A need to fit in and go along with the status quo.
- They must hide their creative ideas and can end up believing they're not good enough.
- Shamed and not valued.

The benefits of psychological safety include:

- Increased likelihood of successful innovation, resulting in quicker time-to-market.
- An increased ability to learn from mistakes, resulting in fewer problems or outages, higher quality, and improved governance and controls.
- Increased reporting of concerns and security issues, resulting in decreased risk of security, health and safety, or non-compliance incidents.
- Increased engagement, resulting in lower churn rates and decreased costs related to recruitment and absenteeism.
- Improved reputation resulting in an increased ability to recruit the best people.
- People feeling able to bring their whole self to work, without fear of embarrassment or recrimination.
- Taking risks and innovating rather than "playing it safe."
- Admitting mistakes and learning from them rather than hiding them, resulting in fewer failures.
- Highlighting problems, dangers, and opportunities as they arise.
- More inclusive, resulting in greater diversity and more voices being heard.

- More stable and happier, resulting in lower absence, increased retention, and improved recruitment.
- Increased profitability because of all the above.

Psychological safety sounds like:

- "This is new territory for us, so I am going to need everyone's input."
- "There are many unknowns/things are changing fast/this is complex stuff. So, we will make mistakes."
- "OK that is one side. Let's hear some dissent/who's got something to add/let's have some give-and-take."
- "What assumptions are we making? What else could this be? Could we investigate? Have we left anything out?"
- "Did everything go as smoothly as you would have liked? What were the friction points? Are there systems we should rethink?"
- "I really appreciate you bringing this to me. I'm sure it was not easy."

Focus on Response Systems before Psychological Safety

People need to feel heard. They need to have confidence when they speak up that someone will be listening and that there will be the necessary systems in place to capture, track, and feedback a response. They need to trust that speaking up will be taken seriously and not be ignored. This can only occur when formal feedback mechanisms are put in place and made reliable in providing quality feedback to individuals' voices (Figure 3.30).

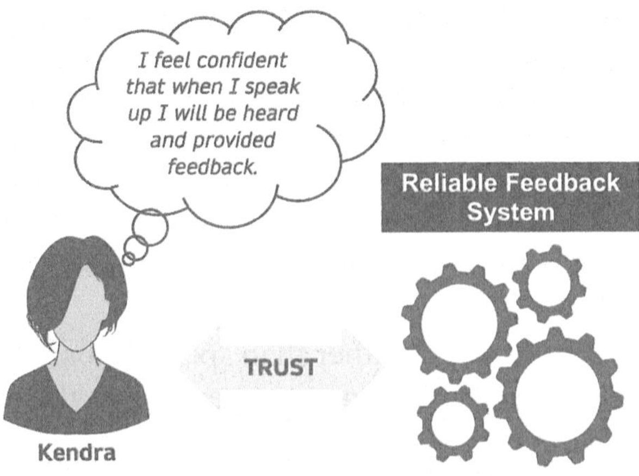

Figure 3.30 A reliable feedback system ensures people feel heard.

> Being psychologically safe is reliant on building trust that is earned through responding consistently when individuals raise issues to demonstrate they are being heard. Leaders can be hamstrung if all they're provided with is training with no systems to support implementation when they go back to work. Don't put the cart before the horse. Consider the systems needed to support leaders to make necessary changes when individuals speak up rather than trying to train your way into an outcome that typically is reliant on systemic changes.
>
> **(Jason van Schie, *Flourish DX*, 2023)**

Psychological Safety Assessment

There has been much written about how to foster psychological safety. The authors have developed a Psychological Safety Assessment (Figure 3.31) that can be used at any time to determine what needs to stop, start, and/or continue to increase psychological safety within a team.

2. Embed a Psychological Health and Safety System across the Organization

Psychosocial hazards reduce PWB. Reducing PWB reduces psychological capacity. Reducing psychological capacity reduces the ability of individuals to perform well in their job and implement improvements. Psychosocial hazards drastically reduce the momentum of improvement within an organization.

These hazards or workplace stressors draw people away from what matters most—being focused on their job. It takes them out of psychological flow and disengages them from their work. The individual's attention is

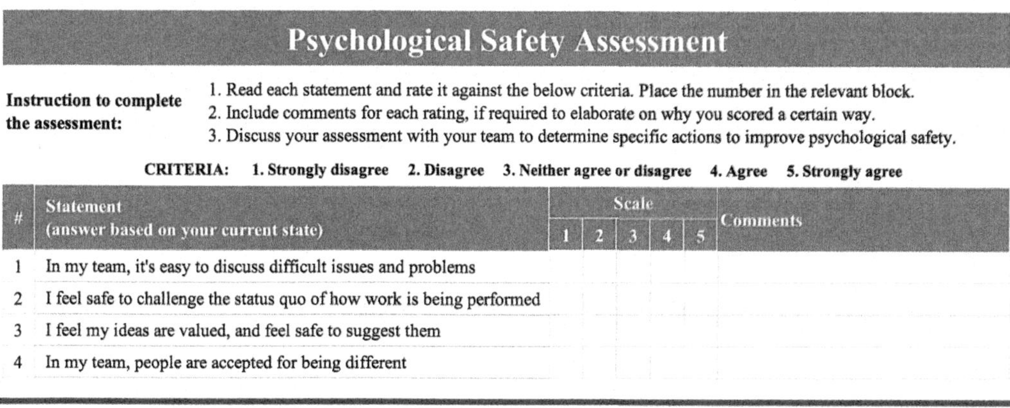

Psychological Safety Assessment

Instruction to complete the assessment:
1. Read each statement and rate it against the below criteria. Place the number in the relevant block.
2. Include comments for each rating, if required to elaborate on why you scored a certain way.
3. Discuss your assessment with your team to determine specific actions to improve psychological safety.

CRITERIA: **1. Strongly disagree** **2. Disagree** **3. Neither agree or disagree** **4. Agree** **5. Strongly agree**

#	Statement (answer based on your current state)	Scale					Comments
		1	2	3	4	5	
1	In my team, it's easy to discuss difficult issues and problems						
2	I feel safe to challenge the status quo of how work is being performed						
3	I feel my ideas are valued, and feel safe to suggest them						
4	In my team, people are accepted for being different						

Figure 3.31 Psychological Safety Assessment extract. Full version available at www.whycarebook.com.

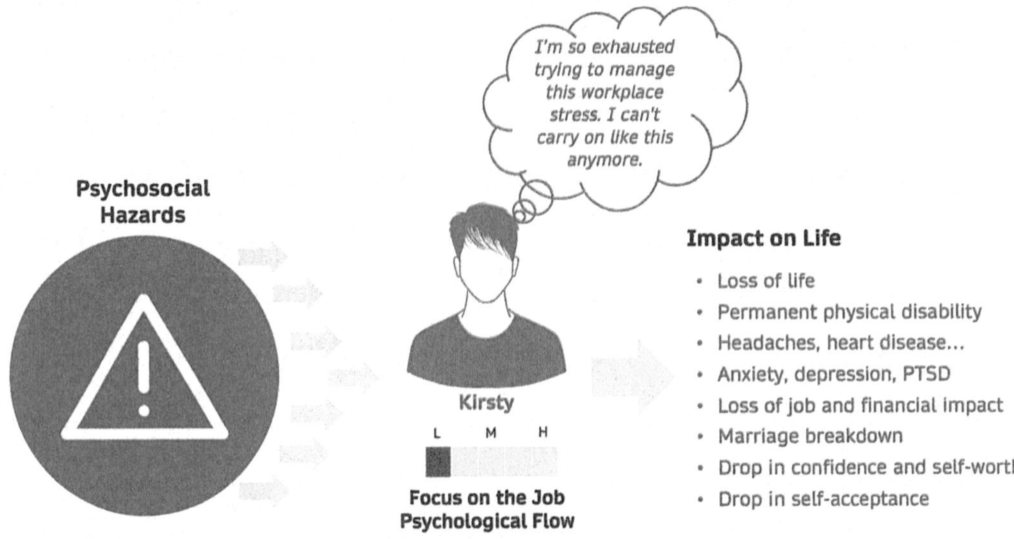

Figure 3.32 Psychosocial hazards reduce focus on the job and psychological flow.

focused on guarding themselves, surviving the onslaughts of stress caused by severe and/or prolonged exposure to psychosocial hazards.

The implications of being drawn away from the job can be severe, including loss of life at work. It can also lead to life-altering physical injury or disability. It can lead to physical illness such as headaches, high blood pressure and heart disease, and mental breakdown including anxiety, depression, and PTSD. The ripple affect can further lead to a drop in confidence and self-worth, reduced self-acceptance and compassion, and instability in work-life integration. Individuals can lose their jobs due to factors out of the individual's control, leading to relationship breakdown and financial loss (Figure 3.32).

There has never been a more important time to embed a PH&S system within an organization. Life has become more challenging for people, especially post-COVID-19. Ensuring that people can go to work without worrying about their health and safety is a right that should be afforded to every individual.

Psychological Health and Safety (PH&S)

As previously stated in this chapter, PH&S is the application of a risk-management framework for identifying, risk-assessing, eliminating, and/or controlling sources of work-related stress. The risk assessment is designed to help organizations meet their legal obligations to manage risks associated with psychological injury.

A psychological injury or mental injury includes a range of cognitive, emotional, and behavioral symptoms that interfere with a person's life and can significantly affect how they feel, think, behave, and interact with others. These injuries are caused by various psychosocial hazards associated with the design, management, and social context of work.

ISO 45003 is the first global standard that helps organizations identify and control work-related hazards and manage psychosocial risks within an occupational health and safety system. Much of ISO 45003 sets out how psychosocial hazards arise, addressing how the workplace is organized, the social factors at work, and the work environment itself.

The risk management process (Figure 3.33) consists of four steps: (1) identify the hazards; (2) assess the risks; (3) control the risks; and (4) review control measures. The process is dependent on deep consultation with every individual within the organization as well as commitment from leaders.

Figure 3.33 Psychological health and safety risk management process.

1. Identifying the Hazards

This step includes identifying aspects in the design, management, and social context of work that have the potential to cause harm to individuals and why they are occurring. This step should also help the organization and leaders identify where and when individuals are exposed to psychosocial hazards, and if controls are not adequately eliminating or minimizing risks from known hazards.

Identifying these hazards can be done in various ways. The authors advocate a simple process to start. This can include easy-to-complete surveys sent to individuals and/or focus groups, where groups of people discuss the matter collectively. Leaders should use their observations during Gemba walks to help identify hazards/wastes individuals are dealing with. The organization can include, for example, additional sources of information such as culture surveys, safety and well-being data, records of injuries, complaints, previous psychosocial risk assessments, and turnover/absenteeism rates.

Types of Psychosocial Hazards

Numerous types of psychosocial hazards have been identified over the past decade by various subject matter experts and regulators. The authors have provided a consolidated view of these hazards (Table 3.4) based on a comprehensive global review.

The authors do not put forward any recommendation on which of these hazards should be prioritized by an organization. This should be an outcome of the organization's internal risk management process. There may be hazards/combinations of hazards that are more prevalent within one organization than another. It is, however, important for the individual and organization to be aware of the various types of hazards and their possibility to cause harm.

Psychosocial Hazards Combine and Interact with Each Other to Impact PWB

An individual may be more susceptible to the impact of different factors combining and interacting with each other versus a singular factor.

> Consider psychosocial hazards collectively rather than in isolation. Individuals may be exposed to more than one psychosocial hazard

Table 3.4 Psychosocial Hazards

Category	*Workplace Psychosocial Hazards*
Organizational	• Poor organizational culture and practices • Poor organizational change management • Poor organizational communication • Poor organizational justice and fairness
Job Design and Environment	• Low role clarity • High job demand (overload) • Low job demand (unfulfilling work) • Low job control and/or autonomy • Low job security and/or precarious work • Remote and/or isolated work • Lack of work flexibility • No policies and/or procedures (inconsistent application) • Unrealistic expectations of competency • Poor working conditions (e.g., lack of space, lighting, noise) • Inadequate resources to perform the job (e.g., equipment, systems, data) • Working in extreme conditions
Leadership	• Inadequate leadership support (e.g., no one-on-one routines) • Poor leadership behaviors and role-modeling • Poor leadership engagement and/or presence • Poor leadership style (e.g., abuse of power, command and control) • Poor leadership communication (lack of and/or withholding information) • Lack of fairness and inconsistent/poor decision making • Inadequate praise, recognition, and reward • Inadequate professional development • Poor or inadequate coaching
Team	• Poor interpersonal relationships • Lack of inclusion and belonging • Poor levels of trust • Poor co-worker support
Behavioral	• Bullying and/or victimization • Harassment (including sexual) • Discrimination (e.g., race, gender, sexual orientation, religion) • Work related violence and/or aggression • Low civility and respect

at a time and hazards can interact or combine. For example, an individual exposed to aggressive customer behavior is more likely to be harmed if at that time they do not have other peers present to support them and do not have the controls to alter the way they work to de-escalate the situation.

(Safe Work Australia, *Managing Psychosocial Hazards at Work*, 2022)

The joint effect of controlling various psychosocial hazards on improving mental health was greater than simple scenarios. Managing the combination of lack of job control, role conflict, lack of co-worker support, and job insecurity achieved highest probability (77%) of good mental health amongst four-hazard scenarios. Based on this scenario, further managing poor physical environment resulted in the highest (83%) of good mental among five-hazard scenarios.

(Sun et al. 2023)

2. Assess the Risks

Once psychosocial risks have been identified, the next step is to assess the risks they create. This will help determine what is reasonably practical in managing the risks.

Risk assessments should be done in consultation with individuals and health and safety representatives. If risks and how to control them effectively are already known, then controls can be implemented without conducting a risk assessment, and checks done to see if they are effective.

To assess the risk of harm, individuals affected need to be identified and the severity, frequency, and duration of exposure to a specific psychosocial hazard or combination thereof assessed (Figure 3.34).

- Severity—how severe are the hazards and individuals' exposures?
- Frequency—how often is the individual exposed to the hazards or risks?
- Duration—how long is the individual exposed to the hazards or risks?

Psychosocial risks increase when exposure to hazards is more severe (traumatic events), more frequent (regularly performing tasks without adequate support), or longer in duration (high job demand over weeks or months).

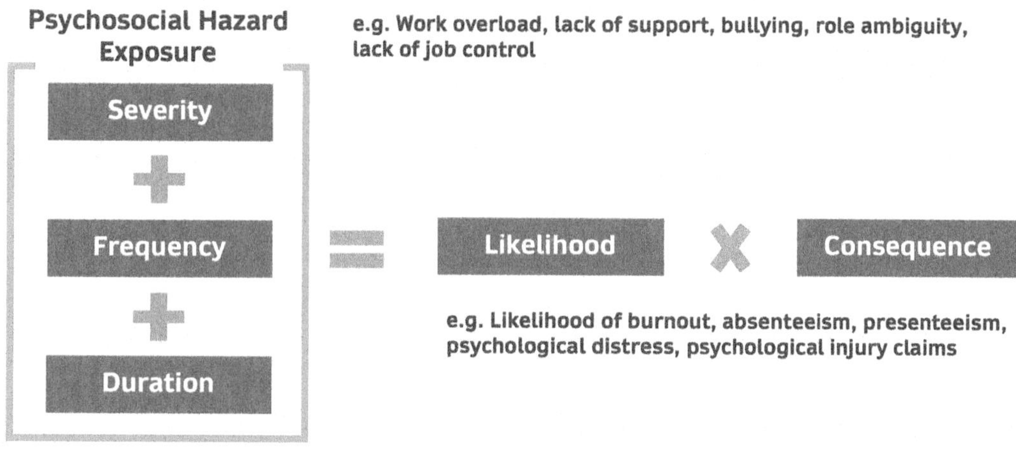

Figure 3.34 Psychosocial risk assessment.

Psychosocial risks cause both physical and psychological injuries. The severity of psychological injuries varies, but in comparison to physical injuries, on average, they require more time off work and are more costly.

> Workers' compensation mental health claims average 17 weeks of lost time and a median total cost of $27,700 for serious claims, compared to $10,700 for serious physical injury claims.
>
> **(Deloitte, "The Cost of Ignoring the Mental Health and Wellbeing of Your Workforce," 2019)**

3. Control the Risks

Once psychosocial hazards have been identified and the risks they create assessed, it is time to control them. Risks to health and safety need to be eliminated if it is reasonably practical to do so. If it is not reasonably practical to eliminate the risks, then they need to be minimized so far as reasonably possible. Every workplace is different, and the combination of control measures needs to be tailored to the organization's size, type, and work activities.

To determine what is reasonably practical to manage psychosocial risks:

(a) Identify as many possible control measures.
(b) Consider which of these control measures are most effective.
(c) Consider which controls are reasonably practical in the circumstances.

The first objective is to eliminate the risk, so identify any control measures which would achieve this. Then order the remaining controls, or combinations of controls, from most to least effective at minimizing the risks. Controls that are reliable and offer the highest level of protection are the most effective.

Implement the controls in a structured manner. It may require time to test the controls first before they are deemed to be effective. Assess the effectiveness of the controls through frequent engagement with individuals. Make sure the implementation of controls is managed well and coordinated appropriately, so it does not create any further hazards.

4. Review the Control Measures

The last step of the risk assessment process is to review the effectiveness of the implemented control measures to ensure they are working as planned. If a control measure isn't working effectively, it must be reviewed, modified, or replaced.

Reviewing control measures should be done regularly and is required:

- When the control measure is not eliminating or minimizing the risks so far as reasonably practicable.
- Before a change at a workplace that is likely to give rise to a new or different health and safety risk that the control measure may not effectively control.
- If the results of consultation indicate a review is necessary.
- If a health and safety representative requests a review because they reasonably believe one of the above has occurred and it has not been adequately reviewed already.

Reports, complaints (including informal complaints), or grievances from individuals may identify new psychosocial hazards or risks that are not adequately controlled. This should trigger a review of whether existing control measures are effective, if the response procedures worked, and whether new risks have been identified that also need to be managed.

Risk Register

A risk register (Figure 3.35) is an ideal tool to have available within the workplace to help manage control measures and/or trigger new risk

Risk Register

Enter Location: **Enter Date:**

Hazard	How frequently are people exposed to this hazard?	How long does the exposure last?	How severe is their exposure?	Are other hazards present this may interact with?	How effective are the current controls?	What further controls are required?	Actioned by	Date Due	Date Complete	Review Period

Figure 3.35 Risk Register extract. Full version available at www.whycarebook.com.

assessments. The register can be located at the team's Performance Board for review during team meetings.

Psychosocial Injuries Need to Be Treated a Lot More Seriously

A return-to-work comparison between psychological and physical injury claims indicates that there is still a lot more work to be done to improve how organizations manage psychological injuries. Table 3.5 shows the disparity between how physical and psychological injuries are dealt with during the claims process. Only 27% of respondants said that their employer did what they could to support them during the claims process for psychological injury versus 75% for physical injuries. Only 23% of respondents agreed that their employer helped them with their psychological injury recovery versus 67% for a physical injury. Only 35% of respondents agreed that their employer treated them fairly after the claims process for a psychological injury versus 79% for a physical injury.

Respondents were asked if they had positive responses to certain statements regarding physical and psychological injury (Table 3.6). Only 30% had a positive response to how their employer responded to their psychological injury versus 73% for a physical injury. Only 20% of the respondents said they had pre-claim assistance from their employer versus 60% for physical injuries.

Respondents were asked to rate their experiences based on specific concerns (Table 3.7). Almost 60% of respondents said they felt their supervisor thought they were exaggerating their psychological injury versus 23% for physical injuries. More than 70% of respondents said that they felt they would be treated differently by people at work for a psychological injury claim versus 36% for physical injuries.

Table 3.5 Responses Based on the Injury Claims Process

Percentage Who Agreed with Employer Response Questions		
Claim Lodgment Concern Questions	*Physical*	*Psychological*
Your employer did what they could to support you	75%	27%
Employer made an effort to find suitable employment for you	72%	34%
Employer provided enough information on rights and responsibilities	68%	32%
Your employer helped you with your recovery	67%	23%
Your employer treated you fairly *during* the claims process	79%	30%
Your employer treated you fairly *after* the claims process	79%	35%

Table 3.6 Positive Responses to Key Statements

Percentage of Employees Reporting Positive Responses to Key Influencing Factors		
Key Influencing Factors	*Physical*	*Psychological*
Employer response to injury	73%	30%
Early contact (within three days)	47%	18%
Employer pre-claim assistance	60%	20%
Absence of disagreement/dispute	25%	49%
Low level of concern about lodging a claim	76%	47%
Workplace culture prior to injury	86%	59%
Interaction with system/claims organization	78%	52%
Higher levels of resilience	71%	49%
Medical care focused on RTW	84%	87%

Table 3.7 Responses Based on Specific Concerns

Percentage Who Agreed with Individual Questions about Claim Lodgment Concerns		
Claim Lodgment Concern Questions	*Physical*	*Psychological*
Felt supervisor thought you were exaggerating injury	23%	59%
Concerned that you would be fired if you submitted a claim	19%	38%
Thought you would be treated differently by people at work	36%	73%
Difference of opinion with employer/claim organization	25%	51%
Feel employer discouraged you from putting in a claim	15%	43%

Key Points from Chapter 3

- The psychological well-being of any individual is impacted by their unique personal and workplace factors, which are constantly changing.
- The ability of an organization to help individuals manage their psychological well-being is a key enabler to how well they can improve performance.
- Psychological safety and psychological health and safety are significant enablers for making sure the psychological well-being of every individual in the workplace is protected and supported.

Chapter 4

Why Care about Thriving Individuals?

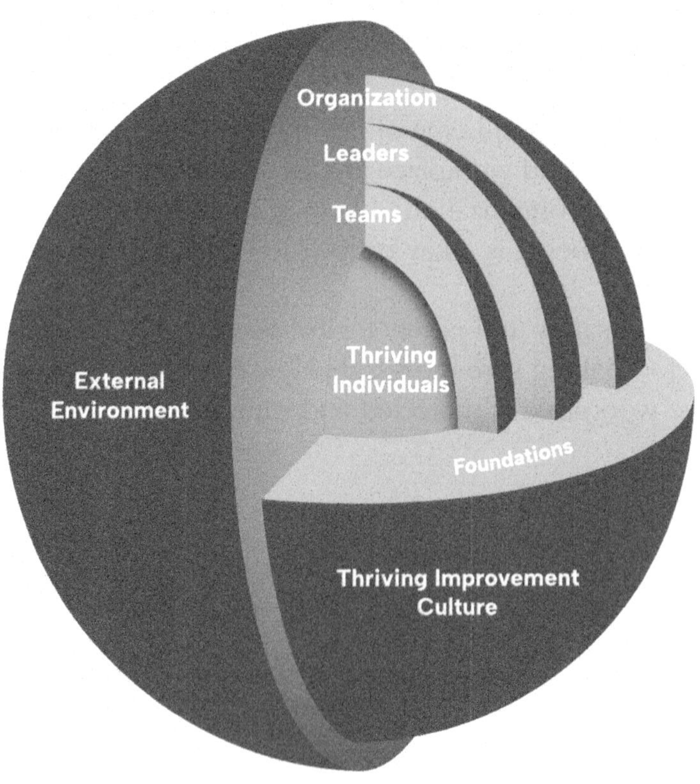

Figure 4.0 **The Why Care Model—Thriving Individuals.**

DOI: 10.4324/9781003413479-5

Introduction

Chapter 4 will focus on thriving individuals as the nucleus of the Why Care Model. The authors believe that organizational resilience is built from inside out, starting within the hearts and minds of every individual within the workplace.

Why care about individuals? Firstly, because it is the right thing to do; and secondly, because caring about every individual provides the organization with an abundance of psychological capacity (emotional and cognitive energy) that can be leveraged to succeed.

Psychological well-being (PWB) is an input into psychological capacity, which is the fuel for an organization to keep moving forward, ideally ahead of the pace of change. A thriving culture of improvement cannot be achieved without thriving individuals (Figure 4.1).

Thriving improvement is the outcome of every individual in the organization having enough psychological energy to not only do their job well but also improve it at the same time. This energy needs to be created and maintained; it is not limitless. It also fluctuates, based on the many events and circumstances that people face daily. Thriving individuals think, feel,

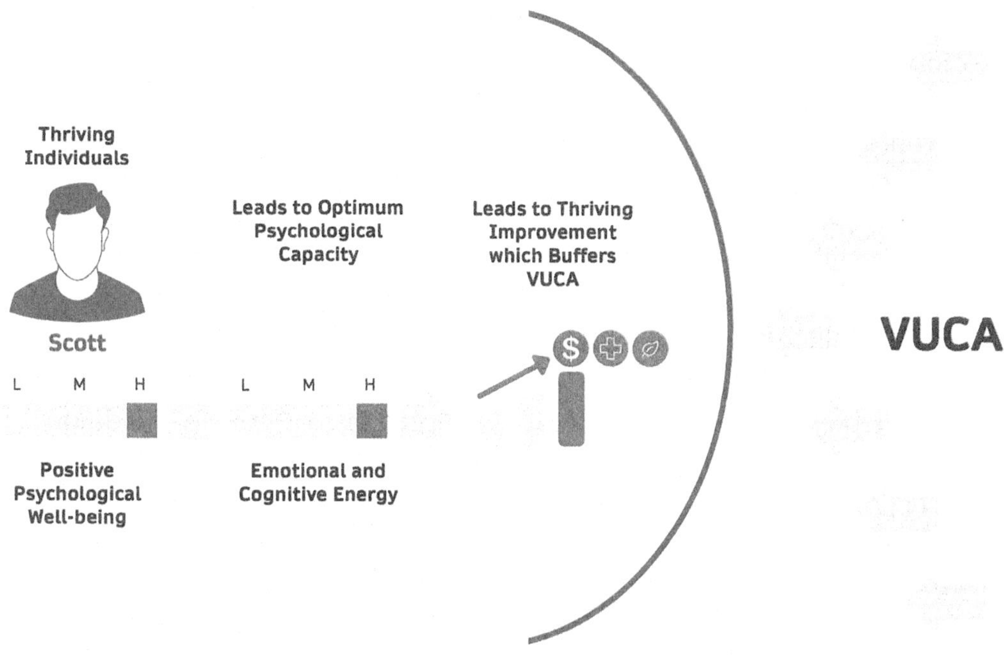

Figure 4.1 Thriving individuals help the organization buffer VUCA.

and behave in a manner that enables them to perform effectively at work, in their personal lives, and society at large.

As stated in Chapter 3, the future of the workplace will demand that organizations be very good at managing the increasing levels of Volatility, Uncertainty, Complexity, and Ambiguity (VUCA). Their ability to do this well will depend on how proficient they are at helping every individual thrive at work.

Every individual needs to be helping the organization move forward into the grey zone of unprecedented VUCA. They need to be looking for business/process risk, relentlessly eliminating waste, and utilizing their growing knowledge and skills to create breakthrough improvement. Creating this culture in mass requires a very deliberate focus on ensuring that the emotional and cognitive energy and stamina of every individual is optimized. This can only be done through regular monitoring of every individual's PWB.

Ensuring that positive PWB is maintained requires focus from the individual and organization; it is a dual responsibility. Individuals need to be doing constant assessments to determine how personal and workplace factors are influencing the various elements of their PWB.

This in turn can be used by the person for discussion with a trusted peer, coach, their leader, a friend, and/or a family member for feedback and guidance. Positive factors need to be locked in and negative factors eliminated and/or controlled. Actions need to be defined and implemented by all parties involved.

The organization has a responsibility to understand the unique impact that workplace factors have on different people within their teams. The leadership skills, management practices, systems, and controls required to proactively protect individuals from psychological harm need to be prioritized above all else. This rapidly emerging organizational requirement and capability has become a critical ingredient for success and a non-negotiable expectation from individuals, investors, shareholders, families, and communities.

The chapter is not intended to be a comprehensive "how-to" guide on how to manage and improve PWB. The focus will be on the ten "why care" elements of PWB stated in Chapter 3 that the authors believe are critical to ensuring that individuals thrive. This will include how personal and workplace factors influence the ten elements. The goal is to help people monitor their PWB in a structured manner. The tools that will be shared in this chapter to help individuals manage their PWB can also be shared with their family, friends, and colleagues to help them improve their own PWB.

Managing PWB, to optimize psychological capacity, is step one in ensuring individuals help the organization manage VUCA. Step two is ensuring that this capacity is integrated into the improvement system for producing knowledge for use—knowledge that can be turned into solutions for problems and drive breakthrough performance and innovation. Managing PWB creates energy and stamina. Connecting people to the improvement system mobilizes this energy in the pursuit of excellence.

Individuals Should Assess the Impact of Their Unique Personal Factors

Organizations can never be expected to understand the intricate details of every individual's life. It is the individual's responsibility to spend regular time reflecting and assessing their unique personal history and makeup. This includes their biopsychosocial blueprint and how it influences their day-to-day life (Figure 4.2).

The state of an individual's PWB is constantly being influenced by micro and macro life factors, obtained from their past and present. These factors either build or break down PWB. Being aware of these factors and their impact allows people to plan for any future situations that may trigger tough emotions.

A large proportion of an individual's life is lived at a subconscious level.

My Personal Factors

Biological	Psychological	Social
• Age	• Self-acceptance	• Cultural traditions
• Gender	• Grief	• Family history
• Lifestyle	• Emotions	• Living environment
• Neurochemistry	• Behaviors	• Access to care
• Genetics	• Perceptions	• Socio-economic status
• Physical health	• Past trauma	• Support network
• Immune function	• Beliefs	• Education
• Flight-fright response	• Coping skills	• Marital health
• Body mass index	• Self-worth	• Work relationships
• Temperament	• Mental health	• Working conditions
• Physiology	• Learning and memory	• Domestic violence
• Stress reactivity	• Meaning in life	• Financial resources
• Disability	• Motivation	• Marginalised group
• Nutrition	• Attitude	• Community support
• Fatigue / Burnout	• Resilience	• Social causes

How do my past and present personal factors impact my PWB and fulfillment in life and at work?

John

Figure 4.2 Personal factors need to be assessed to help manage PWB.

> Today's science estimates that 95% of our brain's activity is unconscious, meaning that the majority of the decisions we make, the actions we take, our emotions and behaviors, depend on the 95% of brain activity that lies beyond conscious awareness.
>
> **(Gail Marra, *9 Interesting Facts about Your Subconscious Mind*, 2021)**

This means that many factors influencing day-to-day emotions, thoughts, and behaviors are governed unconsciously. For example: if the word "suicide" was mentioned amongst a group of friends, some may become very uncomfortable with the term because of an experience where someone died by suicide within their family, whereas others would experience no emotional trigger.

There are many other personal factors, besides words, that can have an impact on an individual's life. These include, for example, their beliefs, family situation, trauma, grief, shame, socio-economic status, gender, education, coping mechanisms, cultural traditions, mental and physical health, self-acceptance, and neurochemistry.

Individuals have a responsibility to understand, as much as reasonably possible, their biopsychosocial makeup and how it impacts on their emotions, and the way they think, behave, and interact with others. The goal isn't to understand every deep-seated nuance but, rather, the core personal themes and how these influence their PWB. Self-reflection is an important input into ensuring that people can have an informed, constructive discussion within the workplace on what increases and decreases their PWB.

Leaders need this base level of information so that they can tailor their support and management of workplace factors. The changing nature and intricate interdependencies between personal factors require that individuals constantly assess how these factors are impacting their PWB. Sharing these assessments with others at work and/or at home can help test their assumptions. Sharing is, however, dependent on trust, feeling heard, and the quality of relationships, most importantly with the individual's one-up leader. Individuals should feel safe to be vulnerable and confident they will be heard.

Individuals Should Assess the Impact of Their Unique Workplace Factors

In the same way that individuals have a personal history and biopsychosocial makeup, they also have a unique workplace narrative. This includes both past and present workplace history and experiences. These experiences, combined with their personal factors, have a substantial impact on their current psychological state. These can include both positive and negative workplace events and experiences that have shaped the way the individual sees the workplace and their role in performing and improving work.

The impact of past workplace experiences, such as workplace trauma (e.g., sexual harassment, bullying, discrimination), is particularly important to understand because of their potential to have a prolonged impact on the individual's health (emotional, mental, and physical). Many of the psychological scars from these events remain hidden within the individual's subconscious and can be triggered at any moment. Individuals need to understand how these past events influence their emotional state and the knock-on impact to their thinking, behaviors, and social interactions.

This self-reflection helps people to be very clear on the type of work that best suits their needs, including how the job can be crafted to get the best out of them. Individuals cannot expect their leader to provide the appropriate protection and support when they are unaware of their workplace journey and needs.

In the same way as with sharing personal information, the communication of workplace factors is dependent on an atmosphere of care, trust, and certainty that the individual will be truly heard when sharing this sensitive information. Individuals will never be open and share their workplace reality if they have previously done so and had negative outcomes, or if they have seen others do so only for it to be used against them.

In addition to any traumatic workplace events, it is also important for individuals to understand the impact of prolonged exposure to various other workplace factors. These can include factors associated with the organization, job design, leadership, team, and workplace behaviors (Figure 4.3).

Examples include the level of leadership and peer support; methods for managing the demand and capacity of the individual work; the amount of job control they had; their opportunities for learning and growth; the amount of training and coaching they received; the level of autonomy they had; and how respected, included, and valued they felt.

Factors such as these, left unresolved for long periods of time, could have eroded the individual's PWB. This could have depleted their ability to cope, thereby reducing their tolerance to stress. This stress could have led to psychological harm such as depression, anxiety, and post-traumatic stress disorder (PTSD). In worst cases, this could even have led to thoughts of suicide. This psychological strain could in turn have impacted the individual's

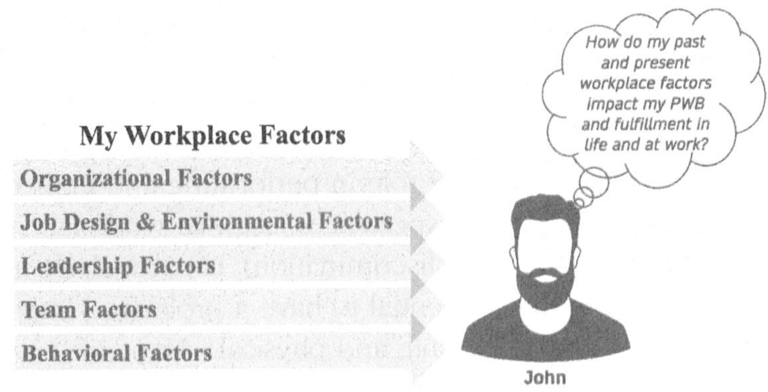

Figure 4.3 Workplace factors need to be assessed to help manage PWB.

physical health (fatigue, headaches, heart disease) as well as reduced their confidence and self-worth.

Understanding past events and communicating these appropriately, where it is safe to do so, is step one. Step two is ensuring that the current condition of the individual's working environment isn't compounding past psychological harm and/or introducing new psychosocial hazards. The link between past and current workplace conditions needs to be understood. The risk of not spending time in thinking this through is that previous workplace trauma is left to continue causing harm. Individuals need to call out anything in the design, management, and social context of their workplace that is having a positive and/or negative impact on their PWB.

List of Workplace Factors

There are numerous workplace factors that can impact an individual's PWB. As mentioned in Chapter 3, these manifest as psychosocial hazards and can be categorized into organizational, job design, environment, leadership, team, and behavioral factors (Table 4.1). Knowing about the factors allows the individual to apply a structured approach in determining how the workplace is impacting their health. An Assessment Tool can be used to help the individual conduct these periodic reviews.

Individuals Should Become More Informed about the Various Elements of PWB

The more that individuals learn about the various elements of PWB and practice self-reflection, the more they can understand how their unique

Table 4.1 Workplace Psychosocial Hazards

Category	*Workplace Psychosocial Hazards*
Organizational	• Poor organizational culture and practices • Poor organizational change management • Poor organizational communication • Poor organizational justice and fairness
Job Design and Environment	• Low role clarity • High job demand (overload) • Low job demand (unfulfilling work) • Low job control and/or autonomy • Low job security and/or precarious work • Remote and/or isolated work • Lack of work flexibility • No policies and/or procedures (inconsistent application) • Unrealistic expectations of competency • Poor working conditions (e.g., lack of space, lighting, noise) • Inadequate resources to perform the job (e.g., equipment, systems, data) • Working in extreme conditions
Leadership	• Inadequate leadership support (e.g., no one-on-one routines) • Poor leadership behaviors and role-modeling • Poor leadership engagement and/or presence • Poor leadership style (e.g., abuse of power, command, and control) • Poor leadership communication (lack of and/or withholding information) • Lack of fairness and inconsistent/poor decision making • Inadequate praise, recognition, and reward • Inadequate professional development • Poor or inadequate coaching
Team	• Poor interpersonal relationships • Lack of inclusion and belonging • Poor levels of trust • Poor co-worker support
Behavioral	• Bullying and/or victimization • Harassment (including sexual) • Discrimination (e.g., race, gender, sexual orientation, religion) • Work-related violence and/or aggression • Low civility and respect

personal and workplace factors influence their life. It affects how they think, feel, and act. Self-reflection, stepping back, and spending time reflecting on a person's thoughts and feelings is an important part of understanding their PWB.

Self-reflection, however, takes courage. It can be uncomfortable and confronting to shift the attention from what's happening around us onto ourselves. There may be aspects of a person's life they like and other things they don't.

As they shine a light on parts of their internal world that feel uncomfortable and confronting, it is essential that they counter this with self-care and self-compassion. Practicing self-reflection without self-compassion is a recipe for feeling bad about themselves. Individuals should remind themselves that self-reflection is not self-judgement.

The ten elements of PWB are split into three categories: Foundational, Relational, and Developmental. Although all elements are essential to ensure holistic well-being, the four foundational elements are regarded as critical for making sure a person has the key building blocks in place to develop the other two categories of relationship building and personal growth.

The Ten Elements of PWB

Four Foundational Elements

Elements one to four ensure that individuals have the building blocks in place upon which to establish a fulfilling life. These are referred to as the foundational elements (Table 4.2). Focusing, as a priority, on these elements sets up the other elements for success.

At the very core of living a fulfilling life is having good physical and psychological (mental) health. Without our health, we have a cracked foundation upon which to build a life of longevity and meaning. All other elements of PWB depend on our ability to prioritize, above everything else, our overall health. This needs to be complemented by a foundation of self-acceptance and compassion.

Health will deteriorate without an individual constantly embracing and reaffirming their whole self. Health (and self-acceptance) needs to be directed toward a meaningful life. The individual does this by defining a

Table 4.2 Foundational Elements

#	*Well-Being Element*	*Description*
1	Physical and Mental Health	• Physical health is the normal functioning of your body. It represents one dimension of your total well-being; it's about how your body grows, feels, and moves, how you care for it, and what you put into it. • Mental health is a state of mental well-being that enables you to cope with the stresses of life, realize your abilities, learn well and work well, and contribute to your community. It's an integral component of health and well-being that underpins your ability to make decisions, build relationships and shape the world you live in. Mental health is the state of your mind, feelings, and emotions.
2	Self-Acceptance and Compassion	• Self-acceptance is an act of embracing all of who you are, whether mental or physical, and positive or negative, exactly as they are. • Self-compassion is the process of turning compassion inward toward yourself. You are kind and understanding rather than harshly self-critical when we fail, make mistakes, or feel inadequate.
3	Purpose and Direction	• Your purpose is your personal why—it's your reason for living, your passion, what you are on this earth to do; something that is unlikely to change over the long run. • Your direction is your short- and medium-term goals that define the direction you will take in your life and career.
4	Resilience and Integration	• Resilience is your ability to successfully adapt to difficult or challenging life experiences, especially through mental, emotional, and behavioral flexibility, and adjustment to external and internal demands. • Integration is your ability to seamlessly weave together different aspects of your life. It's like building a jigsaw puzzle from the individual pieces of work, family, friends, health, and hobbies and it means making conscious choices about what we will prioritize and why.

clear life purpose and setting goals to move toward. Once momentum has been created, the individual needs coping and integration skills to deal with challenges in the pursuit of their goals. This is developed by practicing resilience and work-life integration.

Two Relational Elements

The foundational elements are focused on the individual. Relational elements five and six are focused on how the individual utilizes their foundational capabilities to develop relationships with others that will support them in achieving their purpose in life (Table 4.3).

These trusting, caring, and supporting bonds with others are the fuel that increases the momentum with which the individual can live a fulfilling, meaningful life.

Firmly establishing an individual's foundational capabilities of self-acceptance and compassion, combined with a strong ability to adapt to challenges, allows them to integrate within groups much more easily. They move forward with humble confidence, clear on who they are and what they are called to accomplish in life. This inner strength allows them to actively help

Table 4.3 Relational Elements

#	*Well-Being Element*	*Description*
5	Inclusion and Belonging	• Inclusion is feeling valued and respected, having access to opportunities and resources, and being able to contribute your perspectives and talents. It's not only being at the table but having a voice that matters in the conversation and decision-making that takes place at the table. • Belonging is being accepted and valued for your whole self, a feeling of being happy or comfortable as part of a particular group and having a good relationship with the other members of the group because they welcome you and accept you.
6	Quality of Relationships	• The quality of the relationship between you and another person where there is mutual support and encouragement, where you help each other practically as well as emotionally through listening, communicating openly and without judgement, and trusting and respecting each other's unique opinions ideas and way of doing things.

others feel valued, respected, and included. This in turn enables them to foster quality relationships, where the individual can support others in moving forward toward achieving their own purpose in life.

Four Developmental Elements

The growth elements seven to ten pick up momentum once the individual and relational capabilities have started to mature (Table 4.4). The individual defines very clear expectations—for themselves and others—as

Table 4.4 Developmental Elements

#	*Well-Being Element*	*Description*
7	Autonomy and Boundaries	• Autonomy is your ability and capacity for self-governance and self-direction. It's the capacity to be your own person, to live your life according to reasons and motives that are taken as your own and not the product of external forces. • Setting boundaries is your ability to set and hold limits about what's ok, and not ok, even if this means disappointing others. It's a form of self-care and includes the "right to disconnect."
8	Engagement and Flow	• Engagement is the level of involvement and commitment you bring to a task. • Flow is a specific type of engagement that occurs when you are fully immersed (in the zone) in an activity and experiencing a state of optimal engagement. It's required to meet stretch or challenging tasks.
9	Growth and Competence	• Personal growth is the process of understanding yourself entirely, followed by taking steps to address the behavior, attitudes, values, actions, and habits that you wish to change. • Competence is your ability to do something well. You are capable (knowledge and skills) of performing a task effectively.
10	Accomplishment and Self-Validation	• Accomplishment is feeling good about something that has taken you effort to successfully achieve (e.g., finishing a degree, completing a project, helping someone succeed). • Self-validation is the internal process of encouraging yourself, and acknowledging your strengths, successes, progress, and effort.

to how they want to achieve their goals. This includes their right to self-govern and direct their decisions and behaviors; plan and prioritize the use of their time to stay in flow; define the steps they need to take to keep growing and increasing their skills; and, finally, determine how they will recognize the progress they've made. This includes practicing self-validation.

Factors Combine and Interact to Impact PWB

As stated in Chapter 3, it is the combination and interaction between various factors that can have the biggest impact on PWB (Figure 4.4). This occurs in various ways:

1. Element-on-element interactions (e.g., a lack of purpose can have a negative impact on growth and a high level of self-acceptance can lead to increased levels of self-validation).
2. Personal factor combinations (e.g., good nutrition, exercise, and lifestyle can have a positive impact on mental health).
3. Workplace factor combinations (e.g., low job control, low role clarity, lack of co-worker support, and job insecurity can negatively impact mental health).
4. Personal factor and workplace factor combination (e.g., low coping skills, family conflict, lack of inclusion, civility, and respect at work can negatively impact self-acceptance).

Examples of Two-Factor Combinations

Table 4.5 illustrates examples of two-factor combinations and the associated PWB element they could impact.

This includes two personal factors, two workplace factors, and a personal and workplace factor combination. The quantity of possible combinations is vast. There could be three-, four-, or five-factor combinations, impacting multiple PWB elements. The goal isn't for the individual to over-analyze every possible scenario but, rather, to understand what their top five combinations are and how they have had, and/or continue to have, an impact on their PWB.

Figure 4.4 Elements combine and interact with each other to impact PWB.

Understanding these interactions and their associated impacts can help the individual put in place coping mechanisms/actions to reduce their impact. They can proactively assess risk based on current or upcoming events in their lives. For example, if someone has prolonged family conflict, is susceptible to low self-worth, and knows that they will be retrenched in three months' time, they can put in place coping mechanisms that will help them manage the upcoming uncertainty.

Table 4.5 Examples of Two-Factor Combinations and Their Impact on a PWB Element

Factor 1	*Factor 2*	*Impacted PWB Element*
Low Self-Worth	Lack of Inclusion	↓ Self-Acceptance
Past Workplace Trauma	Workplace Aggression	↓ Mental Health
Good Co-worker Support	Good Psychological Safety	↑ Accomplishment
Low Meaning in Life	Low Job Demand	↓ Growth
Lack of Exercise and Nutrition	High Work Demand	↓ Physical Health
High Job Control	High Meaning in Life	↑ Purpose
High Work Demand	Poor Capacity and Demand Management	↓ Engagement and Flow
Education	Adequate Coaching	↑ Competence
Poor Communication	Job Isolation	↓ Quality of Relationships
Good Coping Skills	Self-Validation	↑ Resilience
Low Job Security	Family Conflict	↓ Mental Health
Good Flexibility	Good Coping Skills	↑ Integration
No Policies and Procedures	Poor or Inadequate Coaching	↓ Engagement and Flow
Poor Psychological Safety	Low Self-Worth	↓ Self-Validation
Good Leadership Communication	Good Leadership Support	↑ Direction
Poor or Inadequate Coaching	Inadequate Professional Development	↓ Accomplishment

The Links between Individuals and the Ten Elements of PWB

1. Physical and Mental Health

Physical and mental health is foundational to living a fulfilling life. Without good health, we can't unlock our full potential and be the best versions of ourselves to our family, friends, and colleagues at work. Prioritizing health is the foundation upon which the other nine elements of PWB are built.

Health does not mean that everything is perfect, but it does mean that the individual is taking steps to maintain and improve it. Physical and mental health can be impacted by someone's unique personal (biopsychosocial) factors. These can have a positive and/or negative influence on their health. For example, regular exercise, good nutrition, and enough sleep can increase physical and mental energy; positive emotions can help maintain stable mood; and good coping skills can help manage stress.

On the other hand, neurochemistry can leave individuals vulnerable to mental ill health; immune dysfunction can leave people exposed to certain sicknesses; low self-esteem can make individuals doubt themselves, which can lead to depression and anxiety; and financial stress can lead to panic attacks and not being able to cope.

Individuals need to understand the impact of these personal factors on their health and ensure they are taking the necessary steps to ensure they don't cause severe and/or prolonged harm. This can include professional help in dealing with trauma, life/family coaching, marriage counseling, mentorship, participating in support groups, improving eating habits, exercising, taking regular breaks to re-energize, and being disciplined in their physical check-ups. Physical and mental health can also be impacted by severe and/or prolonged exposure to psychosocial hazards (anything in the design, management, or social context of work that has the potential to cause psychological harm/injury) within the workplace.

It is important for individuals to upskill themselves on the different types of psychosocial hazards and regularly conduct their own self-assessments on whether any of these hazards are having a negative impact on their health. They need to determine to what degree any exposure to these hazards has made them stressed, overwhelmed, angry, or upset in the past three months.

Individuals shouldn't wait for the organization or their leader to prompt these reviews. It is important for the individual to take responsibility for themselves in determining how the workplace can impact their health by conducting regular PWB assessments (Figure 4.5).

The more that people become informed about the different types of psychosocial hazards and the unique impact they can and/or are having on their health, the better will be at having an informed discussion at work on what is required to ensure their health is maintained and improved.

This does not mean the organization is absolved from responsibility for preventing psychosocial hazards from harming individuals. It remains a moral and legal duty of care. Leaders, especially, need to take very seriously any feedback on harm being caused by the workplace. It should never be

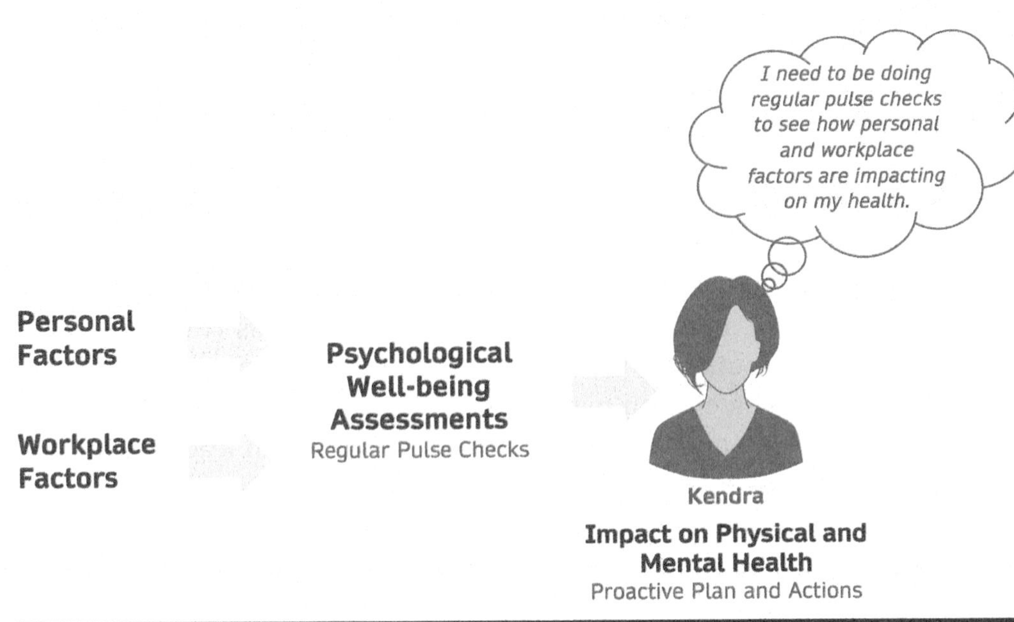

Figure 4.5 Conduct regular pulse checks of how factors are impacting health.

ignored or trivialized. When individuals share any concerns regarding the workplace and its impact on their health, they should be taken seriously and prompt action should be undertaken to prevent further continuation of the harm.

2. Self-Acceptance and Compassion

A lack of self-acceptance and compassion denotes dissatisfaction with oneself, with our past, or with certain aspects of ourselves. Unconditional love, self-acceptance, and kindness toward oneself have proven to make us happier and increase PWB. Self-acceptance involves having compassion and viewing every aspect of ourselves without judgment. Self-acceptance is about accepting ourselves exactly as we are today, living according to our own set of values, and not others. It is avoiding negative self-talk about past mistakes and setting our own standards for personal growth and development. An individual's achievement enriches them but their self-worth does not depend on their success and failures.

There are many ways to become more self-accepting, including working to stop being so hard on oneself. An individual looking at those aspects of themselves that they feel guilt, shame, or embarrassment about will help shed light on areas they try to avoid. They can then start decreasing feelings that may be exaggerated from their avoidance of these aspects. Not judging oneself, accepting things we have no control over, or thinking about what we can learn from our experiences helps us to make peace with our past and to have compassion for oneself.

Unconditional self-acceptance is understanding that you are separate from your actions and your qualities. You accept that you have made mistakes and that you have flaws, but you do not let them define you.

Self-acceptance and compassion toward oneself need to be practiced. It is a habit that needs to be developed (Figure 4.6).

For some people, they have been told they are worthless their entire lives, whether by a family member, partner, teacher, or manager. This has led to constant self-criticism and loathing that has become a norm in the person's life, reducing their emotional stability and resilience.

Entering the workplace with fragile self-acceptance and compassion can be filled with danger. Exposure to psychosocial hazards can very quickly dissolve low reserves of acceptance. If an individual is bullied or experiences sexual harassment at work, it may further reduce feelings of self-worth. If they never receive recognition for work well done, they may start feeling insecure and question their abilities. If they are discriminated against because of their race, it could amplify their feelings of isolation and exclusion, further reducing self-acceptance.

This could trigger feelings of not being enough, being less than others, and not deserving the same level of dignity and respect as others do.

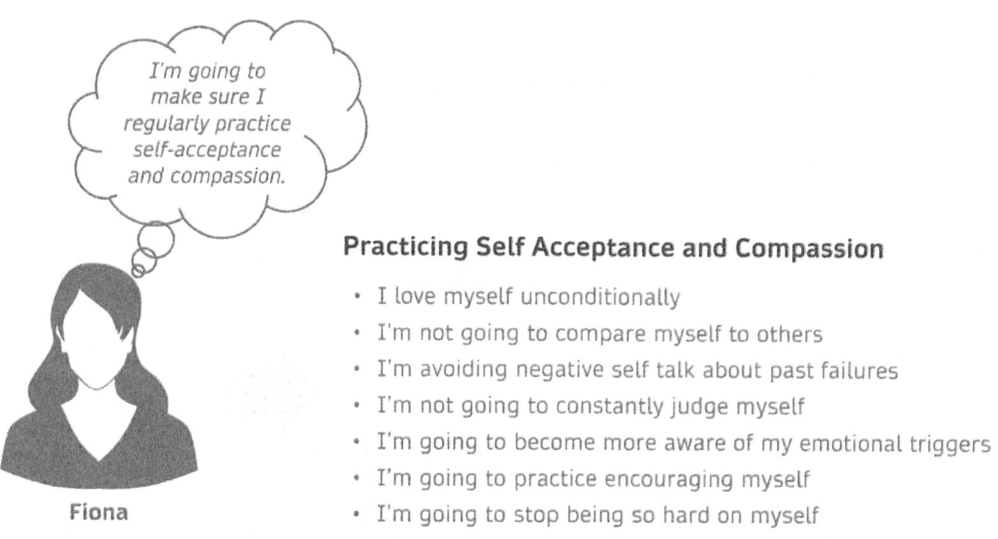

Figure 4.6 Self-acceptance and compassion need to be practiced.

Individuals need to understand what their level of self-acceptance and compassion is, including which personal and workplace factors have the biggest likelihood of triggering feelings of self-criticism. This knowledge will allow them to pre-empt situations or events that could cause harm and plan for how they will respond if they do occur.

3. Purpose and Direction

Individuals with a strong sense of purpose tend to be more content, have a positive outlook on life, have healthier relationships, live longer, and are more psychologically resilient. They have a clear sense of direction in life, with strong goal orientation and a conviction that life holds meaning.

This does not mean that they don't have problems in life; on the contrary, it is living a purposeful life that helps people navigate these difficulties and come out the other side stronger. Self-reflection is the key ingredient for determining a personal why. It is an internal journey of self-discovery, where the individual asks themselves some specific questions. A Purpose Questionnaire can be used to help an individual answer these questions and help to define their purpose in life (Figure 4.7).

Questions like these help people step outside of their current reality and reflect on what they stand for and what brings them happiness in life. Finding meaning in life provides context for everything else. It helps individuals stay focused and motivated, determine priorities, make important

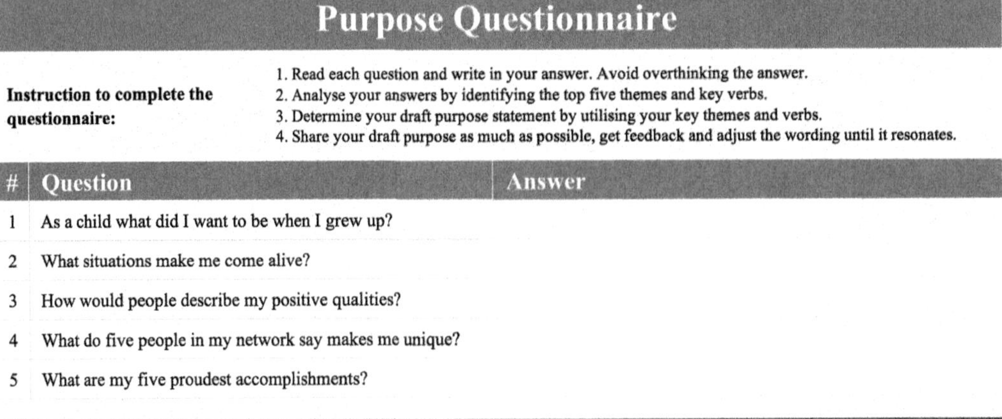

Purpose Questionnaire

Instruction to complete the questionnaire:

1. Read each question and write in your answer. Avoid overthinking the answer.
2. Analyse your answers by identifying the top five themes and key verbs.
3. Determine your draft purpose statement by utilising your key themes and verbs.
4. Share your draft purpose as much as possible, get feedback and adjust the wording until it resonates.

#	Question	Answer
1	As a child what did I want to be when I grew up?	
2	What situations make me come alive?	
3	How would people describe my positive qualities?	
4	What do five people in my network say makes me unique?	
5	What are my five proudest accomplishments?	

Figure 4.7 Purpose Questionnaire extract. Full version available at www.whycarebook.com.

decisions, persevere through hard times, build enduring relationships with the right people, and guide them through difficult challenges.

Purpose is the individual's true north. It is the lighthouse that guides them through stormy seas. Whenever there are hardships, they can look at their purpose and have it remind them of their greater calling, beyond the circumstantial volatility of the present.

Linking personal purpose to organizational purpose ensures that the individual can come to work deeply invested in helping the organization become better. They can clearly communicate to their leader and work colleagues what they value and want to get out of their job. This context helps them have an informed discussion with their leader on how to craft the job to best suit them and the organization. Leaders should periodically assess whether the type and scope of the job is continuing to help the individual fulfill their purpose and career aspirations.

Individuals who have a clear sense of meaning and direction in life are more confident to speak up at work. This does not mean that they are free from all fear, but their inner drive allows them to step out with courage and lead change. They challenge the status quo with confidence, energized from within rather than being constrained by their external environment.

4. Resilience and Integration

Resilience is the individual's ability to successfully adapt to difficult or challenging life experiences by having mental, emotional, and behavioral flexibility and being able to adjust to external and internal demands (Figure 4.8).

Integration is the individual's ability to seamlessly weave together different aspects of their life. The constantly changing personal and workplace

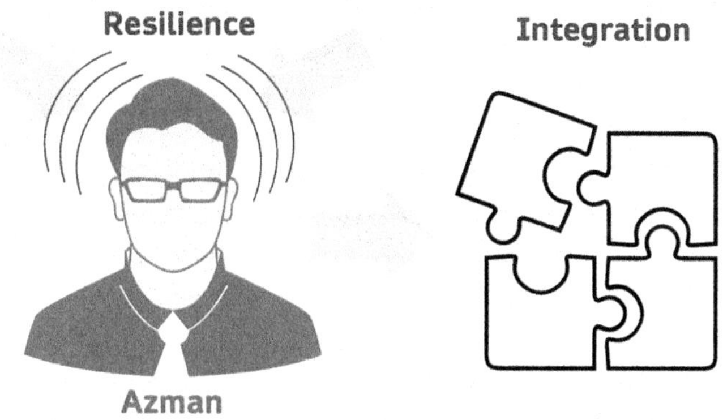

Figure 4.8 Individuals need resilience and integration abilities.

factors can very easily destabilize PWB. The ability to adapt and integrate well can help people absorb and manage the constant flow of life's challenges in the most effective manner.

When an individual has access to resilience, they can harness their inner strength to help themselves rebound from a setback or challenge, such as a job loss, an illness, a disaster, or the death of a loved one. If they lack resilience, they might dwell on problems, feel victimized, become overwhelmed, or turn to unhealthy coping mechanisms, such as substance abuse, eating disorders, or risky behaviors.

An individual's PWB comes under increased attack when they are faced with sudden or prolonged exposure to difficult life challenges. Increasing the number of pulse checks during difficult periods is helpful because it ensures people stay on top of factors that could cause further harm.

The Resilience Checklist (Figure 4.9) can help individuals determine which aspects of their Resilience Profile (Figure 4.10) they need to maintain and/or improve. The checklist consists of 15 specific statements that need to be rated from one to five. These include statements associated with key components of resilience, such as connection to a support network, focus on meaning in life, not worrying about things out of a person's control, not overanalyzing, not catastrophizing, short-term goal setting, self-acceptance and compassion.

Regular resilience check-ins help individuals stay flexible and adaptive; they offer perspective during these times of uncertainty. The Resilience Checklist helps to pinpoint areas within their resilience profile that are helping them to remain stable and areas that are working against them.

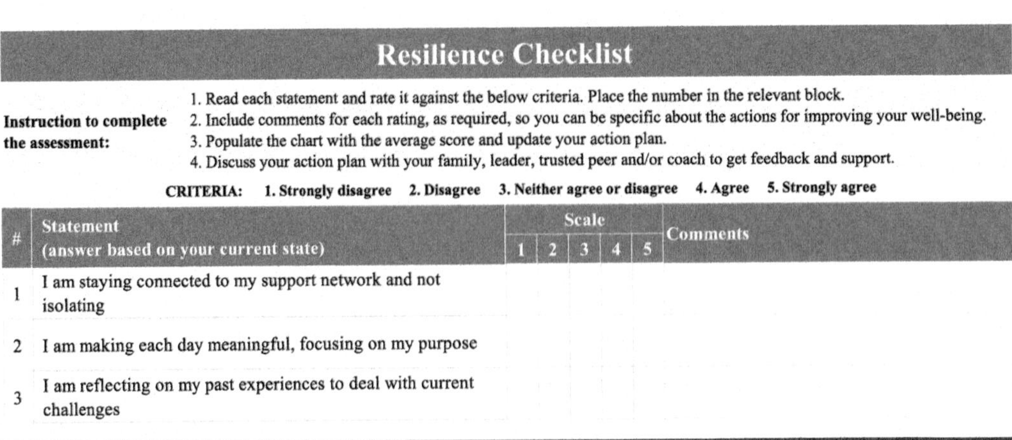

Resilience Checklist

Instruction to complete the assessment:
1. Read each statement and rate it against the below criteria. Place the number in the relevant block.
2. Include comments for each rating, as required, so you can be specific about the actions for improving your well-being.
3. Populate the chart with the average score and update your action plan.
4. Discuss your action plan with your family, leader, trusted peer and/or coach to get feedback and support.

CRITERIA: 1. Strongly disagree 2. Disagree 3. Neither agree or disagree 4. Agree 5. Strongly agree

#	Statement (answer based on your current state)	Scale 1	2	3	4	5	Comments
1	I am staying connected to my support network and not isolating						
2	I am making each day meaningful, focusing on my purpose						
3	I am reflecting on my past experiences to deal with current challenges						

Figure 4.9 Resilience Checklist extract. Full version available at www.whycarebook.com.

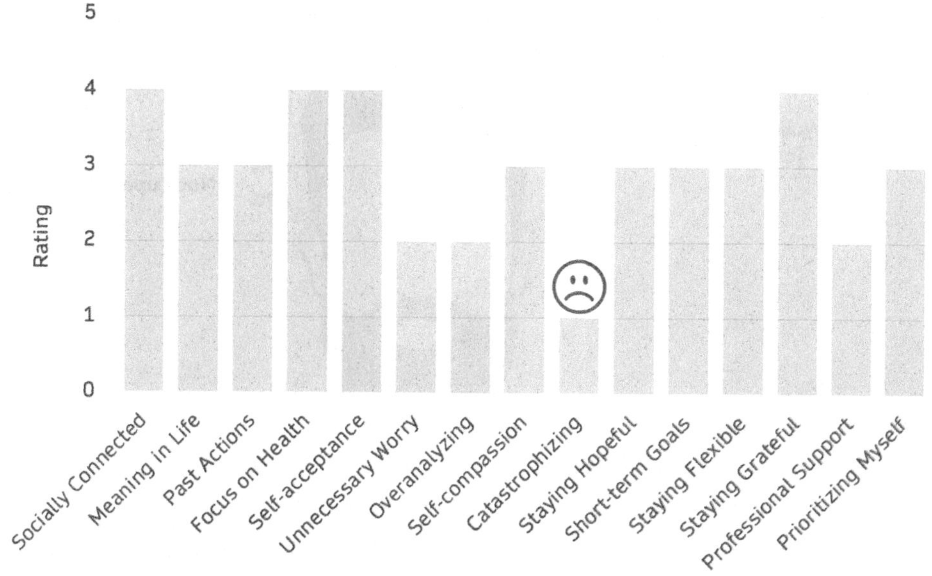

Figure 4.10 Resilience Profile extract. Full version available at www.whycare book.com.

The checklist will help the individual visualize their overall profile and see which areas score the lowest so that they can implement specific gap-closing actions. These actions may be small changes in habits and thought processes. It does not need to be big, drastic life changes but rather slight adjustments in how they regulate their emotions and thoughts throughout the day.

Resilience Isn't a Solution for Dealing with Psychosocial Hazards

Individuals should not be expected to continuously increase their levels of resilience when they are constantly being exposed to psychosocial hazards within the workplace. Resilience isn't an open tap that can just be switched on to fill a person with the required skills and energy to manage ever-increasing workplace hazards. The organization has a responsibility to help people thrive by protecting them from the negative impacts of psychosocial hazards. These hazards drain emotional and cognitive energy, reducing a person's ability to buffer stress (Figure 4.11).

Many organizations have resilience programs in place that focus on the individual's role in building inner strength to deal with difficulties. What these organizations don't realize is that the biggest cause of why individuals need inner strength is having to constantly deal with hazards within their workplace that the organization is responsible for eliminating and/or controlling.

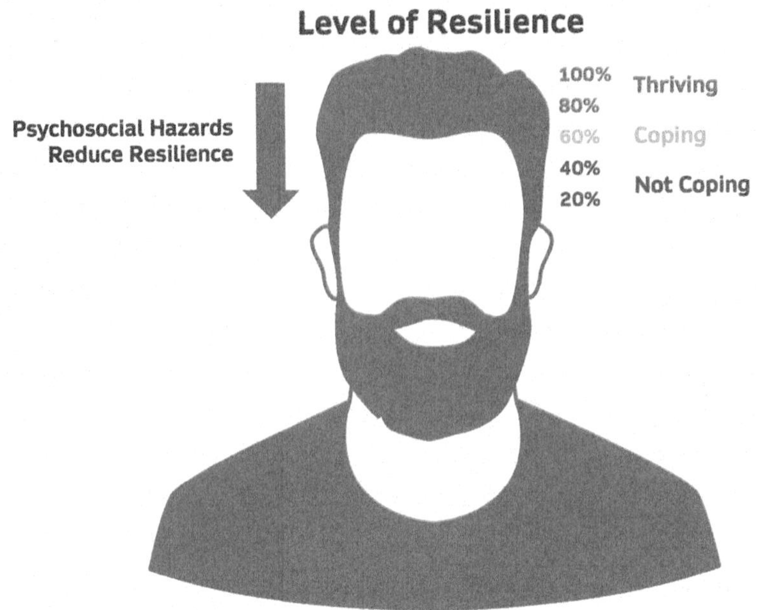

Figure 4.11 Psychosocial hazards reduce resilience.

Organizations and their leaders need to rapidly eliminate and/or control these hazards so that people don't need to be constantly using their limited psychological capacity for surviving. People should be thriving at work, not barely hanging on because their resilience buffer has been bashed around and dissolved because of inappropriate workplace stress. The focus should move more toward the organization's ability to provide a workplace that is safe from psychological harm.

The Difference between Work-Life Balance and Work-Life Integration (Harmony)

> There is a difference between work-life balance and work-life integration, and it is one that many people are struggling with as we look to come out of our pandemic work situations. Work-life balance is focused on keeping your work life and your personal life separate, but equal, whereas work-life integration is centered on the belief that there is no distinction between the two and that both must coexist in harmony.
>
> **(Stephen Kohler, *Work-Life Balance vs. Work-Life Integration: What's the Difference?*, 2021)**

Table 4.6 Work-Life Balance Differs from Work-Life Integration

Work-Life Balance	*Work-Life Integration*
• Creating barriers between work and home so they don't overlap.	• Synergy instead of balance. Managing the boundaries between your personal and work life so that they co-exist.
• Time needs to be equitably distributed and if the scale tips, you are failing.	• Emphasizes gentle pivots rather than hard boundaries between different areas of life.
• Presumes the organization is responsible for prioritizing the person's time—instead empower yourself to meet obligations in ways that best suit you.	• Enjoying the time you spend working as much as the time when you're not. Finding fulfillment in your personal life as well as in work life.

Work-life integration involves blending both personal and professional responsibilities. Rather than viewing work and personal time as separate entities, busy professionals can find areas of compromise (Table 4.6).

This might look like doing some exercise during lunchtime at work or bringing children into the office when schools are closed. "I get asked about work-life balance all the time," Bezos told Axel Springer CEO Mathias Döpfner. "And my view is, that's a debilitating phrase because it implies there's a strict trade-off." He said the reality is, if he's happy at home, he has "tremendous energy" when he goes into the office. And if he's happy at work, Bezos said he comes home with the same energy.

5. *Inclusion and Belonging*

One of the most basic needs for any individual is to feel valued, to feel part of the group, and to feel heard. Social belonging is a fundamental human need, hardwired into our DNA. Without it, we feel isolated and alone. Every person has the right to expect inclusion and belonging, to have a seat around the table (inclusion), and to have a voice at the table that matters (belonging).

The quickest way for people to feel accepted and integrated into a group is to ensure that everybody takes personal ownership for creating it. Every person within the team needs to see it as their responsibility to make others feel seen, accepted, heard, and valued as an equal, irrespective of job title or level within the organization. This includes the person who is longing for inclusion and belonging.

Every individual should wake up every day to make sure they play their role, through small acts, in making others feel they are part of the group and that they matter. These small acts can include simple words of encouragement, seeking out opportunities for recognition, showing an interest in their work, praising an improvement idea, listening to their concerns, offering help to remove obstacles, and learning more about their cultural backgrounds.

In addition, they should also focus on not being a silent bystander when they see any disrespectful, non-inclusive behavior. It is usually the build-up of small, seemingly insignificant actions that can make people feel devalued and isolated over time. Stamping out these behaviors needs to be seen as the responsibility of every person within the team. New norms are formed when everybody plays their part in creating a culture that deeply values everybody's unique nature and input.

The truth, however, is that within some workplaces, personal responsibility for making people feel included, as well as ensuring nobody is a silent bystander, will just not emerge as a priority. Toxic behaviors may be tolerated, leading to a workplace atmosphere that is saturated by cliques, unfair decision making, harassment, nepotism, racism, discrimination, and isolation. This type of culture is extremely damaging and, left unresolved, can cause real harm to a person's PWB.

Individuals should ensure that they explain the impact that the workplace is having on their health, including suggestions for how it can be improved. If they have done this multiple times, without support, then they would have no other option but to consider finding another job. The risk of long-term health problems is just too high to continue working within a workplace that does not prioritize, above everything else, the individual's PWB.

Worrying about why the toxic workplace is left to continue will only further increase the individual's stress, when it is, most often, out of their control. Inclusion and belonging are rights that every person should expect from the workplace. Those rights are brought to life by every person taking personal responsibility for creating them (Figure 4.12).

6. *Quality of Relationships*

Developing relationships with others is a basic human need and a key contributor to PWB. We all want to feel connected to others. It makes us feel significant, accepted, and valued. It is about creating trust and closeness with another person. It is about empathy and caring about the welfare of others. Good interpersonal relationships require giving and receiving.

It is something that needs to be built (Figure 4.13).

Quality relationships don't just happen. They need to be worked on and developed to offer meaning to people. Poor interpersonal relationships are a psychosocial hazard that can be caused by factors such as frequent disagreements between people, disparaging or rude comments, talking behind people's backs, not following through on commitments, trivialization of personal or workplace events, and not getting adequate support from leaders. A breakdown in care and trust, specifically within a team, is one of the leading causes of work-related stress.

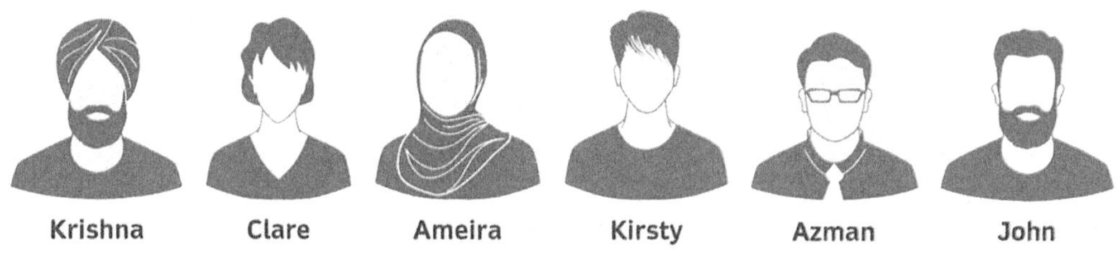

Figure 4.12 Creating inclusion and belonging is everybody's accountability.

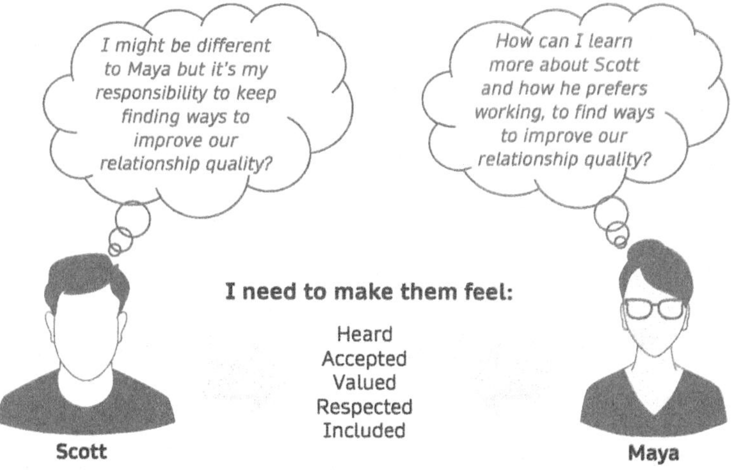

Figure 4.13 Quality relationships need to be deliberately built and maintained.

We need to be aware that stress, irrespective of source, can leave us susceptible to inappropriate behaviors toward others. In the same way that we need to take responsibility for fostering inclusion, so too do we need to take responsibility for constantly assessing our levels of stress and making sure it does not trigger inappropriate behaviors toward others.

Strong relationships are built one person at a time, and everyone should play their part in role-modeling behaviors that promote care and trust amongst people. Showing care and trust is a developed skill and should be encouraged as an improving capability for every person.

Whether stress originates at home or work, the fallout is often seen at work, simply because that is where we spend most of our day. People seldom go to work with the intention of creating stress for their teammates: It naturally occurs when people are overwhelmed.

Regardless of the reason, stress creates communication barriers and breakdowns when people are focused on their individual points of pain. This can quickly lead to misunderstandings and conflict. Once people begin to struggle with overloaded schedules and misunderstandings, they're likely to end up with feelings of resentment toward teammates and leaders.

Even if the cause of the discontent isn't warranted, the person's beliefs will nonetheless show in how they interact with others. Their negative interactions will lead to further resentment by other teammates. Deep-rooted resentment will inevitably damage the entire team and the support they provide to each other. Once teammates stop supporting each other, productivity will begin to decline sharply. The flow of information will become less frequent and limited, leading to missed deadlines and poor-quality deliverables. The continuous stress and resentment can result in a never-ending cycle (intentional or unintentional) of withholding of support. Eventually, the lack of support can turn into blatant sabotage.

Everybody is responsible for building and protecting relationships within the workplace. Leaders need to promote the need for teamwork and stamp out any divisive and toxic behavior.

7. Autonomy and Boundaries

Autonomy means maintaining your personal independence and your convictions. It means feeling that you can choose for yourself and make your own decisions even if it goes against the opinions of others. It means you know how to resist social pressure. People with high autonomy know how to regulate their behavior and assess themselves against personal standards instead of the expectations of others.

Individuals with a low level of autonomy succumb to social pressure. They settle for what others tell them to do. They are influenced and guided by the criteria of others. They also worry about the expectations and evaluations of others. When making decisions, they trust the judgments of others. Every person wants to feel that they are in control of their life and freely make decisions about how they think and behave. They want to feel like they are coping well in their personal life and in the workplace.

Not being able to cope, due to personal and/or workplace factors, can have a devastating impact on a person's health. In addition, it destroys confidence and the ability to manage life. The ability to cope and make decisions for oneself is a basic human right. The implications of not being able to do so can leave people broken and empty of any self-worth and value.

Low job control is a psychosocial hazard, where people have little control over or input into their work, including how or when they do the job. It becomes a hazard when it is severe (very low job control), prolonged (long-term), or frequent (happens often). This hazard disempowers individuals from owning and improving their work because they need to be constantly asking for permission. Leaders become the decision-making bottleneck because every workplace decision needs to pass over their desks.

Individuals become disillusioned by the lack of trust in their abilities. They end up merely complying, coming to work to earn a paycheck versus applying their unique genius. Improvement grinds to a halt when ownership of work is taken away from people doing the work. It is the highest form of disrespect to detach individuals from what they value so much—being great at their job.

Individuals can, however, play a role in making sure this does not happen to them or is reduced. The more that they show initiative in speaking up about their work—what's working and not working—the more control they take back. Instead of relying on others to define every aspect of how their job is performed and improved, they do it themselves and communicate the gains to their leader. The more that individuals do this, the more leaders will see that the people doing the work are the true experts and need to be given more autonomy to manage and improve their jobs.

Individuals need to be open and transparent with their leaders on the level of autonomy they need. Any capability gaps at an individual level can be picked up by the diverse skills of the team. An autonomous team is self-governing and self-regulating.

Setting boundaries is also recognized as a key enabler for supporting PWB. Setting boundaries is a form of self-care by outlining how the individual would like to be treated. They let others know what is and what is not okay or acceptable. It honors our needs and wants, so that we feel respected and safe.

The right to disconnect is also important. People need the ability to disconnect from their work and not engage in work-related electronic communications such as emails or messages during non-work hours.

Autonomy, setting boundaries, and the right to disconnect (Figure 4.14) are key ingredients for self-fulfillment at work and effective work-life integration.

8. Engagement and Flow

Engagement is an individual's level of involvement and commitment they bring to a task. Flow is the outcome of total absorption in what a person is doing—being "in the zone"—with limited distractions. It is the time when people feel most connected to what they are doing, utilizing every bit of their knowledge and skills to perform a task exceptionally well. This can be executing a task or engaging in a one-on-one conversation. In both cases, the individual needs to be in the moment and present, consumed by what needs to be accomplished.

Figure 4.14 Autonomy, boundaries, and disconnecting are all enablers of PWB.

It is within this "flow state" that people achieve their best results. Being in flow means that they are very clear on the activity that needs to be performed and have the necessary resources at "point of use" to complete the task. The more that they are in flow, the more fulfilled they feel. The individual gets more done in less time and feels like they have made progress or achieved something worthwhile.

Increasing engagement and flow is dependent on how well the individual's job connects with their purpose and meaning at work. Their job needs to bring a sense of satisfaction and accomplishment that is linked to what the individual values and wants to get out of their job. The more that people find meaning in their work, the more they will focus on being engaged and striving to be in flow as much as possible. Optimum engagement and flow are dependent on how well the individual plans, executes, and improves their work. It requires that they spend adequate time proactively planning the goals they need to achieve, identifying the specific activities required, and allocating time needed to achieve them.

How Can Individuals Increase the Amount of Time They Are Engaged and in a Flow State?

1. Firstly, they need to find meaning in their work.
2. Secondly, they need to be clear on what needs to be prioritized in their work.
3. Thirdly, they need to structure their time to focus on these priorities.
4. Finally, they need to track compliance with adhering to their plan.

Achieving optimum engagement and flow is the outcome of very clear prioritization of work and allocation of sacred time to accomplish these priorities (Figure 4.15).

Prioritization should include involvement from the individual's leader. The more that they can align on the key deliverables with their leader, the better. It reduces ambiguity, potential conflict, and stress. This alignment should be for a specific period (e.g., monthly priorities).

Regular one-on-one routines should be used between the person and their leader to assess how they have progressed against these agreed priorities. This should include what proportion of time they were in flow and what distracted them from achieving their prioritized deliverables.

Actions should be defined to close gaps, including what the leader's role is in ensuring minimal interference. There may be cases where the

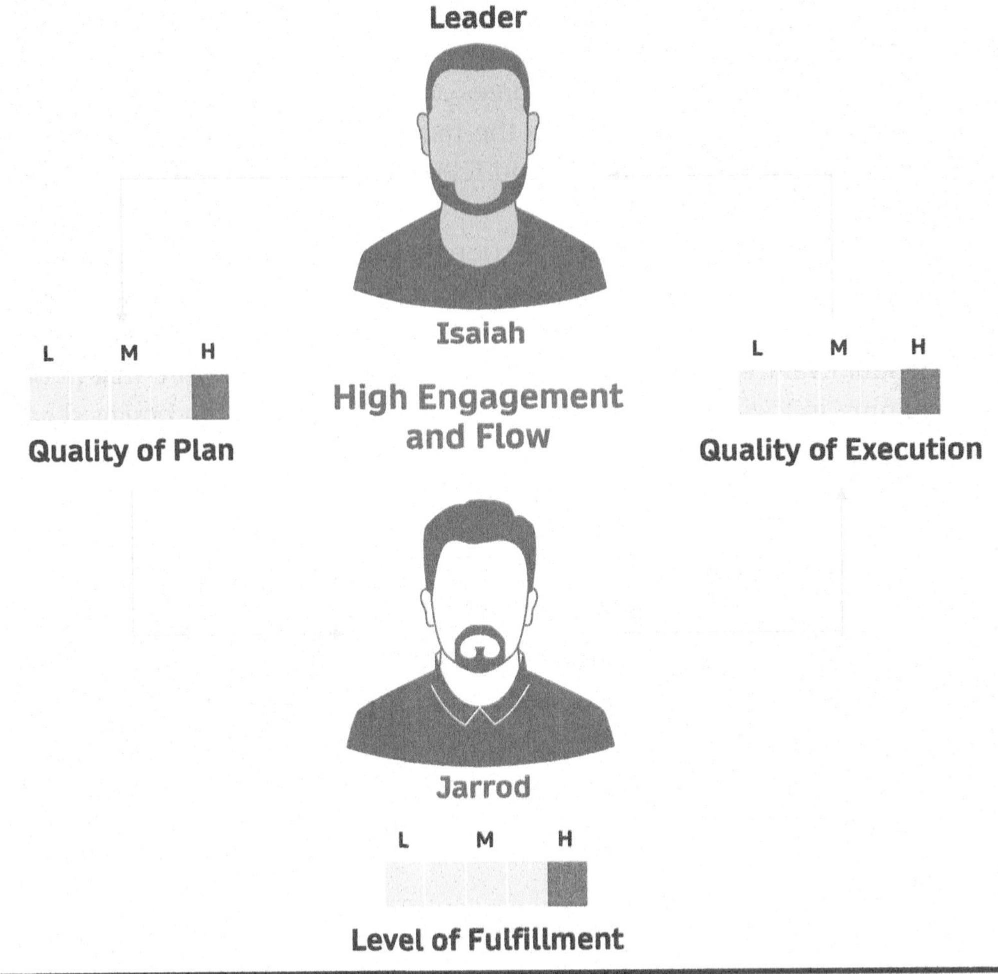

Figure 4.15 Optimum engagement and flow need to be deliberately created.

leaders themselves have been a reason for distraction by expecting urgent, unplanned requests to be actioned immediately. These leadership interruptions, known as managerial variability, should be captured when they occur and discussed at one-on-one meetings. Individuals need to take control of their time; nobody else will.

Staying engaged and achieving optimum flow is an outcome of the individual taking personal responsibility for how their time is used. Utilizing time well to achieve their goals will have a positive impact on the way they feel about themselves and their accomplishments.

Leaders need to understand that high and low work demands are psychosocial hazards. Achieving optimum engagement and flow in work is best achieved when there is a balance between the demand (work tasks) placed on someone and the capacity (time, resources, skills) to complete these tasks.

Planning and prioritization of tasks, including the appropriate capacity to do so, ensure individuals have the best opportunity to achieve engagement and flow in their work—a key enabler for achieving positive PWB.

9. Growth and Competence

Growth and competence are elements of well-being that make us feel like we are moving forward in life and unlocking our potential. They make us feel valuable and give us a sense of fulfillment. Personal Growth is about evolving and is a continuous process of assessing where we are against the development goals we set for our lives. These include personal and career aspirations.

Growth requires that we step outside of our comfort zone and accept that we have gaps in how we think, behave, and engage with others. This can be confronting and may require courage to accept. Accepting we have opportunities to improve can make us feel a little vulnerable. It is easy for an "imposter mindset" to take hold when we are thinking about what areas we still need to develop in.

Growth, however, cannot occur without a growth mindset. A growth mindset is an approach to life in which an individual believes that their talents, intelligence, and abilities can be developed further. People with a growth mindset seek opportunities to learn, gain new skills, and enhance their existing skills (Figure 4.16).

A fixed mindset means that people believe that their abilities, talents, intelligence, or personality traits are given and unchangeable. They're born with what they're born with—and that's it.

Acknowledging that we have opportunities to improve and not letting perceived failure and/or mistakes get us down is the first step toward moving forward and becoming better versions of ourselves. Growth is reduced when we are validated by our education, past ways of doing things, and/or successes. Growth requires an open mindset, a willingness to accept that how we currently think about ourselves and how we perform work may not be conducive for our future.

Constant self-reflection (Hansei) is a central theme for ensuring growth. Hansei is an important part of Japanese culture—a continuous form of subtle meditation undertaken to look at past mistakes, outline the lessons, and pledge to act on those lessons. "Han" means to change, turn

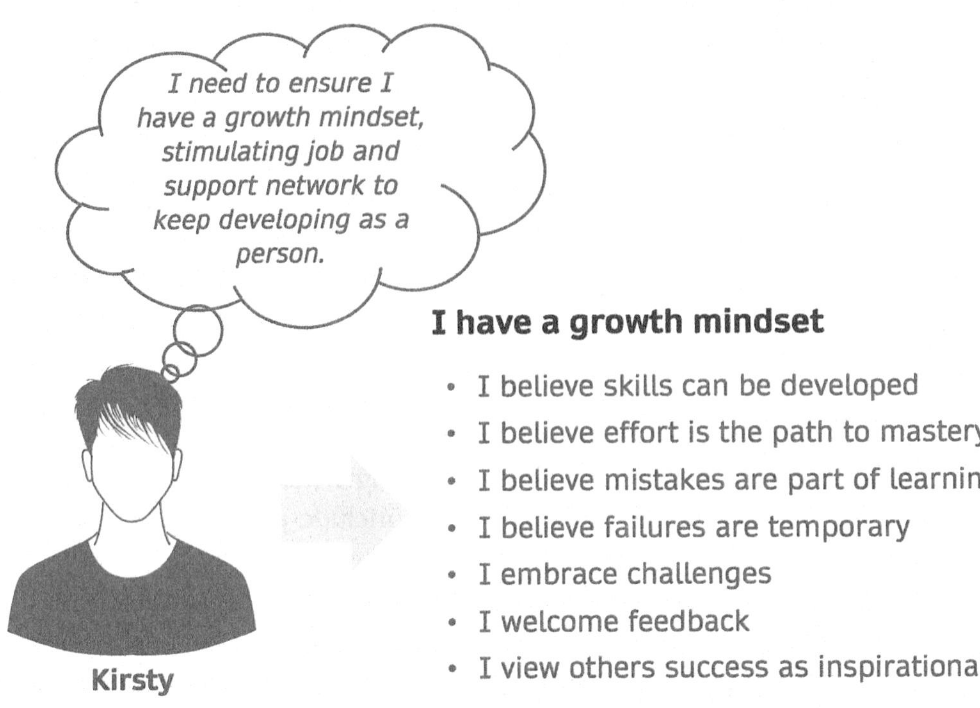

Figure 4.16 A growth mindset is critical for personal development.

over, or turn upside-down. "Sei" means to look back upon, review, and examine oneself. A Hansei Mindset of introspection to improve the self ensures that people remain humble and always focused on continuous self-development.

> Success is not final; failure is not fatal: It is the courage to continue that counts.
>
> **(W. Churchill)**

Growth, however, requires a support network. Individuals should establish a trusted network of people to help them navigate the uncertainty associated with personal development. This can include their leaders, trusted peers, coaches, and—if required—professional support.

Low job demand and/or unrewarding work are psychosocial hazards that can impact a person's growth and competence. These should be discussed in one-on-one meetings between the individual and their leader to ensure the scope of the job is conducive to development of growth and skills.

10. Accomplishment and Self-Validation

Accomplishment is feeling good about something that has taken the individual personal effort to successfully achieve (e.g., finishing a degree, completing a project, helping someone succeed). Self-validation is the internal process of encouraging oneself and acknowledging one's strengths, successes, progress, and effort.

Everyone needs validation—to feel accepted and understood. However, we can't always get validation from others. Therefore, it is important to know how to validate ourselves. It feels good to be praised, to have our feelings affirmed, to be told we did a good job, and to be appreciated. It is normal to want validation from others—our parents, spouse, boss, and friends.

But some of us seek external validation to an unhealthy level. We rely on others to make us feel good. We doubt our abilities if we're not explicitly told we're doing well. We obsessively check our social media posts, looking for approval. And we question our worth if others do not value us.

Relying on external validation can make us anxious or depressed. Constantly waiting for someone to make us feel good about ourselves can be exhausting. If we do not get this external validation frequently enough, we can start feeling anxious that we are not good enough, which can lead to low mood and depression. A lack of self-confidence may cause us to make more errors and have trouble concentrating. And disapproval and criticism are especially painful because we put so much stock into other people's opinions.

We can't rely on others to make us feel good. When we do, we allow others to dictate our worth. And we don't trust our own thoughts, feelings, and judgments; we assume others know more than we do, and their opinions matter more. We become needy and ask for validation in ways that turn others off—in ways that scream, "My self-esteem is lacking and I need you to tell me I'm okay." Instead, a person can learn how to validate themselves. A "Self-Validation Practice Sheet" (Figure 4.17) can be used to get better at this.

The Importance of Dealing with Emotional Hurt

Emotional hurt caused by workplace events can be all consuming. It can flow through and permeate every aspect of a person's work and personal life. People go to work to do a good job, to be valued and recognized for their contributions. So much time and energy are invested in doing the best we can at our work.

Self-validation Practice Sheet

Four Steps for Self-validation:

1. I have identified how I am feeling and what I need (I feel angry, I need space).
2. I have accepted my feeling and needs without judgement (its ok to feel ok).
3. I am not allowing my feeling to define me (I feel angry vs. I am angry).
4. Practice self-validation everyday by using some of the listed example below.

#	Examples that can be used for self-validation	Practice Comments
1	I was born enough and this will never change	
2	I know what my purpose is in life, I just need to keep focusing on it	
3	I can do this, even if people may not think so, I believe in me	
4	I don't need to be perfect in front of people, I just need to be me	

Figure 4.17 Self-Validation Practice Sheet extract. Full version available at www.whycarebook.com.

There is a high likelihood of emotional hurt within the workplace, considering the many interactions people have with each other and the vast number of decisions that need to be made. Every time there is an engagement with another person or a decision made in the workplace, there is an opportunity for hurt. These could include:

- Being sent a rude e-mail.
- Being made to feel incompetent in a meeting with others.
- Being spoken about behind our backs.
- Being told we are not capable of a promotion.
- Being told we aren't performing to standard.
- Being sexually harassed with no repercussions.
- Being discriminated against because of race.
- Not being accepted because of gender identity.
- Being left out of key decisions regarding work.
- Having our ideas used by someone else for recognition.

There is no excuse for abusive behaviors and these need to be treated appropriately, based on their severity, duration, and frequency. Organizations have their own values, guidelines, and systems for dealing with inappropriate behaviors.

The fact is, however, that no matter how big or small an issue is, it can still linger as a painful experience. The longer this hurt is left unresolved, the longer it will continue to impact on a person's PWB.

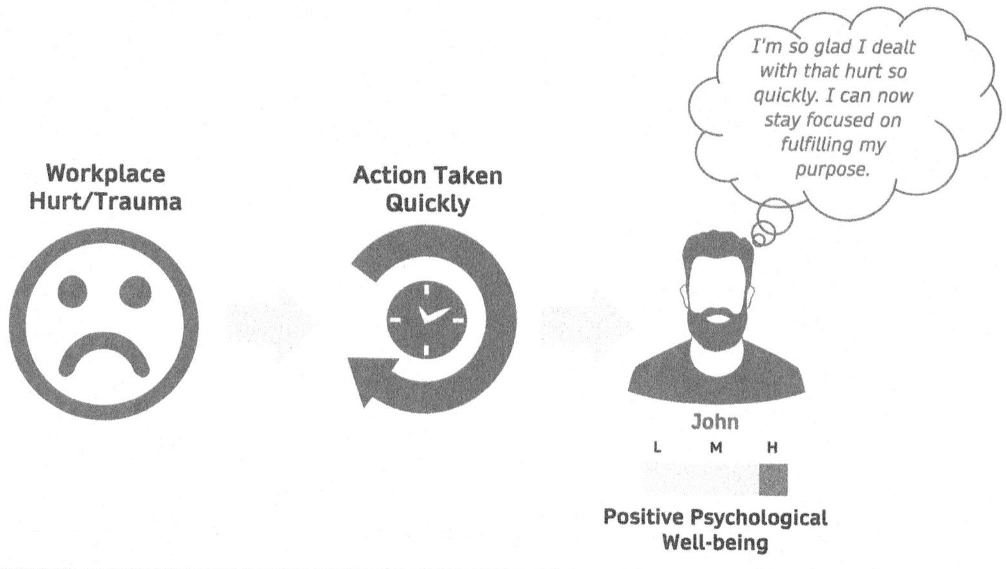

Figure 4.18 Take action to deal with workplace hurt/trauma as soon as possible.

Workplace hurt/trauma can have a devastating impact on a person's life. People spend much of their time at work and invest much of their energy and skills in being the best they can be at their job. The pride people gain from progressing their career makes them feel good about themselves and fills them with a sense of growth and accomplishment. Workplace hurt/trauma can dissolve all these gains in a single moment. They can turn positive thoughts about work into negative thoughts of bitterness, anger, and resentment.

The best way to avoid spiraling into negative thinking and prolonged pain is to deal with the situation as soon as possible (Figure 4.18). This could be speaking to the person who caused the hurt, talking to a leader, raising the issue for formal investigation, or speaking to a mental health professional.

There is nothing worse than when a person goes to work, dreading having to walk past the person who has caused them the hurt and then letting the flood of negative emotions ruin their day. It may require courage to act, but courage is a decision. Just don't let it linger.

A Thriving Plan for Every Individual

A Thriving Plan is the key message of the book. For organizations to thrive, they need a great culture of CI. This culture is the outcome of a mature improvement system leveraging the optimum psychology capacity that has been made available through a deliberate focus on every person's PWB.

The goal is to get every person to realize the importance of being conscientious in managing their psychological health. The best way to do this is to get individuals to regularly evaluate their PWB by using simple tools such as those already discussed in the chapter (Table 4.7).

These tools are used to help the person apply a structured approach for assessing, tracking, and actioning their PWB. The goal is to track these results over time and build up a history of this information, to see which personal and workplace factors are having the biggest impact on the person's ability to thrive. This will help them determine things such as the thoughts, habits, behaviors, and decisions they need to stop, start, and/or continue.

Specific actions can be defined and implemented to improve specific elements of PWB. The Thriving Plan is designed to be owned by the individual. Taking ownership means they prioritize self-care and ensure that they regularly identify opportunities to improve.

Individuals are, however, not solely responsible for these improvements. It will require their entire village (organization, leader, colleague, coach, family,

Table 4.7 Tools to Help Manage PWB

#	*Tool*	*When to Use*
1	Psychological Well-Being Assessment	Whenever you want to assess your PWB.
2	20 Point—Personal Factors Assessment	Whenever you want to assess the impact of personal factors on your PWB.
3	30 Point—Workplace Factors Assessment	Whenever you want to assess the impact of workplace factors on your PWB.
4	Purpose Questionnaire	When you want to determine your life purpose.
5	Resilience Checklist	When you want to determine if you are doing everything you can to stay resilient.
6	Self-Validation Practice Sheet	Whenever you are feeling insecure, self-critical, low confidence, and/or doubtful about your capabilities.

All available at www.whycarebook.com. Tools 2–6 can be used on their own or they can be used to provide a more accurate assessment when doing the PWB Assessment (#1).

and friends) to help implement the specific actions identified from assessments. The fact that an entire village has an impact on their PWB means that every person within their village should also be responsible for helping to improve it.

The Purpose of the PWB Assessment

The purpose of the assessment is for the individual to reflect on each one of the ten elements of PWB and rate them in terms of their personal health (Figure 4.19). These results are then visualized on a timeline and radar chart for further reflection (Figure 4.20).

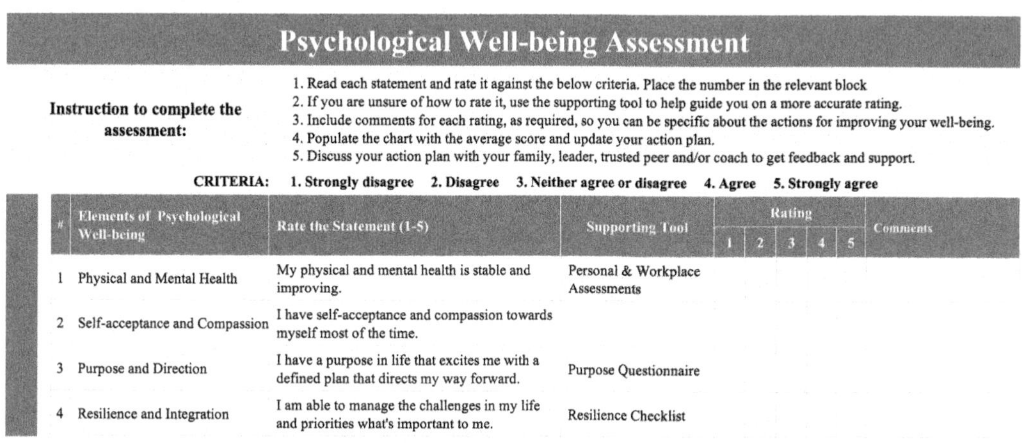

Psychological Well-being Assessment

Instruction to complete the assessment:

1. Read each statement and rate it against the below criteria. Place the number in the relevant block
2. If you are unsure of how to rate it, use the supporting tool to help guide you on a more accurate rating.
3. Include comments for each rating, as required, so you can be specific about the actions for improving your well-being.
4. Populate the chart with the average score and update your action plan.
5. Discuss your action plan with your family, leader, trusted peer and/or coach to get feedback and support.

CRITERIA: **1. Strongly disagree 2. Disagree 3. Neither agree or disagree 4. Agree 5. Strongly agree**

#	Elements of Psychological Well-being	Rate the Statement (1-5)	Supporting Tool	Rating					Comments
				1	2	3	4	5	
1	Physical and Mental Health	My physical and mental health is stable and improving.	Personal & Workplace Assessments						
2	Self-acceptance and Compassion	I have self-acceptance and compassion towards myself most of the time.							
3	Purpose and Direction	I have a purpose in life that excites me with a defined plan that directs my way forward.	Purpose Questionnaire						
4	Resilience and Integration	I am able to manage the challenges in my life and priorities what's important to me.	Resilience Checklist						

Figure 4.19 PWB Assessment extract. Full version available at www.whycarebook.com.

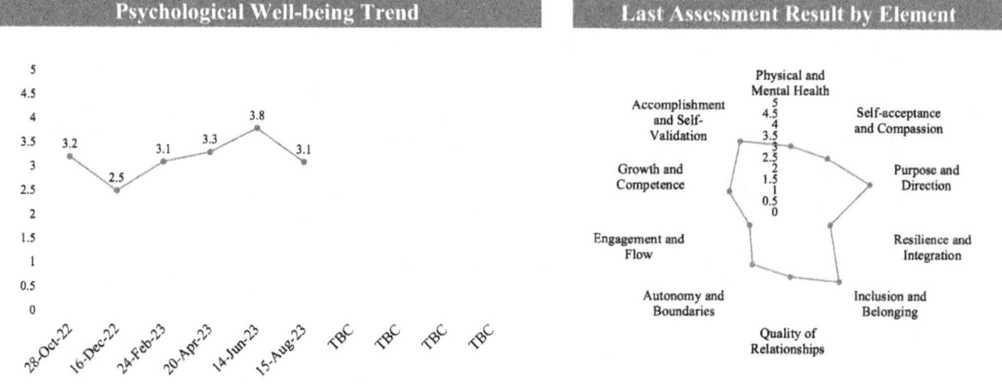

Figure 4.20 Visualization of PWB Assessment results extract. Full version available at www.whycarebook.com.

Once the assessment is complete, they then define the specific activities they want to stop, start, or continue based on the assessment outcomes. This will include the support that they need to implement actions. There are also supporting tools that can be used to further understand the state of each element of PWB.

Guidelines for Conducting a PWB Assessment

There are six simple guidelines for helping an individual think through and complete a PWB Assessment:

1. The individual can conduct an assessment at any time to determine their state of PWB. This is particularly relevant when they are experiencing psychological strain and need to determine what to stop, start, or continue doing.
2. When rating each statement, the individual should think through their unique personal and workplace factors (see start of chapter) and consider how these are impacting on each of the ten elements of PWB.
3. They should also consider how their unique personal and workplace factors are combining and interacting to increase or decrease their PWB. These can be captured on the Factors Worksheet (Figure 4.21).
4. They should make sure the actions they identify are specific and practical, ideally actions within their control. If their PWB is on a steep decline, they should implement short-term containment actions to avoid further harm. The individual should then focus on how these actions can be embedded as habits to support their PWB over the longer term.

Factor 1	Factor 2	Factor 3	Factor 4	PWB Element	Comments
Sickness in Family	Financial Instability	Lack of Leader Support	Low Job Security	- My mental health is in decline - I feel like I am losing direction in life - I'm isolating myself from work colleagues	Conduct a Psychological Well-being Assessment to see what actions I can take to improve my situation

Figure 4.21 Factors Worksheet extract. Full version available at www.whycarebook.com.

5. Individuals can share their assessment with a trusted colleague, coach, family member, or friend. This can be helpful if they want to get feedback on any actions identified. This can include asking for feedback on how workplace factors should be discussed with their leader.
6. The assessment can be used as part of the regular one-on-one meetings between the individual and their leader. This is particularly valuable when they need to communicate any personal or workplace factors that may be impacting their health. This should include the support they need from their leader in eliminating or controlling psychosocial hazards from impacting on them. Where the risk is high for short-term decline of well-being, they should talk to their leader about how they can manage work demand to get through the difficult period.

Every Individual Is Responsible for Being Involved in the Improvement System

A maturing improvement system, combined with maturing PWB, provides the foundation upon which an organization can create a thriving culture of improvement. The more that PWB is increased, the more that people need to be using their increasing psychological capacity to increase the rate of improvement.

This is done by actively engaging with each social (Table 4.8) and technical (Table 4.9) element within the improvement system. This includes receiving the necessary training and coaching on the intent of each element and how each person's role contributes to it. The improvement system will not mature unless individuals use and improve it. It requires that every individual role-model the behaviors to ensure the improvement system flows. In addition, every individual should relentlessly practice applying the principles, processes, tools, and techniques within the system.

Leaders need to lead the way and act as coaches of the system. They need to teach, coach, and role-model the behaviors associated with each element. They need to be the first to practice and apply each element for themselves so that they can learn firsthand what it feels like. This will help them understand the nuances when introducing the behaviors and the empathy required when coaching.

Table 4.8 Social Responsibilities

#	*Social Elements*	*Individual Responsibilities*
1	Lead with Purpose	• Ensure the work you do is meaningful and links to the purpose of your team.
2	Lead with Humility	• Be willing to share any mistakes you have made so others can learn. • Ask for support from your team if you are struggling.
3	Develop Trust	• Be trustworthy, avoid gossip, build people up. • Develop your skills in building trust (care, sincerity, reliability, and competence).
4	Show Respect for Every Individual	• Make sure everybody has a voice and is heard within your team. • Don't be a silent bystander when seeing disrespectful behaviors.
5	Listen to the Voice of the Individual (VOI)	• Provide feedback on what's working well and not so well in your job. • Share successes, challenges, and concerns with your team and leader.
6	Cultivate Teamwork	• Actively participate in team routines. • Be willing to support a peer who needs help.
7	Constantly Challenge the Status Quo	• Help others speak up by being an example yourself. • Relentlessly eliminate waste from your work. • Don't accept bureaucracy.
8	Look, Listen, and Learn at the Gemba	• Share your knowledge, skills, and improvement ideas with peers. • Spend time with other people involved in your process to understand their issues and how you can help them.
9	Develop People through Coaching	• Be clear on those areas you need coaching on and seek support. • Make sure you have formal time set aside for regular coaching sessions.
10	Lead Effectively through Leaders Standard Work	• Provide feedback to leaders on their effectiveness when attending any of your routines.
11	Foster Diversity, Equity, Inclusion, and Belonging (DEIB)	• Actively participate in ensuring everybody feels included within your team. Make them feel like they belong. • Don't be an active bystander when seeing any form of exclusion, harassment, and/or discrimination.

Table 4.9 Technical Responsibilities

#	*Technical Elements*	*Individual Responsibilities*
1	Conduct strategy development and deployment	• Ensure your work is clearly linked to the team's success factors.
2	Listen to the Voice of the Customer (VOC)	• Know who your customer is and engage with them regularly. • Get feedback on how your work is meeting their needs. • Implement improvements to your work based on customer feedback.
3	Listen to the Voice of the Process (VOP)	• Make sure your processes have clear metrics for tracking their health. • Make sure any delays/issues within your process are captured for improvement.
4	Focus on horizontal value streams	• Make sure you understand which value stream you work in. • Understand how your work impacts the value stream.
5	Standardize work and ensure quality	• Execute your work to the current standard. • Look for opportunities to improve the standard.
6	Embed continuous improvement	• Relentlessly eliminate waste from your work. • Share your improvement ideas with others for possible replications.
7	Develop structured problem-solving	• Participate in structured problem-solving activities. • Help the team assess whether solutions to problems have worked.
8	Manage visually	• Actively participate in team huddles (review of KPIs and KBIs).
9	Develop and use knowledge and skills	• Develop your own skills matrix with development goals. • Ensure regular dialogue with your leader to ensure you achieve your development goals.
10	Manage capacity and demand	• Have a formal mechanism in place to manage your capacity and demand. • Communicate to your leader when you are over- or underloaded.
11	Create workplace organization (5S)	• Ensure all resources are available to you at point of use.

Key Points from Chapter 4

- Maintaining and improving PWB is the responsibility of both the person and the organization they work for.
- Understanding a person's unique personal and workplace factors will enable them to take the steps required to ensure they maintain positive PWB.
- The most effective way to manage and improve PWB is to have an individual Thriving Plan and conduct regular PWB Assessments.

Chapter 5

Why Care about Thriving Teams?

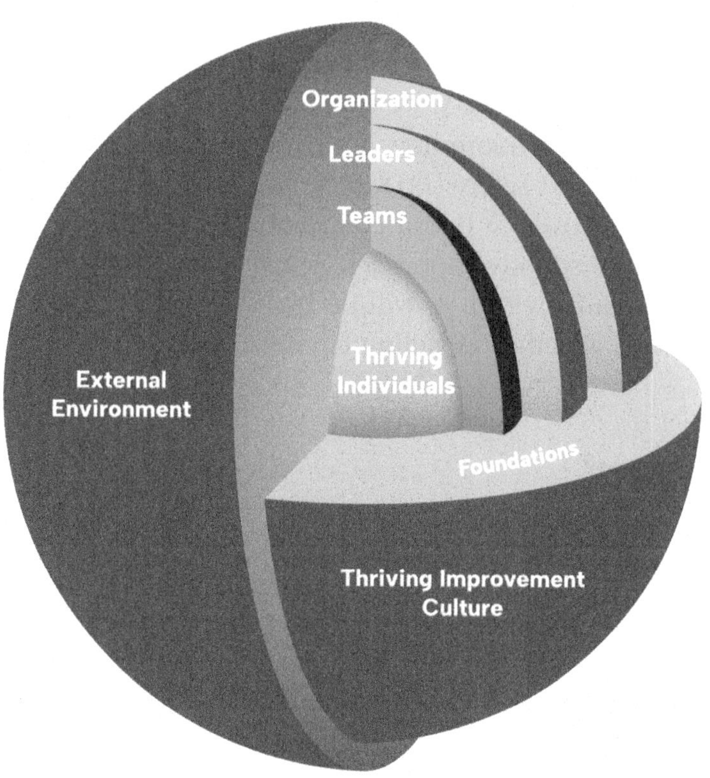

Figure 5.0 The Why Care Model—Teams.

DOI: 10.4324/9781003413479-6

Introduction

In the authors' experience, most organizational well-being initiatives have tended to focus on creating healthy individuals and, somewhere along the way, we've forgotten the ancient wisdom of our ancestors of the power of the collective. The collective matters not just for performance, but for creating an environment for people to flourish and thrive. Chapter 3 highlighted the importance of teamwork for psychological well-being (PWB), illustrating how teams can both create and mitigate psychosocial hazards. Team psychosocial hazards impact both individuals and the team's collective psychological capacity. Continuous improvement (CI) is not usually mentioned in the same sentence as PWB, with well-being often the preserve of HR, and CI reporting to a different function, such as Operations, or a tactical performance unit.

But might we be missing a trick? What if we were to reframe our thinking and see CI not as separate from well-being, not as something to be managed and contained to prevent psychosocial hazards, but as an enabler for PWB? CI could be used to help create a thriving environment with high levels of PWB and psychological capacity.

In this chapter, we'll explore how teams impact well-being, what team psychological health and safety (PH&S) is, and how CI practices and tools can help create collective PWB and contribute to psychological flow. This is not designed as a prescriptive approach because what works for your organization, and the teams within it, will be highly contextual based on your needs, preferences, and the prevailing circumstances.

What Is a Team?

At work today, we're all part of multiple teams, from our "home team" (the one where we do most of our work), to project teams, cross-functional teams, leadership teams, and the list goes on. But are these really all teams? And what is a team, anyway? Peter Hawkins et al. (2017) have built on the work of Jon Katzenbach and Douglas Smith (1993) and have enlarged the definition of a team to focus on the seemingly disparate elements of both individual and collective. Holding this tension between these two is crucial and, in real teams, there is an interdependency between all members, not just between individuals and the leader. The complexity of this interconnectedness increases exponentially as the number of team members increases, as illustrated in Figure 5.1.

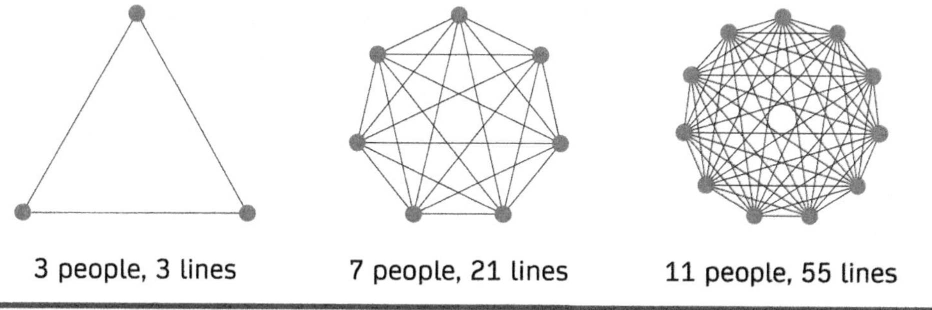

Figure 5.1 Lines of communication and team size—applying Brook's (1995) Law.

When I reflect on my personal experience working in an organization, I was a member of four different teams with little, if any, overlap with the other team members. That is a lot of connections to manage and nurture. In addition, I was a member of different international working groups. So, what were the differences between my roles as a team member and a group member? I found the distinction from Peter Hawkins (2017) particularly helpful in highlighting the differences. In a work group there is strong, clearly focused leadership, with a focus on task and individual accountability. Meetings are efficient, agenda-based, task-focused and issues are discussed, decided, and delegated by the leader. The effectiveness of the work group is measured indirectly by its influence on others, e.g., the financial performance of the business. In a real team, however, there are shared leadership roles with both individual and collective accountability. Meetings involve open discussion, generative dialogue, and active problem-solving with a focus on task, process, and learning. Performance is measured directly by assessing collective work outputs.

You may well be asking why this seemingly pedantic distinction is important. It matters for understanding our roles and responsibilities, how we will do the work, and our level of performance. Will decisions be discussed and the leader decide, or will we have an open discussion, generate ideas, assess risks, and collectively decide and be held accountable for that decision? Will I be expected to bring my best ideas and contribute, or nod and go along with what everyone else says for fear of conflict and disturbing the status quo? And beyond what is expected of me, how safe do I feel to voice what I really think? Do I feel a sense of psychological safety with my colleagues? Are they high-trust relationships? And, at a deeper level, do I feel I belong? Without creating a true team, where everyone feels they belong and are cared for, an individual's and the team's psychological capacity and performance potential will never be realized.

Continuous Improvement and People

CI, at its core, relies on people, and people giving their best to solve problems and come up with new ideas, whether small incremental improvements, or disruptive innovation. Toyota is often quoted as saying, "people are the most important asset of Toyota and the determinant of the rise and fall of Toyota"—a quote ascribed to Eiji Toyoda (Jeffrey Liker and Michael Hoseus 2008). There have been reams of paper devoted to how to recreate the Toyota culture, but what we are proposing here is an inside-out approach, starting with the individual. The inside-out approach involves the individual working in partnership with the organization and, for most of us at work, the organization is our team and our leader. Teams are key enablers for creating a high-trust, psychologically safe environment, with the high-quality relationships needed for resilient, thriving individuals and thriving cultures of CI.

Teams and Well-Being

We all know inherently that the environments we operate in have a profound impact on our emotional well-being. Most of us have worked in, or have seen, environments which are stressful. Often, there is a singular focus on targets and outputs, where people get burned out and are replaced, and are regarded as weak if they can't keep up with the relentless pressure. The strongman trope was a key symbol in the 1980s, with a focus on rugged individualism. Turns out, that was all wrong and we now need to unlearn and relearn. Again, our ancestors had a wisdom that we've lost, as we deified money, technology, consumption, and self-interest. As the ancient proverb says, "If you want to go fast, go alone. If you want to go far, go together."

Team Psychological Health and Safety

Chapter 3 explored how PWB is impacted by personal and workplace factors. As teams are made up of a collection of individuals, team PH&S will need to consider what individuals need from the team to thrive. Team PH&S will also need to take account of how the team can create, or exacerbate, psychosocial hazards and the impact of those on both an individual's and the team's collective psychological capacity. The team's collective psychological capacity, in

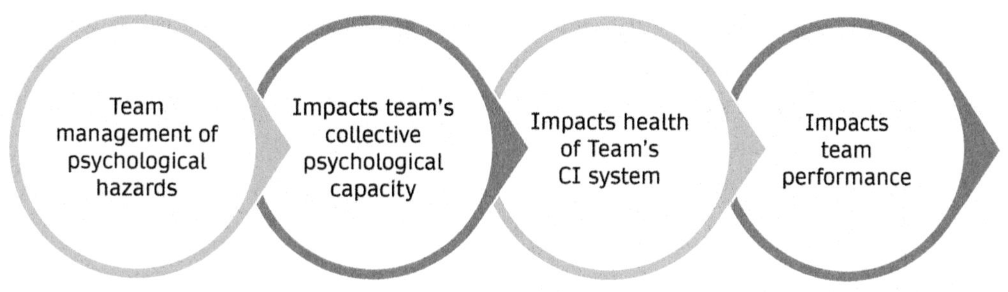

Figure 5.2 Link between team psychological health and safety and performance.

turn, negatively impacts on the team's CI system, with a consequent impact on the team's performance as illustrated in Figure 5.2.

We'll now consider the psychosocial hazards that teams can create or exacerbate; the impact of those on the team's collective psychological capacity; the health of its CI system; and the knock-on impact on performance.

Workplace Hazards

The focus here is on team workplace hazards, which can be divided into two categories:

1. Job design and work environment.
2. Social and behavioral factors at work.

We will now consider how teams create and/or intensify each of these categories and what that means for team performance.

Job Design and Work Environment

How work is organized includes clarity on roles and responsibilities, expectations, job control or autonomy, job demands, organizational change management, remote and isolated work, workload, work pace, working hours, and schedule.

Roles and Responsibilities

In teams with role ambiguity, at best, there is a gap between the performance potential and actual performance of the team. At worst, there is the performance gap coupled with destructive conflict and tension between team members. This involves people pulling in different directions, or people themselves being pulled in different directions with conflicting demands and priorities. Destructive conflict saps an individual's psychological capacity, which could be much better invested in improving work and maturing the team's CI system to help it manage the VUCA external environment.

Communication

In the authors' experience, poor communication is one of the most often cited problems in organizations. Poor top-down communication includes no sharing about changes to work, either in terms of what's expected or how the work is to be completed. Poor bottom-up communication is where people don't have a voice and aren't consulted or listened to regarding decisions which impact the team.

Poor top-down communication leads to confusion and wasted time and energy, which, in turn, leads to frustration and disengagement. Poor top-down communication reduces the team's psychological capacity and wastes valuable resources which could be put to good use to move the team's performance to higher levels. Poor bottom-up communication leads to people feeling that they are not respected, or valued, that their voice and ideas don't matter. This results negatively on the team's psychological safety, with the consequence that valuable improvement ideas are missed, risks are not identified and rectified, or managed.

Once again, the team's collective performance suffers and, in environments where individuals feel that they don't matter, they armor up and play it safe. They don't grow and develop. Relationships become transactional, impacting on the individual's and the team's PWB and resilience.

Workload Planning and Scheduling

As we saw in Chapter 1, patterns of stress activation can build resilience or lead to sensitization and vulnerability. In teams where there is unpredictability about work availability, work hours, or the possibility of redundancy, these high levels of uncertainty prime our fight or flight response, reducing an individual's psychological capacity. This reduced psychological capacity impairs analytic thinking, creative insight, and the ability to problem-solve—all negatively impacting the CI system—and the team's performance declines.

This sensitization, vulnerability, and fight-or-flight response is also evoked when there is a mismatch between the level of challenge and the team's capacity or skill to manage it. That could be when there is work overload; when individuals are asked to complete tasks for which they are not trained; when everything is a priority and should have been done yesterday, causing individuals to work on their own time; or when conflict is created between work life and home life. This prolonged stress has the same impact on the team's collective psychological capacity as a depleted battery trying to still perform at optimum. We know that we can't get the same performance level from a battery at 30 percent as we would from one at 90, yet we unreasonably expect teams to perform when, in reality, we are burning them out.

Under-stress—where there is capacity in the team for people to do more, to be challenged, to be stretched, or to contribute more of their strengths—leads to apathy and boredom. Teams that do not rotate tasks or jobs, particularly sharing out repetitive or boring tasks, prevent individuals from getting into psychological flow. Teams that do not have skills matrices with clear targets stunt growth and development and reduce the collective potential for performance and resilience.

Work Environment

The work environment consists of the physical space, and whether team members are asked to work in environments that are conducive, or detrimental, to PWB in terms of temperature, light, noise, and space. It also consists of whether team members have been given all the equipment, tools, and resources necessary to complete the tasks and whether these are suitable, available, and reliable. Noisy, hot, freezing cold, dark, or cramped environments have obvious impacts on physical well-being and PWB, and deplete team members' psychological capacity. Cognitive and emotional energy is consumed in trying to return to optimum working conditions or is focused on when the work will end.

When team members are distracted and their attention is elsewhere, productivity decreases, quality decreases, and CI is non-existent—the focus is on surviving and not thriving. A lack of suitable equipment, tools, and resources demonstrates a lack of respect, which leads to team members feeling devalued, with the consequent impacts on psychological capacity and team performance.

Stress and Resilience

The continual pressure of being asked to do more, faster, with fewer resources, and with no end in sight causes stress. If the early 2020s have taught us anything, they have taught us the importance of resilience. As we saw in Chapter 4, resilience is not the ability to be armor up when difficult circumstances arise.

> It is the capacity to remain flexible in thoughts, behaviors and emotions when under stress.
>
> **(Carole Pemberton 2015)**

Resilience isn't something which you're either born with, or without, rather it is a combination of genes, early life experience, and learning through adversity.

Pediatric health expert W. Thomas Boyce identifies two personality types: dandelions and orchids. He argues that four-fifths of children appear to be dandelions; those who can thrive in most environments. The remaining fifth are orchids; those who are more exquisite and unusual and have a higher potential than dandelions—but for this to be realized they require a particular environment and careful gardening (*The Guardian* 2019).

You might wonder why we're talking about children, given that this is a book focused on the workplace. But all of us carry with us what happened to us as little people, impacting our personal factors in terms of psychological capacity. In designing workplaces and teams, we need to be aware and mindful of personal factors and that statistically one-fifth of the workforce are orchids who require special care. Individual PWB assessments and thriving plans demonstrate the inside-out approach needed.

Social and Behavioral Factors

Social factors at work center on teams and teamwork, including social and physical isolation, the quality of interpersonal relationships, team culture, and behaviors.

Social and Physical Isolation

In the authors' experience, only now are business and psychology catching up with what our ancestors understood deeply—the need to feel connected and a part of something bigger than ourselves. We've even taken on anthropological terminology—see the ubiquitous use of "work tribes"—to try and buffer against social isolation. But belonging isn't something which can be forced and mandated. It is personal and it is deep and it is related to how you feel.

The ancient tribes gave this connectedness and belonging a name. For the Māori, it is called "whakapapa." "Ubuntu" is a Zulu word meaning "humanity to others." It is often described as reminding us that "I am what I am because of who we all are."

As we saw in Chapter 2, belonging has a huge impact on a team's psychological capacity and performance. There are a lot of teams where people don't feel they belong. The EY Belonging Barometer, a study in belonging of 1,000 employees in the US, suggests that 40% of adults experience feelings of isolation at work. These feelings of isolation lead to serious health problems, affecting both physical and mental health. When we are lonely, our fight-or-flight response is activated, which we've seen negatively impacts on a team's psychological capacity, resilience, and performance.

Interpersonal Relationships

We are each other's environment. How we show up matters as it affects not only our own PWB but the PWB of those around us:

> we are profoundly influenced by micro expressions from others. We are particularly attentive to emotional information. Within milliseconds we interpret signals from others, toggling through facial expressions, tone of voice, body language, confidence levels, energy levels, physical proximity of people to each other, status symbols. We are motivated and incentivized by smiles, attentive eyes and warm words.
>
> **(Owen Eastwood 2022)**

We need to pay constant attention to the quality of relationships. Transactional relationships, where someone will only give if they get something in return, do not build social support in the team. Instead, they erode trust and psychological safety. They also prime our threat response, as we are constantly on the lookout for the real motivation behind someone's actions. A huge amount of psychological capacity is invested in scanning and interpreting what is said, what is not said, and the non-verbal cues. These cues are interpreted based on the context of the conversation/situation, the history of the relationship, the power differential, and the congruence between words, tone, and gestures. When this happens at scale within a team, its collective psychological energy for CI decreases, members become risk averse, and self-protection is primordial, taking precedence over team performance.

This decrease in psychological energy is exacerbated when there is destructive interpersonal conflict between team members. Conflict can be passive-aggressive in style, which involves withholding information. Or the conflict may be overt with arguing, talking rather than listening, where one side wins and the other loses. Conflict consumes a huge amount of psychological energy, and not only impacts those directly concerned but also has a ripple effect on the rest of the team, negatively impacting morale, team performance, and productivity.

As we saw in Chapter 4, quality relationships matter not just for team performance, but also for PWB. Research shows that the pain and feelings of disconnection are often as real as physical pain and the need to belong in the workplace comes second only to the need to belong at home (Jerome Nyameh 2013).

Feeling connected to colleagues is vital in today's knowledge economy—David Epstein (2022) says that what efficiency was to the Industrial Revolution, relationships are to the present era. Gallup has repeatedly shown that having best friends at work is key to employee engagement and is strongly linked to positive business outcomes, including profitability, safety, inventory control, and retention (2022).

In teams, it is critical to build time and space to form, and deepen, relationships during both work activities and social time. As we know from the adage, "families who eat together, stay together," studies show that co-workers who eat together feel more connected (Noreena Hertz 2022). Staff need to feel seen and valued and their efforts appreciated. Contrary to popular practice, this does not need to involve grand gestures from senior leaders with monetary reward. It is about thanking people. As Workhuman research (2022) found, when people were thanked in the last month, they're half as likely to be looking for a new job, more than twice as likely to be highly engaged, and more than twice as likely to feel respected at work. Powerful statistics to rebuff all the naysayers.

Team Culture

Culture in teams is the "way we do things around here," what's acceptable and what's not. Team culture is a microcosm of the organizational culture and may be aligned with the organization's values, norms, and practices, or it may not. In the authors' experience, we have come across high-performing, caring teams in otherwise dysfunctional organizations and dysfunctional teams in high-performing, caring organizations. Team culture centers on space and power: who has a voice, who is listened to in decision-making, who has the power to make decisions, and whether those decisions are fair and consistent, or unfair and inconsistent.

As we saw in Chapter 3, Google's Project Aristotle (2012) found that psychological safety was the number one determinator of high-performing teams. Two behaviors linked to that are conversational turn-taking—equality in distribution of conversational turn-taking, meaning members speak in roughly the same proportion—and a high social sensitivity, i.e., an ability to tap into the non-verbal cues. Stephen Levinson's and Francisco Torreira's (2015) study showed that in conversational turn-taking, each turn lasts for approximately two seconds, with the typical gap between turns at just 200 milliseconds, which is the minimum human response time to anything. That figure is almost universal, existing across cultures, with only slight variations.

So, what does that mean? It means we are planning our responses while our partner is speaking, metaphorically listening with one ear while constructing our hypothetical reply. This means that we are not only reducing the team's psychological safety, but also sending signals to team members that their ideas, suggestions, and feedback don't matter. This behavior displays an inherent lack of respect for the individual, which is the top attribute of a toxic culture, according to research by Donald Sull et al. (2022). When team members feel disrespected, they self-preserve, hide, and turn inward to protect themselves, rather than outward toward their colleagues and the challenges the team faces. This turning inward can lead to rumination, repetitive thinking, or dwelling on negative feelings and distress, which negatively impacts on PWB and further reduces the team's performance and capacity to problem-solve and to deal with the unexpected.

Research shows that teams have their own level of intelligence—dubbed "collective intelligence." It is a measure of the group's ability to perform a wide variety of tasks and this collective intelligence can only fully be harnessed when there are high levels of trust and psychological safety. Without high levels of trust and psychological safety, the team's collective psychological capacity is reduced.

Patrick Lencioni (2008) identified lack of accountability as one of the five dysfunctions of a team. It is where team members are unable to tolerate the discomfort of being candid with a colleague about his or her behavior and where brave, or difficult, conversations are avoided. This breeds resentment among team members, when those who are not respectful of others are not held accountable. In turn good performers then start to think why should they bother, why should they carry others? This further leads to a consequent negative spiral in terms of performance, an increase in antagonism, and the likelihood of destructive interpersonal conflict. The manager becomes the sole arbiter of performance, and the culture is one characterized by discipline and compliance versus problem-solving and innovation.

Behaviors

Which behaviors are tolerated within a team has a huge impact on team members' psychological capacity. Harassment, bullying, victimization, and racism, including microaggressions, prime the body's threat response. If these behaviors are persistent, the associated prolonged and unpredictable stress leads to sensitization and vulnerability, depleting PWB. Even team members who are not the direct targets of harassment, bullying, offensive, and intimidating behaviors are impacted. No-one wants to step out of line, to be different, to challenge the status quo for fear of repercussions, and trust and psychological safety are eroded. This act of fitting in is the opposite of true belonging and, without true belonging, people cannot be their true selves. Precious psychological capacity is depleted just to self-protect and fit in.

Continuous Improvement and Team Well-Being

CI is a team sport. It requires everyone to work together, share information, ideas, and support one another. For CI to thrive, individuals need to have psychological capacity for improvement, and the team needs to have created a psychologically safe work environment. To date, CI has primarily tended to focus on tools, processes, goals, and transactional encounters. Yet, it has an incredible untapped potential as a positive force to create thriving teams with thriving individuals and a thriving culture of CI.

Table 5.1 provides a summary of the team's responsibilities, and desired behaviors, for the 11 social elements of CI and Table 5.2 does so for the technical elements.

Table 5.2 considers the team's responsibilities, and desired behaviors, for the 11 technical elements.

Now, let's explore how some of the CI practices and tools could be reorientated so that they are eliminating the eighth Lean waste of lack of thriving

Table 5.1 Team Responsibilities for CI Social Elements

#	*Social Elements*	*Team Responsibilities*
1	Lead with Purpose	• Co-create the team's purpose aligned to the organizational purpose and their stakeholders' needs.
2	Lead with Humility	• Share leadership roles—distribute power across the team versus power sitting with the leader.
3	Develop Trust	• Choose what is right even when no one is watching and be generous and non-judgmental with others.
4	Show Respect for Every Individual	• Foster a culture of respect within the team by valuing each person for their unique strengths and demonstrating empathy and compassion.
5	Listen to the Voice of the Individual (VOI)	• Actively listen when team members are speaking, seeking first to understand, rather than be understood and stay out of judgment.
6	Cultivate Teamwork	• Dedicate time and space to form and deepen relationships both during work activities and social time. • Ask for and offer help, recognizing that each individual has a different threshold and noticing when colleagues are in struggle.
7	Constantly Challenge the Status Quo	• Help create a safe space for others to have a voice, to bring ideas, and to express dissent. Recognize that to create equal access to psychological safety, we must address different needs for different people so that they feel that what they say matters.
8	Look, Listen, and Learn at the Gemba	• Model curiosity, empathy, and compassion. Recognize the importance of Gemba to build, and enhance, high-quality relationships characterized by high levels of trust and psychological safety.
9	Develop People through Coaching	• Cultivate a relationship of equals and act as thinking partners for one other, providing time and space to explore through open questions and active listening.
10	Lead Effectively through Leaders Standard Work	• Intentionally use elements of LSW for personal growth and competence, recognizing the value of peer-to-peer learning, coaching, and support.
11	Foster Diversity, Equity, Inclusion, and Belonging (DEIB)	• Value difference and create an environment of belonging where it is safe for people to bring their whole self to work. Model that through micro belonging cues—eye contact, body language, tone, and inclusive language.

Table 5.2 Team Responsibilities for CI Technical Elements

#	*Technical Elements*	*Team Responsibilities*
1	Conduct strategy development and deployment	• Help the team to understand how they fit into the bigger picture. • Collectively agree what the vital few Measures of Success and KBIs are for the team to achieve the strategy and ensure everyone is pulling in the same direction. Agree together how these will be tracked.
2	Listen to the Voice of the Customer (VOC)	• Involve a diverse group in listening to the voice of the customer. Ensure the people involved are representative of current, and potential future, customers. Ensure equitable and inclusive practices and language are used.
3	Listen to the Voice of the Process (VOP)	• Collectively analyze if there is an optimum balance between process capability and the expectations of the customer. Ensure all voices are heard and taken into account.
4	Focus on horizontal value streams	• Actively lead from every seat by working with cross-functional peers.
5	Standardize work and ensure quality	• Collectively agree the current best-known standard to ensure quality and productivity. Adhere to that standard when completing tasks.
6	Embed continuous improvement	• Encourage, positively challenge, and support one another to eliminate waste, to innovate, and to make lots of tiny improvements.
7	Develop structured problem solving	• Model a learner mindset—be humble and curious, ask lots of open questions, and listen ostentatiously.
8	Manage visually	• Ensure all Visual Management and measures of success provide a holistic view of team performance, balancing qualitative, as well as quantitative, measures.
9	Develop and use knowledge and skills	• Co-create development plans for each individual with an inside-out approach, linked to their personal "why" and with the "Goldilocks" level of challenge to enable flow.
10	Manage capacity and demand	• Support one another, recognizing that collective team capacity starts with an inside-out focus on each individual's psychological capacity.
11	Create workplace organization (5S)	• When considering the workplace environment, team psychosocial hazards and relevant workplace factors should be included. These will increase collective psychological capacity.

individuals and instead are used to increase individuals' psychological capacity, PWB, and team psychological health and safety.

5S

5S is a methodical process of reducing waste to make your workplace more organized and efficient. When considering the workplace environment, psychosocial hazards should be included, as well as relevant personal and workplace factors, if we are to increase psychological capacity. Measures of success for 5S should be broadened to include increased PWB.

KBIs

The Key Performance Indicators (KPIs), or measures of success, are what the business needs to achieve. Critically, we need to measure the "how" as well as the "what." The how needs to be teachable, observable behaviors which people are held accountable for, and ideally would be at both individual and team levels. As we saw in the Introduction, these are called Key Behavioral Indicators (KBIs).

Chris Butterworth et al. (2021) recommend that the people being measured should be involved in co-creating the KBIs to ensure the measures are meaningful and impactful, and there is a high level of buy in. Using Chris Butterworth et al.'s (2021) framework in Table 5.3 helps to show the linkages between lag KPIs, lead KPIs, and KBIs.

Visual Management Boards and Huddles

Visual Management Boards (VMB) are often introduced in the early stages of CI, as it is believed that sharing the performance metrics of the team and making them visible will induce higher performance. The top-down cascade of KPIs, without input from the team, can feel like something which is being

Table 5.3 Lag KPIs, Lead KPIs, and KBIs

Target Area	Lag KPI	Lead KPI	KBI
What are you trying to achieve?	How might you measure that?	What is the key influence on making this improve?	What behavior is most likely to make this happen?

done to, rather than with, people. The associated huddle tends to be facilitated by the leader, who invests a huge amount of energy trying to engage and interest the team in what is being discussed, and actions are delegated to the team by the leader.

However, there is another way, where the individuals are at the heart of the business and their input is valued, heard, and acted upon. The team in its entirety, including the leader, co-create measures of success. This ensures that everyone's voice is heard, that there is shared decision making, and that there is clarity and transparency about expectations, roles, and responsibilities. When the team can ask for access to the information they need to make informed decisions, it creates transparency and equity—information is not hoarded as a source of power.

This will help eliminate, or mitigate, some of the team's psychosocial hazards. Team psychosocial hazards can be further reduced by balancing the performance measures between those the team needs to excel in to achieve the business strategy, as well as those related to areas of annoyance and frustration for team members. By helping the team resolve the micro annoyances, the team's collective psychological capacity is freed up to allow them to solve bigger problems and continuously improve processes, leading to better business results.

Qualitative Measures of Success

Ensuring that the VMB measures the qualitative, as well as the quantitative, aspects of success provides a holistic view of team performance. This could include measures for team growth and performance, as well as skills matrices, with defined targets to cross-train team members across roles and tasks, and then to rotate around those roles/tasks on an agreed frequency.

VMBs often include a section for recognition. Organizations often have recognition awards for folks who exemplify values and go the extra mile, i.e., linked to performance and achievement. Creating an environment where peers can recognize one another helps strengthen quality relationships within the team. Gratitude—being thankful for what is—focuses one's mind on what is good and also on how connected we all are. Being grateful also helps people to connect with something larger than themselves as individuals.

In positive psychology research, gratitude is strongly and consistently associated with greater happiness. Closing meetings with what we're grateful for today can help build the team's gratitude muscle.

Huddles

In organizations which care about their people, meetings and huddles start with an inside-out focus on the individual. Some ways this can be done is a two-word check-in on how everyone is feeling, e.g., "grateful and focused," or "apprehensive and overwhelmed." Another way is a temperature check. At the beginning of every meeting, ask everyone to state their energy levels on a scale of one (low) to five (high). This simple and fast exercise that will quickly determine whether there is someone who needs attention or is outside their normal range and is suffering from fatigue and frustration.

This is not simply a one-off at the start of the meeting; rather, the attunement to what people are feeling is constant: team members' PWB matters. When it feels like there is an elephant in the room, leaders of high-performing teams create so called "candor breaks" to encourage team members to share their thoughts and feelings. At Ferrazzi Greenlight, they refer to these as "Yoda in the room" moments. Any team member can call one and, if necessary, they break into smaller groups (using breakout rooms if the meeting is virtual) to further encourage frank and honest discussion (HBR 2021).

Huddles are a great opportunity to ensure that there is conversational turn taking; active listening; offering feedback, particularly positive feedback and praise; that decisions and actions are co-created; and that team members are given autonomy where possible.

Some behaviors for huddles to enhance PWB and psychological capacity include:

- No one speaks for a second time until all team members have spoken.
- We listen more than we speak.
- Actions and decisions are co-created and shared among all team members, with the leader owning no more than 30% of actions.
- We hold each other accountable to our commitments.
- We always treat each other with respect.

Team Resilience and Team Learning

Huddles are a fantastic forum to build team resilience and team learning. Research by Lee Hecht Harrison (LHH) and Ferrazzi Greenlight (HBR 2021) identified four characteristics of resilient teams: candor, or psychological safety; resourcefulness; compassion; and humility. At huddles, teams can demonstrate candor through open and honest dialogue with each other. Resourcefulness involves remaining solution-focused, even in the face of challenge, and concentrating on what the team *can* control and influence. Compassion and empathy mean that team members truly care for each other and share both success and failure. There is a "we culture," not a "me culture." Finally, team members are humble enough to ask for, and offer each other, help.

Being prepared to be the learner and not the knower is crucial in today's VUCA environment. The World Economic Forum (2017) identified that the half-life of skills is five years, meaning that every five years a particular skill is about half as valuable as it was before. This means that the learning must be extracted from every opportunity and huddles are a prime opportunity to build this practice. In his best-selling book, *The Fifth Discipline*, Peter Senge (2006) outlines the concept of the "learning organization," where it is important to learn not just in order to survive (adaptive learning), but also to create the conditions to thrive. He calls this "generative learning" and states that teams are at the heart of the learning organization. He defines the three components of core learning capabilities for teams as understanding complexity, aspiration, and reflective conversation.

Understanding Complexity: Systems Thinking

Helping teams to understand how they fit into the bigger picture, and the cause-effect of their actions is crucial for CI. Understanding how teams fit into the wider system helps for problem-solving, for selecting KPIs, and for decision making.

Aspiration: Personal Mastery and Shared Vision

Organizational learning starts with individual learning and how to achieve personal mastery and flow, leading to growth and competence. This echoes the inside-out approach and the importance of starting with individual. Increasing individual PWB builds psychological capacity to enable learning and improvement.

Shared vision is about co-creating a shared picture of the future for the team. The CI system can be used to communicate the vision, delineate it into practical steps, and be clear about the "how"—as well as the "what"—through KBIs. Using tools, such as VMBs and huddles, to set and track goals related to the vision, allows for PDCA, collective accountability, and problem-solving.

Reflective Conversation: Mental Models and Dialogue

> Team learning is vital because teams, not individuals, are the fundamental learning unit in modern organizations. This is where the rubber meets the road; unless teams can learn, the organization cannot learn.
>
> **(Peter Senge 2006)**

Team learning is vital for building organizational learning. Team learning starts with psychological safety, fostering open dialogue to allow the team to discover collective insights not attainable individually.

Workload Leveling

Heijunka, or production leveling, is used to reduce the *Mura* (unevenness) in workload between team members and *Muri* (overburden). We would propose that production leveling focuses on not only ensuring there is no overburden or unevenness in terms of production and tasks, but also in terms of psychological capacity. No team members should have a greater workload than they can individually sustain. Production leveling could also consider PWB and how to share out boring and repetitive tasks to allow everyone the opportunity to get in flow. This, in turn, will reduce the eighth waste of lack of thriving.

Problem-Solving

Problem-solving has tended to focus on technical competence by using myriad problem-solving tools—5-Whys, A3, 8-D, Ishikawa, to name but a few. Generally, little attention is given to setting the stage for the problem-solving group. Problem-solving should start with creating psychological safety and using coaching skills to solicit and ensure that a diversity of viewpoints is listened to and taken into account. When individuals feel heard, respected, and valued, they will offer their ideas and solutions, they will take risks; the team will be more agile, resilient, and innovative. Further, its members will have higher levels of PWB and psychological capacity.

Companies like Atlassian have inverted problem-solving and framed it as an innovative challenge and run Hackathon-style events, such as "Ship It." They set the stage for creativity and allow participants to model the desired behaviors of innovation, collaboration, and problem-solving.

Some behaviors for problem-solving to enhance PWB and psychological capacity include:

- I set the stage and frame the work by talking about the level of uncertainty we face and communicate that you can't get something brand new right first time every time.
- I clearly articulate why our work matters, why it makes a difference and for whom.
- We are all humble and curious—asking lots of open questions and actively listening.
- Solutions and actions are co-created and shared between team members.
- The person doing the job is seen as the expert.

A Thriving Team Plan

In the same way that each individual needs a personalized, tailored plan for how to thrive, so too does the team. This is not simply an amalgamation of all of the team members' individual plans, but rather a plan for the PWB of the team. The Thriving Team Plan takes account of the bigger picture, taking the organizational vision, strategy, and scan of the external environment, and considering what part the team can play in making that happen. So far, so traditional.

The inside-out approach starts with every individual offering their perspective on where the team sits on a scale from surviving, where the team is saturated with psychosocial risks, to thriving, with high levels of collective PWB and psychological capacity, as illustrated in Figure 5.3.

This can be measured by each team member completing the Team Thriving Assessment, which considers psychosocial risks, a measure of the team's level of psychological safety, and level of trust (Brené Brown 2018). Each team member ranks where they believe the team is on the scale. The average of the individual team member's results and the range is displayed for the team to consider as part of the Team Coaching. An extract is shown in Table 5.4 by way of an example. The full Team Thriving Plan Assessment can be found at www.whycarebook.com.

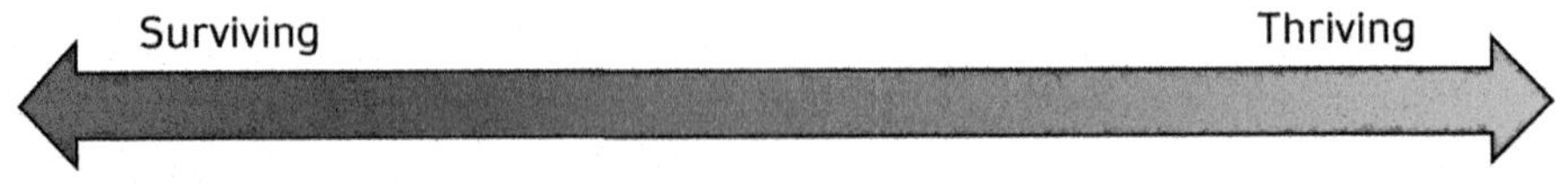

Figure 5.3 Scale of team thriving.

Table 5.4 Team Thriving Plan Assessment Extract

Team Thriving Plan Assessment									
				Rating					
				Not at all	*To little extent*	*Some what*	*To a large extent*	*To a great extent*	
	#	*Factor*	*Please rate each statement (1–5) and add any comments you wish.*	*1*	*2*	*3*	*4*	*5*	*Comments*
Psychosocial Hazards	1	Job Design and Work Environment	Everyone has clarity regarding roles and responsibilities and performance expectations on the team.						
	2		Workload planning and scheduling means that tasks are shared equally between team members.						
	3	Social and behavioral factors at work	I feel connected to my colleagues.						
Psychological Safety	4	Mattering	Working with members of this team, my unique skills and talents are valued and utilized.						
	5	Challenge	I feel safe to challenge the status quo.						
Trust	6	Reliability	Colleagues on this team do what they say they'll do. They don't over promise and they balance competing priorities.						

These results should then be analyzed and used as inputs into a team coaching session. This would ideally be facilitated by someone outside of the team, so that all team members—including the leader—can take part. Some questions for teams to consider as part of the team coaching are:

- If you were to describe this team as an animal, how would you describe it?
- When do you do your best work (i.e., in which circumstances)?
- What do you really value from each of the team members? (Take each person in turn.)
- Considering the results of Team Thriving Assessment, as well as any other contextual issues, the team coach could help the team walk through the following questions:
- What is already working well in this team and we should **CONTINUE**?
  - What in the CI system, practices, and tools would help to lock in these habits/behaviors?
- What are we not doing and it would be really helpful to **START**?
  - What in the CI system, practices, and tools would help to build these habits/behaviors?
- What is no longer serving us and we should **STOP**?
  - What in the CI system, practices, and tools needs updated/altered to reflect this change?

The team would then use the output from the team coaching session to create a thriving team action plan. This needs to be aligned with available resources (who will do what, why, by when, and with what expected result) and should consider how the CI system and practices can be leveraged for optimum effect. To help increase transparency and accountability, the thriving team action plan is displayed on the team's VMB and discussed in monthly team meetings. This helps to ensure that the DCA steps of the PDCA cycle are completed, and any learning is taken on board to enrich the next version of the plan.

Sample Coaching questions framework for the Planning phase to agree on what needs to happen:

- What's most important?
- What would you (collectively) like to do?
- What might the first step be?
- What might stop you (collectively) from making progress?
  - What can you do to get past that?

Sample Coaching questions framework for the DCA phase to ensure that actions have been completed, and that there is time and space for reflection and learning:

- Where have you made most progress?
  - Why is that?
- Where have you made least progress?
  - What is stopping you from progressing?
  - What might you do differently?
  - What would make a difference?
- What have you learned?
  - What would you do the same next time?
  - What would you do differently?

Conclusion

Teamwork is crucial for creating PWB, and teams can both create and mitigate psychosocial hazards. Mitigating, or eliminating psychosocial hazards, impacts on an individual's and the team's collective psychological capacity. The increase in the team's collective psychological capacity can be utilized to create thriving cultures of CI, which creates an organizational buffer to the VUCA external environment. CI philosophies, practices, and tools can be a huge lever for creating collective PWB and contributing to psychological flow if they are reimagined and reorientated with PWB, psychological safety, and psychological capacity in mind.

A Personal Story

When he heard about this book, a personal friend of one of the authors kindly offered to share their own story. It is very moving and is an illustration of the kind of things many people face every day. We would like to thank Indi Ray for sharing this and reprint his story unedited, as he wrote it, below.

One of my closest friends recently commented to my wife: "Your husband will take on three things at the same time and do two of them badly." As I reflected on how true his comment was, I was reminded of my personal journey through distraction, procrastination, and overthinking. I've recently read about ADHD and how individuals on the spectrum have trouble prioritising, are often poorly organized and frequently miss deadlines—indeed I'm writing the final version of my contribution to this book a week before the draft needs to go to the editors.

I've not been clinically diagnosed yet, but I'm convinced I'm on the spectrum. I understand that ADHD tends to run in families; my father always struck me as an incredibly determined individual who suffered from mental restlessness.

My research into ADHD was prompted by recognising my daughter's physical and mental restlessness. Although she is still too young for a clinical diagnosis, I'm preparing myself should that eventuality come to pass. She needs to read whilst having breakfast, she pirouettes whilst attempting maths homework, she provides a verbal narrative whilst playing with LEGO. My mother reminded me that I was the same in my early childhood.

Over the years, I've developed coping mechanisms that have helped me overcome my restlessness. Some have been healthier than others—exercise and mindfulness have certainly helped. Although binge watching TV shows, comfort eating, and one too many beers have provided temporary relief and distraction—especially through COVID lockdowns—I now realize that I needed a set of daily behaviors to keep me on the level and on track with my life.

A few years ago, my coping mechanisms failed, and I struggled with my mental health. My wife had been in hospital for about 4 months with a difficult pregnancy. Our daughter was at risk of being born prematurely and we'd just moved into a new house. I was worried about paying the mortgage and I was struggling to sleep due to anxiety. My parents had come over from India to help me look after our 4-year-old son whilst I was trying to hold down a job.

A large departmental transformation project had kicked off, implementing a new IT system. I was leading the process management workstream, workshopping the change impact on different roles and designing new workflows and future state processes with the IT Vendor.

On Monday mornings, the team reviewed the workstream plan with our new manager. This started out OK, but questions around milestones, dependencies and risks became more and more pointed. After a few weeks, the Monday reviews became like interrogations to ensure we were all sufficiently "across" our tasks. Our explanations were not sufficient and soon we were chastised and ridiculed in front of each other at the meeting with comments like, "I've had new analysts, fresh out of university, better than you."

We struggled as a team, and we struggled as individuals. I became anxious, especially around planning sessions. I've never been an effective planner and now I was being shown up on a weekly basis. After a particularly bad session, I found my head spinning from disappointment and the savagery of the verbal attacks. I locked myself in a toilet cubicle on different floor, held my head in my hands, and cried. A week later, Phil Hughes tragically passed away from being hit by a cricket ball in a Sheffield Shield match. I was in tears again, this time at my desk.

At home, I found I couldn't switch off from work and couldn't fall asleep. I became so tired, I struggled to get to work on time and started to experience episodes of microsleep. I was parking the car at the station on the way to work and nodded off just before the car stopped and ran into a pillar. The damage was bad enough to write-off my aging Subaru Forrester but thankfully I was physically OK, if a bit shaken. In the end, I called the Employee Assistance Program (EAP) line at work to receive counselling on sleep and relaxation techniques.

Members from other teams started to notice I was struggling and asked me if we were OK. They asked how they could help—and then crucially found ways in which to support:

- Reduce work overload—by suggesting that each change champion could map their own processes in VISIO and review their workflows with myself. This freed me up to focus on process structure, rather than content.
- Promote teamwork and collaboration—by suggesting that I work ideas through on a whiteboard and review/adjust these ideas with teams, before committing content to PowerPoint etc. This helped me iterate quickly and filter out ideas that wouldn't work.
- Encourage CI—by suggesting that I sometimes share unfinished work so it could be tested early. This helped me learn quickly from end-user feedback.
- Provide opportunities for autonomy and decision-making—by suggesting that Process Owners should be introduced to own new processes as they were being implemented. This helped me promote empowerment and decision-making, which in turn, gave end-users the support they needed before the system went live.

- Foster a culture of openness and transparency—by suggesting that the artefacts from my workstream be shared by other transformation workstreams, such as scenario testing, training, change management, reporting etc. This helped me "join the dots" in the transformation program.

Fast-forward 8 years—I now recognize that my ex-colleagues helped me through my struggle, by suggesting and engaging in lean behaviors. Learning from this experience (and others since), I've now implemented my personal daily lean management system—where I've tried to codify some of these behaviors into anchor habits. As an aside, I highly recommend James Clear's book, *Atomic Habits*—this has formed the basis of my new strategy to cope with my latent ADHD, even through crisis periods:

- Start my day before anyone is up by going for a morning walk, often listening to an audiobook.
- Make coffee for my wife and myself and plan the day for 5 mins together, whilst the children think about getting out of bed.
- Make breakfast and pack lunches, reminding myself how grateful I am that I can provide for my family.
- Review my virtual MIRO kanban board to prioritize my daily work activities and reflect on yesterday's achievements and missed opportunities.
- Try and take all my notes with my tablet and electronic pen, rather than create a mess of post-its, multiple pieces of paper and various notebooks.
- Keep a physical whiteboard in my home office where I can work through ideas, often talking to myself; I sometimes take photos and send them to collaborators.
- Keep a full water bottle next to my standing desk—it really helps to keep hydrated!
- Follow an evening meal ritual, encouraging everyone to share how their day has gone and if anything is bothering them.
- Play table tennis with my son before bed, so we can both unwind without speaking (especially useful if he's annoyed with me).
- Listen to classical music with my daughter, whilst tucking her into bed—helping to calm us both before sleep.

I often fail at one or many of the above, every day—but at least now I have something to anchor back to, something to remind me of my purpose, if/when things go to **** (insert appropriate expletive).

I'm frequently reminded of the power of connection. I have regular check-ins with mentors, at least monthly, who help me think through my challenges and uplift my thinking so that I continue to grow personally, as well as professionally. I try to distract myself from my distractions, calling friends in different time zones instead of succumbing to Netflix. I catch up with other Dads from my son's cricket team, although I have to endure frequent ribbing when England underperforms in the Ashes.

It helps to have other people hold me accountable; sometimes I lack the discipline to hold myself accountable—whether that be (ex-) work colleagues, family, or friends. Technology can help too—apps on my phone hold me accountable to following weekly Tabata exercise routines and intermittent fasting goals.

I'll leave you with two quotes. They've resonated with me over the years and have helped me get past my mental setbacks.

Oscar Wilde remarked, "Life is too important to be taken seriously." My daily routine helps me have fun along the way—to get over myself when I become anxious and put too much pressure on myself to succeed.

John Lennon apparently said, "Everything will be okay in the end. If it is not okay, it is not the end." Regardless of how messed up things are, today—I'll always have tomorrow to ask for help and make things better.

Key Points from Chapter 5

- Teamwork is crucial for PWB, as teams can mitigate psychosocial hazards and it starts with an inside-out approach focused on the individual.
- Teams with high levels of trust, psychological safety, and high-quality relationships have thriving individuals with high levels of PWB, and high levels of psychological capacity. This psychological capacity can be dedicated to creating thriving cultures of CI, which positively impacts team performance.
- Reorientating CI philosophies, practices, and tools can create, and enhance, collective PWB and contribute to psychological flow, creating thriving cultures of CI and high levels of performance.

Chapter 6

Why Care about Thriving Leaders?

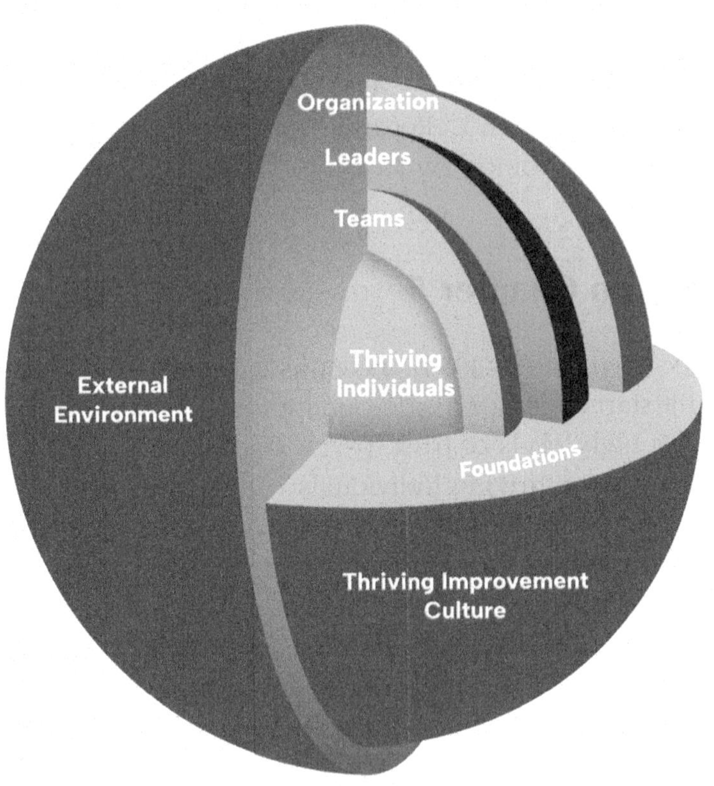

Figure 6.0 **The Why Care Model—Leaders.**

DOI: 10.4324/9781003413479-7

Introduction

This chapter will focus on the role of leaders in supporting the development of a culture of care where people thrive through a focus both on psychological well-being (PWB) and the ongoing nurturing of a culture of continuous improvement (CI).

Leaders are accountable for embedding systems of work and improvement that ensure the conditions are in place to support both PWB and CI.

Risks and opportunities to either of these things are openly discussed with proactive correction action visibly managed. This requires a very different approach and different set of skills and competencies to those traditionally associated with leadership.

As we discussed in the Introduction, the world of work is changing. This increasingly means that traditional perspectives of leadership and how to lead organizations' need to change.

In a recent global survey "It Starts with the CEO 2021" of almost 1,000 CEOs, Egon Zehnder found that "83% of leaders find it essential to reflect on their own leadership style" and that:

> CEOs recognize that today's unprecedented business complexities require a significant shift in leadership—and that change must begin by looking inward with new levels of self-reflection and personal development. This isn't self-indulgent naval gazing; it is what our teams, organizations and stakeholders expect of our CEOs. Now, more than ever, traditional business acumen must be equally balanced with empathy and compassion in order to gain their teams' and organizations' emotional commitment, navigate business complexities and build productive, inspiring workplaces.
>
> **(Jill Ader, Global Chairwoman of Egon Zehnder)**

Co-authors of the Egon Zehnder "It Starts with the CEO 2021" survey Kati Najipoor-Schuette and Dick Patton noted that

> Navigating through these complex environments demands CEOs increase their personal capacity to be adaptive, relational, and self-aware. Especially today, these capacities need to be increasingly balanced with traditional leadership strengths, strategic planning, and a relentless performance orientation. Mastering these

> skills requires leaders to increase their capacity to listen, trust in a broader network of stakeholders, and communicate more authentically than ever before.
>
> As a result of honing these skills and taking a more human-centric approach to leadership, CEOs will evolve the resiliency, leadership, and adaptability of themselves—and their organizations.

Unfortunately, there is often a gap between leaders' perceptions and employees' felt experience. In a recent global survey covering 3,400 people in ten countries, The Workforce Institute UKG (2023) found that:

> Leaders see things one way, employees see things another. While 9 in 10 HR and C-suite leaders believe that working for their company has a positive impact on employees' mental health, only half of employees would agree.

The survey also identified many ways in which work is impacting mental health on a global scale:

- 60% of employees worldwide say their job is the biggest factor influencing their mental health.
- Managers have just as much of an impact on people's mental health as their spouse (both 69%)—and even more of an impact than their doctor (51%) or therapist (41%).
- 81% of employees worldwide would prioritize good mental health over a high-paying job, and 64% admit they would take a pay cut for a job that better supports their mental wellness.
- 38% of employees would not wish their job on their worst enemy.

These shocking findings demonstrate that the focus of leaders in many organizations needs to change. The authors' view is that a key accountability for leaders is to create and nurture the environment where people are thriving, realizing their full potential. Not only is this good for the leader and good for their people, but it is also good for the organization, shareholders, and wider stakeholders.

There is a plethora of literature covering the critical importance of leaders in driving cultural change. It is widely recognized that how leaders behave will have a direct impact on the organization's culture. As Rensis

Likert pointed out over 60 years ago: "Nothing changes until leader behavior changes."

To put it simply, for many people, what is important to their boss is important to them.

It would be impossible to cover all the very extensive literature related to leadership, so instead we have attempted to focus on the elements that have the most impact on creating a culture of PWB and CI where people are able to thrive.

Stages of Maturity

Hines et al. (2022) identified three stages of maturity in organizations in relation to CI culture. These stages are discussed in more detail in Chapter 8 about the organization, but it is worth summarizing how the leadership styles change through these stages.

Stage 1: Traditional Approach

In Stage 1, the Leadership approach can be summarized as "Command and Control." Empowerment and autonomy sit with senior leaders and subject-matter experts (SMEs). In a militaristic fashion, they impose deadlines, determine strategy, and are target-driven and focused on output and productivity.

This "natural order of things," where managers tell and direct, emerged during the Industrial Revolution, when most workers were illiterate, and aligns with McGregor's (1960) Theory X's assumptions that the average person has an inherent dislike of work and will avoid it if (s)he can, thus requiring a hierarchy of managers to control, plan, organize, and lead.

Employees are regarded as "resources," and the legacy of Taylorism persists, despite the nature of much work having shifted to a knowledge economy. There is, typically, little involvement of local individuals, with activities being "pushed" onto them. This approach "relies upon fear and intimidation to help ensure compliance" (Hafey 2015).

> These Companies spend their time telling workers how to do their jobs. This has two consequences. The first is that you end up judging employees by everything except what counts, which is whether the job gets done and the customer is happy. The second is that it becomes difficult, if not impossible, to change any of the myriad

> rules about how to get things done. The result is that it becomes impossible to get the work done without disobeying somebody in the chain of command.
>
> **(Carney et al. 2009)**

In these organizations, development and personal growth is restricted to senior leaders and subject matter experts with a task focus for the wider workforce. Their CI is focused on checking compliance to standards, with a dominance of certain voices—position and rank carry more authority than knowledge. According to Carney et al. (2009),

> Good ideas die every day in command-and-control companies. Asked whether their current job brings out their most creative ideas only 17% of those not engaged and 3% of actively disengaged employees answered affirmatively… these two groups of employees make up 73% of the American workforce.

Stage 2: Classic Lean Organizations

In Stage 2, the leadership approach can be summarized as delegation, with "carrot and stick" rewards and sanctions.

Leaders recognize there are benefits to soliciting input from the wider workforce and this is management led, using "Kata style" coaching. This coaching focuses on organizational targets and using formulaic style questions, with input sought only on very specific areas (Rother 2010).

There is typically a focus on safety, based on lead measures such as the number of near misses, the number of safety walks undertaken, or the percentage of physical (and sometimes mental) health first aiders.

Employees are invited to participate in problem-solving activities, but their voice often does not carry as much weight as a leader/expert: "many traditional bureaucracies must rely on innovation 'heroes' or on special 'creativity' programs and platforms to ensure that ideas are heard" (Carney et al. 2009). As a result, there may be low stress among some team members who are not being challenged to grow and develop, leading to apathy, boredom, and disengagement. In others, there may be higher stress to do things better or come up with ideas. As we discussed in the brain and psychological safety chapters, any form of stress needs to be carefully managed.

This may also be accompanied by negative physical issues, as work pace is increased as "waste" (or in-cycle rest periods) is reduced. This contrasts with the high levels of burnout in front-line leaders, who often feel CI is an addition to their job, rather than a system and philosophy to achieve their targets and engage all team members.

Personal development is event-based and does not always translate into on-the-job performance, as it would using a model such as 70/20/10 (Lombardo et al. 1996). Employee development is typically focused on organizational needs linked to the strategy and vision, rather than individual preferences.

Leaders recognize that bringing together the collective intelligence of the whole workforce is vital, but they benchmark systems and processes with best performing organizations focused on the comparison of results, missing the vital culture piece which means that their own results are often below potential and suffer from sustainability issues (Lucey 2006).

Stage 3: "People Value Stream" Organizations

Leaders in Stage 3 organizations (described by Hines et al. as "People Value Stream Organizations") exhibit high levels of emotional intelligence and there are high levels of psychological safety across the organization (Edmondson 2019), which is consciously built into all systems and practices.

As a result of this, and the coaching style of leaders, there are high levels of employee engagement and autonomy.

> As far back as 1924, William L. McKnight, the legendary CEO of 3M, put the matter succinctly: "If you put fences around people, you get sheep. Give people the room they need."
>
> **(Carney et al. 2009)**

Authority and responsibility are devolved to the most appropriate level and leaders create an environment of co-creation of goals, targets, and how they will be achieved. There is, therefore, a congruence between the individual and the organization (Brown and Trevino 2009).

Meetings are co-facilitated by the leader and the team and Gemba walks are an opportunity to Look, Listen, and Learn using Appreciative Inquiry (Cooperrider et al. 2008) and a coaching approach based on the needs of the individual, thereby helping team members to develop and grow.

Southwest Airlines, for example, regard their frontline supervisors as the most influential leaders in the company, and having the "highest supervisor-to-employee ratio in the industry enables supervisors to… take on a 'player-coach' role" (Gittell 2003).

At firms like FAVI, teams approve candidates for the leader's role (Zobrist 2020). Employees feel a sense of belonging to the organization and sense that it is safe, permitted, and desired for them to bring their "whole selves" to work, and the leaders work to create an environment where people can belong and flourish. Leaders stop trying to motivate people and "instead, build an environment that allows people to grow and self-direct—and let them motivate themselves. If they understand the vision… they'll take care of the rest if you let them" (Carney and Getz 2009).

Key Features of Leaders in Stage 3

Leaders in Stage 3 organizations lead with humility and demonstrate respect for every individual. This approach to leadership is often described as "servant leadership" and was first advocated by Robert K. Greenleaf in his book published in 1973. Greenleaf talks about servant leadership, resulting in employees becoming healthier, wiser, freer, more autonomous, and more likely themselves to become servants.

His first premise signifies the act of altruism. Altruism is defined as the belief in or practice of disinterested and selfless concern for the well-being of others. The second premise of servant leadership is "I am the leader because I serve."

This concept is often misunderstood, and many leaders find themselves stuck in a cycle of overburden trying to solve everyone else's problems. They initially feel good because they have helped someone by solving the problem for them but unintentionally build dependency, reducing the ability of people to learn and think for themselves. This vicious cycle eats into leaders' time and they become "rescuers," forever firefighting.

Servant leadership does not mean solving people's problems for them. Leaders best serve their people by ensuring they have good processes/systems to work with, the tools needed to do their job, and the skills and time to make improvements and solve problems for themselves. Rather than focus on the specifics of a problem, leaders need to focus on what improvement/problem-solving approaches have been applied and coach people on these to build competency, confidence, and self-reliance.

One of Steven Covey's quotes on leadership is also very relevant to this approach:

> Leadership is communicating people's worth and potential so clearly that they are inspired to see it in themselves.
>
> **(2004)**

At a high level, the key activities of the leader within the context of a Stage 3 organization are to:

- Demonstrate a passion for people and champion employee needs.
- Focus the organization on excellence, not just on the delivery of the product or service provided but also on PWB and CI.
- Lead by example, coach, and support completion of Thriving Plans for Every Individual.
- Ensure there is a clear expectation and systems in place to support leaders focusing a significant proportion of their time on the development of people and nurturing the desired culture.

Skills and Competencies of Leaders for Stage 3 Organizations

There are a range of skills and competencies that leaders need in Stage 3 organizations. The list below is not intended to be the complete list, as each organization is likely to have some specific requirements (for example, technical knowledge), but is useful input regarding considering the implications for leadership expectations and future development.

Building Trust

The importance of building trust cannot be overemphasized. It can take years to build trust and seconds to destroy it. All leaders need to proactively build trust within the whole organization, as trust is not something limited to hierarchical relationships but rather needs to be built at all levels and across all teams and peers. We explore the role of leaders in building trust for PWB in Chapter 3 and in the CI system in Chapter 7.

Listening

Listening skills were identified by van Dun (2017) as the most important area for middle managers when applying Lean. However, listening does not always come easily to many people, especially as they progress in their careers, and it requires skills in listening empathically (Tietsort et al. 2020). It is only when we listen that we support others and help them solve problems and develop themselves.

Hence, it is important that listening skills increase as people flow through their careers. In a survey of employees' views, Qualtrics (2020) found that 63% of employees believe that it is very important that their employers listen to their feedback. This is particularly important in times of change.

There are several opportunities for leaders to practice listening skills, such as in general discussions, coaching conversations, and in the application of "Gemba" walks, which are discussed in more detail below. Another opportunity to apply listening skills is in one on ones. Recent research by Castro et al. (2022) found that "one on ones increase psychological safety and even more so if focused on the needs of the individual rather than task support focus."

Look, Listen, and Learn (Gemba) Walks

Gemba walks are an inquiry process that leads to greater understanding and are, therefore, the foundation for further learning, development, and improvement, not just of the people met on the walk but also of the walker themselves. They help distinguish between "the process" and "the people."

However, they are not about checking on the people. A better way to think about the activity is a "Look, Listen, and Learn" walk. To do them correctly, they require humility—for example, a leader checking if people understand the company goals should be checking the effectiveness of the deployment system, not the person they are talking to. They are learning about the effectiveness of a particular system from the person who is a participant in it.

An effective Look, Listen, and Learn walk provides a way to help understand why the existing process may not be capable enough and help people understand that they are not to blame. For leaders, it is about asking the five whys, not the five whos. What Look, Listen, and Learn walks provide is the opportunity to learn first-hand what is really happening in the workplace. Ideally, they are not random wanders through the workplace but are scheduled at a regular frequency and with a clear purpose every time they are undertaken.

They are not so much about ensuring that targets are being met but what support people need to help achieve the targets. We need to look at what is happening and listen to what people are saying, both to us and to each other.

Typical things leaders could learn are listed in the below examples. These are not the questions to ask but are intended to illustrate the understanding the leader needs to seek.

- How well do people understand the business purpose and connect to it?
- Do people feel they get the support they need to achieve their targets?
- Are people skilled in how to solve problems in a structured way that addresses the root cause?
- Do people feel psychologically safe?
- Are people living and breathing the organization's ideal behaviors?
- Are our systems making it easy to do the job in the right way or not?

Some example questions to help this understanding are listed below and many more are given in Chapter 3:

- What does the organization's purpose mean to you?
- Is there anything that frustrates you in getting the job done?
- How are problems solved in your team?

Understanding will also come from observation of team meetings/huddles. Again, these are not questions to ask but things to look for and learn from. For example:

- Is everyone actively engaged and contributing?
- Are suggestions welcomed and positively encouraged by peers?
- Are there open discussions about behaviors?

When these questions are asked, it is important that leaders take the approach that they are not testing the person they are talking to. If the desired answers are not forthcoming, then this highlights potential issues with one or more of the organization's systems which leaders are accountable for. In other words, what is being tested is the effectiveness of the systems the leaders own to help people to effectively and efficiently serve the customer. The leader is accountable for ensuring the systems are supporting the ideal behaviors that deliver outcomes valued by the customer. Look, Listen, and Learn walks provide a very effective Plan, Do, Check, Act cycle to help leaders understand the effectiveness of the systems in supporting ideal behaviors and what improvements might be needed.

If this approach is taken, then the "walker" will understand the current target and current state of the topic under review. They then discuss the desired improvement, any specific obstacles, what has been learned, and what the next steps are. This then allows for appropriate coaching conversations about how to reach the target state and whether this target should be extended. Also, it should be followed by personal reflection time on what changes the "walker" might need to make personally to the ways of working, leadership style, and preconceptions.

In Stage 3 organizations, Look, Listen, and Learn walks are regularly reviewed for effectiveness, with leaders honing their skills in shared lessons learned reviews. They are part of all leader's standard work and are valued by both leaders and employees across the organization. Key Behavior Indicators are well established and in place to measure and track effectiveness.

Effective Look, Listen, and Learn walks are an essential element to sustaining a culture of CI and supporting PWB. Undertaken correctly, they will support the development of leaders, managers, and colleagues at all levels. These aspects of Gemba activity are discussed in more detail throughout the book.

They should be undertaken with humility and viewed as a process of discovery. It is important that people have an open mind and maintain curiosity—it should never be about validating preconceptions, but rather discovering what is going on.

Anyone undertaking a walk must maintain respect for those working on the process and engage people by directly listening and learning.

Planning is essential for an effective walk. They need preparation so that the purpose of the activity is clear, and they need reflection time on what has been learned about the topic or system studied and what the leader has learned about themselves.

As we discussed in Chapter 3, leaders should use their observations during Gemba walks to help identify hazards and wastes individuals are dealing with. To do this we need to think about Gemba conversations in a different way and shift the focus from a very structured technical approach to more of a people-orientated approach.

A typical approach to "Gemba" assumes a deficit in something and uses a Kata coaching approach with five questions:

- What is the target condition?
- What is the actual condition now?

- What obstacles do you think are preventing you from reaching the target condition? Which one are you addressing now?
- What is your next step? What do you expect?
- When can we go and see what we have learned from taking that step?

Whilst this can be useful for technical issues, there is an opportunity to move Gemba to a relational basis one where its purpose is two-fold:

1. To build, and enhance, high-quality relationships characterized by high levels of trust and psychological safety, which will increase team members' PWB and psychological capacity.
2. To Look, Listen, and Learn if the system is working as intended, and if it is producing the required outcomes. If not, to co-create ideas and actions to improve the system.

Gemba need not always be leader-led but could be an opportunity to develop skills and connections across the team. A relational Gemba walk model is illustrated in Figure 6.1.

Leaders, or peers, coming every day with a mindset of curiosity, humility, and respect, with the intention of enhancing high-quality relationships and

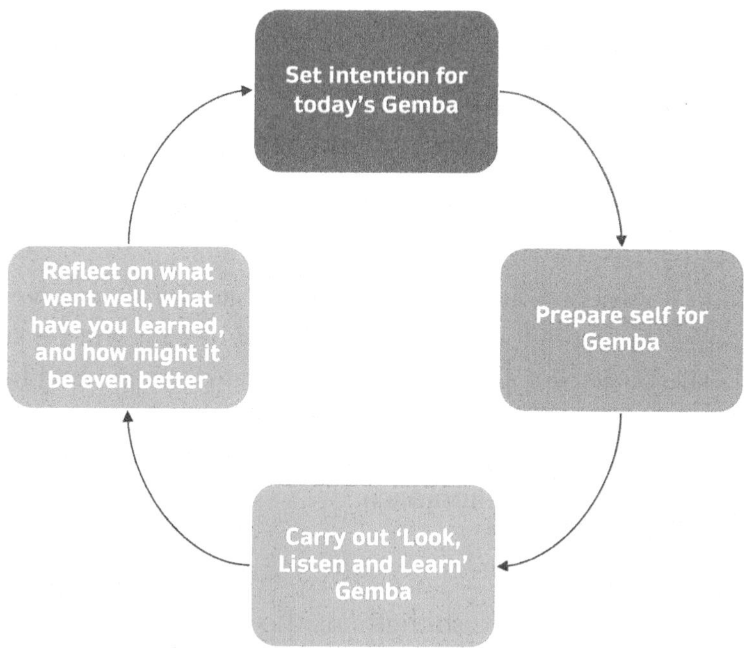

Figure 6.1 Relationship Gemba walk model.

balancing a focus on the system and the individual's PWB, could create a seismic shift in team members' psychological capacity and team performance—a continuous well-being pulse check, if you will. Carrying out "Look, Listen, and Learn" puts the focus not on the deficit and the gap, but rather on how to amplify what's already working well—not to ignore the potential for improvement, but to accentuate and reinforce the positive and where both parties learn from each other. This draws on the work of positive psychology and Appreciative Inquiry (Cooperrider) where teams and organizations are viewed as the solutions, rather than the problems. Some potential questions could be:

- How are you feeling today?
- What's your news?
- What went well in the last 24 hours?
- What opportunities can you see?
- What do we still need to learn about your situation?
- What needs our immediate attention moving forward?
- What assumptions do we need to test, or challenge, about ...?
- What's possible here, and who cares?
- What challenges might come our way, and how can we meet them?
- What seed might we plant together today that could make the most difference to the future of your situation?
- If our success was completely guaranteed, what bold steps might we take?

The person carrying out the Gemba would be acting as a coach, with the focus on the other person and their learning and progress. A coaching relationship is one of equals, and coaches

> place value on people's ability to think and act for themselves, or on creating the conditions in which their own team will be successful. The basic start point might be "What do they need to succeed?" rather than "How do I make sure everyone's doing the right thing?" It may not appear to be a huge difference, but over time it shapes both attitude and approach.
>
> **(Starr 2017)**

Building the reflection practice strengthens the Gemba walker's self-awareness, and continuously improves the Gemba itself. This could be done with a peer or mentor/coach to offer a different perspective and provide the Gemba walker with a thinking partner. Coaching builds on the inside-out approach of focusing on the individual and what they need to increase their PWB, and their psychological capacity, and unleash their potential for improvement.

Some example behaviors for Gemba walks to enhance PWB and psychological capacity:

- I use a coaching approach, actively listening, asking open questions, and seeking first to understand.
- I look for what is working well and offer praise and encouragement for effort as well as outcomes.
- I pay attention to how people are feeling and consider this as important as tasks and results.

Recognition

Recognition is one of the key aspects of respecting people (Miller 2018; Edgeman 2019). "The greatest specific benefit of recognition is its ability to replicate behavior; that is, make it more likely to occur again… unprompted" (Marciano 2010). We explored why this is in Chapter 1.

Ogden Lindsley's (1990) research in behavioral psychology showed that, in order to achieve the highest rate of learning, the optimum ratio of praise to criticism of children in a classroom was 3.57:1. More recent research by the O.C. Tanner Institute (2015, 2017) found that the greatest enabler of great work was recognition and that it increased engagement and encouraged innovation and productivity, with 41% of the people surveyed citing recognition for going "above and beyond" as their first choice. They also showed that 50% of employees said that recognition for ongoing work effort would be the most important thing in improving the relationship with their manager. Perhaps their most interesting finding was that recognition had a major impact on attracting and retaining employees, with people staying 6.7 years in organizations with service awards and only 4.7 in those that do not.

Many leaders struggle with recognition. A common attitude in many organizations can be summarized as "why do we need to recognize people for doing their job?" with the implication being that recognition is reserved for when people go above and beyond what's expected. Why not recognize that people are doing the right thing in the job we have asked them to do?

This is not about formal recognition programs linked to high value monetary reward—indeed, as highlighted by Marciano in his book *Why*

Carrots and Sticks Don't Work (2010), these programs often drive the wrong behavior.

We should never underestimate the power of a simple "thank you" or "well done." By leading by example in giving recognition, leaders set the tone for culture and support a positive environment where everyone feels more able to recognize each other.

Hines and Butterworth (*The Essence of Excellence*, 2019) recommend that recognition should be considered one of the key elements of Leaders Standard Work.

The Value of Kindness

In some ways linked to recognition, the importance of kindness in the workplace is being increasingly understood. O.C. Tanner promotes "20 acts of random kindness," ranging from "Give a shout-out to an employee during a meeting" to "starting a kindness wall." Several organizations have introduced "kindness trees," where employees call out colleagues for recognition for acts of kindness. This in itself is seen as a further act of kindness.

In-depth research summarized in an article by Dr Pragya Agarwal (2019) in Forbes showed that:

> acts of kindness don't go unnoticed, and it had a huge impact on the overall positivity in the workplace, and on the employees' sense of well-being… In addition, the receivers felt in control at work and reported significantly higher levels of happiness. The acts of kindness, however small and insignificant they might have seemed acted as a buffer even during a period of stress, and difficult work conditions.

Genuine kindness makes both the giver and receiver feel good and reinforces self-esteem. We discussed why this is in Chapter 1, when we looked at the way our brains work.

The *Harvard Business Review* (May 7, 2021) published an article "Don't Underestimate the Power of Kindness at Work," which expands on this:

> A commitment to be kind can bring many important benefits. First, and perhaps most obviously, practicing kindness will be immensely helpful to our colleagues. Being recognized at work helps reduce employee burnout and absenteeism, and improves employee

> well-being, Gallup finds year after year in its surveys of U.S. workers. Receiving a compliment, words of recognition, and praise can help individuals feel more fulfilled, boost their self-esteem, improve their self-evaluations, and trigger positive emotions, decades of research have shown. These positive downstream consequences of compliments make intuitive sense: Praise aligns with our naturally positive view of ourselves, confirming our self-worth.

We explored burnout and its causes and implications in more detail in Chapters 1 and 3.

Coaching

Since 2010, there has been a growing realization of the importance of coaching within Lean literature (Rother 2010). Particularly important has been the application of Kata coaching (Rother and Aulinger 2017), Gemba walk conversations (Bremer 2014), and the GROW approach (Landsberg 2015). However, what is important here is that coaching is not an episodic event but is instead related to the learning and developmental needs of the individual in order to meet their own, the team's, and the wider organization's needs.

Whilst some leaders may be natural coaches, most need to train and continuously practice honing their skills. Coaching and mentoring are often confused, and indeed are used interchangeably, yet they are very different. Coaching could be regarded as "hands-off" and mentoring as "hands-on." A coach is a thinking partner offering space to think, reflect, and challenge underlying assumptions. Mentoring, on the other hand, offers information, advice, and assistance.

From the authors' perspective, whilst both are essential skills, they are not the same. In her book *Brilliant Coaching* (2017), Julie Starr defines them as below:

Mentoring

> A mentor gives relevant opinions or advice because their own professional experience matches yours in some way. So, a mentor is more of a "wise guide" because of their relevant skills or knowledge. Generally, a mentor is more involved in the content of a conversation, whereas a coach is more focused on the process of it.

Coaching

> A good coach can coach most people in most situations, because they are able to support a person's own thinking processes, using advanced skills of listening, questioning and observation or feedback. They are less likely to offer expert advice or guidance, as they are more committed to the other person's finding their own solutions.

Coaching is a conversation, or series of conversations, that one person has with another. A coaching conversation can last a few minutes or a couple of hours. The duration is not what defines it; rather, it is the style of conversation and its impact. Some clues as to whether you are having a coaching conversation include the following:

The focus is on the other person, i.e., you regard them as the expert.
You believe the other person is resourceful and can figure out what they need to do.
It is characterized by questions, listening, and reflection.
The conversation helps the other person to think, feel, and/or do things differently.

On the other hand, a mentor will offer advice and suggestions, share knowledge and experience, and give examples and ideas. Many leaders think they are coaching when they are in fact mentoring. Whilst both are needed, it's important to make a conscious choice between the two and coach wherever possible.

What It Means to Be a Coaching Leader

A coaching leader learns to adopt a less directive style when working with others, consciously asking open questions even when we think we know the answer. It requires high levels of trust and rapport, and a belief that it is a relationship of equals, rather than manager and subordinate. Sometimes people need direction and guidance but if directive is a leader's default style, they will soon find themselves overwhelmed with everyone looking for advice and direction.

Mindset and Beliefs of a Coaching Manager versus a Directive Manager

The likely skills and behaviors linked to those values and beliefs are detailed by Julie Starr in her highly recommended book *Brilliant Coaching* (Starr

2012). To summarize some of her key points, Directive managers tend to believe that their seniority means that they are expected to have all the answers and make all the decisions, whereas a Coaching manager believes that the team can generate great solutions. Skills that a Directive manager tends to develop are around problem solving and decision making, whereas a Coaching manager will focus more on developing skills around listening, reflection, and feedback.

When leaders encourage people to think, act, and learn for themselves, they are more likely to thrive and be less dependent on the leader.

Skills of a Coach

A coach will cultivate trust and safety and facilitate growth. There are a wide range of skills needed for effective coaching but the two cornerstone coaching skills are listening attentively and asking questions.

Listening

As we noted earlier, listening is a key skill for many reasons. It is vitally important in coaching conversations. Starr devotes a whole chapter in her book to listening but some of the key points she highlights are:

- Good listening demands we make a conscious effort to listen.
- The person we are listening to requires our sole focus.
- "Listen from nothing"—presume nothing.
- Make the other person more important than yourself.
- "Listening is linked directly to our attention, and it starts with intending to listen, being focused and present, and concentrating. Really good listening means that we don't get distracted by our own thoughts and ideas, instead, we stay totally focused on the other person, making them more important than ourselves" (Starr 2012, p. 62).
- If you have any doubt about the power of listening, then pause and reflect on how you felt the last time you realized that someone was really listening to you.
- Another aspect of coaching in leadership conversations is the need to focus on deepening the understanding of the why more than the how. This enables people to think independently, reduces uncertainty, and improves creativity.

Questioning

Asking questions, especially open questions, gets better quality answers. Open questions generally start with who, what, where, when, and how but can also start with "tell me..." or "help me to understand..." A quality question is one which:

- Is simple.
- Has a clear purpose.
- Influences through or learning—without being controlling (Starr 2012, p. 70).

The GROW Model

The GROW model (Goal, Reality, Options, Will) (Whitmore 2017) is one of the simplest and most effective frameworks for a coaching conversation and this is explained in more detail in Chapter 7.

Appreciative Inquiry

Appreciative Inquiry (Cooperrider 2008) focuses on building on what's working well rather than trying to fix what's broken. It has four phases which are paraphrased below:

- Discovery—identify and appreciate the best of what is.
- Dream—what might be? Imagine and envision the future state.
- Design—agree what could be in a shared vision.
- Destiny—agree steps needed to achieve the design.

Whilst often discussed in terms of major organizational change or complex problems, it can also be used as an effective approach for more day-to-day issues.

A simple example of the application is to apply to the management of workforce absenteeism. This is traditionally measured and discussed as a percentage absent from work and has negative connotations, often creating feelings of anxiety and a reluctance to actively engage in constructive discussion across the whole team.

Taking an appreciative enquiry approach, the opportunity is to focus on measuring and managing attendance rather than absenteeism. Whilst we are, essentially, looking at the same issue, how people will engage in trying to find solutions will be very different. Focusing on attendance and working out what are all the good things we are doing to get attendance, an attendance rate of 96% is a much more engaging experience for people than focusing on trying to fix what's wrong and causing 4% absenteeism.

What we are trying to do is understand what's working well, expand on this, and, in the process, come up with even more ways to increase attendance. This approach means that people are striving for a positive outcome rather than fixing a negative issue, which most people find more personally rewarding. It also helps engage the whole team to find solutions that they can support rather than pointing the finger at particular individuals. This approach can be applied to many of the KPIs used on Visual Management Boards. A good question to ask about any KPI is: how can we measure this to focus on the positive target we are aiming for?

Emotional Intelligence

Whilst the term emotional intelligence (EI) has been around for several decades, it became widely known with the publication of Daniel Goleman's book *Emotional Intelligence: Why It Can Matter More Than IQ* (1995). Goleman described emotional intelligence as consisting of five factors:

1. **Self-awareness**. Understanding your own strengths and weaknesses and how your actions affect others. People with self-awareness are usually receptive to and able to learn from constructive criticism.
2. **Self-regulation**. Demonstrating restraint and control when expressing emotions and being able to determine when the right time and place is to express them.
3. **Motivation**. Self-motivation or intrinsic motivation driven by an inner passion rather than external rewards, such as money or fame.
4. **Empathy**. The ability to understand how other people are feeling and the ability to connect with other people on an emotional level, responding genuinely to other people's concerns.
5. **Social skills**. The ability to build meaningful relationships and connections with other people.

EI starts with self-awareness. Afton (2023) recognizes that "compassionate leaders work to lift themselves above any unconscious biases to value all people in the organization." Self-awareness is related to not only educating oneself about diversity, difference, and bias, but also recognizing how you are feeling. Self-awareness is about understanding the subtleties of those emotions and how they impact on what we think and do. Self-awareness is about treating ourselves with self-compassion and not beating ourselves up when we make a mistake.

Resilience is a core component of EI and belonging leadership—the willingness to adapt and respond, effectively, to change and challenging situations, and the capacity to cope with and recover from disruption, challenge, and loss.

This can be loss of identity or loss of community, as you become more aware of bias. A network of support is vital for resilience, as is the ability to be vulnerable and reach out and ask for help. Staying flexible and optimistic, and adapting to the unpredictable and unfamiliar, while remaining hopeful that better times are coming, will help leaders to lean into tough conversations and to choose courage over comfort.

Today, EI is widely recognized as a key factor in successful leaders. While not universally agreed, most psychologists put forth the view that emotional intelligence can be practiced, and the skills developed. The authors' view is that a high level of emotional intelligence in leaders is critical for the development of DEIB, PWB, and CI and that leaders need to be prepared to invest time in developing these skills. This is even more important, as "State of the Heart EQ research," which has been monitoring levels of EQ (Emotional Quotient) globally since 2011, is seeing a downward trend in levels of workplace EQ.

Leadership Behaviors

There are many hundreds of studies into the characteristics of good leaders. Here, we select just two of them, which independently identified several common factors.

In a major study of their own leadership approach, Google identified ten key attributes of their most effective leaders. These are:

1. Is a good coach.
2. Empowers teams and does not micro-manage.
3. Creates an inclusive team environment, showing concern for success and well-being.
4. Is productive and results orientated.
5. Is a good communicator—listens and shares information.
6. Supports career development and discusses performance.

7. Has a clear vision/strategy for the team.
8. Has key technical skills to help advise the team.
9. Collaborates across Google.
10. Is a strong decision maker.

There are many similarities to research undertaken by Zenger and Folkman (2019), who identified "9 vital leadership behaviors that boost employee productivity":

1. Inspire and Motivate Others.
2. Driving for Results.
3. Strategic Perspective.
4. Collaboration.
5. Walk the Talk.
6. Trust.
7. Develops and Supports Others.
8. Building Relationships.
9. Courage.

Whilst neither of these lists explicitly uses the words "psychological well-being" nor "continuous improvement," these behaviors are good examples of the kinds of behaviors needed to support a thriving culture.

Informing all these behaviors are two key principles from the Shingo Institute: Respecting Every Individual and Leading with Humility, which are foundational principles that inform ideal behaviors for any organization. Some of the specific behaviors for leaders linked to these principles are explored in depth in Chapter 7.

Whilst the use of skills matrixes is relatively common for technical skills, it is less frequently seen for leadership and CI skills. One example organization that has extended the leadership skills matrix to include the "cultural enabler skills" and the "continuous improvement skills" is the Thermo Fisher site in Lithuania (Shingo Prize winner, 2019) (Hines and Butterworth 2019).

The skills matrix shows, for example, the ability to coach problem-solving tools and leader standard work. These and other skills are assessed and coached as leaders move up through the competency levels. This is a very effective leadership tool and is used by the Thermo Fisher team as a key enabler of leadership development. Whilst every organization will need to define its own skills matrix requirements, we believe the concept is very powerful.

DEIB and Leaders

We discussed DEIB in Chapter 2, so here we will explore the key role of leaders in supporting DEIB. Leaders need to start with respecting and valuing individuals for the unique perspective which they bring.

> Unfortunately, employees do not feel nearly as respected as leaders believe: While 60% of HR leaders say employees are respected at work, only 44% of employees feel respected. Further, Gallup research shows that 90% of employees who don't feel respected say they have experienced some form of discrimination at work.
>
> **(Brecheisen 2023)**

Leaders need to believe that feelings matter in the workplace:

> Leaders must either invest a reasonable amount to time attending to fears and feelings, or squander an unreasonable amount of time trying to manage ineffective and unproductive behavior.
>
> **(Brown 2018)**

We saw in Chapter 1 that we are, essentially, feeling beings who can sometimes think, rather than thinking beings who sometimes feel. Attending to feelings requires leaders to lean into vulnerability and believe that brave leadership requires discomfort and a learner mindset—"here to get it right, not to be right" (Brown 2020).

It is critical that leaders adopt an inside-out approach to creating cultures of belonging—they need to start with the individual and listen daily with all five senses to what individuals need to thrive at that moment in time. It is critical that the leader can build high levels of trust with individuals one-on-one and psychological safety with the entire team to ensure that individuals feel comfortable sharing what is really going on.

Looking at the outputs of all individuals' Thriving Plans and the Team Thriving Plan will be crucial to creating a tailored approach. Wharton (2021) recommends leaders "avoid a 'one size fits all' mentality," and Washington for Gallup (2022) recognizes that this is "probably one of the most frustrating things for leaders who are used to having a playbook." There can still be a framework but it should be less prescriptive and focus more on a leader's beliefs and values, skills, and behaviors, trusting and empowering them to do the right thing.

That does not mean that DEIB should not be systematized—it absolutely needs to be codified, as this is what creates sustainability and consistency from one leader to the next and from one team to the next. Codification enables the organization to operationalize DEIB because the processes, practices, skills, and behaviors are in place.

A framework for a belonging leader, which codifies the key elements and yet allows for flexibility and autonomy, is illustrated in Figure 6.2.

Developing the skills to become a belonging leader needs to be integrated into leadership development at its core, and not an add-on, or what Brown and Bethea (2021) call "'parachute' training that is a 'one and done.'"

Skills development starts with developing leaders with high levels of emotional intelligence. Coaching skills—being curious, asking questions, and active listening—are vital for belonging leaders, as is a focus on strengths and how amplifying what is already really good, rather than trying to "fix." The final components are the skills to create cultures of trust and psychological safety. Belonging leaders regard power as something to be shared—they believe in power to and power with, in empowering and collaborating with people in their team and across teams.

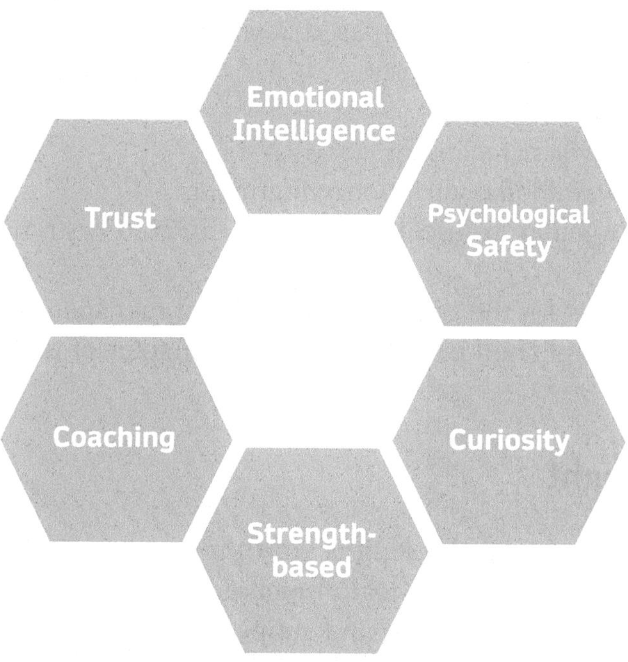

Figure 6.2 A framework for a Belonging Leader.

Summary Role of Leaders in PWB And CI

In Chapter 3 we explored the role of leaders in supporting PWB and in Chapter 7 we explore in more detail the role leaders play in supporting a culture of CI. Tables 6.1 and 6.2 show a summary of key leader activities to support CI from a Social and Technical Perspective.

Leader Thriving Plan

One of the core enablers we have focused on is the Thriving Plan for every individual. The Psychological Well-Being Assessment and the other five key tools explained in Chapter 3 apply to leaders as individuals along with everyone else in the organization and are key components of the leader's Thriving Plan. However, as we have explored above, leaders have additional responsibilities. To help with this, we have suggested a Psychosocial and Continuous Improvement template for a leader to complete as input to their own Thriving Plan, which is shown in Figure 6.3. We recommend that this is reviewed and updated on a regular basis and discussed in one-on-ones with any leader's one-up.

Additional input to a leader's Thriving Plan that some people may find helpful could also be a strengths-based assessment. There are many of these available. Here are three examples:

- https://www.viacharacter.org/
- https://www.redbull.com/int-en/wingfinder
- https://www.gallup.com/cliftonstrengths/en/254033/strengthsfinder.aspx

The overall process for the creation and ongoing management of the Thriving Plan is explained in the Introduction chapter of this book.

A Final Thought

Whilst leaders play a critical role, it is worth remembering that PWB is a shared responsibility among all team members, with every individual having a role in helping to ensure a safe and supportive environment. Leaders are not just accountable for the PWB of their teams—they need to ensure they have a focus on their own PWB as well as their peers.

Table 6.1 Leader Responsibilities for CI Social Elements

#	*Social Elements*	*Leadership Responsibilities*
1	Lead with Purpose	• Connect your personal why to your team and/or organization's purpose. • Ensure the broader team has a compelling purpose that can be linked back to the individual's job. • Ensure the purpose is brought to life by integrating it into the team's systems of work and artifacts.
2	Lead with Humility	• Role model humility by involving people in key decisions regarding their work. • Be curious, ask questions, and show others that you don't suppose to have all the answers. • Abandon bias and prejudice, be open to alternatives.
3	Develop Trust	• Role model behaviors of integrity, empathy, and care. • Develop your skills in building trust.
4	Show Respect for Every Individual	• Treat each person as unique with specific needs and capabilities. • Actively listen when team members are speaking, seek to understand. • Involve people in decisions regarding their work.
5	Listen to the Voice of the Individual (VOI)	• Actively listen when team members are speaking, seek to understand, and act on what's heard. • Ensure everyone's voice is heard.
6	Cultivate Teamwork	• Regularly communicate the need for teamwork to achieve the team goals. • Role model behaviors that ensure people work together and not against each other.
7	Constantly Challenge the Status Quo	• Help create an atmosphere within the team where it's safe to speak up. • Be open to new ideas, promote curiosity, and the need to eliminate waste. • Avoid taking challenges to the status quo personally.
8	Look, Listen, and Learn at the Gemba	• Schedule time to go to the Gemba (the area people do their work) to connect with people. • Use this time to also assess the well-being of individuals.
9	Develop People through Coaching	• Prioritize regular time for one-on-one coaching of your direct reports. • Develop your coaching skills by using a structured approach (GROW Model).
10	Lead Effectively through Leaders Standard Work	• Prioritize time to role-model ideal behaviors • Prioritize time to regularly coach individual and teams' systems of work and improvement.
11	Foster Diversity, Equity, Inclusion, and Belonging (DEIB)	• Ensure KBIs are in place to support DEIB. • Proactively coach DEIB.

TABLE 6.2 Leader Responsibilities for CI Technical Elements

#	*Technical Elements*	*Leadership Responsibilities*
1	Conduct strategy development and deployment	• Ensure formal processes are in place for strategy development and deployment. • Make sure the strategic objectives, performance measures, and improvement initiatives are effectively operationalized.
2	Listen to the Voice of the Customer (VOC)	• Support the team to put in place formal mechanisms for regularly obtaining the VOC. • Support the team to integrate/operationalize the VOC into their performance and improvement systems.
3	Listen to the Voice of the Process (VOP)	• Support the team to embed a system for understanding how their processes are performing (KPIs, Waste Trackers, Delay Capture).
4	Focus on horizontal value streams	• Promote and help mobilize horizontal value streams by engaging and working with cross-functional peers. • Role-model behavior that ensures the team doesn't work in a silo.
5	Standardize work and ensure quality	• Help the team determine what standards are required that are fit for purpose for their type of work. • Support the team to embed a system for doing a regular review of standards.
6	Embed continuous improvement	• Support the team to embed a CI system. • Ensure every individual in the team understands their responsibility to make improvement part of what they do every day.
7	Develop structured problem solving	• Ensure the team does structured problem solving when root causes of problems aren't known. • Practice problem solving for yourself to help you coach others.
8	Manage visually	• Help embed systems for understanding the current state of the team's performance applying the 1-3-10 principle. • Ensure the KPIs and KBIs that teams track are within their control.
9	Develop and use knowledge and skills	• Ensure that each individual has a plan on how they develop their skills.
10	Manage capacity and demand	• Ensure a formal system is in place to manage the capacity and demand of the team's workload. • Use one-on-one time to assess individuals' workload against capacity.
11	Create workplace organization (5S)	• Help the team ensure resources required to do their job are available at point of use.

Leadership Psychosocial and CI Assessment								
Instruction to complete the assessment:		1. Read each statement and rate it against the below criteria. Place the number in the relevant block. 2. Include comments for each rating, as required, so you can be specific about the actions for improving your and your teams well-being. 3. Populate the chart with the average score and update your action plan. This plan is designed for you to work through yourself, and/ or with someone else - a coach, a manager, or a peer whom you trust to get a snapshot of where you are today and what are the top 3 actions which would serve you well over the next agreed time period. 4. Discuss your action plan with your family, leader, trusted peer and/or coach to get feedback and support.						
		CRITERIA: 1. Strongly disagree 2. Disagree 3. Neither agree or disagree 4. Agree 5. Strongly agree						
#	**Factors**	**Statement (answer based on your current state)**	**Scale**					**Comments**
			1	**2**	**3**	**4**	**5**	
1	Leadership Support	I have regular one-on-one routines with each direct report and, in all interactions, I start with an inside-out approach, tailoring my style to the individual's needs at that time, avoiding rescuing or fixing.						
2	Well-being	I regularly discuss the individual physical and psychological well-being including the presence of psychosocial hazards that may be causing them harm and I consider what that means for me and how I lead.						

Figure 6.3 Leaders Psychosocial and CI Assessment extract. Full version is available at www.whycarebook.com.

Key Points from Chapter 6

- Do not underestimate the power of Look, Listen, and Learn activities and the need to train leaders in how to do these effectively through coaching.
- Leaders need a skills matrix supported by a personal development plan that tracks their progress in the cultural enabling and CI skills they need.
- Leaders need to look after themselves as much as their teams and ensure they complete their own Thriving Plan.

Chapter 7

Why Care about a Thriving Improvement Culture?

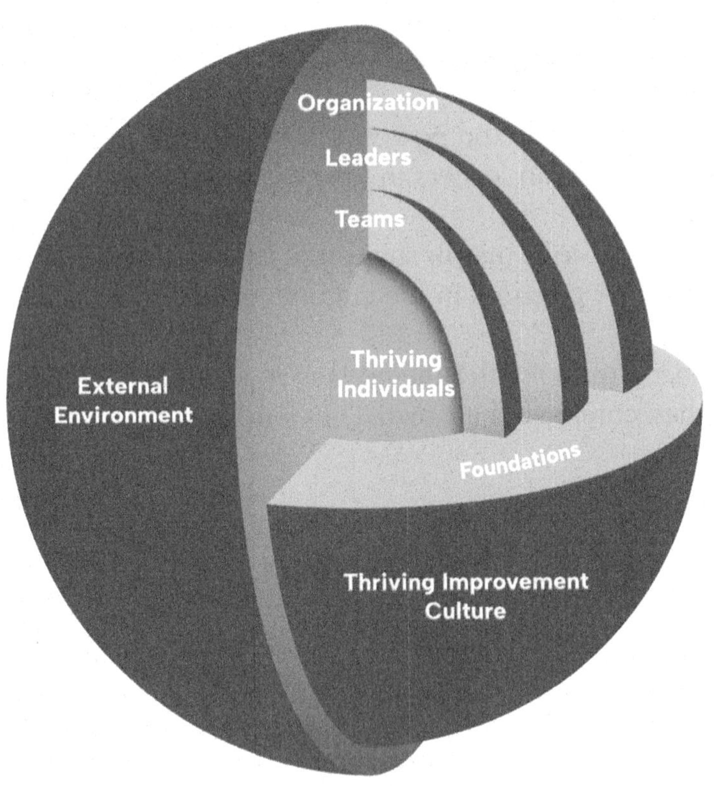

Figure 7.0 **The Why Care Model—Thriving Individuals.**

 DOI: 10.4324/9781003413479-8

Introduction

Chapter 7 will focus on the importance of creating a thriving culture of continuous improvement (CI) to help the organization achieve internal performance targets and effectively manage external volatility, uncertainty, complexity, and ambiguity (VUCA).

A thriving culture of improvement is deliberately created. It needs to be prioritized as a critical organizational capability to meet the constantly changing needs of customers, shareholders, investors, regulators, communities, families, and individuals. Organizations that do not prioritize the need for defining, deploying, and maturing an internal improvement system as a strategic business imperative will risk being taken over and consumed by rapidly changing global priorities, shifting customer needs, agile competitors, emerging technologies, and social/workplace activism.

Organizations will not be able to proactively pre-empt and adequately respond to change without an ability to be adaptive, agile, and flexible. This ability is enabled by solidifying an improvement system within the organization that stimulates, harnesses, and applies proactive learning.

Learning cannot be reactive. Every person within the organization needs to apply their knowledge and skills toward the relentless improvement of their work. In doing so, they will learn new things about what needs to change in their workplace to provide better products and services to their customers. This learning will also trigger breakthrough innovation, which will help the organization to lead the way within their industry.

Learning cannot occur in a vacuum. It requires a system to ensure it becomes a lived experience for every individual. A learning culture is one where the collective knowledge and skills of every individual within the organization are valued and desperately required to manage change. People are expected to think and not just do. They are recognized for constantly using the improvement system to identify, capture, and implement ideas for improving their work.

A transformation occurs when every person in the organization takes responsibility for using the improvement system to improve their work. The entire atmosphere within the organization changes. Individuals are trusted to work more autonomously; this makes them feel more valued because they have ownership of their work, which releases a cognitive energy that catapults the organization forward.

The more that people use the system and improve it, the better the system becomes at managing change. People are expected to suggest improvements to the various elements of the system as they use it. The improvement capabilities of people grow as the capability of the improvement system matures. The two are linked.

The system is only as good as its weakest link, and it is the people using the system who can find and improve these weak points. In doing so, the individual's improvement capabilities grow. This constant cycle of applying, learning, and improving, matured over time, represents one of the most lucrative capabilities the organization can invest in to sustainably achieve performance aspirations and stay ahead of change.

As stated in Chapter 3, psychological capacity needs to be made available through the proactive management of the psychological well-being (PWB) of every individual. People need emotional and cognitive energy to use within the improvement system (Figure 7.1).

Expecting people to use the improvement system when they are being constantly exposed to psychosocial hazards is unrealistic. The organization cannot expect individuals to contribute their intellect and time to improvement when they are in a survival mode, guarding themselves against workplace harm. People will use whatever psychological capacity they have for coping and not improving if they work within a toxic environment.

Psychological capacity, therefore, cannot be liberated for the purpose of CI without a deliberate focus on PWB. This includes the elimination and/or control of psychosocial hazards. The organization and its leaders need to proactively help the individual optimize their psychological capacity and then promote the use of it within the improvement system. The improvement system needs to be used daily to mature and achieve its purpose of making improvement part of every individual's job. This use is dependent on emotional and cognitive capacity.

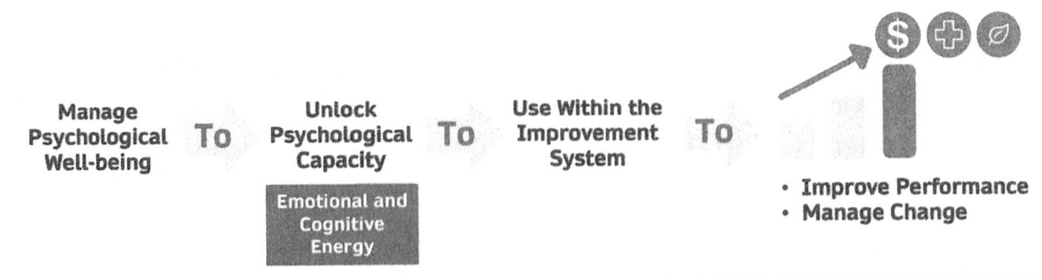

Figure 7.1 Emotional and cognitive energy is needed to improve performance.

The Improvement System

A system consists of a collection of elements, an interconnection of parts functioning as one complex whole. A system has a specific purpose, and each element plays a role in achieving this purpose. When thinking about organizational systems, we consider both social and technical elements and how they work interdependently to achieve the system's purpose. The way these social and technical elements interact with each other is complex and constantly changing and therefore needs to be regularly verified for effectiveness.

A system's maturity is reflected as a continuum. At one end of the continuum, we have the system elements weak and disconnected, working in isolation. At the other side of the continuum, we have the system elements well developed and working as conjoined cogs. They each have their own purpose and function harmoniously with each other to consistently meet the purpose of the system. The goal is to achieve seamless flow between all the social and technical elements.

Increasing flow is the result of increasing the maturity of ideal behaviors within and across each element of the system. These ideal behaviors serve as the lubricant between the social and technical elements (the oil that makes the cogs work well together). The better that a system flows, the more chance it has of achieving its objectives.

The CI system needs to be periodically assessed to determine how well it is flowing. This is done through structured maturity assessments, highlighting the strengths and opportunities between elements. A purpose of a CI system is to ensure that all the people are improving all processes, all the time, at all levels. The goal is to make sure that improvement becomes part of what people do every day and that this improvement is focused on what matters most for the individual and the organization.

A CI system, illustrated on the Thriving Matrix (Figure 7.2), consists of its own, specific collection of social and technical elements. The selection of elements can look slightly different across various organizations. The goal is to internalize the design based on a review of various improvement methodologies, such as the Shingo model, Lean manufacturing, Six Sigma, and theory of constraints. The elements stated in the book have been selected as being universally applicable to any industry and organization, based on the authors' experience.

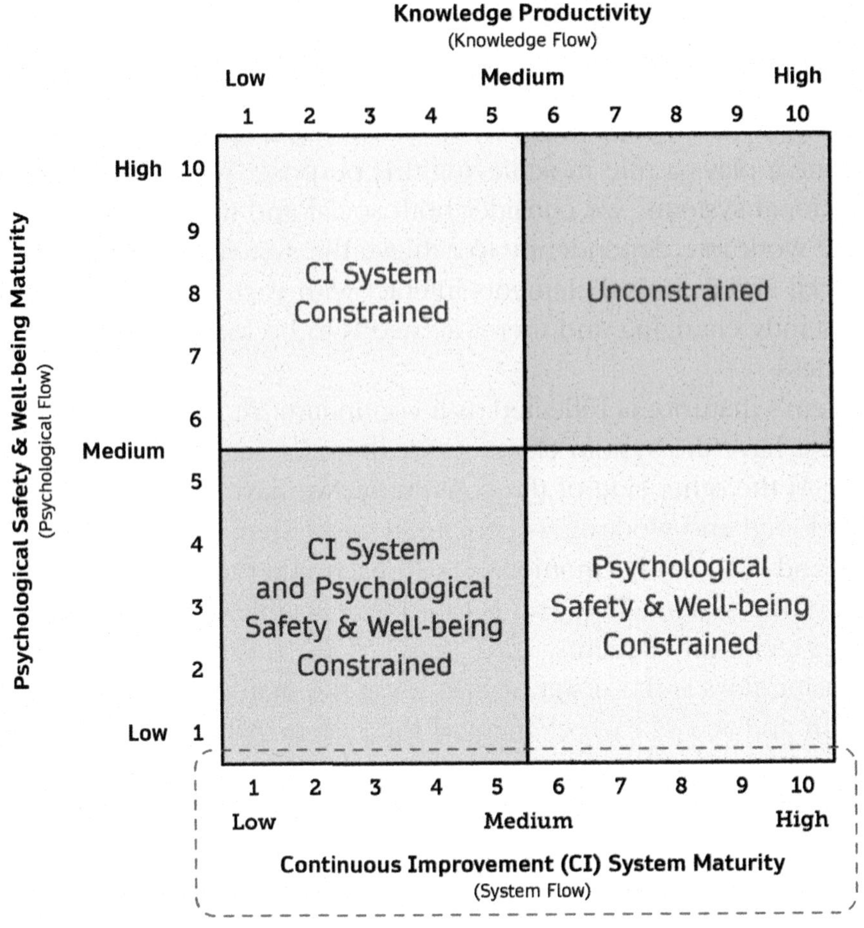

Figure 7.2 **The CI system is a key enabler for knowledge productivity.**

The Role of Ideal Behaviors

The effectiveness of any CI system, as a self-reinforcing mechanism, is dependent on how saturated the system is with ideal behaviors, within and across system elements.

> A behavior is something you can see and/or hear. An effective way to think about this is that a behavior must be something that you could video—demonstrating what future-state behaviors (ideal) would look and sound like.
>
> **(Chris Butterworth, Morgan L. Jones, and Peter Hines, *Why Bother*, 2022)**

Drenching the system with ideal behaviors will have a direct impact on the pace and quality of improvement, including the maturity of psychological safety and well-being in the organization. Ideal behaviors lead to ideal results. This includes how people feel about their work, their contributions, and their ability to achieve their full potential. Embedded KBIs are used to measure and track the maturity of these behaviors within the workplace.

Social and Technical Elements of the CI System

There are 11 social elements and 11 technical elements (Table 7.1) that the authors have selected to represent an ideal improvement system. The

Table 7.1 Social and Technical Elements of the CI System

#	*Social-Enabling Elements*	#	*Technical-Delivery Elements*
1	Lead with purpose	1	Conduct strategy development and deployment
2	Lead with humility	2	Listen to the Voice of the Customer (VOC)
3	Develop trust	3	Listen to the Voice of the Process (VOP)
4	Show respect for every individual	4	Focus on horizontal value streams
5	Listen to the Voice of the Individual (VOI)	5	Standardize work and ensure quality
6	Cultivate teamwork	6	Embed continuous improvement
7	Relentlessly challenge the status quo	7	Develop structured problem solving
8	Look, Listen, and Learn at the Gemba	8	Manage visually
9	Develop people through coaching	9	Develop and use knowledge and skills
10	Lead effectively through Leader Standard Work	10	Manage capacity and demand
11	Foster Diversity, Equity, Inclusion, and Belonging (DEIB)	11	Create workplace organization (5S)

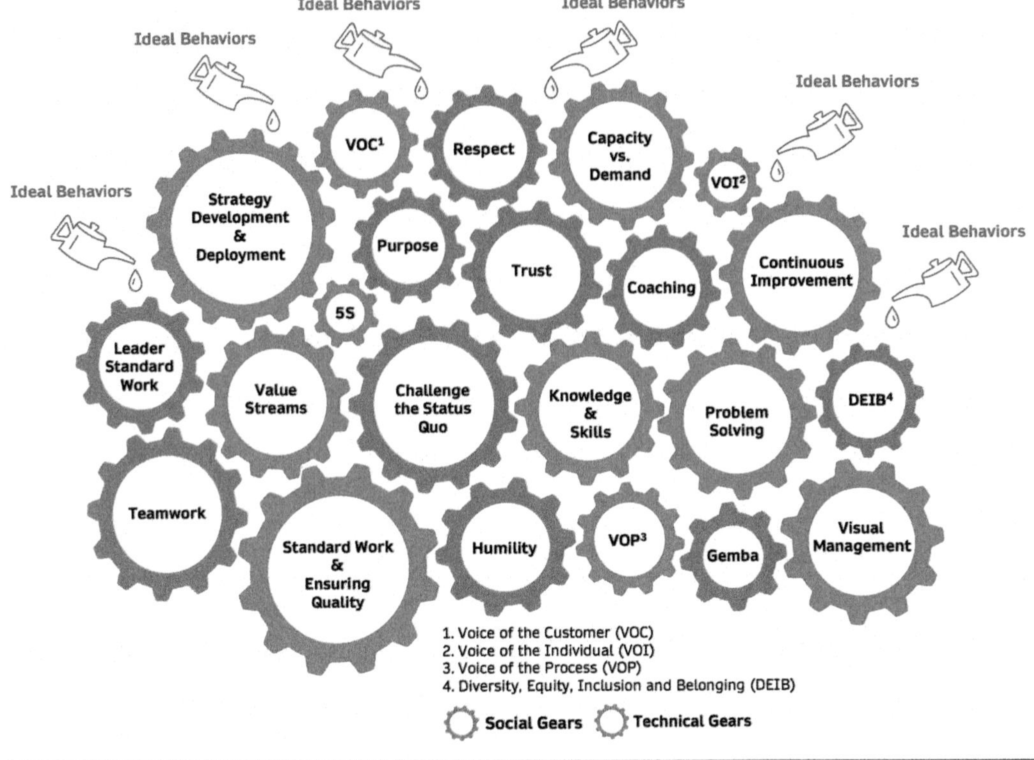

Figure 7.3 Ideal behaviors ensure the improvement system flows as a self-reinforcing engine.

22 self-reinforcing elements operate seamlessly as a whole in producing improvements from every individual.

Elements have been split between those that are enablers (social) and those that help deliver improvement (technical). Enabling elements/cogs are those that are required to make the delivery cogs work well. Delivery cogs are those that produce improvement and tangible performance outcomes. Ideal behaviors are the oil that makes all the enabling and delivery cogs flow as one self-reinforcing engine (Figure 7.3).

Social Elements of the Continuous Improvement System

1. Lead with Purpose

Leading with purpose is an enabling cog within the CI system which ensures an organization has a clear view of its true north, its reason for being. Purpose represents the "why" for an organization, its higher calling. Organizational purpose is necessary to bring people together and inspire them to be part of something bigger than themselves. It is an anchor point that is brought to life regularly in the course of daily work to help focus people on what matters most.

Organizational purpose is essential for helping provide meaning for people at work. The absence thereof can leave individuals lost and not connected emotionally to the organization and their work. Meaningful work includes individuals feeling pride in a job well done, a sense that they are fulfilling their potential and working to the best of their ability, a belief that their work is either interesting, creative, and/or absorbing, and receiving praise, recognition, or acknowledgment from others.

Meaning, however, differs for every person. People are different and should have their own purpose in life. Leaders therefore need to apply a personalized approach when engaging with every individual to determine how their "personal why" connects to the purpose of their team/organization. Purpose is what gets people out of bed each day.

Linking "personal why" to "organizational why" is the goal (Figure 7.4).

It takes time to fuse together. It requires a deeper conversation, one that involves a different set of questions. These questions are focused on getting to know what motivates the individual, what they value and are passionate about. The leader is in fact trying to understand what makes the individual tick, their personal and workplace history, what they stand for, their beliefs and convictions, development goals, and how these fit in with their work.

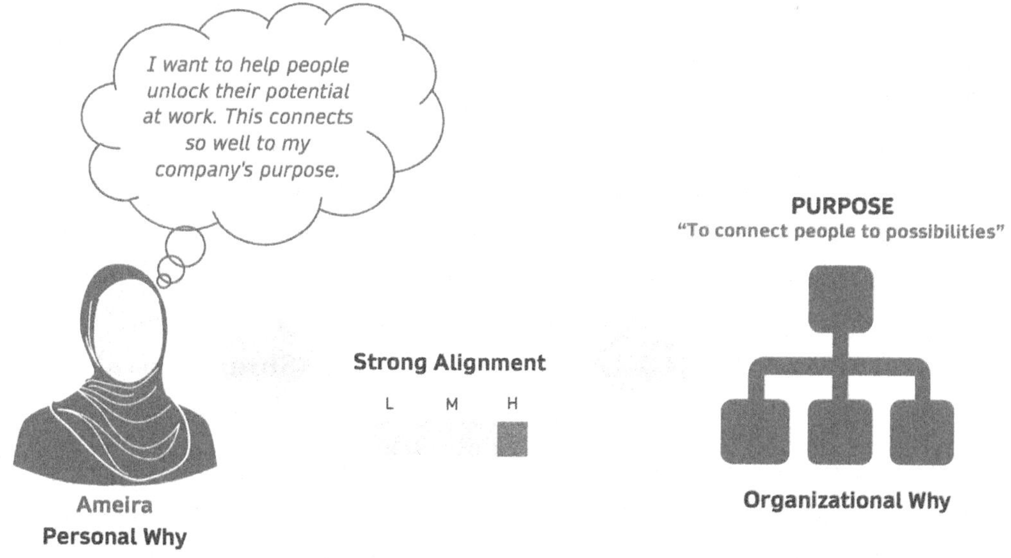

Figure 7.4 Connecting personal why to organizational why.

The individual can use the Purpose Questionnaire to help them think through their purpose in life and share it with others, including their leader. This can then be used to craft their job to link as closely as possible to what their passions and aspirations are in life.

People aren't motivated by money alone. They want to understand the bigger picture, the greater goal of the organization, beyond merely increasing shareholder returns. They want to play a part in something larger than themselves, to make a difference, to feel part of something special. The leader has an ideal opportunity to use a personalized approach to understand the individual's unique purpose for life and help connect this to their work, values, and moral compass.

Purpose and direction are important foundational elements of PWB. Having a clear sense of direction in life with strong goal orientation and conviction that life holds meaning is a key element of PWB. The more people find meaning in life, the more likely they will improve their PWB. Positive PWB allows people to invest their psychological capacity toward helping their team/organization fulfill its purpose. Understanding personal why and linking it to organizational why is, therefore, a big enabler for positive PWB, which in turn unlocks psychological capacity for improvement.

2. Lead with Humility

Leading with humility is an enabling cog within the improvement system that ensures a conducive atmosphere is created for people to feel valued and contribute with confidence.

> Humility is an enabling principle that precedes learning and improvement. A leader's willingness to seek input, listen carefully, and continuously learn creates an environment where people feel respected and energized and will give freely of their creative abilities. Improvement is only possible when people are willing to acknowledge their vulnerability and abandon bias and prejudice in their pursuit of a better way.
>
> **(Shingo Booklet)**

People take pride in what they do at work, especially if it is linked to their personal why. They invest their time, emotions, and cognitive capabilities toward doing the best they can at what they are passionate about. They enjoy sharing what they have learned and how they are making a difference and adding value to the organization.

Psychological Well-being Impact

- People feel seen & heard
- People feel appreciated
- People feel valued
- People grow through learning
- Builds trust & relationships
- It reduces workplace stress

Figure 7.5 Leadership humility makes people feel valued, appreciated, and heard.

Leaders need to stimulate this sharing by going to the place people work and looking, listening, and learning. People's level of energy and focus is increased when they feel heard. Humility is best practiced by leaders asking questions and listening with the sincere intent to understand. When a leader engages with humility, seeking to understand the nuances, the "knack" that people are applying to their work, it boosts the emotional state of the individual (Figure 7.5).

People feel that they matter and that others are interested in what they do. This in turn makes them feel valued. Humility is about curiosity; it is about learning and deeply valuing the contributions of others, even if they contradict deep-seated beliefs. Humility is jet fuel for igniting psychological capacity because people feel recognized as the true experts of the work they perform.

3. Develop Trust

Developing trust is an enabling cog within the improvement system that is split into two categories—relationship trust and element trust.

Relationship Trust

Trust is needed to ensure that people can express their ideas for improvement without fear that the idea will be judged or trivialized. As previously stated, trust is defined as "choosing to risk making something you value vulnerable to another person's actions" (Charles Feldman, *The Thin Book of Trust*, 2021).

For people to put forward their unique ideas for improvement requires them to be vulnerable. They are making something they value (the idea) vulnerable to the scrutiny of others. Vulnerability, if not treated appropriately, can either build or breakdown PWB. Thriving improvement is the outcome of thriving psychological safety.

Psychological safety allows people to speak with confidence. Confidence is an outcome of people working within a trusting environment, where it is ok to put forward ideas without fear of what others may think of them. Mistrust, on the other hand, reduces PWB because people worry that who they are, and their unique contributions, will be judged. They end up constantly looking over their shoulder, worried about what someone may say of them and/or their work.

A toxic workplace is synonymous with one where there is a lot of mistrust. Mistrust is the ultimate uncertainty because nothing can be predicted. When people don't trust their peers, leaders, and/or organization, they focus their energy on self-preservation rather than improvement. Mistrust gets people looking inward, constantly analyzing their environment and adjusting what they say or do to avoid scrutiny. Mistrust drives up workplace stress and, if left unattended for long periods, can cause psychological instability and harm.

People thrive in a workplace atmosphere where trust has been deliberately put on the table for discussion as a key PWB enabler. Trust cannot be assumed but, rather, needs to be evaluated and developed as a skill. Open and transparent dialogue becomes the norm, with regular role modeling of what good trust looks like.

This atmosphere of trust means that people will not waste their energy on guarding themselves but will instead direct their psychological capacity toward making their job easier and helping the organization prosper. Relationship trust is, therefore, critical to enable improvement.

Element Trust (Reliability)

For the improvement system to achieve its purpose of making improvement part of what people do every day, it needs to trust that all the elements (cogs) can perform their role in service of the whole (engine). Elements operate interdependently and rely on each other to be effective (Figure 7.6).

Examples of element relationships include:

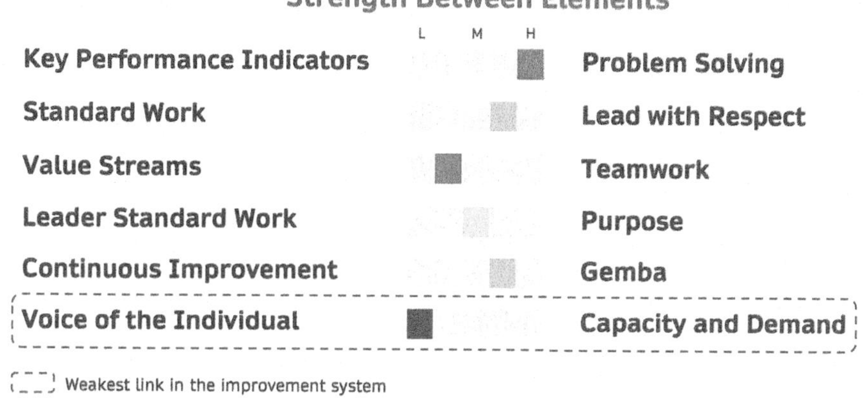

Figure 7.6 People need to trust that the elements of the CI system have the capability to support each other.

- If key performance indicators (visual management) are trending in the red and a problem-solving activity is generated. The leader/team need to be confident that a structured approach (problem-solving) will be followed to identify root causes and solutions.
- If operating standards (standard work) are being developed, does it include input from the people who perform the work (lead with respect)?
- If core business processes (value streams) are being improved, is there good engagement and collaboration (teamwork) between cross-functional teams to solve interface problems?
- Are leaders scheduling time (Leader Standard Work) to reinforce the team's purpose (purpose) and are they scheduling time to provide their team with guidance (coaching) on how to make improvement part of what they do every day?
- If the rate of idea implementation (continuous improvement) is dropping, are leaders going to the place where people work (Gemba) to determine whether they are continuously looking for waste in their work (challenging the status quo)?
- If people are saying they are struggling to cope (voice of the individual), are leaders assessing the work demand for the individual and their capacity to fulfill this demand (capacity and demand)?

4. Show Respect for Every Individual

Respect is an enabling cog within the improvement system that can have one of the biggest impacts on ensuring the system achieves its purpose.

People will not make improvement part of what they do every day if they do not feel respected.

Respect is not merely being nice to somebody but also the full spectrum of acknowledging their unique nature and role within the workplace. It is about having empathy for others, and thinking about the impact of actions and behavior on others (owed respect).

To have empathy for someone, you need to be able to walk in their shoes and understand their perspective. This can only be done at a personal level through strong, trusting relationships. It requires regular visits to the Gemba (place where people work) to Look, Listen, and Learn. It is about treating the person doing the work as being the true expert of their work, and not some internal specialist or external consultant.

Respect is a deep regard for an individual's unique biopsychosocial factors, an acceptance of their unique characteristics. It is the recognition of their unique knowledge, experience, and skills. It is about providing them with the necessary autonomy to control their work and opportunities to learn and grow. It is about providing them with a work environment where their physical and psychological health and safety is always protected (Figure 7.7).

Respect for every individual is a transformational activity. The intent is to use the improvement system to transform the lives of people. Implementing breakthrough improvement and solving complex problems provides people with opportunities to be unique and achieve accomplishments that make

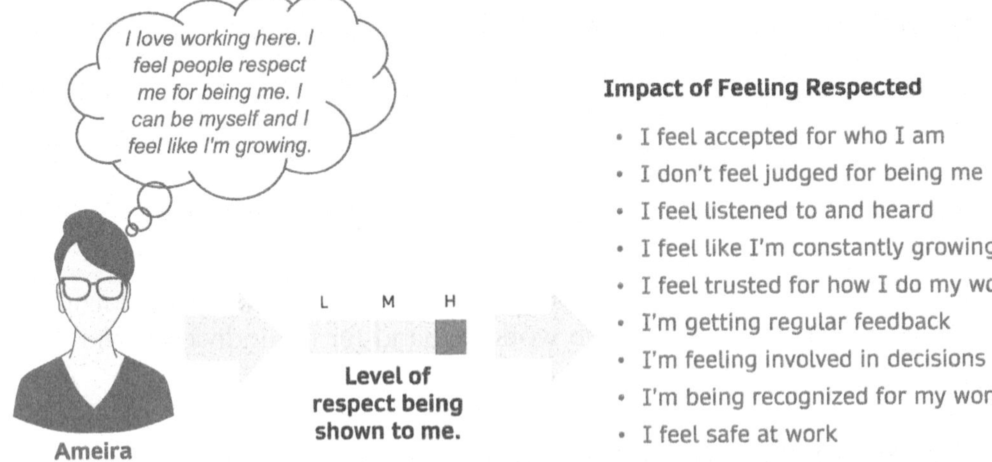

Figure 7.7 Feeling valued and respected has a big impact on how people feel at work.

them stand out (earned respect). The more people make improvements to their work, utilizing the improvement system, the greater the opportunity for them to shine, to express themselves and show what they can achieve.

> The better we do as leaders creating an environment where continuous improvement is practiced "every day, everywhere, (and by) everybody," the better we enable a culture where inspired and engaged team members transform their energy, passion, and performance into organizational results."
>
> **(Masaaki Imai)**

Transforming lives means that we need people to accept challenging goals and tough problems to solve. These challenges create the conditions for people to accomplish great things and, once accomplished, those become a source of pride. Meeting these challenges builds confidence and self-worth. People feel good about themselves, which promotes self-acceptance.

A lack of respect can have a material impact on almost every element of well-being. People can question their meaning at work; it can make them doubt their competence, break down relationships, make them feel excluded, and reduce their productivity.

Creating a thriving culture of improvement is the outcome of every person believing that who they are and what they have to offer is enough. The workplace should be a place that builds people up, that develops and encourages them, that offers them the dignity and respect they deserve. Anything less is abuse and a trigger for workplace harm.

There are many psychosocial hazards in the workplace that can reduce respect for every individual. These include, for example: low role clarity, low job involvement, lack of inclusion and belonging, bullying, harassment, discrimination, inadequate recognition, and poor capacity and demand management. All these hazards, and more, reduce people feeling valued and respected in the workplace and need to be eliminated and/or controlled.

5. Listen to the Voice of the Individual (VOI)

The voice of the individual is an enabling cog within the improvement system that ensures the facts are always known about the health of the individual and their workplace. Without knowledge of these facts, the condition of the individual's PWB cannot be known, and true improvement cannot be made.

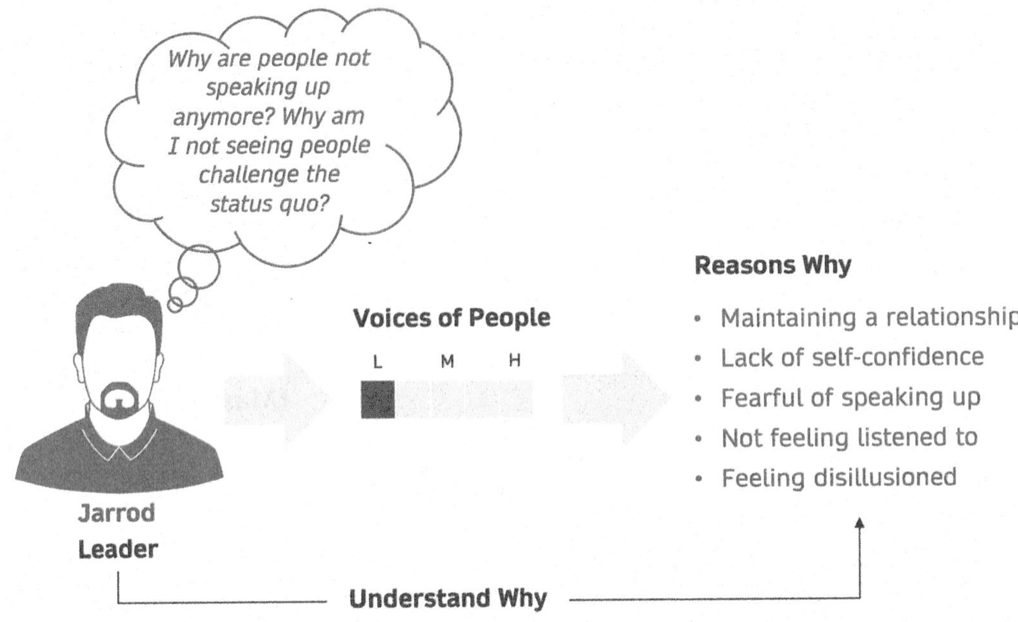

Figure 7.8 Leaders need to be constantly checking for workplace silence.

A leader needs to make it a daily practice to listen for pockets of quietness (Figure 7.8).

Once found, it should be dealt with immediately. Silence could mean something is wrong with the PWB of an individual or the momentum of improvement within the team.

People who are being exposed to psychosocial hazards often suffer in silence. They fear being open about how they are feeling. They don't want their leader or other people to think they are weak or not coping. This fear drives up stress, reduces PWB, and can cause psychological harm.

The voice of the individual is a critical input for proactively managing PWB and the state of improvement within the workplace. When people aren't talking, then the organization isn't moving forward. Freedom of expression, obligation to dissent, and liberty to challenge the status quo are essential ingredients for CI. Leaders need to help create an atmosphere that is conducive to every individual feeling that their voice is valued and heard, irrespective of where they sit in the hierarchy. The voice of a graduate needs to be valued as much as the voice of a CEO.

CI cannot mature without seeking out the contributions of all individuals within the organization. CI requires continuous listening.

> Continuous improvement is synonymous with a constant, rhythmic, and diverse sound emanating from confident individuals who know they are valued and listened to.
>
> **(Chris Warner, *Flick the Switch*, 2014)**

The voices and inputs of individuals are reduced when they have low job control (a psychosocial hazard). People will not proactively look for waste within their processes if they are constantly being controlled, with little say over their work. Individuals need to feel they are safe to challenge the status quo by using their voices.

In addition to formal methods for acquiring the voice of the individual (surveys, one-on-one routines), informal approaches should be used as much, if not more. It is within the informal, day-to-day interactions that people feel most comfortable articulating the truth about how they feel and the condition of their work. It is the short engagements at the coffee machine, on the shop floor, and in the elevator that can provide a wealth of information on how people are feeling about the workplace and the impact it is having on their PWB.

"The ear of the leader must ring with the voices of people" (Woodrow Wilson 1915).

Well-being is best determined within the regular visits that leaders make to where the person works, to just say hello and ask them how they are doing. It is the sincere, personal interest shown between people in the workplace that can draw out a wealth of knowledge about the workplace and its impact on individuals. Be interested in others, be prepared to be amazed, listen intently; it makes people feel valued.

6. Cultivate Teamwork

Teamwork is an enabling cog within the improvement system that ensures people feel connected to a common purpose and goals. As humans, we have this inner need to belong, to be in relationship with others, to share stories that make us cry and laugh together. Isolation from others—no more exposed than during COVID-19—can break the spirits of people.

Prolonged isolation at work is seen as a psychosocial hazard that needs to be eliminated and/or controlled. It is the people in the organization—and the teamwork that results from people working together—that bring fulfillment and give an organization its competitive edge.

Teamwork can include people focusing on improving their common key performance indicators, people working together on improvement projects, people engaging together in cross-functional value stream improvement, people being brought together to solve complex problems, or people focusing together on promoting diversity, equity, inclusion, and belonging within the workplace.

It is the collective utilization of a diverse set of knowledge, experience, and skills that makes teamwork so powerful. It is diverse thinking, brought together behind a singular purpose, that can differentiate the good from the great. Teamwork allows for ideas to be turned into solutions rapidly. It ignites innovation by creating a vibrant atmosphere for every individual to contribute with confidence.

Thriving teamwork is, however, dependent on psychological safety (Figure 7.9).

> When a work environment has good psychological safety, good things happen, mistakes are reported quickly so that prompt corrective action can be taken, seamless co-ordination across groups or departments is enabled, and potentially game-changing ideas for innovation are shared.
>
> **(Amy C. Edmondson, *The Fearless Organization*, 2019)**

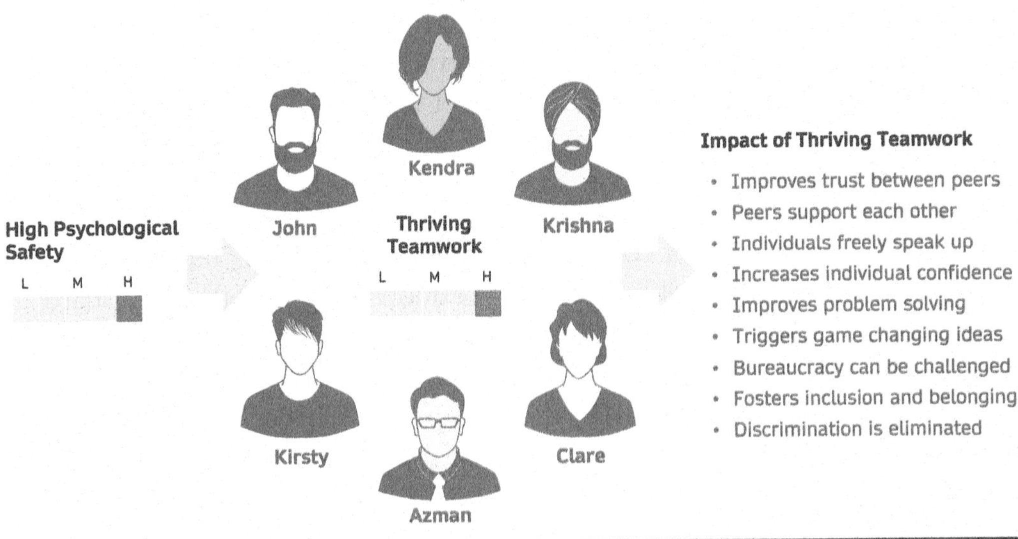

Figure 7.9 Psychological safety enables thriving teamwork.

The absence of teamwork can have a detrimental impact on PWB.

> Poor workplace relationships or interpersonal conflict is regarded as a psychosocial hazard. It can occur between managers, supervisors, co-workers, or others with whom workers are required to interact. It can appear as frequent or excessive disagreements, or rude comments—either from one person to another or between multiple people.
>
> **(WorkSafe Qld 2023)**

A lack of trust between people working closely together creates unnecessary stress. The constant worry that people working in your close inner circle may not have your back, gossip about you, misrepresent your intentions, or deliberately accept recognition for your ideas can be emotionally exhausting.

The energy exerted to manage a lack of teamwork draws the individual away from working freely with others. Everybody is responsible for improving their teamwork skills. It requires a commitment from every individual. Teamwork can never be assumed; it needs to be cultivated and matured to reap the benefits. "Don't tolerate brilliant jerks, the cost to teamwork is too high" (Reed Hastings 2018).

7. Relentlessly Challenge the Status Quo

Challenging the status quo is an enabling cog within the improvement system. Without it, there is no improvement. The phrase "status quo" means the "existing state of affairs." It is the short form of the Latin phrase "in status quo."

Challenging the existing state of affairs is non-negotiable for creating a thriving culture of CI and innovation. The way things are, don't need to stay that way. Nothing great has ever been achieved by doing things the way they have always been done. People often refrain from challenging because of fear.

> At some point during elementary school, children start to recognize that what others think of them matters, and they learn how to lower risk of rejection or scorn. By the time we're adults, we're usually good at it! So good, we do it without conscious thought. Don't want to look ignorant? Don't ask questions. Don't want to

look incompetent? Don't admit to mistakes or weaknesses? Don't want to be called disruptive? Don't make suggestions.

(Amy C. Edmondson, *The Fearless Organization*, 2019)

Self-preservation is an enemy of improvement. Whenever people are guarding themselves, they are not confidently making things better. Confidence is a key ingredient for disruptive dialogue. A lack of confidence is often an outcome of a lack of psychological safety. Leaders play a critical role in building confidence through their one-on-one routines with individuals and role-modeling behaviors that promote the need for everybody to have courage and conviction to offer alternate ideas that may disrupt workplace norms.

Disrupting norms is crucial to finding waste and finding waste is a responsibility of every person in the organization. The word "waste" needs to become common language in the organization, from the CEO to every person working within a process. Continuous and breakthrough improvement is an outcome of relentlessly challenging sacred cows—not occasional curiosity, but constant critical review of every decision, system, and process.

Waste is everywhere. It is in every workplace process, non-excluded. It does not matter how long organizations have been on their CI journey; waste will always hibernate, like a disease, within every one of their processes. Whether these are operational, human resources, technology, finance, or health and safety processes, waste exists throughout the entire eco-system.

People work with these processes every day. They come to work to do a good job, to feel fulfilled at the end of a day's work. The condition of their systems and processes can, however, be extremely frustrating to work with. Prolonged exposure to waste can cause unnecessary stress that can reduce PWB and subsequent psychological capacity.

Waste can present itself as a psychosocial hazard which, in turn, can lead to psychological harm. Waste does not need to be big things. It is usually the small, lingering things that cause the most frustration and discouragement, especially when the person has asked for help many times with no support. It can lead to absolute exhaustion and burnout. "A bad system will beat a good person every time" (Edward Deming 1950).

Some of the most destructive wastes hurting people are those associated with waiting and rework. Waiting and constant rework dissolves PWB

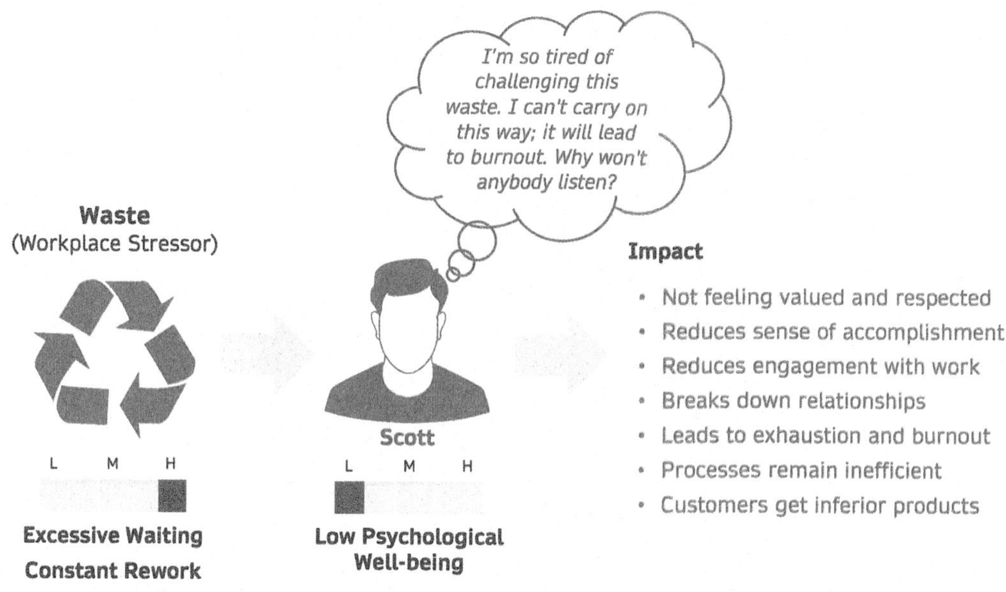

Figure 7.10 Challenging the status quo without feeling heard can reduce PWB.

because it inhibits people from feeling fulfilled at the end of each day's work (Figure 7.10).

It reduces a sense of accomplishment and pulls people out of psychological flow. Individuals must feel empowered to challenge this waste. Systems need to be put in place for people's voices to be heard and feedback to be provided rapidly once waste is identified.

8. Look, Listen, and Learn at the Gemba

The process of going to the place where people do the work (Gemba) to Look, Listen, and Learn is an enabling cog within the improvement system. Experience shows that a small percentage of a leader's time gets allocated for frontline observations, especially senior executives (typically five percent or less). "The Iceberg of Ignorance" (Figure 7.11), a study popularly attributed to consultant Sidney Yoshida, concludes:

> Only 4% of an organization's front-line problems are known by top management, 9% are known by middle management, 74% by supervisors and 100% by individuals executing the process.

So much vital information, required by senior leaders to make informed decisions, gets diluted when communicated up through the hierarchy.

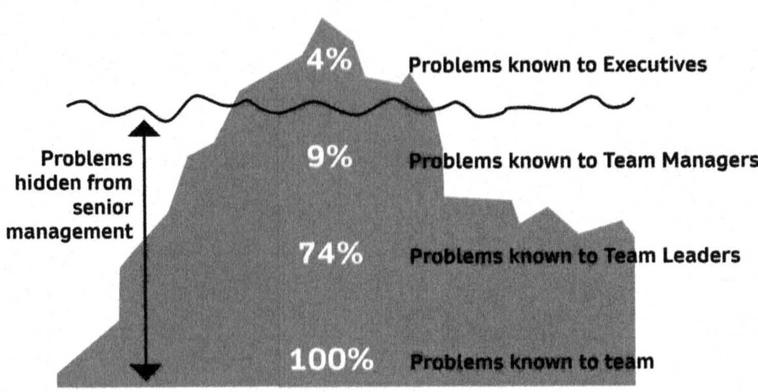

Figure 7.11 The Iceberg of Ignorance.

> It would be naïve to think that some leaders don't subtly conceal results in monthly reports, represent half-truths on PowerPoint presentations and/or memorandums, or cunningly avoid difficult discussions for the sake of self-preservation.
>
> **(Chris Warner, *Flick the Switch*, 2014)**

The result of managing from glass towers and reports is that decisions regarding the workplace can be ill-informed and disconnected from the "real" situation. These decisions destabilize processes and the PWB of people. Leaders scheduling time to regularly go to where the work occurs, to observe reality for themselves, is critical for understanding the facts—the actual workplace condition. Individuals feel honored, valued, and grateful when leaders take the time to come and engage with them at the place they work. It makes them feel like they are important, that their work is important.

Leaders should schedule regular time to:

1. Engage with individuals to determine if they feel safe to challenge the status quo, raise concerns, and acknowledge mistakes freely. Leaders should find out if people are struggling to deal with recurring waste and what help they need to eliminate it.
2. Engage with individuals to determine their state of PWB. Asking questions to see if there are any personal and workplace factors that may be impacting their emotional and cognitive capacity. This includes any

specific psychosocial hazards and what the leader can do to help eliminate and/or control them.

3. Assess the quality of how the psychological health and safety system has been embedded within their workplaces. This could include:
   (a) Integration of any policies relating to PWB.
   (b) Tracking of specific PWB KPIs/KBIs in team routines.
   (c) Tracking and implementation of PWB initiatives.
   (d) Assessing the quality of the controls that have been put in place to manage psychosocial hazards and if any improvements are required to these controls.

Leaders going to the place where people work to Look, Listen, and Learn lifts the spirits of individuals and teams. It is a simple but very effective way for leaders to connect with their people, develop trust, and offer support. Going to the Gemba is one of the best ways for leaders to increase the levels of PWB within others.

9. Develop People through Coaching

Developing people through coaching is an enabling cog within the improvement system. People need to be treated as living, feeling beings versus variable costs. Assets such as machines, equipment, and infrastructure are maintained. They have strategies set for them for regular preventative maintenance. They are cared for as critical resources in creating value for the organization.

If people are an organization's most valuable "resource," then they should be looked after even more than machines. It is humans who design and maintain machines, so why not make sure their PWB is prioritized above all else?

The condition of any individual's emotional, cognitive, behavioral, and social state cannot be maintained merely through one-off training and online tools. It requires regular face-to-face time between a coach and an individual. Leaders need to be coaches but not all coaches are leaders/managers of people.

Coaching can be contrasted with a "command and control" leadership style (Grant 2017). A command-and-control leader is highly directive, decides without consultation, rewards performance, and punishes failure (Wheatley 1997).

Leaders need to be able to see hidden potential within people and draw it out. Leaders who are only interested in short-term results will use people as objects to get actions completed versus sources of creative genius to help them sustainably improve performance over time.

Coaching is a skill that needs to be practiced. It is the art of connecting with another human being on a personal level, considering their unique personal and workplace factors. People need to feel like they are important contributors within the organization. They need to feel that they matter, and that their unique input is valuable and worth developing further. "Workplace coaching is a professional helping relationship, focused on the goals of the individual" (Passmore and Lai 2019).

It is based on reciprocal actions between the two parties.

> Workplace coaching unlocks the potential of the individual. Coaching is a facilitative approach, in which the coach enables future self-directed learning and development.
>
> **(Passmore and Lai 2019)**

Workplace coaching can occur internally, with managers and leaders engaging with individuals in either formal, "sit-down" coaching sessions or informal, "on-the-run" coaching sessions. When coaching occurs internally, it becomes a leadership style.

The GROW (Goal, Reality, Options, What's Next) Model is ideal to help structure formal coaching sessions (Figure 7.12).

The coach helps the coachee define what their goals are for a set period. These can be personal development goals, performance goals, health goals, family relationship goals, career goals, and more. The question to be answered at this initial stage is "What do I want?"

The second step is for the coach to help the coachee determine their current state as it relates to their stated goal. The question that should be answered at this stage is "What is happening?"

The third step is for the coach to help the coachee think through options for closing the gap between the current state and the stated goal. The question to be answered at this stage is "What might I do?"

The final stage of the GROW model is for the coach to help the coachee determine what their way forward is, their immediate next step. The question that should be answered is "What will I do next?"

Coaching is not about telling, and it is not about short-term results. Coaching is the process of developing capability over time. It is a journey of self-reflection and discovery. Coaches help build awareness, empower choice, and lead to change.

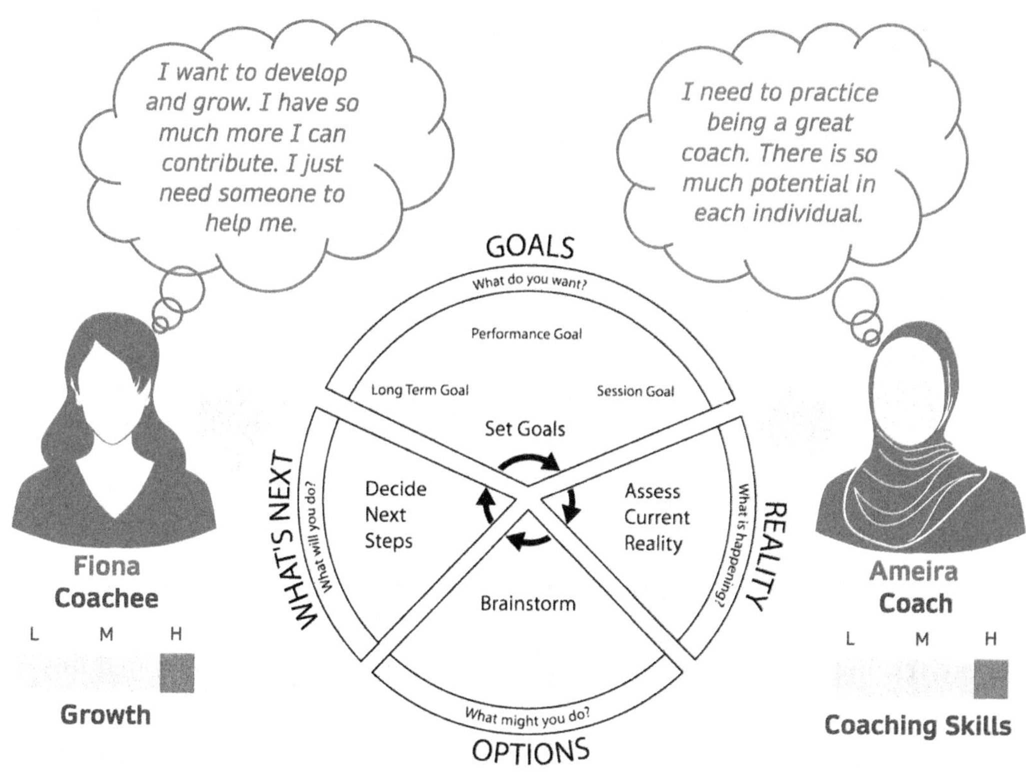

Figure 7.12 The GROW Model.

Three elements of PWB (growth, competence, and accomplishment) are directly impacted by regular coaching. The ability to grow, to improve capabilities and skills, and to accomplish goals can be linked back to the quantity and quality of coaching that an individual receives.

Coaching needs to be prioritized as a non-negotiable right for every person.

> Everyone needs a coach. It does not matter whether you're a basketball player, a tennis player, a gymnast, or a bridge player. We all need people who will give us feedback. That's how we improve.
>
> **(Bill Gates 2013)**

Inadequate professional development and inadequate or poor coaching is a psychosocial hazard. One of the ten elements of PWB is "growth and competence." Individuals need to feel that they are growing their knowledge and skills. It makes them feel valued and an important contributor to the organization. The coach and coachee can use the GROW template to help define and plan development opportunities.

10. Lead Effectively through Leader Standard Work

Leader Standard Work (a structured behavior-focused organization of a leader's time) is an enabling cog within the improvement system. The improvement system is dependent on ideal behaviors to improve, and leaders need to help define and role model these behaviors.

A behavior is something a person can record. It is an action that can be seen or heard. Examples are observing a leader providing encouraging feedback in a performance dialogue, observing leaders speaking to the people doing the work about what their issues are, and observing leaders making sure every individual has a voice in a team meeting.

Leaders prioritize time to role-model these behaviors. This is done by the leaders reflecting on their time allocation and re-aligning it to focus on prioritizing time for those behaviors that will develop their people and mature the improvement system. If behaviors are the lubricant for making the improvement system flow seamlessly, then Leader Standard Work is the mechanism to plan and track these behaviors.

Tools to track the day, week, or month in the life of a leader can be used to plan and track the use of a leader's time. Leaders need to track compliance with these predefined, sacred activities to ensure nothing gets in the way of them leading the culture change required for thriving improvement.

Inappropriate behaviors (psychosocial hazards), on the other hand, can destroy PWB. These include sexual harassment, bullying, low civility or respect, deliberate exclusion, any form of discrimination, work-related violence, and aggression. This includes micro-aggression, which is a term used for commonplace daily verbal, behavioral, or environmental slights, whether intentional or unintentional, that communicate hostile, derogatory, or negative attitudes toward others.

Leaders, therefore, have two responsibilities. Firstly, they need to be deliberate at defining and role-modeling ideal behaviors; and secondly, they need to be deliberate at stamping out behaviors that reduce the safety and PWB of individuals.

Behaviors are not easy to change or introduce, so they need to be clearly defined, deliberately prioritized, and consciously practiced until they become a habit and new workplace norm.

Examples of activities that should be included in a Leader Standard Work:

- Time for developing and cascading the team strategy and operational plan (e.g., purpose, KPIs, improvement initiatives).
- Time for regular communication, context setting, and reaffirming purpose.
- Time for coaching key routines within the improvement system (e.g., team huddles, improvement routines, problem-solving routines, and customer feedback meetings).
- Time to go to the Gemba and engage with individuals and teams to Look, Listen, and Learn the facts for themselves, including recurring issues/wastes people are having to deal with.
- Time to go to the Gemba to assess how well the controls for managing psychosocial hazards are working, including whether they require improvement.
- Time for one-on-one meetings with direct reports to provide help, support, and coaching for personal and workplace development. This should include an assessment of the individual's PWB and career aspirations.

Leader Standard Work helps the leader to not be held hostage by the ebbs and flows of changing organizational priorities. It drives up effectiveness and impact (Figure 7.13).

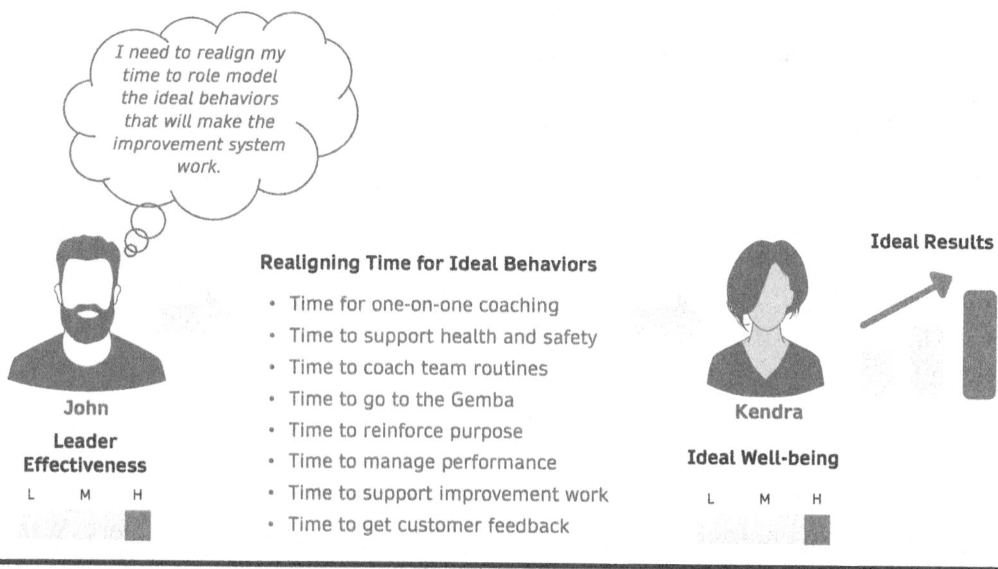

Figure 7.13 Leader Standard Work helps improve PWB and performance outcomes.

11. Foster Diversity, Equity, Inclusion, and Belonging (DEIB)

Fostering diversity, equity, inclusion, and belonging is an enabling cog within the improvement system. DEIB was covered in detail in Chapter 2 and here the focus is on how DEIB relates to the CI system, both the social and the technical elements.

Diversity is about human difference. Difference is essential for ensuring that we have a holistic view of the environment in which we operate and that we understand the voice of all potential customers. Without different perspectives, different mindsets, and different viewpoints, we will be unable to break out of this paradigm.

Equity is about fairness in allocating the required resources and opportunities needed to reach an equal outcome. Fairness is foundational for respect and teamwork. Without allocating the resources needed fairly and providing opportunities to reach an equal outcome, there cannot be equal development of knowledge and skills. Managing capacity and demand requires fairness to ensure equitable distribution of tasks and to allow optimum levels of challenge to enable flow. Without equity, strategy deployment and problem-solving are strangled as favored initiatives and groups thrive while others flounder. We know that psychological safety, the number one factor in determining team effectiveness, is impacted by equity. Psychological safety is not distributed equally by default and equal access to psychological safety must be tailored to meet every individual's needs.

Inclusion is about space and voice, being treated with dignity and respect. Inclusion and respect go hand-in-hand. Without space and voice, you don't have true teamwork—you have dominance and compliance. Inclusion—listening to the voice of the individual and creating a safe space for dissent—are essential for problem-solving, challenging the status quo, and truly listening to the voice of the customer. Without inclusion, you cannot leverage the power of diversity. With inclusion, people feel respected, valued, and that they matter. This has a huge positive impact on every individual's PWB, increases psychological capacity, and strengthens psychological safety.

Belonging is about *feeling* that you belong, and you can show up as your whole self. The opposite of belonging is fitting in. Cognitive dissonance, the mental conflict that occurs when your beliefs don't line up with your actions, saps psychological capacity and damages psychological safety. When consumed with "fitting in" and code-switching to do so, PWB and physical health suffer enormously. When this happens, the vital cognitive energy needed to innovate and continuously improve is lost—strategy deployment, problem-solving, innovation, and capacity versus demand all suffer. When there is no belonging, and no psychological safety, there is no real teamwork, no respect, no humility, no trust, and no challenging of the status quo. In fact, lack of belonging causes suffering—the pain and feelings of disconnection are often as real as physical pain and psychosocial hazards are in abundance.

Fostering DEIB as a key component of the improvement system can create environments where individuals feel respected and that they matter. A DEIB environment has high-trust relationships and is characterized by psychological safety and true teamwork. Here everyone has space, voice, and power. It is an environment of power to and power with. This unleashes huge amounts of PWB and psychological capacity. Here diverse perspectives, mindsets, and approaches are listened to and acted upon. Including DEIB as a key element of CI allows the organization to solve problems faster, to innovate, to respond quickly to the Voice of the Customer and create thriving cultures of CI.

Technical Elements of the Continuous Improvement System

1. Conduct Strategy Development and Deployment

Strategy development and deployment is a delivery cog within the improvement system. The organization should use its annual strategy development process to define its psychological health and safety policy, strategic objectives, targets, and aspirations.

The strategy development process should include the development or review of the organization's psychological health and safety policy, including how it intends to implement and govern the policy. The strategy development process includes guidance on how to integrate the psychological health and safety policy into the organization's improvement system. The strategy needs to be developed in close collaboration with people at all levels within the organization. People need to own the strategy and commit to it at a personal level.

Psychological health and safety KPIs and KBIs need to be defined and operationalized. Strategic improvement initiatives need to be defined and resourced appropriately to improve KPI outcomes. The improvement system needs to be used to manage and improve the psychological health and safety system. Reports should be generated and published across the organization showing the progress being made in embedding the psychological health and safety system.

2. Listen to the Voice of the Customer

Listening to the voice of the customer (VOC) is a delivery cog within the improvement system. People come to work to provide goods and services to customers. Understanding the needs of their customers is important because it provides people with the context they need for how their work adds value to the organization.

The VOC helps provide meaning to work. Meaning gets people out of bed each day. Getting regular feedback from the customer on how work is being performed, against set expectations, helps people to gauge the impact they are having. Everybody wants to have impact, to feel that their work is making a difference. Customer feedback, although sometimes confronting, is an ideal source for evaluating impact, including what the person needs to stop, start, or continue doing.

The VOC is represented as the target lines that individuals/teams need to achieve on their KPIs. These targets should be agreed on between the individual/team and their customer through formal dialogue. Understanding these targets helps people to understand what is most important.

Targets should be challenging and motivate people to relentlessly question the status quo and stretch their creative thinking to solve problems that lead to breakthrough performance. These ambitious targets, although daunting at the start, ignite people's inner need for growth and accomplishment (element of PWB).

Customers and their agreed delivery expectations should be treated as ideal reference points for coaching, learning, and development. Receiving recognition for solving complex problems and closing gaps in performance fills people with confidence and pride (Figure 7.14).

Confidence, in turn, is the key ingredient for the continued disruption of the status quo. The impact of positive customer feedback on an individual work can be significant. When people know that their work is meeting the needs of their customers, it gives them self-assurance that they have the necessary skills to be excellent at what they do. This increases psychological capacity that can be used to keep improving their skills and eliminating waste from their processes. Small, regular gestures, of gratitude, compliments, and appreciation by the leader and/or customer are vital for energizing individuals.

A lack of recognition is a psychosocial hazard. The VOC is an ideal source for finding opportunities to recognize individuals for a job well done.

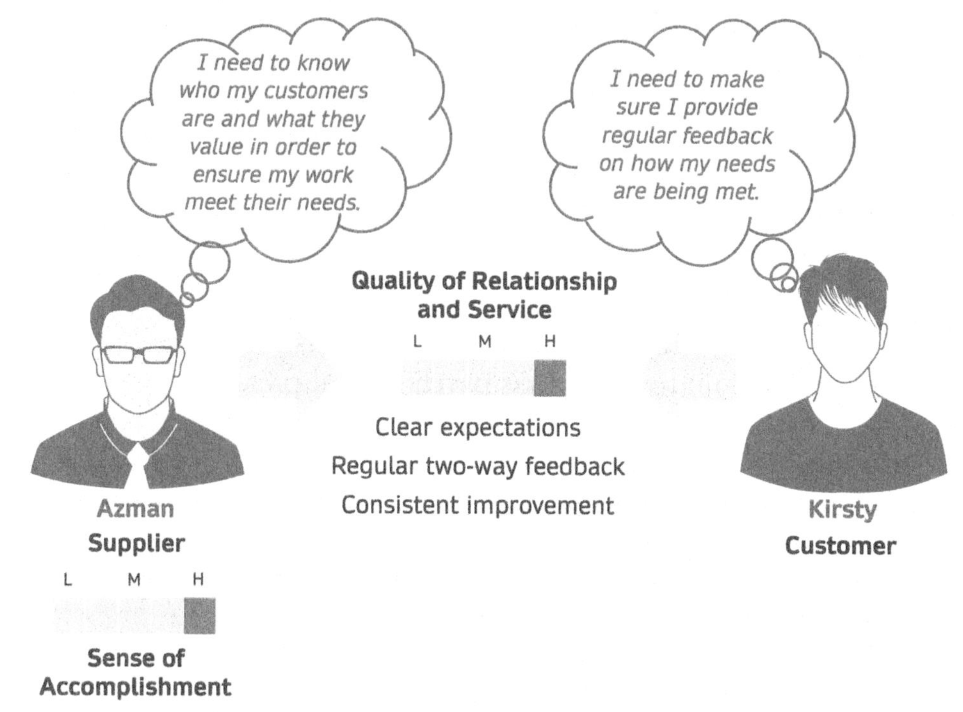

Figure 7.14 Good customer relationships drive up a sense of accomplishment.

Building a trusting and supportive relationship with customers is also an important contributor to positive PWB. When relationships break down between the people executing the work and the people who receive the outcomes of their work, it can be tremendously demoralizing and psychologically draining. Leaders need to help people think through who their customers are. They need to provide coaching on how people can build strong relationships with those they serve.

3. Listen to the Voice of the Process

Listening to the voice of the process (VOP) is a delivery cog within the improvement system. The VOP represents the actual performance of the process against the agreed targets on KPIs.

A process is only as good as its ability to consistently meet the output expected by the customer. This consistency is produced when individuals focus on the means to an outcome and not merely the outcome itself. An over-infatuation with outcomes draws people away from what is most important, understanding the capability of the processes that produce these results. The right process will always produce the right results.

People work within processes that consist of a lot of wasted activity—activity that adds cost but creates no value. This waste demoralizes, frustrates, and exhausts people. Too often, people are blamed for inconsistent results when in fact the process is weak and unable to meet expectations. People are then forced to create workarounds, which further destabilize processes and negatively impact on the customer's experience.

The VOP needs to be visualized. "The worst kind of waste is the waste that cannot be seen" (Shigeo Shingo). Not seeing waste within a process places the individual under enormous psychological pressure.

> We get into a rut of firefighting simply because we have weak, poorly designed processes. This leads to waste blindness, the inability to see evidence of inefficiency within a process. How do we expose waste? By firstly teaching people how to see it and secondly finding ways to destroy it.
>
> **(Chris Warner, *Flick the Switch*, 2014)**

Waste increases work demand. High work demand (a psychosocial hazard) is often the result of poorly designed processes. The additional hours of work required to mitigate process waste take the individual out of psychological flow, which causes frustration, leading to a drop in PWB. It consumes scarce psychological energy, energy that could be better focused on performing the job well and improving it.

Measuring and tracking the VOP through KPIs and waste tracking sheets helps people locate sources of inefficiency within their processes and focus improvements on eliminating waste (Figure 7.15). Eliminating waste increases PWB because people feel more in flow.

Individuals need to feel empowered to own and improve the processes they work with. Low job control is a psychosocial hazard. Individuals need to be empowered to be able to identify the areas within their processes that are wasteful and eliminate them.

In addition, a lack of work procedures on how the process is intended to operate is a psychosocial hazard. Individuals need to be empowered to develop and improve their work standards to reduce ambiguity and frustration. The impact on PWB is just too great to allow weak processes to continue wreaking havoc on people's emotions and cognitive energy.

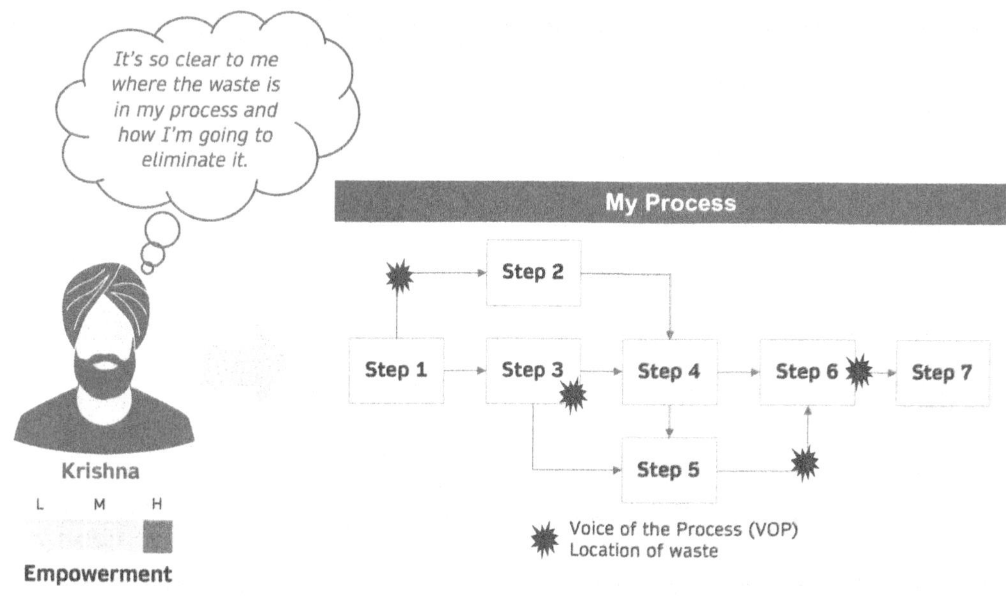

Figure 7.15 The VOP should be visualized, and individuals empowered to eliminate waste.

4. Focus on Horizontal Value Streams

Focusing on value streams is a delivery cog within the improvement system. A value stream represents cross-functional business processes that include multiple groups of people. These people are located within different departments with their own vertical reporting lines, accountabilities, and KPIs.

Horizontal value streams enable and deliver the value for sale to customers. They represent the revenue streams for the organization, including the processes to proactively manage the external environment.

These value streams cannot function effectively without horizontal social and technical integration. People need to be brought together behind one unifying purpose with commitment to common objectives.

This commitment needs to be role-modeled by leaders in their language and behaviors. They need to encourage their people to spend time developing trusting and supportive cross-functional relationships (Figure 7.16).

> Unfortunately, many organizations are not structured to promote value stream thinking. Relationships between independent departments are not linked, causing isolated pools of performance to exist that only benefit the privileged few surrounding that watering

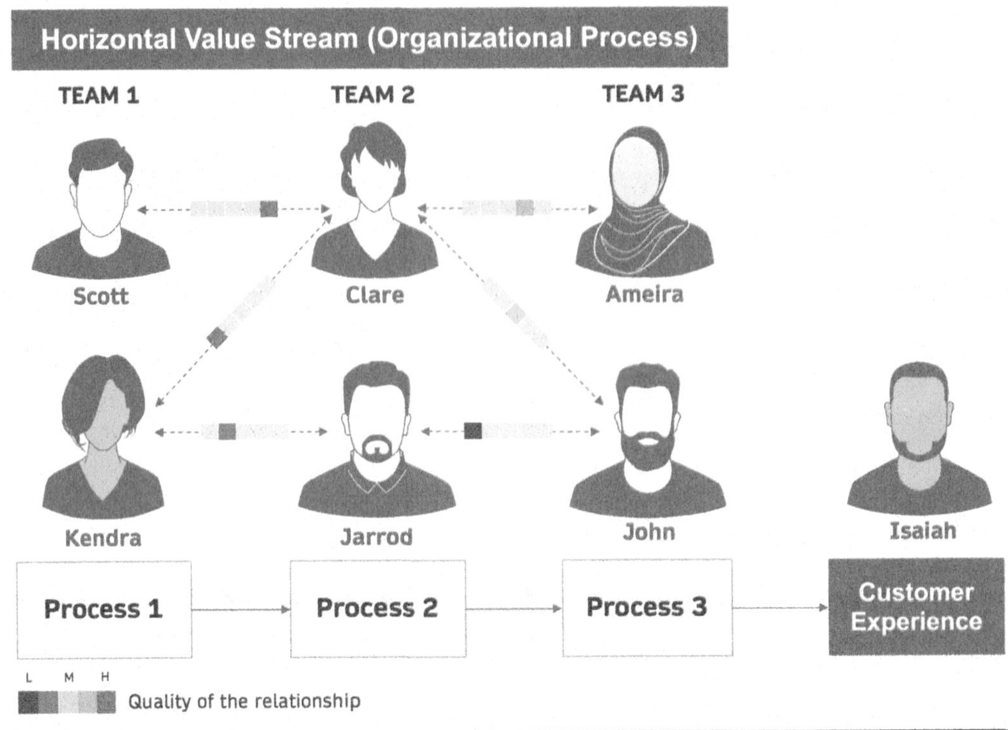

Figure 7.16 Strong horizontal relationships help improve value stream performance.

> hole. For a value stream to flow, relationships and process activities need to be linked, designed in such a way as to benefit the whole and not merely components of the supply chain.
>
> **(Chris Warner, *Flick the Switch*, 2014)**

The stress that is caused by prolonged exposure to poor horizontal engagement can cripple PWB. Feeling included, valued, and respected for who you are and for your unique contributions within the extended value stream is vital for ensuring positive PWB.

Poor interpersonal relationships are a psychosocial hazard. This can include a breakdown in relationships due to horizontal bullying, aggressive behaviors, discrimination, and lack of fairness and equity in dealing with issues, spreading falsehoods about people, an unwillingness to compromise on important decisions, a lack of integrity, poor communication amongst groups, micromanagement, siloed behaviors, and hidden agendas.

All these factors drastically inhibit the organization embedding a horizontal mindset. If value streams performance is the key to breakthrough results, then quality cross functional relationships is the glue that holds it all together. The value stream is only as strong as its weakest social link.

Value stream performance requires:

- The rapid creation and dissolving of groups of people (teaming) that have the unique skills required to solve complex value stream problems.
- Unity and commitment to common value stream objectives and singular purpose.
- An atmosphere where every individual can freely challenge the status quo outside of their team's boundaries.
- The obligation of respectful dissent is stated as a requirement and critical input for improving the value stream.
- An atmosphere where people feel free to take calculated risks and don't fear failure.
- An atmosphere of active listening and respect for every idea raised.
- An atmosphere of frankness, openness, and honesty. The facts need to be exposed without people getting defensive.
- Regular recognition of behaviors that promote cross-functional teamwork.

5. Standard Work and Ensuring Quality

Standard work and ensuring quality are delivery cogs within the improvement system. Standard work defines how to do the job, the expected inputs and outputs, and the targets agreed on with the customer. It ensures that individuals have the necessary training, coaching, and documented guidance on how to perform their work well. Standards include the specific quality requirements agreed on between the individual/team and their customer.

People cannot be expected to consistently perform their work, to customer expectations, without any guidance on how to do so. Throwing people into the deep end and asking them to figure out how to do the job, with no guidance on how to do so, is workplace abuse.

The lack of work procedures is a psychosocial hazard. The impact on PWB is severe. Individuals wanting to do a good job but not having the resources to do so can be soul-destroying and trigger severe workplace stress.

Work standards provide a level of certainty that allows people to perform their work in a stable and consistent manner. Standards ensure that expectations (time, quality, safety, and cost) are clearly agreed to with the customer and documented, which reduces confusion and ambiguity for the individual. It provides certainty, which allows the individual to be in psychological flow much easier and more often.

Standards are foundational to positive PWB. Knowing what is expected of them, allows individuals to focus on consistently meeting this requirement rather than constantly worrying about whether it is good enough. Standards bring a level of predictability within the individual's work that ensures they can come to work with clarity on what good looks like. This reduces stress. Understanding what is expected allows the individual to focus their energy on doing their job well. It also provides the individual with a reference point against which improving the standard can be made.

The people doing the work must be involved in the design of the standards that will be used to determine the quality of their work. Why? Because they are the true experts of the work they do. Having someone else constantly telling them what they should and should not do is disrespectful and disempowering. Autonomy is an important element of PWB that provides people with the freedom to own their work.

Low job control is regarded as a psychosocial hazard. Not being able to influence the standards with which individuals do their work, including the inability to make decisions about how their work is done, is disempowering. Job control can include control over work tasks, the work environment, where work is done, how it is done, the pace of work, and the ability to work with minimal supervision. It includes the opportunity to participate in decision-making about issues that affect the person's work.

A lack of standard work also leads to role ambiguity (a psychosocial hazard). This is the result of a lack of clarity or uncertainty about role requirements and responsibilities, or a lack of information about a role or task (Figure 7.17).

Constantly changing requirements, objectives, and responsibilities can also cause role ambiguity. This can lead to confusion about what work people should be doing, which can significantly impact PWB.

People draw energy from consistently achieving great results from their work. They go home feeling a sense of accomplishment. The organization needs to enable this outcome by ensuring that individuals are involved in defining how their work is performed and improved.

6. Embed Continuous Improvement

CI is a delivery cog within the improvement system. It is the turbo booster of the improvement system. Without CI, people and the organization do not

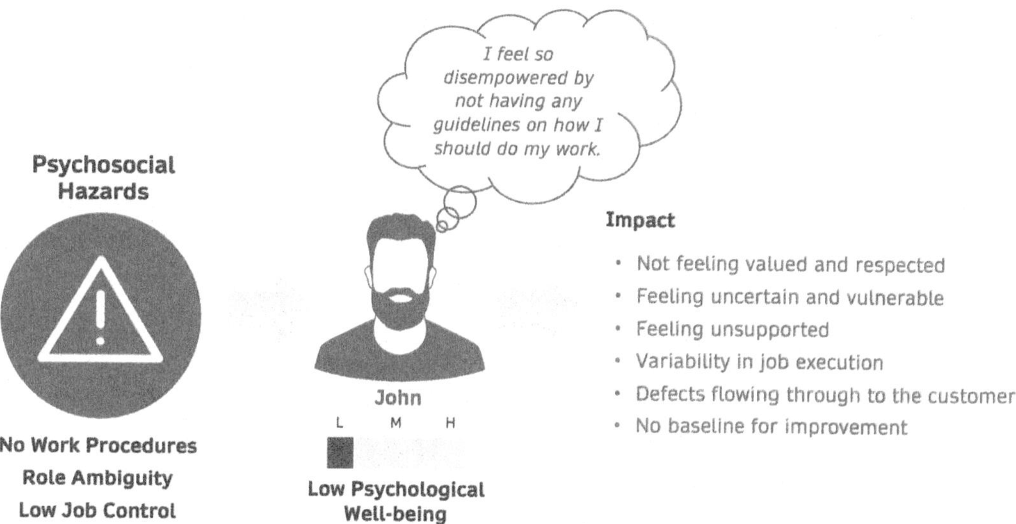

Figure 7.17 A lack of standard work can impact PWB and performance outcomes.

thrive. The definition of the term "continuous improvement" needs to be broadened to remain relevant for a knowledge-based economy.

Creating a thriving culture of CI will not occur if improvement is relegated to a few specialists (for example, six sigma/Lean coaches, reliability engineers, analysts, or technology specialists). Improvement should never be restricted to some people improving some processes every now and then. The knowledge, experience, and skills, however valuable, of this small group of improvement professionals are highly inadequate for managing the vast array of internal and external challenges being faced by the modern organization.

There is too much volatility, uncertainty, complexity, and ambiguity (VUCA) in the world for organizations to not value and leverage all knowledge and skills available for use. Every person within the organization needs to see themselves as having two jobs: their day job and improving their day job (Figure 7.18).

Improvement needs to be treated as equal to everybody's day job (work equals improving work) versus a nice-to-have or an addition to work.

Prerequisites for ensuring everybody owns improvement:

- It needs to be stated as an expectation.
- People need to be told that they are the true experts of their work, acknowledged, and respected for understanding the facts about what works and does not work.

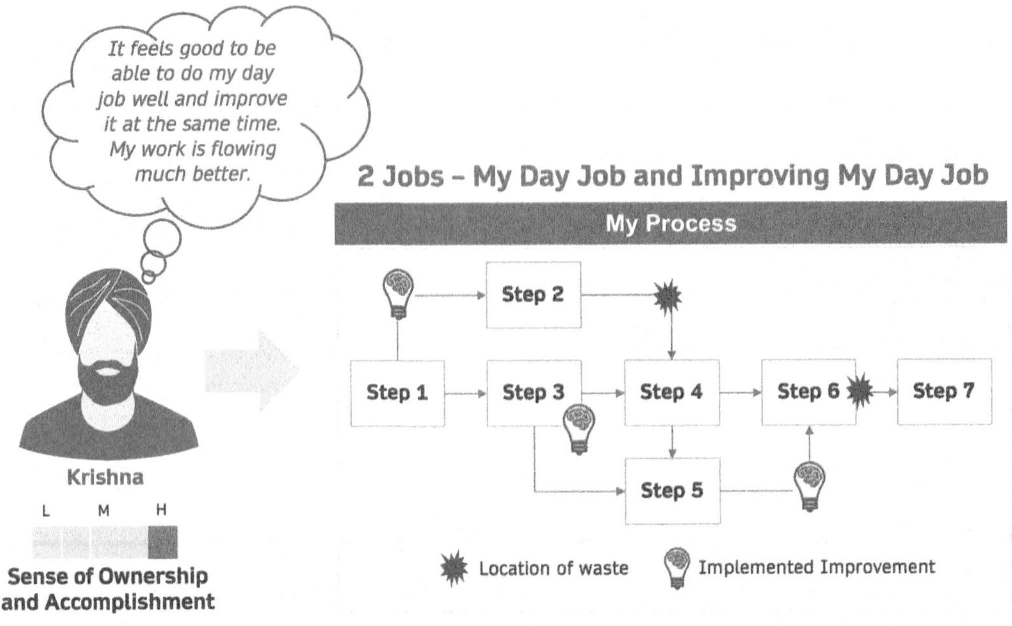

Figure 7.18 Every individual should own improvement and be recognized for it.

- People need to be given the authority to implement micro improvements to their work without having to ask permission, trusted to make good decisions. Micro improvements are small improvements that rarely affect the standard. The boundaries of these improvements are determined by each individual's experience, position, and capabilities.
- No improvement idea should be judged or trivialized, especially if it originated from those doing the work. Utmost respect should be given to every idea that is sourced by those executing work.
- Ideas need to be treated with respect and not discarded because another person or leader disagrees with them. The impact on knowledge flow will be reduced if people feel that their ideas for improvement are constantly dismissed.
- The focus should be on increasing engagement with people and creating ownership for improvement before rushing in to determine just how much value each idea is producing. The goal is to make improvement part of people's everyday work. Once this has been done, then leaders can help people focus their ideas on those areas within their process that have the most waste.
- Recognize an improvement mindset often. Look for examples of where idea implementation has made an impact on culture, health, safety, or productivity. Make it a big deal and celebrate this ideal behavior.

7. Develop Structured Problem-Solving

Problem-solving is a delivery cog within the improvement system. Structured problem-solving is a learned skill and is a critical capability to meet the needs of the knowledge economy. The rate at which unknown events are converted into known root causes and solutions has become a competitive differentiator.

The increase in VUCA requires a parallel increase in problem-solving skills. Many organizations are so consumed by firefighting because of weak processes and disconnected value streams that they do not prioritize time to develop structured problem-solving skills. The focus is more on forcing through results at any cost to ensure that short-term commitments are met.

Developing problem-solving skills requires a long-term mindset. Coaching individuals and teams to become great at problem-solving requires time to achieve and tremendous perseverance.

For some leaders, this time is better served forcing through results while in tenure to build a reputation. The consequence is that problems persist year in and year out. Constantly firefighting systemic problems becomes an embedded norm within the workplace.

Individuals who can be relied on to quickly subdue or resolve these issues are recognized and promoted. They become famous for their ability to conceive workarounds for shoddy processes. In many cases, they are promoted because of their firefighting abilities. The result is nothing changes. Systems and processes remain weak, wreaking havoc on the PWB of people who use them. Frustration increases, morale reduces, and fatigue sets in.

Growth, competence, and accomplishment are three elements of PWB. Problem-solving enables all three. It allows people to grow by teaching them a structured approach to identify root causes. It helps them learn how to collaborate with others in solving complex organizational issues. It allows them to develop and apply their knowledge, skills, and abilities. People feel they are having an impact (Figure 7.19).

The fulfillment of seeing solutions work can be very motivating. Weak processes require a lot of firefighting. It drains valuable psychological capacity that can be better used for problem-solving. People end up working longer hours to get the job completed. This creates fatigue which leads to errors. Errors, in worst cases, can lead to fatalities.

Problem-solving requires emotional, cognitive, behavioral, and social energy. It requires all available knowledge and experience to be made

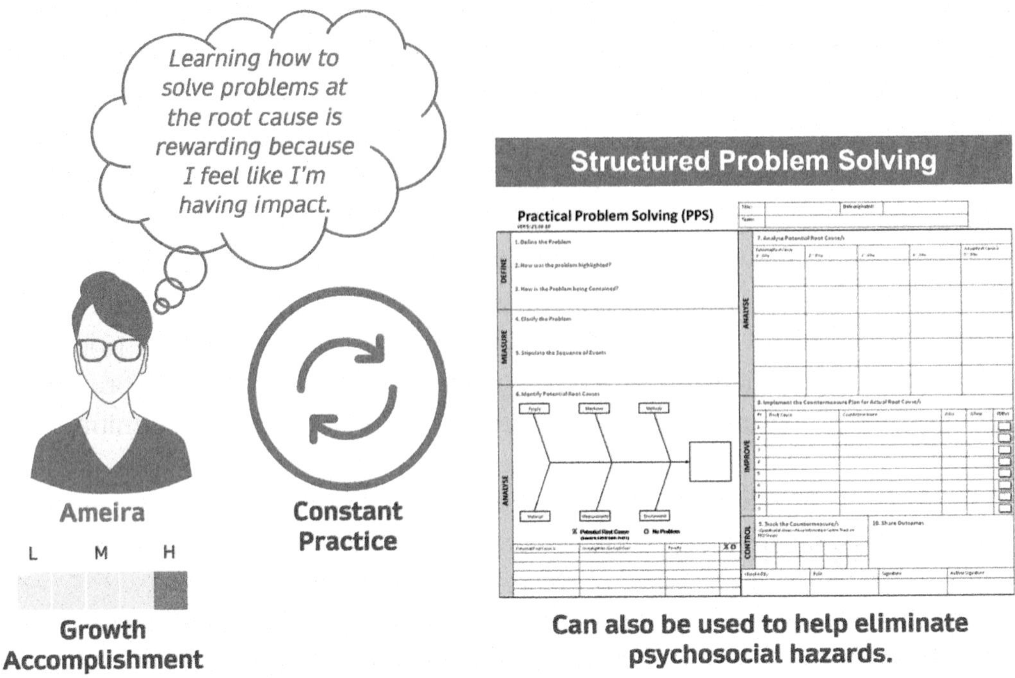

Figure 7.19 Developing problem-solving skills helps improve PWB and performance.

available for use. It requires focus and psychological flow. People are more able to apply their expertise toward problem-solving when they work in an environment that is psychologically safe. Solutions for problems emerge from robust dialogue, candor, and the confidence to challenge the most entrenched beliefs and systems.

Problem-solving skills are especially helpful when trying to eliminate and/or control the many psychosocial hazards within the workplace. Containments (immediate actions) can be put in place quickly to prevent or stop individuals from experiencing psychological harm.

Structured problem-solving activities can then be triggered to understand the root cause of these hazards and countermeasures (permanent solutions) implemented to ensure they are eliminated and/or controlled. Problem-solving can also be used to ensure controls remain robust. Periodic assessments of controls could indicate that they are inadequate at preventing harm.

Problem-solving skills are therefore extremely valuable for not only driving up performance but also developing the skills of individuals and managing psychosocial hazards.

8. Manage Visually

Managing visually is a delivery cog within the improvement system. The key to growing an organization is ensuring that every individual is empowered to take responsibility for their work. Individuals at all levels should understand their role in helping to meet the targets and aspirations of their team and the organization. They should have the autonomy (element of PWB) to make decisions about how their work is performed and improved.

There should be no ambiguity about what is expected by their customers in terms of the time, quality, and cost of their products and/or services. The voice of the customer needs to be explicitly known and visualized for everybody to see. The voice of the process (actual daily performance) needs to be tracked and visualized against these customer expectations (target lines on KPIs).

Good visual management allows every individual to have the information they need at the point of use. It enables them to see how the team is performing at any time, which allows more time for good decision making.

People are taught how to apply the 1–3–10 principle: take one second to know whether you are winning or losing, three seconds to identify what you are winning or losing at, and ten seconds to determine your course of action.

The 1–3–10 principle is particularly important during team huddles (meetings to assess team performance). The team can very quickly determine, based on effective visualization of their KPIs, what actions need to be taken to improve results. Visual management helps the team to see together, know together, and act together (Figure 7.20).

Visual management supports various elements of PWB. It ensures that every individual is clear on what the team's purpose is and their role in fulfilling it. It highlights areas for personal growth and skills development. It brings people together around common goals, fostering inclusion and belonging. It highlights what is most important for the team to focus on, increasing engagement and psychological flow. It also provides individuals and teams with a sense of accomplishment when achieving their targets and objectives.

Team huddles are ideal for visualizing psychological health and safety KPIs, implementing improvements for eliminating or controlling psychosocial hazards, and scheduling assessments of whether controls for hazards are working.

9. Develop and Use Knowledge and Skills

Developing and using knowledge and skills is a delivery cog within the improvement system. A thriving culture of improvement is dependent on a

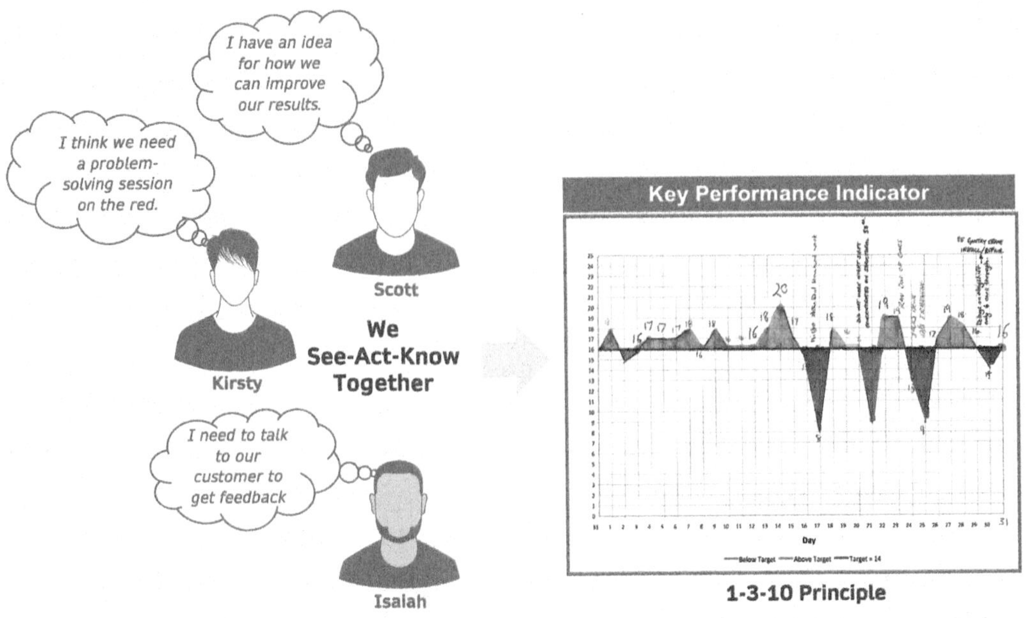

Figure 7.20 Visual management helps the team to see together, know together, and act together.

thriving system for developing the knowledge and skills of every person in the organization.

If people are treated as assets, then they need to be looked after and constantly developed, otherwise the skills of today will not be the skills needed to thrive tomorrow. Organizations need to be clear on what knowledge and skills will be required to meet and exceed internal targets, as well as effectively manage external change. They need to embed capability development systems that can transition skills rapidly. These skills then need to be put to full use to help the organization prosper.

These systems should not merely include one-off training but should be followed up by on-the-job coaching. Individuals should not be expected to perform their work to standard without clarity on the skills required to do so. Poor or inadequate coaching is a psychosocial hazard that can increase workplace stress because people's current skills cannot meet the demands of their jobs.

The job-specific technical and social skills and associated development plans to achieve these skills need to be agreed to by every individual. These should be discussed in one-on-one meetings between the individual and their leader. The leader should support the individual to achieve their development goals by ensuring they are exposed to suitable work activities.

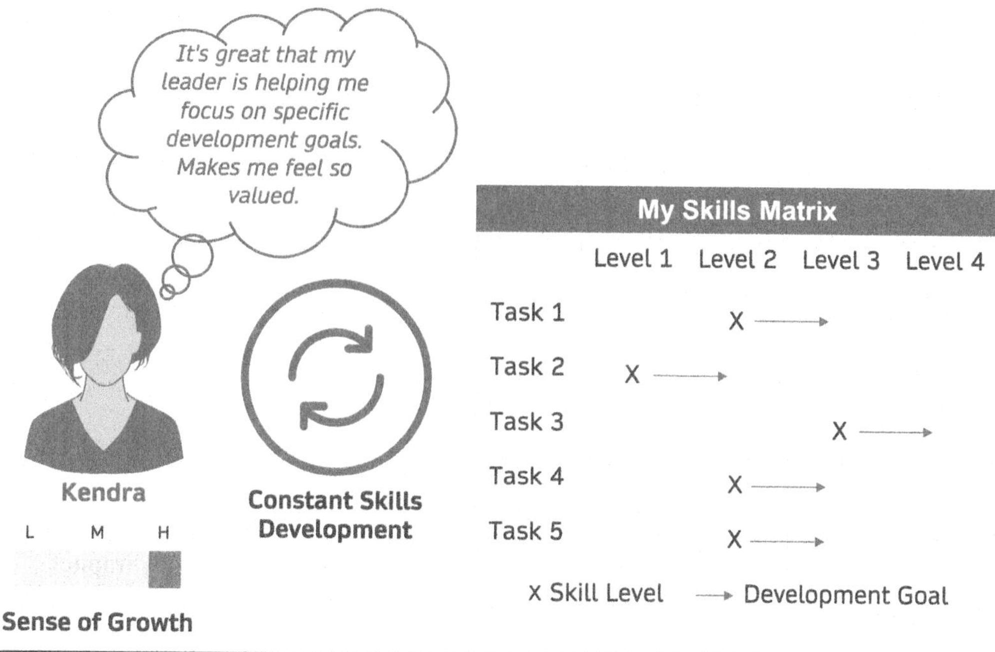

Figure 7.21 **Skills development increases an individual's sense of growth.**

Applying new skills and seeing the positive outcomes in performance makes people feel good about themselves. It increases their positive feeling of personal growth, competence, and accomplishment (Figure 7.21). All of these are important elements of PWB.

10. Manage Capacity and Demand

Managing capacity and demand is a delivery cog within the improvement system. Teams need to regularly assess the relationship between what is expected as an outcome of their work (demand) and the capacity (skills, time, resources) they have available to consistently produce this outcome (capacity). Overburden occurs when the demand on the individual regularly exceeds their capacity to produce this demand (Figure 7.22).

Demand is constantly changing, especially in recent times. VUCA is exacerbating demand peaks and troughs. This, in turn, is making it more difficult for teams to predict the workload heading their way. Uncontrolled demand fluctuations can cause job overload (a psychosocial hazard). Job overload occurs when people feel stress and pressure due to excessive work demands, including high workloads, deadlines that are difficult to meet, and problems meeting unreasonable workplace expectations and objectives.

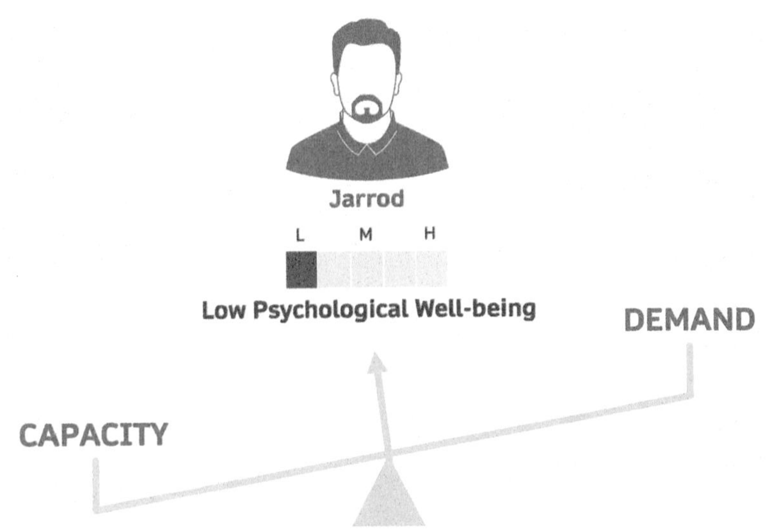

Figure 7.22 An imbalance between capacity and demand can negatively impact PWB.

People who have their psychological capacity fully consumed, without time to reflect and improve, will inevitably get weighed down by the pressure. This will negatively impact their PWB and potentially lead to fatigue, burnout, anxiety, and depression.

Managing capacity and demand is a moral and economic imperative. People cannot be expected to be pushed beyond their physical and psychological limits to achieve performance outcomes they have not been adequately resourced to achieve. The workplace needs to be resourced with the appropriate systems and tools to help people predict demand as much as is reasonably possible. Routines need to be put in place to manage capacity and demand and implement actions to close gaps.

11. Create Workplace Organization

Creating workplace organization is a delivery cog within the improvement system. The work environment, including how the workplace is laid out, can have a direct impact on physical and PWB.

The ergonomics of the workplace—the location of equipment, tooling, and parts to perform the work—need to enable well-being. Individuals want to come to work to do a good job. If the work environment is disorganized, hazardous, or not well designed, it can increase workplace stress.

If people see that the organization is not prioritizing improving the condition of their workplace, they will become despondent and feel devalued and disrespected.

The design, maintenance, and improvement of the workplace goes a long way to show people that they are cared for. People thrive when they believe that the organization cares about their workplace and well-being.

The same is true for people who perform transactional work. Instead of focusing just on the physical design of a workplace, the focus should also be on digital organization. This includes the design, location, and availability of technology systems (digital tools, data sets, and work folders). The frustration caused by not having digital resources available can be as severe as those in a physical location.

The purpose of work organization is to enable work processes to flow. The goal is to design the job and locate resources to execute work in such a way that the person can get into psychological flow as quickly and as often as possible. Psychological flow, or being "in the zone," and being totally consumed by the work at hand helps people to feel they have achieved something at the end of each day. It drives up a sense of accomplishment—an important element of PWB (Figure 7.23).

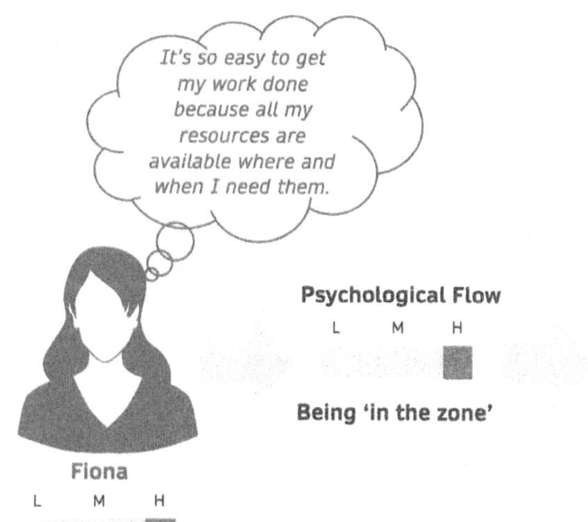

Psychological Flow

L M H

Being 'in the zone'

Impact of Workplace Organization

- I feel valued because I have been provided with what I need
- I don't need to look for things to do my job
- I feel fulfilled after a day's work because my work flowed
- I don't feel frustrated when doing my job, its seamless

Figure 7.23 Workplace organization helps people stay in psychological flow.

The Improvement System Can Be Used to Implement the PH&S System

The improvement system can play an important role in helping the organization develop and deploy its PH&S policy, strategy, KPIs, KBIs, improvement initiatives, risk management process, risk registers, Leader Standard Work, and operating standard.

The improvement system can also be used for PH&S problem-solving, standards development, control verification, Gemba walks, and annual strategy deployment.

KPIs and KBIs can be visualized in team performance boards (visual management boards) and discussed in team meetings (huddles). Any gaps to target can then be closed using structured problem-solving.

PH&S improvement initiatives can be tracked and implemented through improvement routines.

Leaders can lock in time in their Leader Standard Work to see how these KPIs, KBIs, problem-solving, and improvement initiatives are progressing and provide coaching where required.

PH&S standards can be developed, and people coached on how to use them.

The improvement system represents the ideal mechanism for operationalizing the strategic objectives of the PH&S policy and strategy.

The Improvement System Elements Can Be Mapped to Specific Psychosocial Hazards

Social and technical elements of the improvement system have been mapped against specific psychosocial hazards. In some cases, the elements will eliminate the hazard and in other cases they won't. The intent of the mapping exercise is to show which elements can be linked to which hazards. In doing so the organization can leverage their improvement system to strategically focus on specific hazards. As the improvement system matures, then so should the management of psychosocial hazards also improve. The 11 social elements (Table 7.2) and 11 technical elements (Table 7.3) each contribute uniquely to help the organization think through and manage psychosocial hazards within the workplace.

Table 7.2 Social Elements and Psychosocial Hazards

#	*Social Elements*	*Psychosocial Hazards*
1	Lead with purpose	• Poor organizational culture and practices • Poor organizational change management
2	Lead with humility	• Poor leadership behaviors and role-modeling • Poor leadership style (e.g., abuse of power, command and control) • Inadequate praise, recognition, and reward
3	Develop trust	• Poor levels of trust • Lack of fairness and inconsistent/poor decision making • Poor leadership communication (lack of and/or withholding information) • Poor organizational justice and fairness
4	Show respect for every Individual	• Poor organizational communication • Bullying, victimization, harassment, and/or work-related violence and/or aggression • Poor interpersonal relationships • Low civility and respect • Low job security and/or precarious work • Remote and/or isolated work
5	Listen to the Voice of the Individual (VOI)	• Low job control and/or autonomy
6	Cultivate teamwork	• Poor co-worker support • Lack of inclusion & belonging
7	Relentlessly challenge the status quo	• Low job control and/or autonomy
8	Look, Listen, and Learn at the Gemba	• Poor leadership engagement and/or presence
9	Develop people through coaching	• Poor or inadequate coaching • Inadequate professional development • Inadequate praise, recognition and reward
10	Lead effectively through Leader Standard Work	• Inadequate leadership support (e.g., no one-on-one routines) • Poor leadership behaviors and role-modeling • Poor leadership style (e.g., abuse of power, command and control) • Poor leadership communication (lack of and/or withholding information)
11	Foster Diversity, Equity, Inclusion, and Belonging (DEIB)	• Poor interpersonal relationships • Poor co-worker support • Lack of inclusion & belonging • Discrimination (e.g., race, gender, sexual orientation, religion)

Table 7.3 Technical Elements and Psychosocial Hazards

#	*Technical Elements*	*Psychosocial Hazards*
1	Conduct strategy development and deployment	• Poor organizational culture and practices • Poor organizational change management • Poor organizational communication • Poor leadership communication (lack of and/or withholding information)
2	Listen to the Voice of the Customer (VOC)	• High job demand (overload)
3	Listen to the Voice of the Process (VOP)	• High job demand (overload)
4	Focus on horizontal value streams	• Poor levels of trust
5	Standardize work and ensure quality	• No policies and/or procedures (inconsistent application) • Low role clarity
6	Embed continuous improvement	• Low job control and/or autonomy • No policies and/or procedures (inconsistent application) • High job demand (overload) • Poor working conditions (e.g., lack of space, lighting, noise) • Inadequate resources to perform the job (e.g., equipment, systems, data) • Unrealistic expectations of competency
7	Develop structured problem solving	• Low job control and/or autonomy
8	Manage visually	• Low job control and/or autonomy • Poor leadership engagement and/or presence
9	Develop and use knowledge and skills	• Unrealistic expectations of competency
10	Manage capacity and demand	• High job demand (overload) • Low job demand (unfulfilling work) • Lack of work flexibility
11	Create workplace organization (5S)	• Poor working conditions (e.g., lack of space, lighting, noise) • Inadequate resources to perform the job (e.g., equipment, systems, data) • Working in extreme conditions

Key Points from Chapter 7

- The improvement system needs to leverage the optimum psychological capacity of every individual. Psychological capacity can only increase with a deliberate focus on every individual's PWB.
- The ability of the improvement system to leverage psychological capacity is dependent on ideal behaviors. Ideal behaviors ensure the social and technical elements of the improvement system flow seamlessly as a self-reinforcing mechanism to create a thriving culture of CI.
- The improvement system can be used as a mechanism for implementing the organization's PH&S system. This includes eliminating and/or controlling, so far as is reasonably possible, psychosocial hazards from causing harm.

Chapter 8

Why Care about the Thriving Organization?

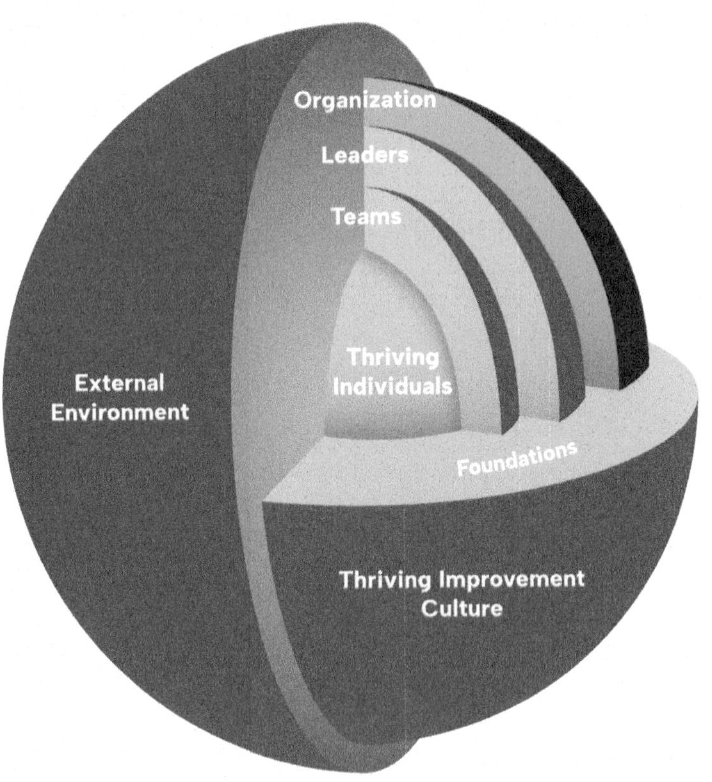

Figure 8.0 The Why Care Model—Organization.

DOI: 10.4324/9781003413479-9

Introduction

As we touched on in the Introduction, with the advent of the Fourth Industrial Revolution (sometimes referred to as Industry 4.0) we are entering an ever-accelerating pace of change.

The situation was summarized by Canadian Prime Minister Justin Trudeau in 2018 at the World Economic Forum at Davos. Here is a longer extract from his speech.

> I was last here at the World Economic Forum in 2016, two months after being sworn in as Prime Minister. And while that might not seem like very long ago, in this new era of perpetual change that we're living in, two years might as well be a lifetime.
>
> Think about it: The pace of change has never been this fast, yet it will never be this slow again.
>
> There's enormous opportunity, and enormous potential, in that realization.
>
> Technology has always brought such promise—a better standard of living, new innovations, remarkable products. Consider that progression from steam power, to electricity, to computers. But it also brings dramatic shifts in our social, economic, and political cultures.
>
> This current step, involving automation and AI, as the obvious examples, will totally revolutionize the world of work—in many ways, they already have.
>
> **(Transcript from the World Economic Forum 2018)**

This was two years before the world was rocked by the COVID-19 pandemic, and since then the global explosion in volatility, uncertainty, complexity, and ambiguity (VUCA), as well as the pace and complexity of work, have continued to accelerate.

As we discussed in Chapter 4, to respond effectively, organizations need to develop ways to engage their workforce in helping to deal with this challenge. Unfortunately, what we are seeing instead is an increase in workplace stress and absenteeism across the globe with "an estimated 12 billion workdays are lost annually due to depression and anxiety costing the global economy nearly US$ 1 trillion" (*World Mental Health Report* 2022). So at a time when organizations need to maximize the intellectual capacity of their people to come up with innovative ways to improve, increasing numbers of people are not able to contribute due to issues related to psychological well-being (PWB).

As we discussed in Chapter 4, thriving improvement is the outcome of every individual in the organization having enough psychological capacity to do their job well and to improve it at the same time. This energy needs to be created and maintained. It is not limitless. It fluctuates, based on the many events and circumstances that people face daily. Thriving individuals think, feel, and behave in a manner that enables them to perform effectively at work, in their personal lives, and in society at large.

Unfortunately, as we have illustrated in previous chapters, many individuals are not thriving at work, and consequently, many organizations are struggling to thrive. In 2020, Deloitte found that "Considering all the available evidence, there is more that employers can do to support their staff. In particular, there is scope for more investment around tackling stigma, increasing awareness of mental health issues, and providing adequate training for employees."

Their survey also highlighted that "1 in 4 employers fear the negative consequences if they make their mental health issues formal" and that only "44 % of respondents said they would feel comfortable talking to a line manager about their mental health" (*Mental health and employers: Refreshing the case for investment*, Deloitte 2020).

Two years later in 2022, CCLA found that whilst "Nine in 10 companies recognize workplace mental health as an important business concern, yet less than half have formalized their commitments to mental health in a policy statement" (*CCLA Corporate Mental Health Benchmark Global 100 Report* 2022).

More recently, in 2023, the American Psychological Association (*Work in America* survey) found that whilst there were "some positive" developments in the workplace—such as "77% of workers reported being very (36%) or somewhat (41%) satisfied with the support for mental health and well-being they receive from their employers"—that "improvements were still needed." Interestingly, 55% of workers surveyed expressed the view that their employer "thinks the workplace environment is a lot mentally healthier than it is."

The report goes on to state that "for employers, a failure to provide the mental health and well-being support that workers are seeking could harm talent recruitment and retention." Among workers overall, 33% said they intend to look for a new job at a different company or organization in the next year. Among those workers who said they were unsatisfied with the mental health and well-being support offered by their employer, that number rose to 57%.

Whilst some progress appears to be being made, there is still a great deal to do.

We have discussed that the inside-out approach—starting with the individual, supported by the team, and coached by their leaders—is essential to creating and embedding a culture of care that enables continuous improvement (CI). This, however, will not happen unless there is a whole-of-organization approach to ensuring that policies, systems, and performance measures (KPIs and KBIs) are implemented and proactively managed. This requires the organization to establish and proactively manage policies and systems that proactively support PWB and CI. There is a need to ensure that these policies and systems are integrated and mutually supportive for individuals and the organization to thrive.

In his 1978 book *Gods of Management*, Charles Handy put forward the theory that organizations mainly have one of four types of culture, which are very broadly summarized below:

1. Club culture, built on power and connections.
2. Role culture, built on hierarchy and bureaucracy.
3. Task culture, built on people's ability to solve problems and deliver results.
4. Existentialist culture, built on the shared understanding that the organization exists to help people achieve their higher purpose.

The existential culture has often been put forward as most relevant for organizations that depend on the skills of experts; for example, legal practices or accountancy partnerships. Today, we are in a very different world to the one Handy was writing about almost 50 years ago and yet we can still recognize these broad cultures in many organizations. The authors' view is that in today's environment, to achieve a thriving culture of CI that delivers a thriving organization, many of the characteristics of Handy's theory of "existentialist culture" need to be applied to every type of organization at every level. To be successful in the long term, organizations need their people to thrive.

Hines et al. (2023) identify three stages of maturity in organizational culture, specifically in relation to physical and mental well-being. In Chapter 7, we explored the different types of leadership seen at each of these stages. Below, we reproduce some of the characteristics of organizations at each stage from this work. Stage 3 organizations' characteristics are very aligned with an existential culture.

Stage 1: Traditional Approach

In Stage 1 organizations, the approach is typically based on the application of minimum standards, where activities are primarily undertaken by specialists from functions—such as Safety, Health, and Environment—to comply with legislation.

Hafey (2015, p. 13) notes:

> Leaders focus on safety because it is the right thing to do or because they are forced to focus by an external influence such as OSHA global business demands, their customers, or serious injuries or deaths that occur in the company.

Here, we are therefore often dealing with failure management borrowing from the classic Prevention, Appraisal, Failure "Cost of Quality" thinking (Keogh and Dalrymple 1995).

This is usually based on lag measures, such as the number of accidents or percentage absentee rate. There is typically little involvement of local individuals, with activities "pushed" onto them. This approach "relies upon fear and intimidation to help ensure compliance" (Hafey 2015, p. xiii).

Stage 2: Classic Lean Organizations

In Stage 2 organizations, activities are either undertaken by specialists or leaders and tend to be periodic or event-based, such as a monthly safety walk or annual health check. Here, there is a move beyond mere compliance toward appraisal management, although activities still tend to be "pushed" onto individuals—such as employee risk assessments, ergonomic assessments, or safety walks—often through an event or short-term project approach dislocated from the general management system (Yazdani et al. 2018; Oakman et al. 2019). This is usually based on lead measures, such as the number of near misses, the number of safety walks undertaken, or the percentage of physical (and sometimes mental) health first aiders. Winkel et al. (2021) have suggested that occupational musculoskeletal and mental disorders cannot be properly reduced by this kind of approach.

The organization has started to evolve and pockets of the population, such as managers and experts, have been empowered. As a result, there is a disparity in levels of equality, trust, and psychological safety, meaning that many in the wider workforce do not feel an alignment between their personal values and the organization's.

Stage 3: People Value Stream

In Stage 3 organizations, there is a move to prevention management and self-reliance by the individuals themselves (and their respective teams), in terms of identifying opportunities for improvement of their mental or physical health, seeking approaches to make such improvements, and "pulling" support from leaders and other support specialists.

This is a far more psychologically positive position, as it allows for autonomy, competence, and relatedness (Ryan and Deci 2000), as well as the possibility of job crafting (Wrzesniewski and Dutton 2001), all of which increase motivation. This is far from saying that leaders are passive. They undertake a great deal of work to enable this to happen and use specialists such as those in Safety, Health, and Environment to create the infrastructure whereby individuals can become self-reliant and highly motivated.

Employees feel a sense of belonging to the organization and know that it is safe, permitted, and desired for them to bring their "whole selves" to work. Further, the leaders work to create an environment where people can belong and flourish. The psychological contract is deeper. It is related to values and behaviors and there is an alignment between the individual and the organization, both at "home team" level and the organization as a whole.

This flourishing environment is beneficial for both the individual and the organization; employees are intrinsically motivated and often put in extra effort for no ostensible reward. There are high levels of innovation and problem-solving, with employees having the permission and expectation to challenge upward. There is an inherently higher level of mental and physical well-being.

There are many examples of organizations around the world that have wonderful cultures that help them to thrive and could be said to be within Stage 3 maturity. We have noted several examples throughout the book and could add many more such as Patagonia, Toms, Gore, USAA, O.C. Tanner, to name just a few. Links to all these organizations' websites can be found in the references at the end of the book. There are countless others that also deserve to be in this list but our purpose in naming these example organizations is just to highlight what's possible. All of them have created cultures unique to them that cannot be simply cut and pasted somewhere else. However, they do have some common features that are worth noting.

They all demonstrate:

- A deep focus on the value and potential of their people.
- Respect for their people and trust in them.
- A big focus on ensuring an environment where people feel safe to speak up.
- A strong focus on connecting people's personal values to the organization's values.
- A strong focus on Environmental, Social, and Governance.
- Humble and respectful leaders.
- Diversity is a key part of their culture.
- Flatter, less hierarchical structures than typical organizations.

In other words, they all care. They also happen to be very successful organizations and places of choice for people to work.

What Organizations Need to Do

As we detailed in Chapter 4, ISO 45003 Standard "Psychological Health and in the Workplace" provides excellent guidance on what is needed to build a system at an organizational level.

In 2022 the US Surgeon General published a "Framework for Mental Health and Well-Being" that not only provided the shocking statistics we shared in the Introduction but also provided a useful framework for mental health and well-being consisting of five core elements. These are:

- Protection from Harm.
- Connection and Community.
- Work-Life Harmony.
- Mattering at Work.
- Opportunity for Growth.

We have taken learnings from both these sources to create the ten elements that make up the PWB assessment detailed in Chapter 4. The organization leadership team needs to understand the ten elements and ensure they are built into policies and systems that support the PWB of everyone in the organization.

However, neither ISO 45003 standard nor the Surgeon General's report make an explicit link to the CI system. What we have tried to demonstrate in this book is that the PH&S system will be sub-optimized if it does not integrate closely with the CI system. Equally, the CI system will fail to deliver its full potential unless the PH&S system is working effectively.

The Leadership team needs to have oversight and proactive management of both these systems and ensure they are integrated for the organization to thrive.

One way to support this is for the organization to use the social and technical elements of its improvement system to promote and embed the ideal behaviors that will support the objectives of the PH&S system. This includes the utilization of various improvement systems and tools to implement the PH&S objectives, KPIs, KBIs, and improvement initiatives. Regular assessments can be conducted on how well the improvement system is helping embed the PH&S system.

The illustration in Figure 8.1 highlights some of the key things that need to be in place and proactively managed to leverage the CI system to support the PH&S system.

In the Introduction, we put forward three key insights:

1. A thriving culture of CI is essential for organizations to successfully respond to opportunities and threats in the volatile, uncertain, complex, and ambiguous external environment. A thriving culture of CI starts with eliminating the eighth waste of individuals not thriving.

ISO 45003 Psychological Health and Safety (PH&S)

Leverage the Improvement System for Implementing the PH&S System

- PH&S Policy D&D
- PH&S Strategy D&D
- PH&S KPI & KBI D&D
- PH&S Improvement Initiatives D&D
- PH&S Risk Management D&D
- PH&S Risk Register D&D
- PH&S Leader Standard Work D&D
- PH&S Operating Standards D&D
- PH&S Problem Solving
- PH&S Controls Verification
- PH&S Gemba Walks
- PH&S Annual Strategy Deployment

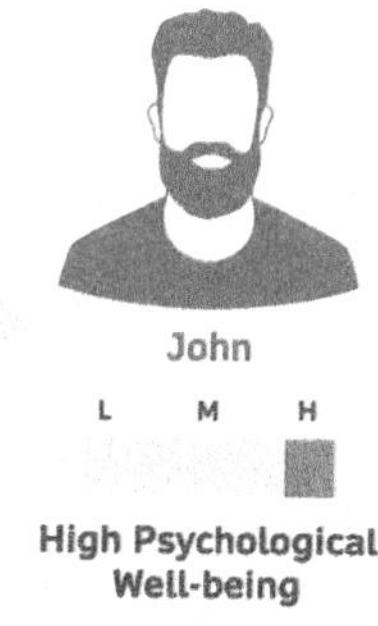

KPI – Key Performance Indicator KBI – Key Behavior Indicator D&D – Development and Deployment

Figure 8.1 Leverage the improvement system for implementing the PH&S System.

2. Thriving individuals can maintain a positive state of PWB, thereby unleashing psychological capacity to work on CI. As everyone is unique, maintaining this positive state will require a partnership approach between the individual and the organization, starting from the inside-out with the individual.
3. To maximize the number of thriving individuals, assessments need to be undertaken at all levels (individual—team—leader—organization), which will feed into thriving plans at each level, linked to the CI system and subject to a never-ending cycle of Plan, Do, Check, Act. Crucially, this starts with the individual and is embedded through ideal behaviors and leveraging the social and technical elements of the CI system to work in synergy.

We have discussed Individual, Team, and Leader Thriving plans in previous chapters. Below is a proposed framework for an organizational thriving plan. The purpose of the organizational thriving plan is for the enterprise leadership team to consider how well each of the systems is either positively contributing to or detracting from the organization's progress in creating PWB. This is essential in order to create psychological capacity for individuals, leaders, and teams that enables them to support a thriving CI culture and a thriving organization.

This is intended as an example and each organization can adapt the concept as is appropriate for their unique context. It would consist of several elements such as:

1. Organization-level psychosocial and CI assessment that is completed by the leadership team and reviewed on a regular (e.g., quarterly) basis. An example is shown in Figure 8.2 Organization Psychosocial and CI assessment.
2. CI maturity systems assessment status (six monthly/annually). See *Why Bother* (Butterworth et al. 2022) for examples of these.
3. Other relevant assessment results/indicators for example:
   a. PH&S results.
   b. Employee engagement.
   c. Recruitment and retention.
   d. DEIB.
   e. Organization psychosocial hazard assessment.

Organizational Psychosocial and CI Assessment

Instruction to complete the assessment:

1. Read each statement and rate it against the below criteria. Place the number in the relevant block.
2. Include comments for each rating, where required, so you can be specific about actions.
3. Populate the chart with the average score.
4. Discuss the results as a leadership team and define specific actions to improve outcomes.

CRITERIA: 1. Strongly disagree 2. Disagree 3. Neither agree or disagree 4. Agree 5. Strongly agree

#	Factors	Statement (answer based on your current state)	Scale 1	2	3	4	5	Comments
1	Leadership Support	As a senior leadership team we regualar share our own personal psychosocial assessments and discuss learnings, coaching and collabortion opportunities.						
2	Well-being	As a senior leadership team we regularly discuss physical and psychological well-being including the presence of psychosocial hazards that may be causing harm at an organisational level and consider what this means for our leadership and systems of work.						

Figure 8.2 Organization Psychosocial and CI Assessment extract. Full version available at www.whycarebook.com.

Like the other thriving plans, progress would be tracked over time and actions prioritized should be agreed upon. The results could even be summarized in a radar chart to give a high level visual of all the chosen elements.

The Leadership team—ideally facilitated by an external Team Coach, to allow everyone to participate—would consider the questions below. Each member of the team would focus on the organization's priorities versus their departmental/divisional responsibilities.

The team would then use the output from the Team Coaching session to create a thriving organization action plan—this plan needs to be aligned with available resources (who will do what, why, by when, and with what expected result). To help increase transparency and accountability, the thriving organization action plan should be displayed on the team's VMB and reviews at Leadership meetings, for example, to ensure the DCA steps of the PDCA cycle are completed, and any learning is taken on board to enrich the next version of the plan.

Sample Coaching questions framework for Planning phase to agree what needs to happen:

- What's most important?
- What would you (collectively) like to do?
- What might the first step be?
- What might stop you (collectively) from making progress?
- What can you do to get past that?

Example Coaching questions framework for DCA phase to ensure that actions have been completed, and that there is time and space for reflection and learning:

- What is already working really well on this team and we should **CONTINUE**?
  - What in the CI system, practices, and tools would help to lock in these habits/behaviors?
- What are we not doing and it would be really helpful to **START**?
  - What in the CI system, practices, and tools would help to build these habits/behaviors?
- What is no longer serving us and we should **STOP**?
  - What in the CI system, practices, and tools needs updating/altering to reflect this change?

Creating a thriving organization cannot be an HR, or any other function's, project. It is something that can only be achieved by a coherent, united focus from the whole leadership team. Organizational leadership team meetings agenda, discussions, and measures need to reflect this. The primary focus should be on managing the whole enterprise culture and behaviors, not on individual departmental performance. Leadership teams need to challenge themselves to trust the departments and functions to deliver, to call out for help when needed, and to leverage cross-team support as required. Hines and Butterworth (*Essence of Excellence*, 2019) advocate that senior leadership teams need to allocate 70% of their time to managing culture and share the example from Cogent Power Inc that illustrates this reproduced in Table 8.1.

Table 8.1 Time Allocation between Different Roles at Cogent Power Inc.

Role	*Level*	*Culture and Behavior*	*Improvement*	*Work*
President	Senior Manager	70%	20%	10%
Value Stream Manager	Manager	30%	50%	20%
Team Leader	Team Leader	20%	40%	40%
Operator	Team Member	2%	18%	80%

Perhaps a good place for any leadership team to start is to reflect and consider if they are allocating enough of their time to managing culture and, if not, what can they do to free up capacity. Completing the Organization Thriving Plan will help to operationalize what is required.

Key Points from Chapter 8

- PWB needs to be a priority for every organization.
- The organization needs to embed a PH&S system to protect its people that is integral to the way the organization operates.
- The organization needs to embed a CI system and ensure this is integrated with the PH&S system so that both can support each other in order to create an environment where individuals and the organization thrive.

Chapter 9

Summary and the External Environment

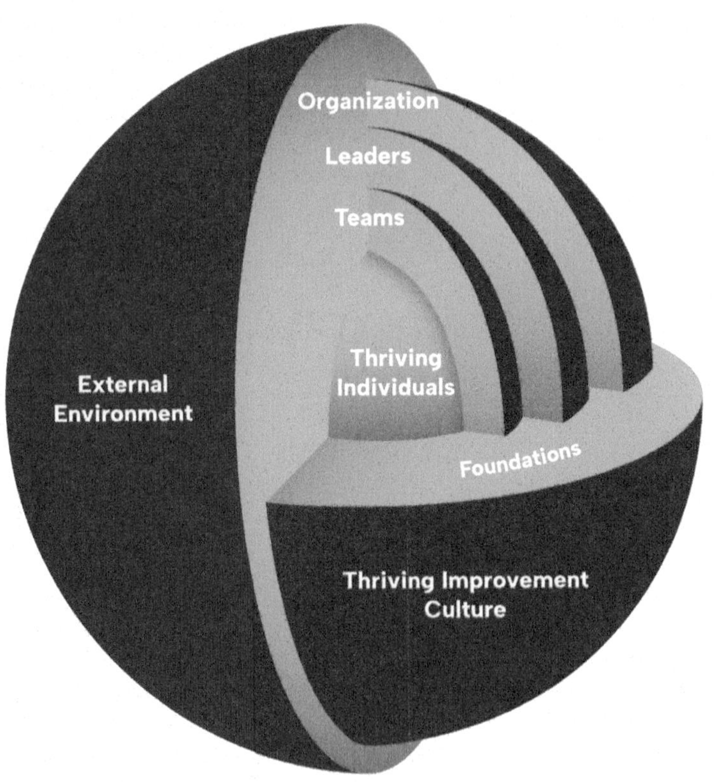

Figure 9.0 The Why Care Model.

DOI: 10.4324/9781003413479-10

We have highlighted how the global explosion in volatility, uncertainty, complexity, and ambiguity (VUCA), and the pace and complexity of work, have continued to increase in the wake of the COVID-19 pandemic. This complexity and uncertainty are accelerating for many reasons, including climate change and the yet-not-fully understood impacts of artificial intelligence.

If organizations are going to thrive in this environment, then they need to be able to adapt and respond quickly. To do this, they need to maximize how they engage and leverage the limited psychological capacity (the amount of emotional and cognitive energy available for use at any point in time) of every person in the workplace. This needs to start with an inside-out perspective focused on every individual. We need to see people as people, not as payroll.

To achieve this, organizations need to ensure the psychological well-being (PWB) of all their people at every level through robust systems of psychological health and safety and continuous improvement (CI). These two systems are intertwined and support each other. Without PWB in place, we will severely limit the full potential of the CI system and restrict the organization's capacity to respond to the external environment. At the same time, if we have a robust psychological health and safety system in place but do not have a robust CI system, we will limit people's potential to make best use of their psychological capacity.

Both systems are essential to a thriving organization. Working together they provide incredible potential for both every individual and the whole organization. They provide a protective shield that helps the organization and its people manage the external environment more effectively. Throughout the book, we have tried to demonstrate the essential elements of both these systems and how to integrate them so that they strengthen each other.

PWB is a human right that needs to be protected, promoted, and supported by everyone. We have discussed the key factors that impact PWB, including how the brain works and responds in different situations and the critical importance of being accepted and valued for 100% of yourself. A deep understanding of and constant focus on DEIB is essential to support this.

PWB is not a constant, and both personal and workplace factors will impact it. We need to recognize this and put things in place that aim to maximize everyone's PWB. Workplace factors can present themselves as psychosocial hazards that need to be proactively managed through the Psychological Health and Safety System to prevent harm.

Negative PWB reduces psychological capacity (our emotional and cognitive energy) and this scarce resource is critical for people to be able to do their work effectively and to improve the way it is done. Psychological capacity is needed to help people stay "in flow" and connected to their work. When people are not in flow, this can have catastrophic consequences, tragically including fatalities.

The CI system needs to be co-designed so that it can leverage the available psychological capacity and needs to be constantly matured and improved to ensure it is maximizing the capacity available. A well-designed CI system will support PWB and help embed the PH&S system. Together, both these systems will create capacity for improvement and make sure everyone can contribute to making tomorrow better than today both through CI and innovation.

As we have discussed, organizations, leaders, teams, individuals, family, and friends all have a role in helping manage PWB. Without it, the individual, the organization, families, and the community will suffer.

This is not just a nice thing to do. It is critical to the future of every organization and its people. Thriving is not a one-off event. It takes constant focus and nurturing, but the rewards are tremendous. We have put forward a range of frameworks and assessments to support individuals and organizations on their journey through the development of thriving plans and we encourage you to try them out for yourselves.

The various topics discussed in the book have been brought together as in the Why Care Implementation Framework (Figure 9.1).

Figure 9.1 The Why Care Implementation Framework.

We hope you have found this book thought-provoking and useful and that you have enjoyed reading it as much as we enjoyed writing it.

Our key message is that thriving individuals create thriving organizations.

For more information on the frameworks and assessments, go to **www.whycarebook.com.**

References

Introduction

Atkinson, W. (2000). Managing Stress. *Electrical World*, 214(6), pp. 41–42.

Australian Productivity Commission Mental Health—Public Inquiry—Productivity Commission. https://www.pc.gov.au/inquiries/completed/mental-health/report. Last accessed January 12, 2024.

Bosma, H., Stansfeld, S. and Marmot, M. (1998). Job Control, Personal Characteristics, and Heart Disease. *Journal of Occupational Health Psychology*, 3(4), p. 406.

Carney, B. and Getz, I. (2009). *Freedom Inc.* New York: Crown Business.

Cartwright, S. and Cooper, C.L. (1997). *Managing Workplace Stress*. Thousand Oaks, CA: Sage.

CCLA Corporate Mental Health Benchmark Global 100 Report 2022. https://www.ccla.co.uk/documents/2022-mental-health-benchmark-global-100-report/download?inline. Last accessed January 12, 2024.

Czikszentmihalyi, M. (1990). *Flow, the Psychology of Optimal Experience*. New York: Harper & Row.

Deloitte (2020). *Mental Health and Employers*. Refreshing the Case for Investment. https://www2.deloitte.com/uk/en/pages/consulting/articles/mental-health-and-employers-refreshing-the-case-for-investment.html. Last accessed January 12, 2024.

Deloitte Insights (2019). https://www2.deloitte.com/us/en/insights/topics/talent/workplace-mental-health-programs-worker-productivity.html. Last accessed 12 January 2024.

Edelman Trust Barometer Special Report (2020). https://www.edelman.com/trust/2020-trust-barometer. Last accessed January 12, 2024.

Gerstner, L. (2003). *Who Says Elephants Can't Dance? How I Turned Around IBM*. London: HarperCollins.

Hines, P. and Butterworth, C. (2019). *The Essence of Excellence: Creating a Culture of Continuous Improvement.* Chaerphilly: S A Partners.

Hines, P. et al. (2022, August). Turning the Lean World Upside Down. *International Journal of Lean Six Sigma*, 13(5), pp. 989–1024. https://doi.org/10.1108/IJLSS-09-2021-0166.

Hines, P. and Butterworth, C. Greenlee & Jekiel (2023). The Mental and Physical Well-Being Flow within the People Value Stream. *Human Resource Management and Services*, 5(1). https://doi.org/10.18282/hrms.v5i1.3367.

Human Centred Lean, Hines. (2022, September). Introducing the People Value Stream. *International Journal of Lean Six Sigma*, 13(5), pp. 961–988. https://doi.org/10.1108/IJLSS-03-2021-0061.

Indeed. Employee Burnout Report: COVID-19's Impact and 3 Strategies to Curb It (indeed.com). https://www.indeed.com/lead/preventing-employee-burnout-report. Last accessed January 12, 2024.

Malini, H., Lenggogeni, D., Windah, A., Qifti, F., Thapa, D., West, S. and Cleary, M. (2021). #Stressed: Covid-19, Chronic Illness and Technostress. *Issues in Mental Health Nursing*. https://doi.org/10.1080/01612840.2021.1958035.

Mann, D. (2005). *Creating a Lean Culture: Tools to Sustain Lean Conversions.* New York: Productivity Press.

Martyn, M. and Crowell, B. (2012). *Own the Gap*, p. 3. Oregon: Sisu Consulting.

Miller, Kelsey (2022 HBS Online). *The Triple Bottom Line: What It Is & Why It Is Important* (hbs.edu). https://online.hbs.edu/blog/post/what-is-the-triple-bottom-line. Last accessed January 12, 2024.

OECD (2022). A *New* Benchmark *for Mental Health* Systems*: Tackling* the *Social* and Economic *Costs* of Mental *Ill-Health*. Paris: OECD Publishing.

Organization for Economic Cooperation and Development (OECD) (2021). *A New Benchmark for Mental Health Systems: Tackling the Social and Economic Costs of Mental Ill-Health, OECD Health Policy Studies.* Paris: OECD Publishing. https://doi.org/10.1787/4ed890f6-en.

Perkbox (2018). How to Kickstart Your Employee Wellness Programme. www.perkbox.com. Last accessed July 17, 2023.

Personal Group (2021). *Physical Well-Being in the Workplace.* Milton Keynes: Personal Group.

Ryan, R.M. and Deci, E.L. (2000). Self-Determination Theory and the Facilitation of Intrinsic Motivation, Social Development, and Well-Being. *American Psychologist*, 55(1), pp. 68–78. https://doi.org/10.1037110003-066X.55.1.68.

Smiles, S. (2017/1866). Self-Help. *Astounding Stories* (Originally Published 1866). www.astounding-stories.com. Last accessed July 18, 2023.

Stevenson, P. and Farmer, D. (2017). Thriving at Work—The Stevenson/Farmer Review of Mental Health and Employers. https://assets.publishing.service.gov.uk/government/uploads/system/uploads/attachment_data/file/658145/thriving-at-work-stevenson-farmer-review.pdf.

Tetlow, G. and Bartrum, O. (2022). *Cost of Living Crisis: Reducing Energy Bill Costs.* Institute for Government. https://www.instituteforgovernment.org.uk/explainers/cost-living-energy. Last accessed July 17, 2023.

The Workforce Institute UKG (2023). *Mental Health at Work: Managers and Money.* https://www.ukg.com/resources/article/mental-health-work-managers-and-money. Last accessed January 12, 2024.
Trudeau, Justin. https://www.weforum.org/agenda/2018/01/pm-keynote-remarks-for-world-economic-forum-2018/. Last accessed January 12, 2024.
UK Government, hse.gov.uk (2019). https://commonslibrary.parliament.uk/research-briefings/cbp-7458/. Last accessed January 12, 2024.

Chapter 1

Brown, B. (2018). *Dare to Lead: Brave Work: Tough Conversations. Whole Hearts.* New York: Random House.
Buckingham, M. and Goodall, A. (2019). The Feedback Fallacy. *Harvard Business Review.* Available at: https://hbr.org/2019/03/the-feedback-fallacy. Last accessed 11 January 2024.
Cacioppo, John T. and Patrick, W. (2009). *Loneliness: Human Nature and the Need for Social Connection.* New York: W. W. Norton and Company.
Cain, S. (2012). *Quiet.* New York: Penguin.
CIPD (2018). *Neurodiversity at Work.* https://www.cipd.org/uk/knowledge/guides/neurodiversity-work/. Last accessed May 7, 2023.
Crum, A. (2022). *Science of Mindsets for Health & Performance, Huberman Lab Podcast.* https://www.hubermanlab.com/episode/dr-alia-crum-science-of-mind-sets-for-health-performance. Last accessed January 11, 2024.
Davis, P. (2021, Fall). QUESTIONS FOR: Paula Davis, CEO, Stress and Resilience Institute. *Rotman Management Magazine.*
Davis, P. (2023). *How Teams Can Help Address Burnout in the Legal Profession.* NALP. https://www.nalp.org/how-teams-can-help-address-burnout. Last accessed January 11, 2024.
Dweck, C. (2014). *TED Talk (2014) on "The Power of Believing That You Can Improve."* https://www.ted.com/talks/carol_dweck_the_power_of_believing_that_you_can_improve?language=en. Last accessed January 11, 2024.
Dweck, C. (2016). What Having a "Growth Mindset" Actually Means. *Harvard Business Review.*
Eisenberger, N., Lieberman, M. and Williams, K.D. (2003, October). Does Rejection Hurt? An fMRI Study of Social Exclusion. *Science,* 302(5643), pp. 290–292.
Fabritius, F. (2022). Most People Are under the Impression That the Brain Alone Controls Stress. LinkedIn Post.
Goleman, D. and Davidson, R.J. (2018). *Altered Traits: Science Reveals How Meditation Changes Your Mind, Brain, and Body.* New York: Avery, an Imprint of Penguin Random House LLC.
Google (2012). Re: Work. *Withgoogle.com.*
Haidt, J. (2005). Wired to Be Inspired. *Greater Good Magazine.*

Hamilton, D. (2020). The Biology of Kindness Online Course. https://david-hamilton.mykajabi.com/thebiologyofkindness. Last accessed February 22, 2023.

Huberman, A. (2021). *How Your Brain Works & Changes*. https://hubermanlab.com/how-your-nervous-system-works-and-changes/. Last accessed May 4, 2023.

Huberman, A. (2022). *Making and Breaking Habits*. https://hubermanlab.com/the-science-of-making-and-breaking-habits/. Last accessed May 4, 2023.

Jones, M., Butterworth, C. and Harder, B. (2018). *4 + 1: Embedding a Culture of Continuous Improvement in Financial Services*. Melbourne: Book Pod.

Killingsworth, M.A. and Gilbert, D.T. (2010). Wandering Mind Not a Happy Mind. *The Harvard Gazette*.

Kross, K. (2021). *Chatter*. London: Vermilion.

Maslach, C. and Leiter, M. (2016) Understanding the Burnout Experience: Recent Research and Its Implications for Psychiatry. https://doi.org/10.1002/wps.20311.

McGonigal, K. (2013). *TED Talk*.

Neff, K. (2011). *Self-Compassion: The Proven Power of Being Kind to Yourself*. Hodder & Stoughton.

NeuroLeadership Institute. *SEEDS Model*. https://neuroleadership.com/your-brain-at-work/unconscious-bias-in-brain. Last accessed April 29, 2023.

Peters, S. (2012). *The Chimp Paradox: The Mind Management Program to Help You Achieve Success, Confidence, and Happiness*. New York: Jeremy P. Tarcher/Penguin.

Pink, D. (2009). TED Talk. The Puzzle of Motivation. https://www.ted.com/talks/dan_pink_the_puzzle_of_motivation. Last accessed April 28, 2023.

Rock, D. (2008, December). SCARF: A Brain-Based Model for Collaborating with and Influencing Others. *NeuroLeadership Journal*, 1(1), p. 44.

Rock, D. (2009a). *Managing with the Brain in Mind*. https://www.psychologytoday.com/sites/default/files/attachments/31881/managingwbraininmind.pdf, Last accessed April 28, 2023.

Rock, D. (2009b). *Coaching with the Brain in Mind*. Hoboken, NJ: Wiley Press.

Rock, D. (2009c). *Your Brain at Work: Strategies for Overcoming Distraction, Regaining Focus, and Working Smarter All Day Long*. HarperCollins.

Rock, D. (2023). *NLI Perspectives, Psychological Safety (2023)*.

Rock, D. and Halverson, H.G. (2015, Autumn). Beyond Bias. *Strategy+Business Magazine*, 80, pp. 1–10. https://www.strategy-business.com/article/00345. Last accessed April 29, 2023.

Siegel, D.J. (1999). *DEVELOPING MIND: How Relationships and the Brain Interact to Shape Who We Are*. SL: Guilford.

Simon, Herbert A. (1971). *Designing Organizations for an Information-Rich World*. Baltimore, MD: Johns Hopkins University Press, pp. 37–52.

Tedeschi, R.G. (2020). Growth after Trauma. *Harvard Business Review*.

The Encyclopedia Britannica (2023). https://www.britannica.com/science/neuroplasticity. Last accessed January 11, 2024.

Wigert, B. and Agrawal, S. (2018). Employee Burnout, Part 1: The 5 Main Causes. *Gallup*. https://www.gallup.com/workplace/237059/employee-burnout-part-main-causes.aspx.

Williams (2012). The Mind's Eye. University of Rochester. https://www.rochester.edu/pr/Review/V74N4/0402_brainscience.html. Last accessed January 11, 2024.
Wood, W. and Ruenger, D. (2015, September 10). Psychology of Habit. *Annual Review of Psychology*, 67, pp. 289–314. https://doi.org/10.1146/annurev-psych-122414-033417.
Zaki, J. and FeldmanHall, O. (2022). *Essential Trust: The Brain Science of Trust.* Wbur. https://www.wbur.org/onpoint/2022/11/29/essential-trust-how-our-brains-process-trust Last accessed April 29, 2023.

Chapter 2

Afzal, N. (2022). *The Race to the Top: Structural Racism and How to Fight It.* UK: HarperCollins.
Avery, D., Ruggs, E., Garcia, L., Traylor, H. and London, N. (2022). Improve Your Diversity Measurement for Better Outcomes. *MIT Sloan Management Review.*
Berreby, D. (2007). *Us and Them: Understanding Your Tribal Mind.* London: Hutchinson.
Bersin, J. (2022). We Are Becoming a PowerSkills Economy. Josh Bersin. https://joshbersin.com/2022/10/we-are-becoming-a-powerskills-economy/. Last accessed June 12, 2023.
Brecheisen, J. (2023). Research: Where Employees Think Companies DEIB Efforts Are Failing. *Harvard Business Review.*
Brown, B. (2021). *Atlas of the Heart.* New York: Random House.
Brown, B. and Eger, E. (2021). Dr. Edith Eger on Recognizing the Choices and Gifts in Our Lives. Available at: https://brenebrown.com/podcast/brene-with-dr-edith-eger-on-recognizing-the-choices-and-gifts-in-our-lives/. Last accessed 10 January 2024.
Brown, B. and Tulshyan, R. (2022). *Brené with Ruchika Tulshyan on Inclusion on Purpose.* https://brenebrown.com/podcast/inclusion-on-purpose/. Last accessed June 20, 2023.
Burey, J.-A. (2021). Jodi-Ann Burey: The Myth of Bringing Your Full, Authentic Self to Work. www.ted.com.
Chin, M.H. and Chien, A.T. (2006). Reducing Racial and Ethnic Disparities in Health Care: An Integral Part of Quality Improvement Scholarship. *Quality and Safety in Health Care*, 15(2), pp. 79–80. https://doi.org/10.1136/qshc.2006.017749.
CIPD (2022). *Inclusion at Work.* https://www.cipd.org/uk/knowledge/reports/inclusion-work/. Last accessed June 20, 2023.
Clear, J. (2018). *Atomic Habits.* New York: Penguin Publishing Group.
Coyle, D. (2019). *The Culture Code.* Random House.
Deming (1993). The Deming Institute. https://deming.org/a-bad-system-will-beat-a-good-person-every-time/. Last accessed January 10, 2024.

De Smet, A., Dowling, B. Mugayar-Baldocchi, M. and Schaninger, B. for McKinsey (2021). How Companies Can Turn the Great Resignation into the Great Attraction. https://www.mckinsey.com/capabilities/people-and-organizational-performance/our-insights/great-attrition-or-great-attraction-the-choice-is-yours. Last accessed June 12, 2023.

Enumah, T. Arauz, M. for August (2023). *Looking at Psychological Safety Through an Equity Lens.* https://3948739.fs1.hubspotusercontent-na1.net/hubfs/3948739/Dec%202022/Equity_Lens_for_Psychological_Safety_-_August_Frontier.pdf. Last accessed April 29, 2023.

Epstein, D. (2022). A Practical Guide to Building Team Culture (Including Remote-Team Culture). https://davidepstein.substack.com/p/a-practical-guide-to-building-team-22-08-14. Last accessed June 23, 2023.

Gallo, A. (2022). *Is Your Co-worker Actually "Difficult"—Or Are You Being Biased?* http://www.amyegallo.com/newsletter/amy-7mzdj-bpff7 Last accessed June 12, 2023.

Global Brands (2022). The Success of Dove's Real Beauty Campaign. *Global Brands Magazine.*

gov.uk (2010). *Equality Act 2010.* https://www.legislation.gov.uk/ukpga/2010/15/contents. Last accessed June 20, 2023.

Henley Business School (2021). *The Equity Effect.* https://www.henley.ac.uk/equity-effect. Last accessed June 20, 2023.

Kepinski, L. and Nielsen, T.C. (2023). *Inclusion Nudges Quick Guide.* https://inclusion-nudges.org/wp-content/uploads/2022/08/Inclusion-Nudges-Free-Quick-Guide.pdf. Last accessed June 20, 2023.

McKinsey (2019). *Women in the Workplace Report.* https://www.mckinsey.com/~/media/McKinsey/Featured%20Insights/Gender%20Equality/Women%20in%20the%20Workplace%202019/Women-in-the-workplace-2019.ashx. Last accessed June 20, 2023.

McKinsey (2020). *How Diversity, Equity, and Inclusion (DE&I) Matter.* https://www.mckinsey.com/featured-insights/diversity-and-inclusion/diversity-wins-how-inclusion-matters?cid=other-eml-dre-mip-mck&hlkid=60bb5287427d4636942a4ef87d3d18d7&hctky=11596947&hdpid=d2e4ffab-e955-4b9c-86f5-3594041718c7. Last accessed June 20, 2023.

McKinsey Global Institute (2015). How Advancing Women's Equality Can Add $12 Trillion to Global Growth. McKinsey & Company. https://www.mckinsey.com/featured-insights/employment-and-growth/how-advancing-womens-equality-can-add-12-trillion-to-global-growth. Last accessed June 20, 2023.

The NeuroLeadership Institute (2023). *Equity, Explained.* NeuroLeadership Institute. https://neuroleadership.com/your-brain-at-work/equity-explained-infographic. Last accessed June 10, 2023.

Purushothaman (2022). Fortune. Commentary: Women of Color Can No Longer Buy into the "Inclusion Delusion." https://fortune.com/2022/03/28/women-careers-color-inclusion-delusion-kbj-supreme-court-gender-power-business-corporate-culture-deepa-purushothaman/. Last accessed June 20, 2023.

Rein, D.P. and Purushothaman, V. (2023). Workplace Toxicity Is Not Just a Mental Health Issue. *MIT Sloan Management R*eview. https://sloanreview.mit.edu/article/workplace-toxicity-is-not-just-a-mental-health-issue/. Last accessed June 12, 2023.

Rother, M. and Shook, J. (1998). *Learning to See*. Brookline, MA: The Lean Enterprise Institute.

Sapolsky, R. (2018). *Behave: The Biology of Humans at Our Best and Worst*. London: Vintage.

Sull, D. and Sull, C. (2023). The Toxic Culture Gap Shows Companies Are Failing Women. *MIT Sloan Management Review*.

Sull, D., Sull, C., Cipolli, W. and Brighenti, C. (2022). Why Every Leader Needs to Worry About Toxic Culture. *MIT Sloan Management Review*.

Tulshyan, R. (2022). *Inclusion on Purpose: An Intersectional Approach to Creating a Culture of Belonging at Work*. Cambridge, MA: The MIT Press.

Tulshyan, R. and Burey, J.-A. (2021). Stop Telling Women They Have Imposter Syndrome. *Harvard Business Review*.

Unerman, S., Jacob, K. and Edwards, E. (2022). *BELONGING: The Key to Transforming and Maintaining Diversity, Inclusion and Equality at Work*. UK: Bloomsbury Business.

Ward, M. (2020). The Psychologist Who Coined the Term "Glass Cliff" Explains What It Is, and Why Companies Need to Be More Wary of It Now. *Business Insider*.

Wikipedia Contributors (2023). *Dove Campaign for Real Beauty*. https://en.wikipedia.org/wiki/Dove_Campaign_for_Real_Beauty#cite_note-AdAge-6. Last accessed June 12, 2023.

World Economic Forum (2023). *Global Parity Alliance: Diversity, Equity and Inclusion*. https://www3.weforum.org/docs/WEF_Global_Parity_Alliance_2023.pdf. Last accessed June 20, 2023.

Chapter 3

Cobb, Ellen Pinkos. (2022). *Managing Psychosocial Hazards and Work-Related Stress in Today's Work Environment*. New York: Taylor & Francis.

Deloitte. (n.d.). *The Cost of Ignoring the Mental Health and Well-Being of Your Workforce—Risk Advisory Blog*. Deloitte Australia. https://www2.deloitte.com/au/en/blog/risk-advisory-blog/2019/cost-of-ignoring-mental-health-and-Well-being-of-workforce.html. Last accessed January 14, 2024.

Employment and Social Development Canada (2016). Psychological Health in the Workplace—Canada.ca. *Canada.ca*. https://www.canada.ca/en/employment-social-development/services/health-safety/reports/psychological-health.html#h2.3. Last accessed January 14, 2024.

flourishdx.com (2023). Psychological Health and Safety Made Simple—FlourishDx. https://flourishdx.com. Last accessed January 14, 2024.

Government of Canada. C.C. for O.H. and S (2023). CCOHS: Mental Health—Psychosocial Risk Factors in the Workplace. https://www.ccohs.ca/oshanswers/psychosocial/mh/mentalhealth_risk.html. Last accessed January 14, 2024.

Living Meanings (2014). Carol Ryff's Model of Psychological Well-Being Living Meanings. https://livingmeanings.com/six-criteria-well-ryffs-multidimensional-model/. Last accessed January 14, 2024.

Madeson, Melissa (2017). The PERMA Model: Your Scientific Theory of Happiness. *PositivePsychology.com*. positivepsychology.com/perma-model/. Last accessed January 14, 2024.

Noigroup (2018). Everything Old Is New Again, on a History of the "Biopsychosocial Model." https://www.noigroup.com/noijam/everything-old-is-new-again-on-a-history-of-the-biopsychosocial-model/. Last accessed January 14, 2024.

Return to Work: A Comparison of Psychological and Physical Injury Claims (n.d.). https://www.safeworkaustralia.gov.au/system/files/documents/1711/return-to-work-a-comparison-of-psychological-and-physical-injury-claims.pdf. Last accessed January 14, 2024.

Safe Work Australia (2022). Psychosocial Hazards | Safe Work Australia. https://www.safeworkaustralia.gov.au/safety-topic/managing-health-and-safety/mental-health/psychosocial-hazards. Last accessed January 14, 2024.

Sun, C., Hon, C.K.H., Way, K.A., Jimmieson, N.L., Xia, B. and Wu, P.P.-Y. (2023). A Bayesian Network Model for the Impacts of Psychosocial Hazards on the Mental Health of Site-Based Construction Practitioners. *Journal of Construction Engineering and Management*, 149(3). https://doi.org/10.1061/jcemd4.coeng-12905. Last accessed January 14, 2024.

www.octanner.com (n.d.). Well-Being and Recognition: The Heartbeat of Thriving Workplace Cultures. https://www.octanner.com/webinars/Well-being-recognition-the-heartbeat-of-thriving-workplace-cultures. Last accessed January 14, 2024.

Chapter 4

Deloitte. (n.d.). *The Cost of Ignoring the Mental Health and Well-Being of Your Workforce—Risk Advisory Blog*. Deloitte Australia. https://www2.deloitte.com/au/en/blog/risk-advisory-blog/2019/cost-of-ignoring-mental-health-and-Well-being-of-workforce.html.

Employment and Social Development Canada (2016). Psychological Health in the Workplace—Canada.ca. *Canada.ca*. https://www.canada.ca/en/employment-social-development/services/health-safety/reports/psychological-health.html#h2.3.

flourishdx.com (2023). Psychological Health and Safety Made Simple—FlourishDx. https://flourishdx.com.

Government of Canada. C.C. for O.H. and S (2023). CCOHS: Mental Health—Psychosocial Risk Factors in the Workplace. https://www.ccohs.ca/oshanswers/psychosocial/mh/mentalhealth_risk.html.

Living Meanings (2014). Carol Ryff's Model of Psychological Well-Being Living Meanings. https://livingmeanings.com/six-criteria-well-ryffs-multidimensional-model/.

Madeson, Melissa (2017). The PERMA Model: Your Scientific Theory of Happiness. positivepsychology.com/perma-model/.

Noigroup (2018). Everything Old Is New Again, on a History of the "Biopsychosocial Model." https://www.noigroup.com/noijam/everything-old-is-new-again-on-a-history-of-the-biopsychosocial-model/.

Return to Work: A Comparison of Psychological and Physical Injury Claims (n.d.). https://www.safeworkaustralia.gov.au/system/files/documents/1711/return-to-work-a-comparison-of-psychological-and-physical-injury-claims.pdf.

Safe Work Australia (2022). Psychosocial Hazards | Safe Work Australia. https://www.safeworkaustralia.gov.au/safety-topic/managing-health-and-safety/mental-health/psychosocial-hazards.

Sun, C., Hon, C.K.H., Way, K.A., Jimmieson, N.L., Xia, B. and Wu, P.P.-Y. (2023). A Bayesian Network Model for the Impacts of Psychosocial Hazards on the Mental Health of Site-Based Construction Practitioners. *Journal of Construction Engineering and Management*, 149(3). https://doi.org/10.1061/jcemd4.coeng-12905.

www.octanner.com (n.d.). Well-Being and Recognition: The Heartbeat of Thriving Workplace Cultures. https://www.octanner.com/webinars/Well-being-recognition-the-heartbeat-of-thriving-workplace-cultures.

Chapter 5

Brooks, F.P. (1975). *The Mythical Man-Month: Essays on Software Engineering* (1st ed., Vol. 1975). Boston, MA: Addison-Wesley Pub. Co.

Brown, B. (2018). *Dare to Lead: Brave Work: Tough Conversations. Whole Hearts.* New York: Random House.

Butterworth, C., Jones, M.L. and Hines, P.(2021). *Why Bother?* Boca Raton, FL: Routledge New York.

Eastwood, O. (2022). *Belonging: The Ancient Code of Togetherness.* London: Quercus Publishing.

Edmondson, A.C. (2019). *The Fearless Organization: Creating Psychological Safety in the Workplace for Learning, Innovation, and Growth.* Hoboken, NJ: John Wiley & Sons, Inc.

Epstein, D. (2022). A Practical Guide to Building Team Culture (Including Remote-Team Culture). https://davidepstein.substack.com/p/a-practical-guide-to-building-team-22-08-14. Last accessed June 23, 2023.

Ferrazzi, K., Race, M.-C. and Vincent, A. (2021). 7 Strategies to Build a More Resilient Team. *Harvard Business Review.*

Gallup Inc. (2022). https://www.gallup.com/workplace/397058/increasing-importance-best-friend-work.aspx. Last accessed June 23, 2023.

Google (2012). Re: Work. *Withgoogle.com.*

Hawkins, P. (2017). *Leadership Team Coaching Developing Collective Transformational Leadership.* London, New York and New Delhi: Kogan Page, p. 160.

Hertz, N. (2022). Noreena Interviewed by Royal College of Physicians about Loneliness & Health. https://noreena.com/noreena-interviewed-by-royal-college-of-physicians-about-loneliness-health/. Last accessed June 23, 2023.

Jones, M., Butterworth, C. and Harder, B. (2018). *4 + 1: Embedding a Culture of Continuous Improvement in Financial Services.* Melbourne: Book Pod.

Kasriel, S. (2017). *Skill, Re-skill and Re-skill Again. How to Keep up with the Future of Work.* World Economic Forum. https://www.weforum.org/agenda/2017/07/skill-reskill-prepare-for-future-of-work/. Last accessed June 23, 2023.

Katzenbach, J. and Smith, D. (1993). The Discipline of Teams. *Harvard Business Review.*

Kellogg Insight (2023). Building Great Teams. https://insight.kellogg.northwestern.edu/building-leading-great-teams-research. Last accessed June 23, 2023.

Lencioni, P. and Okabayashi, K. (2008). *The Five Dysfunctions of a Team: An Illustrated Leadership Fable.* Singapore: John Wiley & Sons. Asia.

Levinson, S.C. and Torreira, F. (2015). Timing in Turn-Taking and Its Implications for Processing Models of Language. *Frontiers in Psychology,* 6. DOI: 10.3389/fpsyg.2015.00731.

Liker, J.K. and Hoseus, M. (2008). *Toyota Culture: The Heart and Soul of the Toyota Way.* New York: McGraw-Hill Education.

Lovett, M. (2022). *Introducing the New Workhuman Survey Report: The State of Human Connection at Work.* Workhuman. https://www.workhuman.com/blog/introducing-the-new-workhuman-survey-report-the-state-of-human-connection-at-work/. Last accessed June 23, 2023.

Nyameh, J. (2013). Application of the Maslow's Hierarchy of Need Theory; Impacts and Implications on Organizational Culture, Human Resource and Employee's Performance. https://www.semanticscholar.org/paper/Application-of-the-Maslow-%E2%80%99-s-hierarchy-of-need-%3B-%2C-Jerome/b0bcc8ca45193eaf700350a8ac2ddfc09a093be8. Last accessed February 4, 2022.

Pemberton, C. (2015). *Resilience: A Practical Guide for Coaches.* Maidenhead: Open University Press.

Perry, P. (2019). The Orchid and the Dandelion by W Thomas Boyce Review—Which Are You? *The Guardian.*

Senge, P.M. (2006). *The Fifth Discipline: The Art and Practice of the Learning Organization.* London: Random House Business.

Sull, D., Sull, C., Cipolli, W. and Brighenti, C. (2022). Why Every Leader Needs to Worry About Toxic Culture. *MIT Sloan Management Review.*

Chapter 6

Afton, M. (2023). How to Cultivate Belonging at Work. Available at: https://www.linkedin.com/pulse/how-cultivate-belonging-work-marissa-afton/. Last accessed 14 January 2024.

Agarwal, P. (2019). Forbes: Making Kindness a Priority in the Workplace. Available at: https://www.forbes.com/sites/pragyaagarwaleurope/2019/08/26/making-kindness-a-priority-in-the-workplace/?sh=6e121fc038f4. Last accessed 12 January 2024.

Brecheisen, J. (2023). Research: Where Employees Think Companies' DEIB Efforts Are Failing. *Harvard Business Review*. Available at: https://hbr.org/2023/03/research-where-employees-think-companies-deib-efforts-are-failing. Last accessed 20 June 2023.

Bremer, M. (2014). *How to Do a Gemba Walk: A Leader's Guide*. Nashville, TN: The Cumberland Group.

Brown, B. and Bethea, A. (2021). Brené with Aiko Bethea on Inclusivity at Work: The Heart of Hard Conversations. Available at: https://brenebrown.com/podcast/brene-with-aiko-bethea-on-inclusivity-at-work-the-heart-of-hard-conversations/. Last accessed 20 June 2023.

Carney, B. and Getz, I. (2009). *Freedom Inc.* New York: Crown Business.

Castro, S. et al. (2022). Fostering Psychological Safety in Teams: Evidence from an RCT. Available at: https://papers.ssrn.com/sol3/papers.cfm?abstract_id=4141538. Last accessed 8 January 2024.

Cooperrider, D., Whitney, D. and Stavros, J. (2008). *Appreciative Inquiry Handbook: For Leaders of Change*. Oakland, CA: Berrett-Koehler Publishers.

Covey, R.S. (2004). *The 8th Habit: From Effectiveness to Greatness*. New York: Covey Publishing.

Edgeman, R. (2019). *Complex Management Systems and the Shingo Model*. New York: Routledge.

Edmondson, A.C. (2019). *The Fearless Organization: Creating Psychological Safety in the Workplace for Learning, Innovation, and Growth*. Hoboken, NJ: John Wiley & Sons, Inc.

Goleman, D. (1995). *Emotional Intelligence*. New York: Bantam.

Hafey, R. (2015). *Lean Safety Gemba Walks: A Methodology for Workforce Engagement and Culture Change*. Boca Raton, FL: CRC Press.

Harvard Business Review (2021, May 7). Available at: https://hbr.org/2021/05/dont-underestimate-the-power-of-kindness-at-work. Last accessed 14 January 2024.

Harvard Health Publishing (2021). Giving Thanks Can Make You Happier. Available at: https://www.health.harvard.edu/healthbeat/giving-thanks-can-make-you-happier. Last accessed 23 June 2023.

Hines, P. and Butterworth, C. (2019). *The Essence of Excellence: Creating a Culture of Continuous Improvement*. Caerphilly: S A Partners.

Hines, P., Butterworth, C., Greenlee, C., Jekiel, C. and Taylor, D. (2022). Turning the Lean World Upside Down. *International Journal of Lean Six Sigma*. DOI: 10.1108/IJLSS-09-2021-0166.

Landsberg, M. (2015). *The Tao of Coaching, Profile Business Classics*. London: HarperCollins.

Lindsley, O. (1990). Precision Teaching: By Teachers for Children. *Teaching Exceptional Children*, 22(3), pp. 10–15.

Marciano, P. (2010). *Carrots and Sticks Don't Work: Build a Culture of Employee Engagement with the Principles of Respect*. New York: McGraw-Hill.

McGregor, D. (1960). *The Human Side of Enterprise*. New York: McGraw Hill.

Miller, R. (2018). *Hearing the Voice of the Shingo Principles*. New York: Routledge.

Najipoor-Schuette, K. and Patton, D. (2021). Egon Zehnder "It Starts with the CEO 2021" Survey. Available at: https://www.egonzehnder.com/it-starts-with-the-ceo.

O.C. Tanner (2023). 20 Acts of Kindness for the Workplace. Available at: https://www.octanner.com/articles/20-acts-of-kindness-to-do-in-the-workplace. Last accessed 12 January 2023.

Qualtrics (2020) 2020 Global Employee Experience Trends. Available at: https://www.qualtrics.com/ebooks-guides/2020-global-employee-experience-trends-report/. Last accessed 14 January 2023.

Rother, M. (2010). *Toyota Kata: Managing People for Continuous Improvement and Superior Results*. New York: McGraw-Hill.

Rother, M. and Aulinger, G. (2017). *Toyota Kata Culture: Building Organizational Capability and Mindset through Kata Coaching*. New York: McGraw Hill Professional.

Senge, P.M. (2006). *The Fifth Discipline: The Art and Practice of the Learning Organization*. London: Random House Business.

Starr, J. (2017). *Brilliant Coaching: How to Be a Brilliant Coach in Your Workplace*. Harlow and New York: Pearson Education Limited.

Tietsort, C.J. et al. (2020). Free Listening: Identifying and Evaluating Listening Barriers through Empathic Listening. *Communication Teacher*. DOI: 10.1080/17404622.2020.1851734.

van Dun, D., Hicks, J. and Wilderom, C. (2017). Values and Behaviors of Effective Lean Managers: Mixed Methods Exploratory Research. *European Management Journal*, 35(2), pp. 174–186.

Washington E.F Gallup Inc (2022). The Necessary Journey and What It Takes. Available at: https://news.gallup.com/podcast/401789/ella-washington-necessary-journey-takes.aspx. Last accessed 14 January 2024.

Wharton 2021–Evidence-Based Diversity, Equity and Inclusion Practices IMPROVING WORKPLACE CULTURE THROUGH (n.d.). Available at: https://www.wharton.upenn.edu/wp-content/uploads/2021/05/Applied-Insights-Lab-Report.pdf. Last accessed 12 January 2024.

The Workforce Institute UKG (2023). Mental Health at Work: Managers and Money. Available at: https://www.ukg.com/resources/article/mental-health-work-managers-and-money. Last accessed 12 January 2024.

Zenger, J. and Folkman, J. (2019). 9 Vital Leadership Behaviors That Boost Employee Productivity. Available at: https://zengerfolkman.com/wp-content/uploads/2019/08/9-Vital-Leadership-Behaviors_WP-2019.pdf. Last accessed 14 January 2024.

Chapter 7

Butterworth, C., Jones, M.L. and Hines, P. (2021). *Why Bother?* New York: CRC Press.

Edmondson, A.C. (2019). *The Fearless Organization: Creating Psychological Safety in the Workplace for Learning, Innovation, and Growth.* Hoboken, NJ: John Wiley & Sons, Inc.

Feltman, C. (2021). *The Thin Book of Trust: An Essential Primer for Building Trust at Work (Edition:2).* Bend, OR: Thin Book Publishing.

flick-the-switch (n.d.). Lean Manufacturing in Mining | Perth | Flick the Switch. https://www.flicktheswitch.com.au/.

Queensland, W.H.S. (2022). Poor Workplace Relationships Including Interpersonal Conflict. https://www.worksafe.qld.gov.au/safety-and-prevention/mental-health/Psychosocial-hazards/poor-workplace-relationships-including-interpersonal-conflict. Last accessed January 14, 2024.

Schultz, J. (2021). What Is Coaching in the Workplace and Why Is It Important? https://positivepsychology.com/workplace-coaching/. Last accessed January 14, 2024.

Shingo.org (2019). Shingo Institute—Home of the Shingo Prize. https://shingo.org/. Last accessed January 14, 2024.

Chapter 8

American Psychological Association (2023). *Work in America Survey-Workplaces as Engines of Psychological Health and Well-Being* (apa.org).

Butterworth, C., Jones, M.L. and Hines, P. (2021). *Why Bother?* New York: CRC Press.

*Gore Our Story | History and Information.*https://www.gore.com/about/the-gore-story. Last accessed January 12, 2024.

Hines, P. and Butterworth, C. (2019). *The Essence of Excellence: Creating a Culture of Continuous Improvement.* Chaerphilly: S A Partners.

Justin Trudeau. https://www.weforum.org/agenda/2018/01/pm-keynote-remarks-for-world-economic-forum-2018/. Last accessed January 12, 2024.

O.C. Tanner. *Culture Cloud™ Employee Recognition Software.* https://www.octanner.com/products/culture-cloud. Last accessed January 12, 2024.

Patagonia Business Unusual—Patagonia. https://www.patagonia.com.au/pages/business-unusual. Last accessed January 12, 2024.

Toms Impact Overview | TOMS. https://www.toms.com/us/impact.html. Last accessed January 12, 2024.

U.S. Surgeon General Releases New Framework for Mental Health & Well-Being in the Workplace. https://www.hhs.gov/surgeongeneral/priorities/workplace-well-being/index.html. Last accessed January 12, 2024.

USAA. *8 Ways to Spot a Great Workplace Culture with USAA | BestCompaniesAZ.* https://bestcompaniesaz.com/8-ways-to-spot-a-great-workplace-culture-usaa/. Last accessed January 12, 2024.

WHO World Mental Health Report (2022, June). WHO and ILO Call for New Measures to Tackle Mental Health Issues at Work. https://www.who.int/teams/mental-health-and-substance-use/world-mental-health-report. Last accessed January 12, 2024.

Index

Page numbers in italic indicates *figure* and **bold** indicate table respectively

Accomplishment, 88, 179–181
Adrenaline, 25
Afzal, N., 56, 58, 61
Agarwal, P., 230
Agrawal, S., 27
American Psychological Association, 294
Appreciative inquiry, 50, 221, 228, 234–235
Autonomy, 27, 28, 36, 37, 46, 50, 67, 75, 88, 108, 151, 172–174

Behaviors, 47, 63, 77, 200, 248–249
Belonging
  benefits of, 65–66
  and inclusion, 88, 169–170
  levels of, 64, *65*
  micro belonging cues, 64–65
Bersin, J., 66
Bethea, A., 239
Biopsychosocial model, 88–90, **89**
Boundaries, 172–174
Brain
  chemicals, 24–25
  and CI
    behaviors, 47
    Gemba, 48–49
  and diversity
    bias, 43–44
    brain, visual management boards, and huddles, 49–51
    introverts and extroverts, 44–45
    neurodiversity, 45–46
  organizational psychological capacity
    brain plasticity and learning, 40
    neuroscience of habits, 40–42
  and problem-solving, 51–52
  psychological well-being, *see* Psychological well-being
  structure of, 23–25
The Brain Friendly Workplace, 27
Brecheisen, J., 61, 77
Broad-brush approach, 95
Brown, B., 61, 64, 67, 239
Burey, J.-A., 59
Burnout, 27–29
Butterworth, C., 203

Capacity and demand management, 285–286
Carney, B., 220
Certainty, 37
Chien, A.T., 60
Chin, M.H., 60
Clear, James, 55
Coaching, 266
Coaching leaders
  defined, 232
  mindset and beliefs, 232–233
  skills
    appreciative inquiry, 234–235
    emotional intelligence, 235–236
    GROW Model, 234
    listening, 233
    questioning, 234
Cogent Power Inc., **302**

Cognitive ability, 35
Cognitive Behavioral Therapy, 32
Communication, 7, 45, 46, 76, 124, 151, 172, 191, 194, 276
Compassion, 38, 48, 56, 87, 136, 162–164, 206
Constant self-reflection, 177
Continuous improvement (CI), 190, 295, 305
  behaviors, 47
  effectiveness, 118–119
  Gemba, 48–49
  key behavioral indicators, 118
  leader responsibilities, social elements, **241–242**
  and people, 192
  psychological capacity, 116–118
  social elements
    coaching, people development, 265–268
    diversity, equity, inclusion, and belonging (DEIB), 270–271
    element trust, 254–255
    Leader Standard Work, 268–269
    lead with humility, 252–253
    lead with purpose, 250–252
    Look, Listen, and Learn at Gemba, 263–265
    relationship trust, 253–254
    respect for every individual, 255–257
    status quo, challenging, 261–263
    teamwork, 259–261
    voice of the individual (VOI), 257–259
  stages of maturity
    classic lean organizations, 220–221
    "people value stream" organizations, 221–222
    traditional approach, 219–220
  and team well-being, 200–203
  technical elements
    capacity and demand management, 285–286
    embed continuous improvement, 278–280
    horizontal value streams, 275–277
    knowledge and skills, 283–285
    problem-solving, 281–282
    standard work and ensuring quality, 277–278
    strategy development and deployment, 271
    visual management, 283
    voice of the customer (VOC), 272–273
    voice of the process (VOP), 273–274
    workplace organization, 286–287
Cortisol, 25, 26, 64
COVID-19 pandemic, 3, 9, 84, 293, 305
Coyle, D., 64
Crum, A., 26
Cynicism dimension, 27

Davidson, R.J., 34
Davis, P., 28
Deloitte, 58, 69, 294
Diversity
  confidence and competence, 59
  defined, 57
  imposter syndrome, 59
  intersectionality, 58
  narrowing of, 58–59
  systemic, 59
  visible and invisible diversity, 57–58
Diversity, Equity, Inclusion, and Belonging (DEIB), 270–271
  for business, 66–68
  and CI, 73–75
  culture and systems, 55–56
  defined, 55
  individual psychological safety, 71–72
  intention and action, 56–57
  levels of change for
    individual, 70–71
    leadership, 69
    organization, 69
    team, 69–70
  PDCA, 75–81
  psychological well-being, 71
Dopamine, 25, 38
Dweck, C., 32

Eisenberger, N., 36
Element trust, 253–255
Emotional and cognitive energy, *246*

Emotional hurt, 179–181
Emotional intelligence
  empathy, 235
  motivation, 235
  resilience, 236
  self-awareness, 235
  self-management in, 24
  self-regulation, 235
  social skills, 235
Emotional thinking, 24
Employee Assistance Program (EAP), 213
Encyclopedia Britannica, 40
Epstein, D., 66
Equity, 60
  current status, 61
  inequity—statistics, 61
  power and status, 59
  psychological safety, 60
  toxic culture, 61
Exhaustion dimension, 27

Fabritius, F., 27
Fairness, 37
Feelings, 97, *256*, *263*
  accomplishment, 179
  belonging, 270
  of discomfort, 59
  and impressions, 24
  psychological capacity, 24, 67
FeldmanHall, O., 35

Gallo, A., 70
Goleman, D., 34
Google, 127
Google's Project Aristotle (2012), 28, 60, 199
Greenleaf, Robert K., 222
GROW (Goal, Reality, Options, What's Next) Model, 234, 266
Growth mindset, 32–33, 50, 52, 177, *178*

Hafey, R., 296
Haidt, J., 38
Hamilton, D., 38
Handy, C., 295
Harari, Yuval Noah, 70
Hawkins, P., 190, 191
Hines, P., 219, 295
Horizontal value streams, 275–277
Huberman, A., 40
Human resources (HR) leaders, 56

Improvement system
  continuous improvement system, *see* Continuous improvement system
  ideal behaviors, role of, 248–249
  PH&S System, 288
  psychosocial hazards, 288–290, **289–290**
Inappropriate behaviors, 268
Inclusion
  and belonging, 88, 169–170
  defined, 62
  inclusive mindset and behaviors, 63
  inclusive organization, 62–63
  inclusive system, 63–64
Inefficiency dimension, 27
Interpersonal relationships, 88, 90, 170, 171, 197–198
Intersectionality, 58, 73
ISO 45003, 7, 8, 92, 113, 137, 298, 299

Job stress, 93
Jones, M., 40

Katzenbach, J., 190
Kepinski, L., 56
Key Performance Indicators (KPIs), 12, 123, 203, 255, 260
Knowledge flow, 102, 105, 124, 280
Knowledge productivity
  cycle time for idea implementation, 106
  flow rate of knowledge, 105–106
  idea implementation plan, **104**, 105
  knowledge utilization, 104
  ownership for improvement, 106–107
  value and respect, 108–109, *109*
Kross, E., 33

Leaders
  coaching, *see* Coaching leaders
  key features of
    building trust, 223
    listening skills, 223–224

Look, Listen, and Learn (Gemba) Walks, 224–229
recognition, 229–230
skills and competencies, 223
mentoring, 231
Leadership
behaviors, 236–237
competence and, 59
DEIB and, 238–239
Leader Thriving Plan, 24
and peer support, 151
strength-based leadership, 40
Leader Standard Work, 226, 230, 237, 255, 268–269
LeDoux, J., 40
Leiter, M., 27
Lencioni, P., 199
Levinson, S.C., 199
Lindsley, O., 229
Listening, 62, 73, 76, 130, 134, 170, 198, 199, 205, 223–224, 233
Logical thinking, 24

McGonigal, K., 26, 58
McKinsey, 61, 67, 78
Maslach, C., 27
Mental health
economic impact of, 3–5
physical and, 87, 160–162
and well-being, 294
Mindfulness, 34–35, 39, 47, 51–52, 212
vs over-identification, 39
Mindset
and beliefs, 232–233
growth mindset, 32–33, *178*
inclusive mindset and behaviors, 63
power of self-talk, 33–34

Neff, K., 38
Nielsen, T.C, 56

Organizational learning, 206, 207
Organizational purpose, 17, 30, 165, 250, 251
Organization changes, 245
Organizations, 85, 100, 245
classic lean organizations, 296–297
people value stream, 297–298
psychological health and safety system, 135–136
traditional approach, 296
Oxytocin, 24, 26, 38, 64

Patton, D., 217
Performance, 15, 17, 26, 59, 66, 73, 74, 84, 93, 104, 106, 119, 123, 127, 191, 193–195, 198, 203, 209, 245, 246, 260, 265, 272, 276, 282–283, 295, 302
Personal development, 178, 221, 266
Personal growth, 29, 94, 162, 177–178, 220, 283, 285
Peters, S., 23
Phillips, T., 61
Pink, D., 23
Plan, Do, Check, Act (PDCA) approach
behaviors, 77
equity value stream mapping, 77–81
Gemba, 76–77
problem-solving, 77
visual management and huddles, 76
Premuzic, T.C., 59
Presenteeism, 93
Pressures, 13, 14, 84, 123
Prioritization, 9, 73, 175, 177
Problem-solving, 77, 207–208, 281–282
Psychological capacity, 30–31, 102, 246, 247, 294
window of tolerance, 30–31
Psychological Health and Safety (PH&S), 90, 136, 190, 288, **299**, 306
control measures, 142
hazard identification, 138–140
risk assessments, 140–141
risk control, 141–142
risk register, 142–143
Psychological safety, 35, 126–127
catastrophic consequences
Boeing 737 MAX crashes, 128
Chernobyl Disaster, 128–129
space shuttle Columbia disaster, 129–135
defned, 91

Psychological well-being (PWB), 23, 190
  accomplishment and self-validation, 88
  autonomy and boundaries, 88
  defined, 125
  elements of, 152–154
    developmental elements, 157–158
    foundational elements, 154–156
    physical and mental health, 160–162
    relational elements, 156–157
    self-acceptance and compassion, 162–164
    two-factor combinations, 158–160
  engagement and flow, 88
  growth and competence, 88
  inclusion and belonging, 88
  organizations, 92–93
  personal factors, 88–90, *149*
  physical and mental health, 87
  positive psychological well-being, 111–113, *112*
  psychological capacity, 96–97
    on continuous improvement, 97–98
    limitation, 98–101
  psychological harm, prevention, 113–114
  Psychological Health and Safety (PH&S)
    control measures, 142
    hazard identification, 138–140
    risk assessments, 140–141
    risk control, 141–142
    risk register, 142–143
  psychosocial injuries, 143–145
  purpose and direction, 87
  PWD assessment
    guidelines for, 184–185
    purpose of, 183–184
  quality relationships, 88
  resilience and integration, 87
  self-acceptance and compassion, 87
  severe and/or prolonged stress, 94–96
  Thriving Matrix
    constraints of, 120–136
    continuous improvement system, 116–119
    factors, 101
    knowledge flow, 102
    knowledge productivity, 103–116
    Thriving Quadrant, 121–125
  workplace factor, impact of, 90–92
Psychosocial hazards
  combining and interacting factors, 138–140
  types of, 138
Psychosocial injuries, 143–145
Purpose Questionnaire, *164*, 252
Purushothaman, V., 55, 71

Quality relationships, 88, 170–172
Qualtrics, 224
Questioning, 232, 234

Rein, D.P., 55, 71
Relatedness, 36, 37, 297
Relationship trust, 253–254
Rest, 28, 127, 198, 220, 222
Rock, D., 26, 36
Rother, M., 78

5S, 203
Sapolsky, R., 56
Self-acceptance, 87, 154, 156, 158, 162–164, 166
Self-compassion, 38–39, 71, 154, 236
Self-kindness *vs.* self-judgment, 39
Self-preservation, 91, 112, 130, 262, 264
Self-reflection, 150, 151, 154, 164, 177, 266
Self-talk, 33–34, 162
Self-validation, 88, 158, 179–181, *180*
Senge, P., 206
Shook, J., 78
Siegel, D.J., 30, 31
Smith, D., 190
Social responsibilities, **186**
Starr, J., 228, 231, 232
Status, 17, 18, 36–37, 60, 61, 84
Status quo, 261–263
Stress, 25–26
  defined, 94
  and resilience, 196
Sull, C., 61
Sull, D., 61, 63, 71, 199

Team
  defined, 190–191

huddles
mental models and dialogue, 207
personal mastery and shared vision, 206
problem-solving, 207–208
systems thinking, 206
team resilience and team learning, 205–206
workload leveling, 207
learning, 207
qualitative measures of success, 204
team psychological health and safety, 192–193
teamwork, 259–261
Thriving Team Plan, 208–211
visual management boards and huddles, 203–204
and well-being, 192
workplace hazards
culture, 198–203
job design and work environment, 193–196
social and behavioral factors, 196–198
Team Thriving Assessment Extract, **209**
Technical responsibilities, **187**
Tedeschi, R.G., 29
Thinking
analytic thinking, 26
focus and clarity of, 35
logical thinking, 24, 247
systems thinking, 206
Thriving individuals, 300
accomplishment and self-validation, 179–181
autonomy and boundaries, 172–174
elements of PWB, 152–154
four developmental elements, 157–158
four foundational elements, 154–156
physical and mental health, 160–162
self-acceptance and compassion, 162–164
two-factor combinations, 158–160
two relational elements, 156–157
engagement and flow, 174–177
growth and competence, 177–178
improvement system, 185–186
inclusion and belonging, 169–170
organizational resilience, 147
personal factors, 149–150
purpose and direction, 164–165
quality of relationships, 170–172
resilience and integration, 165–168
Thriving Plan for, 181–188
VUCA, *147*
work-life balance and work-life integration, 168–169
workplace factors, 150–152
Thriving Matrix, 247
Thriving Quadrant
characteristics, 124–125
goal of organization, 121–124
Toyota, 12, 192
Trauma, 29–30, 151, 152
Trudeau, J., 293
Trust, 35–37, 49, 77, 110, 134, 172, 197, 199, 223, 233, 238
element trust, 254–255
relationship trust, 253–254
Tulshyan, R., 59, 61, 72

UK Equality Act, 57, 62
Unerman, S., 61, 63

Value Stream Mapping (VSM), 76–81
Value streams, 275–277
van Dun, D., 223
Visual management, 283
Visual Management Boards (VMB), 203
Voice of the customer (VOC), 272–273
Voice of the individual (VOI), 257–259
Voice of the process (VOP), 273–274
Volatility, uncertainty, complexity, and ambiguity (VUCA), 84, *147*, 148, 245, 279, 305

Wharton, 238
Why Care Model, *22*, *54*, *83*, *146*, *189*, *216*, *244*, *292*, *304*, *306*
Wigert, B., 27
Work environment, 3, 16, 46, 84, 92, 114, 125, 133, 137, 193–196, 278, 286
Workforce Institute UKG, 218

Workload planning and scheduling, 194–195
Workplace coaching, 266
Workplace factors, 84, *85*, 90–92, *95*, 99–100, 148, 150–152, 158, 164, 182, 184, 185, 203, 266, 305
Workplace organization, 34, 286–287
Workplace psychosocial hazards, **153**
Work-related stress, 9, 91, 95, 100, 114, 136, 171
World Economic Forum, 3, 58, 206, 293

Zaki, J., 35
Zehnder, E., 217